ALANA FAIRCHILD

CRYSTAL ANGELS 444

HEALING WITH THE DIVINE POWER OF HEAVEN & EARTH

BLUE ANGEL®
PUBLISHING

CRYSTAL ANGELS 444
HEALING WITH THE DIVINE POWER
OF HEAVEN & EARTH

This printing 2016
Copyright © 2013 Alana Fairchild

Published by Blue Angel Publishing®
80 Glen Tower Drive, Glen Waverley
Victoria, Australia 3150
Email: info@blueangelonline.com
Website: www.blueangelonline.com

Edited by Chip & Asheyana Richards and Tanya Graham
Artwork by Jane Marin

Blue Angel is a registered trademark of Blue Angel Gallery Pty. Ltd.

ISBN: 978-1-922161-13-0

DEDICATION

For Jon

Special thanks to Toni, with gratitude for the inspiration for this book, and to the earth angels of the Blue Angel team, including my wonderful editor Tanya, for their support in sharing this message of love with others.

"Do not search for us, we will find you.
Do not wait for us, we are here already.
Do not whisper your name, we know it well.
We have loved you forever, we are your Guardian Angels".

CONTENTS

Introduction   7

Colour Section - Crystal Angel Mandalas & Crystals   17

1. CLEAR QUARTZ (The Master Healer)
and ARCHANGEL METATRON (King of Angels)
THE GIFT OF POWER   43

2. ARAGONITE (Sacred Rest)
and ARCHANGEL REMIEL (Carer of the Soul)
THE GIFT OF REST   57

3. PINK CALCITE (Unconditional Acceptance)
and ARCHANGEL ANAEL (Angel of the Heart)
THE GIFT OF UNCONDITIONAL ACCEPTANCE   71

4. SELENITE (Peace)
and ARCHANGEL MELCHIZEDEK (Angel of Peace)
THE GIFT OF HIGHER CONSCIOUSNESS   85

5. LABRADORITE (Uniqueness)
and ARCHANGEL IAHEL (Angel of Solitude)
THE GIFT OF INDIVIDUALITY   99

6. BLUE OBSIDIAN (Clarity)
and ANGEL AMITIEL (Angel of Truth)
THE GIFT OF CLARITY   115

7. POLYCHROME JASPER (Playfulness)
and ANGEL CALIEL (Angel of Laughter)
THE GIFT OF DIVINE PLAY   133

8. LAPIS LAZULI (Insight)
and ARCHANGEL MICHAEL (Protection)
THE GIFT OF VISION   147

9. PICTURE JASPER (Earth Wisdom)
and ARCHON BARBELO (Prosperity)
THE GIFT OF SUPPORT   163

10. CARNELIAN (Life Force)
and ANGEL ISDA (Food)
THE GIFT OF NOURISHMENT   **179**

11. TURQUOISE (Amulet)
and ARCHANGEL GABRIEL (Strength)
THE GIFT OF SPIRITUAL AUTHORITY   **195**

12. PIETERSITE (Knowledge)
and ANGEL RAZIEL (Mysteries)
THE GIFT OF HIGHER UNDERSTANDING   **211**

13. TIGERS EYE (Courage)
and ANGEL ADNACHIEL (Adventure)
THE GIFT OF INDEPENDENCE   **229**

14. BLACK TOURMALINE (Cleansing)
and ANGEL LAHABIEL (Protection)
THE GIFT OF PURIFICATION   **249**

15. MALACHITE (Evolution)
and ARCHANGEL RAPHAEL (Healing)
THE GIFT OF ONENESS   **267**

16. ROSE QUARTZ (Unconditional Love)
and ANGEL BALTHIEL (Healing Jealousy)
THE GIFT OF HEART HEALING   **285**

17. AQUAMARINE (Expression)
and ANGEL BATH KOL (Voice)
THE GIFT OF HIGHER CREATIVITY   **303**

18. SMOKY QUARTZ (Grounding)
and ANGEL UZZIEL (Mercy)
THE GIFT OF EMBODIMENT   **323**

The End is Just Another Beginning   **341**
About Alana   **343**
About the Artist   **344**
Thematic Index by Chapter   **345**
Index   **356**

INTRODUCTION

THE CRYSTAL ANGELS HAVE SPOKEN TO YOU ALREADY!

I believe you have been drawn to this book because you have a special connection with crystals and the angelic kingdom. You may have known this consciously for many years, having worked with the angels privately or professionally. You might have done lots of work with crystals or even be a crystal healer. Or perhaps you are very new to both of these worlds, or at least you think that you are! The truth is, if you felt a pull to pick up this book and read it, this is because the crystal and angelic beings have been calling you closer to them!

This book is for those that are open to loving the crystals of this Earth and the angels of heaven. Whether you are a beginner or an advanced student of the healing arts, you will read at the level of depth that serves you and you will find something new in this book each time you read it.

Whether you think you are a new soul or an old soul, the truth is that you are an advanced soul. You wouldn't be interested in healing and energy if you were not. At some level, either consciously or subconsciously, you are helping humanity to grow in sensitivity and connection to the Earth so that we can all evolve together in harmony, creating a new human culture that celebrates life based in love, rather than fear.

Even those who consider themselves new to the world of healing resonate with the idea of living from love-based consciousness. We all instinctively know that there is much more to life than competition, harshness, fear and suffering. We sense that the qualities of gentleness, compassion, wisdom and love could alleviate so much pain in the world. Bringing these spiritual values into our every day lives and filtering them into mass consciousness takes time and patience. I believe advanced souls, like you, have chosen to incarnate over and over again to live the truth of love and help it gain a foothold in human culture on Earth.

Having real life experiences of the loving crystal beings and angelic beings that are connected to us helps us love more and fear less. We begin to believe that there is more to life than the concrete, physical world that we perceive. We start to act with more faith and trust in the Divine. We become open to divine assistance and intervention, and life becomes more flowing and fun.

This book is in service of that process. As you read about the various crystals and angels that have chose to be a part of this book, living a spiritually-attuned life will feel much more accessible and real for you. If you already live a spiritual life, you may find that you start to interpret your experiences with even greater understanding of how you have been helped and guided throughout your life. As we begin to realise the gift of divine assistance that is already active in our lives, that assistance flows more abundantly and we are able to fast-track our own unique soul awakening, living the life we were spiritually destined to live.

HEALING

In this book we experience the wisdom of the spirit or angel that is alive within every crystal. We delve into the healing power of each stone and explore its spiritual wisdom. We then explore three different healing processes – one for the soul (your spiritual essence), one for the emotional and psychological bodies and one for the physical body (which includes your chakras and energy field and their connection to your physical wellbeing). You can choose to do all three of these healing processes for whichever crystal you are exploring, or simply choose the one that grabs your attention the most.

These healing processes are offered to support you, but you must rely on your own wisdom and take responsibility for your own healing too. This may mean consulting with a health care practitioner in conjunction with your energy work.

Energy work is powerful, and it will have an effect on the physical body, as well as the soul and mind. The effect happens whether you are conscious of it or not. If you are a natural sensitive (who tends to feel a lot and consciously register emotion and psychic energy) then you'll likely feel the effect of the healing processes during the session, as well as noticing clearing and healing effects afterwards.

If you are new to energy work and haven't previously sensed subtle energy, I know it can be hard to trust, but please do have faith. The processes will work for you too, you just won't be as aware of it consciously at first. Your ability to feel energy consciously, to gain awareness of the subtle worlds that exist beyond the physical world – where the crystal beings and angels dwell – will open up to you with practice, patience and persistence.

You are always entitled to ask to be shown more of the subtle world. As you release fear (of being different, of not liking what you see or hear, of being considered strange or crazy) it will open up to you, bringing you into your heart. It may take a little patience, so take your time working through the healing processes. Your abilities will open as you clear your energy through the healings and become more sensitive to that which you may have subconsciously ignored previously. And it is highly likely that you are already far more capable of subtle perception than you think. Often you'll find that your inner voice and loving divine guidance is already communicating with you – you just need to pay more conscious attention to it!

WHAT IS A CRYSTAL ANGEL?

Every crystal has its own angel. It is sometimes called a nature spirit, oversoul or deva (which translates loosely from Sanskrit into English as a 'Shining One'). These crystal angels are the spirit, consciousness, wisdom and vibration of that particular crystal 'species'.

If you were holding a piece of Aquamarine, for example, you would be working with the energy of that individual crystal, plus the entire consciousness of all of Aquamarine everywhere, discovered or undiscovered! That means every piece of Aquamarine that has ever been created, from the bluest blue to the greenest green blue, is energetically linked to every other piece of Aquamarine through the consciousness of the crystal angel of Aquamarine. Although your particular piece will have its own unique energy, particular to its unique colour, shape and size, the overall consciousness of Aquamarine will also be emanating through that stone. This is why even a small piece of crystal can be very powerful. It is a holographic intelligence, whereby even the smallest part contains within it the power and wisdom of the whole.

Calling on the crystal angel helps you tap into the greater power, healing properties and energetic potency of that particular crystal type as a whole, as well as the special personality of the individual piece you are working with. This is why we can work with a particular crystal, by calling on the crystal angel of the crystal we need, even if we don't have it available physically at the time. Through connecting with the angel we can call on the healing energy of the crystal anyway.

I have worked with this technique for many years. If someone is struggling and a crystal intuitively comes to mind, I simply call upon the angel of the crystal and ask for its consciousness to channel into the body and soul of my client through unconditional love. It works! And it saves me from rummaging around in my crystal cupboard mid-session to see if I have the exact stone that holds the vibration my clients may need in the moment!

Working with the crystals physically is fun and beautiful, and can make the experience of learning to sense energy feel more tangible and real to us, yet it is good to know that it is not the only way to tap into the healing intelligence of crystals, especially if we are drawn to a crystal and know instinctively that it can help us, but we just don't have it on hand at that precise moment. We can simply close our eyes for a moment and (silently or aloud) say, "Through unconditional love, I call upon the Crystal Angel for Malachite (or whatever crystal it is that we need) and I ask for you to bring your healing power to my body, mind and soul now, with compassionate grace. Through my own free will, so be it." Breathe in and out slowly, with your awareness in your heart, and an intention to receive. Done!

CRYSTAL ANGELS OF EARTH AND ANGELS OF HEAVEN

Heaven and Earth aren't so far apart as we may feel them to be at times. They are actually spiritual reflections of each other. The crystal angels belong to the Earth. They are to the vast soul that is the Earth exactly what the heavenly angels are to the heavenly spirit – a healing hand that reaches out to those who ask for divine help, healing and love.

The angels we call upon together in this book will help you according to your highest good. They want to help you, and they have great power to help you, but only if you call upon them. You must always ask for angelic assistance through unconditional love. These beings genuinely love and serve you. You may find yourself feeling quite emotional at different points of this book when you resonate with a story being shared or a particular piece of guidance that strikes a chord with you. This is when the truth of love is reaching through all the noise of the day-to-day world and touching your soul. Your heart responds with deep feeling. You may feel like crying, whether out of sadness or some other feeling such as joy, without knowing exactly why. This is nothing to worry about and something to accept and even welcome. It is your soul speaking to you, letting you know that it feels the divine angelic realm helping you, and everything is going to be alright.

The crystal angels and heavenly angels that came forward for this book share a special bond with the healing power and wisdom of each particular crystal in question. They amplify each other in divine synergy. Synergy is when the combined power of two forces is greater than the sum of its parts – the crystal angels and heavenly angels become even more powerful in combination with each other, helping you to connect your spiritual self and earthly self into one, fulfilled being. Together they achieve powerful and effective healing because they call on all parts of us, body, mind, emotions and soul, to be in unison with the healing wisdom.

When I first started writing this book, I was open to receiving the messages about which angels wanted to be paired with which crystals. This "pairing" was a lot of fun and didn't take very long at all. I didn't always know why certain angels and crystals went together until I began to write their chapter. And I didn't know what wisdom they would offer together until the moment of their sharing came. It wasn't until channelling their introductory message that I understood what they would offer in terms of healing. From there, it all poured out relatively quickly. This book has been written from the heart, channelled from divine beings, rather than from the mind, planned in advance.

The process of writing this book was enjoyable but very challenging at times. Calling on a new heavenly energy and a new crystal angel each day was not always easy. It felt amazing, but it also brought up some issues to be cleared! You may find something similar when you read a certain chapter and delve into the energy of a particular crystal-angel duo. You may find that during the reading of that chapter, or slightly after, the relevant issues become clearer to you, more pronounced in your life (especially if you don't rush through the book, but take your time in exploring it). These may be wounds rising up to your awareness so that they can be resolved and released.

If you feel stuck in a chapter, or that you just can't 'get into it,' it may be resistance to the issue within the chapter arising. Give yourself time to read it... and be kind. You don't need to push yourself to heal but you do need to stand your ground and commit to the process. Find the balance between not running away and not forcing the issue. You'll find that balance in your heart, and even having this book around you will help you tune in and become more receptive to your own heart wisdom.

WHY HEAVEN AND EARTH?

The theme of this entire crystal healing series, starting with the book, is the bringing together of heavenly (spiritual) and earthly (physical) aspects of ourselves.

Various spiritual traditions have differing responses to the body and its role in spiritual awakening. There are the tantric traditions (which many Westerners mistakenly assume relates solely to sexuality, but which are more about acceptance of all aspects of life and experience) which place the body at the centre of our spiritual awakening. In these traditions we can call the spirit into the body and begin to integrate them. Then there are more traditional ascetic spiritual traditions that teach the path of transcending of the body as the way to awaken, learning that the spirit is so much vaster than the body.

Whether you end up finding your divinity through your body or beyond your body, or both, it doesn't really matter. The reason the body is included in the healing processes and teachings of this book is because your spiritual life will progress far more quickly, enjoyably and smoothly as you heal your relationship to your body and learn to get along with it. For some lucky ones, this is pretty easy. Perhaps their journey is more in how to connect spiritually, or in how to bring the spiritual connection and the body connection together. For others, getting some mastery around the relationship to the body is where the learning is focused this lifetime, so that their spiritual connection can feel more real in the physical world.

Whatever your learning edge, bringing spiritual energy consciously into the body (through the physical healing processes in each chapter) is what helps bring your inner dreams into physical form, so you can walk your spiritual path this lifetime and really live it, rather than only dream that it was more real for you. When the body-soul connection is working, we feel like we are living heaven and Earth together more and more. This is what this book is designed to help you achieve.

When the body-soul connection is not flowing so easily, we can feel as though heaven is very distant and the Earth is very challenging! This is not a sign of failure, it often means that we are growing beyond what we have known or are comfortable with.

You can imagine that having a body is like the soul having to learn to walk a path in the dark. If you call in the heavenly light of the Divine, it's like getting a powerful torch to help you see where you are going. So rather than stumbling around, hoping you don't fall off ledge somewhere, you can actually see what you are doing and maybe even enjoy the wonders that you behold, essentially becoming more skilled in walking the path, and getting to your destination with more swiftness and clarity.

What this looks like in practical terms is that your life and how you spend your time reflects what you feel is important inside. It can mean confronting a lot of fear and letting go of how you were taught your life had to be, but the freedom this brings you makes taking spiritual responsibility for yourself worth the effort.

When your emotional life and psychological life are in harmony with your soul, with divine light shining through you, your feelings, thoughts and insights help rather than harm you. Even if you have negativity arising, you'll be able to see where it is helping you, learn the lesson and let it go more quickly and with less suffering. You'll be dreaming, thinking and feeling with passion about what is happening in your life, not wishing it would be different.

A final way to get a clear feeling or picture about what heaven and Earth can do in healing together is to imagine that you are a car and your body, soul, mind and emotions are each one wheel on the car, with the divine spark of God-Goddess that lives in you being the driver. When heaven and Earth come together, all four wheels are in alignment and off we go! We could still probably get to where we wanted to go if we had a flat tyre (say our body was out of alignment with our soul) or our wheel alignment was a bit off (with say our mind thinking we should be heading in a different direction to where we are actually going) but it would be a bumpier and less enjoyable ride!

WHAT IS 444?

This brings us to 444 in the title. I'll share a special story with you. My publisher and I had been discussing the idea of me writing an angel book for some months, but we hadn't quite found the approach to the topic that felt right. One evening I asked the angels, "What do you want me to write about in this angel book?" My publisher and I had emailed some thoughts back and forth quite late that evening, but still hadn't quite got it. I let my prayers go and slept soundly.

The next morning I found an email from my publisher saying that he had been awakened in the early hours of the morning (at 4:44 to be exact!) with the specific title of this book and the number 444! The email included an affirmation (used in the Lapis Lazuli chapter) from our beloved Archangel Michael.

I wrote the first chapter two days later and the rest of the book in the following few weeks. The content poured out quickly and powerfully, which was exhilarating and also challenging at times, with a lot of flow and not much thought or planning on my part, apart from setting aside time to allow the magic to happen, without actually knowing what that magic would be.

The angels had answered my prayers, as they always do.

So back to 444!

444 and other repeating numbers or number sequences are a language. The Divine loves to communicate with us. Sometimes amongst the stream of thoughts it is hard to get a word in edgewise, so the Divine uses other techniques too, outwitting our logical mind and getting straight to our hearts. The Divine may speak through colour, feeling, symbols, white feathers on the street (which are your angels saying hello), other feathers (which are the air guardian spirits, part of the great soul of Mother Earth, saying hello and to remember to keep your mind light and free flowing plus whatever else you feel with that feather!), hearing a song on repeat or waking up with song lyrics in your head, hearing a special message in a television show or book you are reading where you just know it is guidance for you. Another technique is messages through numbers. Numbers hold energy and vibration. The number four is associated with stability, earthly reality, building a strong and capable foundation for higher growth and the crystals, angels and ascended masters.

With repetition, the power and emphasis is multiplied. So 444 is really a strong and powerful message from the angels speaking directly to your intuitive and subconscious mind. If you were curious about the meaning of the numbers, or they caused you to pick up the book when the title alone without the numbers may not have grabbed your attention then you are receiving this message from your angelic helpers loud and clear.

They are helping you with all the issues you have and have asked for help in healing. The issues of money, wellbeing, power and relationship, food and body, health and energy, psychic awakening and more that are explored in this book have been channelled for your benefit, from the Angelic beings that love you unconditionally. They are letting you know that they are real, that their help is genuine and offered to you here and in other ways in your life too, so be open to receiving it.

The number sequence 444 is also telling you that yes, you are meant to live your spiritual light in a physical sense.

If you have stumbled in trust, been tested and pushed to the point that you wonder if your spiritual work is just in your head, or destined to remain a dream, not to be lived in the abundant physical manifestation that you had hoped for, you are being told do not give up! You are destined to live your soul light in physical form. Your dreams are manifesting now. This is not the Divine saying 'the cheque is in the mail' and fobbing you off. It IS actually happening and you need to do the inner work provided here and let yourself be loved into peaceful trust, which will make the manifestation so much faster! Follow the signs that present themselves to you. Take risks. Accept discomfort but always stay true to yourself. Growth is about stepping into your truth, not doubting it, believing that you have to step away from who you are to become something or someone else.

444 is also the call to have faith and let it manifest. You'll be safe and it will be OK. You are healing the foundation and the manifestation will be stable, calling heaven and Earth into the one mighty and beautiful zone of divine creation. This is part of your soul healing contract with the Earth. It isn't just about your own life being wonderful but also about being in service to others. It is hard to save a drowning man if you are drowning alongside him. But to heal yourself and to realise that you have something of healing value to offer the world in how you choose to be yourself, helps you fulfil your divine life mission, bringing heaven and Earth together.

This is the healing message of 444 and it is offered to you from the angelic realms now. In summary, 444 essentially means 'the angels have your back'.

HOW TO USE THIS BOOK

You can read this book as you would any self-help healing book and allow yourself to just take the journey.

However you can also use it as an intuitive guidance book.

Simply centre yourself in your heart and ask your question such as "what do I most need to know right now?" or "what is the next step to take to heal my issue with (whatever your issue is)?"

Then close your eyes, hold the book and allow yourself to open it, letting it open at whatever page it does. Read the page carefully noticing what jumps out at you. You might be drawn to one of the images. Let it soak into your being without thinking about it, as you gaze at it.

Notice that even though you are asking for healing about one issue, the chapter you open up to and read may seem to point to a completely different issue. This is not a mistake. Often what we think the issue is about is not where the 'spiritual action' is taking place at all and to heal from a different perspective, or with a completely different mindset or approach can really help shift stuck energy.

It might also be your angels saying, "Just drop it!" and deal with something else. When we really focus on an issue we can unintentionally end up strengthening it rather than dissolving and resolving. Sometimes to let it go is to let it heal of its own volition.

So learn to 'read between the lines' with your intuition when using the book as an intuitive guidance book. You can also assume that if you land on a particular chapter of a crystal angel, that the crystal angel and/or the heavenly angel in question have a soul connection with you now and are waiting for you to ask for their help or confirming that their help is being given to you now. It is their way of waving at your soul saying, 'Hi, yes, it's me, I am with you!'.

Finally if you want help but you really are confused and don't know who to call upon, just use the affirmation prayer for all the crystal angels at the end of the book. You'll be guaranteed to get a response from the right ones for you.

WORKING WITH CRYSTALS

If you are new to working with crystals there are some basic principles that will help you get the most out of their presence in your life.

Choose what speaks to you intuitively. There is no such thing as a wrong choice. If a crystal has come to you, it has come to you for a reason. In a way, it's a little like adopting a pet (or being adopted by a pet – crystals and animals tend to choose us more than we think we choose them!) so don't question it and just trust.

Secondly cleanse your crystals regularly. Some don't do well in sunlight, as they fade, and others (like halite which is essentially a rock salt) don't do well in water because they dissolve! Others get scratched by salt. So my suggestion is to begin with the following simple and effective technique that works with all crystals. Once you learn more about individual stones, you can change your cleansing process if you feel the need to do so.

You can cleanse all crystals by visualising a vibrant violet light, flecked with white. Imagine it sparkling and crackling above the crown of your head, flowing down through your head and into your mouth, then blowing it out on the breath.

Don't just breathe on the crystal, actually gently and intently blow the violet energy out of your mouth, straight into and through the crystal with the intent of cleansing it of all negativity. Do this until it feels clean or for at least seven breaths. When you get very focused you'll be able to clear a crystal with one short sharp breath, but that may take a little practice before you feel confident with it. You can also play beautiful music in your home (a CD with chant or OM is a good option) and burn incense to clear the space and your crystals all at once.

Cleanse your crystals before and after use in healing if the crystal has touched your body. If it is just in your environment and doesn't get handled then every few months, or more frequently if there is a lot of emotional energy or stress in the room, will be fine. Trust your sense of whether the stone is clear or not. The energy will feel vibrant and clear when the crystal is clean. When it is dirty it will feel like sunlight trying to get through a dirty window – you know there is good energy there but it's a bit muddy and hard to really feel it. This means your crystal has been working hard, clearing and absorbing energy and it needs to be cleared so that it can continue doing its wonderful work (which it wants to do).

You can never over-cleanse a crystal and you will never clear its good energy away. Cleansing only removes that which isn't pure in the crystal, like giving it a spiritual shower. It is safe to do and will not harm you or the stone. You may be wondering, "Where does the negative energy go?" When you use the violet light breath technique, the energy gets transmuted from one form into another. This is one of the healing properties of violet light. If you are unsure about the breath technique, then quite simply say, "I call upon the beings of unconditional love who can assist with cleansing my crystal and transmuting negativity energy into unconditional love. Through my own free will, so be it." Then go about burning your incense and/or playing music.

CRYSTAL ANGEL MANDALAS

You'll notice that each chapter in this book features a Crystal Angel Mandala. These are printed in black and white at the beginning of each chapter but they also appear in the full-colour section which begins on page 17. They are a combination of the energy of the crystal angel and heavenly angel connected to each crystal in this book. The Crystal Angel Mandalas were specifically created for this book by artist, Jane Marin.

These mandalas bring the energy of the crystal angels to you immediately, which is especially helpful if you cannot get easy access to any of the stones mentioned in the book. The mandalas are encoded with light, design and colour to create a certain energetic frequency. This frequency is in alignment with the crystal angel for each stone. Feel free to work with these mandalas as substitutes for the actual stone in the healing processes of this book.

Or if you are having trouble connecting with the heavenly angel associated with a crystal, you can gaze at the mandala instead, imagining its energy, its light, pattern and colour flowing into your body and filling it with loving energy.

You can also use the mandalas separately. If there is one that you feel particularly drawn to work with, you may like to place the book open at that page on your altar, if you have one, or even a coffee table or at your desk. You may wish also to place the book near your bedside table to help you absorb the healing at night. Just leave the book open at the page featuring the appropriate mandala, facing upwards. If you have a crystal you can rest it on the mandala too – or just use the mandala on its own. These mandalas hold energies that are loving, kind and healing and those energies will help you. A simple way to use them to best effect is to say, "I call on the unconditionally loving energies of this mandala and ask for healing" and then place it where you feel is best for you. The rest is up to the crystal angels!

WHY THESE CRYSTALS AND ANGELS?

When I began writing this book it wasn't how I thought it would be. The chapters quickly dropped into more depth than I had anticipated and of the 44 crystals and angels that I originally connected with, 18 jumped forward and claimed their place in this book. I didn't choose these beings consciously. They simply called to me on the day that I wrote each chapter. Each day I had experiences that seemed to directly relate to the material I was working through and it helped me know that there was alignment between the energy flowing from the Divine through my soul, into my mind and out through my fingers onto the page for others to share.

After eighteen chapters were written, I wondered if it was completed or if I should do more. My publisher supported me either way and as I sat with it my partner walked in the room.

"What are you thinking about?" he asked me. I described the situation, to which he responded with a question, "Does it feel like its finished? Did the last chapter seem like a natural conclusion?"

I thought of where I started writing, at the Clear Quartz and Archangel Metatron level of divine light and power and where I had just finished writing with Metatron's assisting Angel Uzziel and the grounding gift of Smoky Quartz, the gift of embodiment. I had been guided by the crystal angels without consciously realising it until then. We had travelled together from heaven to Earth. I answered my partner without hesitation, "Yes," I said, "it's done."

These particular crystal angels have stepped forward to offer healing at this time because it is what is needed now. I believe that the crystal angels later in the series will also present themselves as needed, according to a higher wisdom. I trust it completely. May you be served well by their loving presence.

1.
CLEAR QUARTZ (The Master Healer)
and ARCHANGEL METATRON (King of Angels)
THE GIFT OF POWER

2.
ARAGONITE (Sacred Rest)
and ARCHANGEL REMIEL (Carer of the Soul)
THE GIFT OF REST

3.
PINK CALCITE (Unconditional Acceptance)
and ARCHANGEL ANAEL (Angel of the Heart)
THE GIFT OF UNCONDITIONAL ACCEPTANCE

4.
SELENITE (Peace)
and ARCHANGEL MELCHIZEDEK (Angel of Peace)
THE GIFT OF HIGHER CONSCIOUSNESS

5.
LABRADORITE (Uniqueness)
and ARCHANGEL IAHEL (Angel of Solitude)
THE GIFT OF INDIVIDUALITY

6.
BLUE OBSIDIAN (Clarity)
and ANGEL AMITIEL (Angel of Truth)
THE GIFT OF CLARITY

7.
POLYCHROME JASPER (Playfulness)
and ANGEL CALIEL (Angel of Laughter)
THE GIFT OF DIVINE PLAY

8.
LAPIS LAZULI (Insight)
and ARCHANGEL MICHAEL (Protection)
THE GIFT OF VISION

9.
PICTURE JASPER (Earth Wisdom)
and ARCHON BARBELO (Prosperity)
THE GIFT OF SUPPORT

10.
CARNELIAN (Life Force)
and ANGEL ISDA (Food)
THE GIFT OF NOURISHMENT

11.
TURQUOISE (Amulet)
and ARCHANGEL GABRIEL (Strength)
THE GIFT OF SPIRITUAL AUTHORITY

12.
PIETERSITE (Knowledge)
and ANGEL RAZIEL (Mysteries)
THE GIFT OF HIGHER UNDERSTANDING

13.
TIGERS EYE (Courage)
and ANGEL ADNACHIEL (Adventure)
THE GIFT OF INDEPENDENCE

14.
BLACK TOURMALINE (Cleansing)
and ANGEL LAHABIEL (Protection)
THE GIFT OF PURIFICATION

15.
MALACHITE (Evolution)
and ARCHANGEL RAPHAEL (Healing)
THE GIFT OF ONENESS

16.
ROSE QUARTZ (Unconditional Love)
and ANGEL BALTHIEL (Healing Jealousy)
THE GIFT OF HEART HEALING

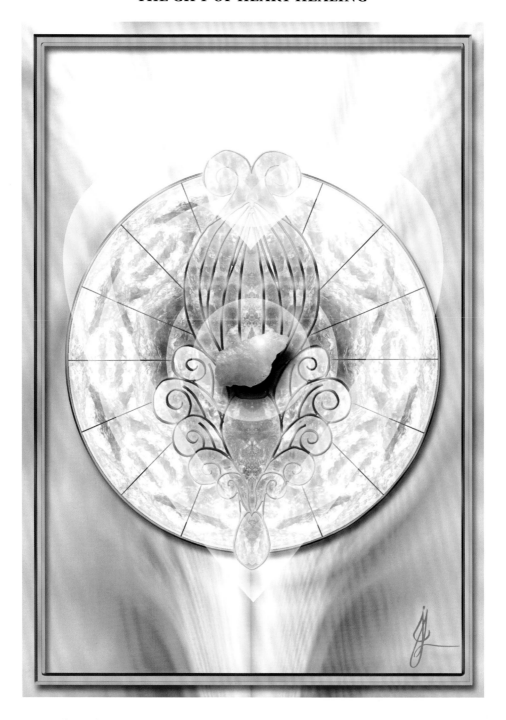

17.
AQUAMARINE (Expression)
and ANGEL BATH KOL (Voice)
THE GIFT OF HIGHER CREATIVITY

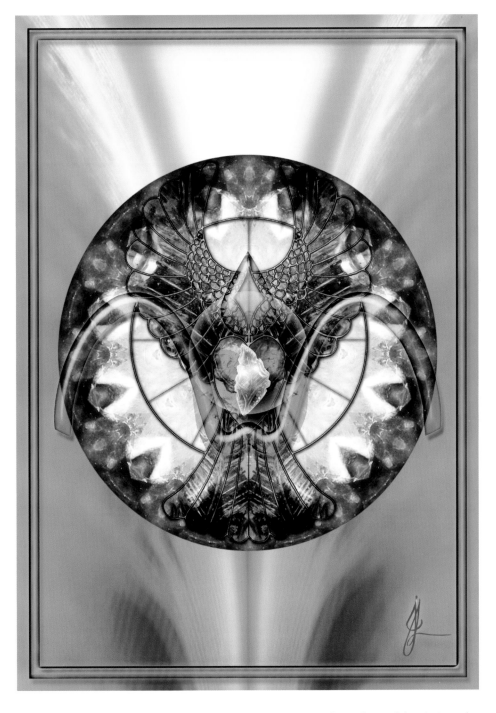

18.
SMOKY QUARTZ (Grounding)
and ANGEL UZZIEL (Mercy)
THE GIFT OF EMBODIMENT

THE CRYSTALS:

Clear Quartz

Aragonite

Pink Calcite

Selenite

Labradorite

Blue Obsidian

Polychrome Jasper

Lapis Lazuli

Picture Jasper

Carnelian

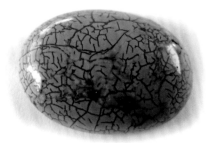

Turquoise

Pietersite

Tigers Eye

Black Tourmaline

Malachite

Rose Quartz

Aquamarine

Smoky Quartz

1.

CLEAR QUARTZ (The Master Healer) and ARCHANGEL METATRON (King of Angels)

THE GIFT OF POWER

SPIRITUAL GUIDANCE FROM THE ANGEL OF CLEAR QUARTZ AND THE ARCHANGEL METATRON

We bring to you the healing power of light. Neutral it is, until your intention is given. Then for greater or lesser purpose, the power grows and the manifestation unfolds. Always you have the power to create, and with this gift of Clear Quartz and the Archangel Metatron, your power grows stronger now. What do you wish for? Pray for that. Pray by dreaming of it, aligning your heart with it and knowing that you are worthy. Pray without attachment. Surrender it to the greater universal power and allow it to return to you without fear or concern for failure. All will manifest in time. This is the power that lies within you. Use it wisely and from your heart, and you will be gifted a second time – also with peace.

PICTURING CLEAR QUARTZ

Clear Quartz is probably the best-known crystal. It is sometimes clear like glass or has a softer, milky or opaque tone. It can contain inclusions (other minerals within it – often evidenced by various flecks of colour or internal structures visible within the Quartz) or even rainbow refractions of light. You may find quartz sold in individual pieces or in clusters with one base and many crystals growing out.

Quartz can be massive in size. Live growing quartz sources have been found where even just one individual part of the quartz cluster is many times larger than a human being, yet even small pieces of quartz hold the potential for great power.

HEALING PROPERTIES

Clear Quartz is a Master Healer. It amplifies energy – hence the teaching from the Angel of Clear Quartz is to become clear and aware of your energy, intention and thoughts.

Our thoughts can be positive or negative and Quartz is a teacher of the power of thought. Often those that are still learning this lesson will be spiritually protected by an absence of interest or belief in the healing power of crystals. It is as though they are not yet prepared to handle the power of them, and so the crystals veil themselves from the awareness of the person until the divine timing is appropriate. Many of us at least begin to get a handle on our negativity before a real passion for crystals develops.

If you find that you are interested in working with crystals but are still learning how to manage your thoughts (as most of us are to at least some degree!), it is a great idea initially to "program" your Quartz. You do this by simply holding it in your left hand and placing your right hand over the top of the Quartz. You then say, "Of my own free will, with gratitude, I ask that all energy or programming not of unconditional love be cleared from this crystal now." Perform the cleansing method of your choice (outlined in the introduction) such as breathing in violet light through the top of your head and breathing it out into the crystal with an intention to cleanse it. When the crystal feels clean, after one or more breaths, say, "I program this crystal with the task to dissolve negative energy and amplify unconditional love, through my own free will, so be it". When you are done, just be in your heart with gratitude. You have completed your programming of the Quartz crystal.

Not only does Quartz amplify energy, but it unlocks, regulates and releases it. It is an excellent healer for almost any condition, cleanses the energy field and helps the soul release past life issues that would hold it back from being more fully in this present moment of earthly incarnation.

ABOUT THE ARCHANGEL METATRON

Archangel Metatron is often considered the most powerful of all the Archangels, a Prince or King of the Angels, as large as the world and responsible for serving all of Humanity with a massive team of angels in service to him so that he may complete his task.

One of the most beautiful aspects of Metatron is his ability to teach us about power as a form of great love. His strength doesn't come from creating fear or domination, although when I first connected with him many years ago, he was quite intimidating! I was in a New Year's Eve ritual on the edge of an ocean-washed cliff two hours south of Sydney when I called out his name into the night skies, and had an instant response – thunder crackled and lightning flashed! It was intense to say the least. But in my heart, I just loved him and felt no fear.

This is the key to honouring the presence and spiritual gifts of this powerful archangel, and to learning how to honour power itself as a part of our life. By responding with love and openness, rather than fear or distrust, we stay in our heart and our use of power will be wise, with nothing to fear.

ATLANTEAN SOUL HEALING WITH CLEAR QUARTZ AND THE ARCHANGEL METATRON : PROCESS FOR CLEARING FEAR AND STEPPING INTO YOUR SOUL POWER

Deep within many old souls on the Earth are Atlantean memories, which consciously or unconsciously affect the human lifetime of that soul even now.

During the Atlantean era there was a growth of power without an equal growth of love. As a race, we had been learning to balance love and power and to bring them together with wise intention. The wisest of all intentions is that anything we wish to manifest be for the greatest good of all in how it unfolds.

In Atlantis, there was an abuse of technology and a lust for the power that it could create, which was not matched by a connection to the natural world and its wisdom. The addiction to power was so strong, and so disconnected from heart-centred intention and presence, that great catastrophe and destruction occurred and an entire civilisation was destroyed.

Within many old souls today, there is a subconscious recognition of this pattern still healing itself, and a fear that history will repeat itself. The more disconnected from feminine earth wisdom we have become as a species, the more fear there is that we could once again destroy ourselves and even our beautiful Mother Earth. Once we discovered that we literally do have this destructive power at our fingertips in the form of nuclear power, the fear of power leading to destruction of the world rose – particularly in old souls that carried unresolved past life trauma from Atlantis.

At the time of Atlantis, many tried to speak up but those that were more intent on personal gain than the greater good used their authority to silence wiser voices and act out their lust for power and domination. From that wounded frustration, those who were suppressed at the time may have come to believe that power led to corruption and destruction, although they could equally choose to build their own power so that their voice of love may always be heard, no matter what kind of obsession may be blinding those around them in positions of leadership. Ultimately, in order to stay present and true in their leadership from a place of love, they would need to use power, not shy away from it, therefore demonstrating a higher choice and contributing towards a hopeful future for the human species.

The job of the soul with Atlantean experience is to heal this fear of power within and to redefine power as an expression of love. As we do this within ourselves, we create a new template for human behaviour, a viable alternative for the wounded obsession with power as dominance and technology. There are many spiritual teachers helping the old souls on Earth to do this. The Archangel Metatron is one such divine teacher. Others include the Dalai Lama and previously Mother Teresa. These beings teach love, the path of the heart, and a connection to Mother Earth (another great spiritual teacher) so that we may learn to live in a more balanced fashion, creating wellbeing rather than destruction.

HOW DO YOU KNOW IF YOU ARE HEALING
AT A SOUL LEVEL IN THIS WAY?

You will sense that you carry within you a general fear of becoming powerful if you feel distrust of those who are in positions of authority and power this lifetime. You may find that you fall easily into fear and distrust and wish to opt out of the current framework of politics and financial power struggles altogether.

This is not necessarily negative. In fact, it is often those that dare to live outside of what is considered to be currently 'normal' that allows for new ways of being to be explored, developed and then introduced into society, helping it to grow. You will need to be ready to bring your unique viewpoints back to the collective when they are stable and secure enough to withstand possible criticism and rejection until the wisdom of your difference can be received.

Archangel Metatron will help you with this process, but first you must do your own healing so that you can come from an empowered place of positivity and hope for the human race, rather than fear or despair, or judgement for how things are going for humanity on Mother Earth at this time. We are just learning balance as a species.

Much like a tightrope-walker who may wobble a bit from one side to the other before finding that point of balance, we have to learn from our 'wobbles' as a culture and move forward, appreciating technology, and using it to support world healing (it can bring many together as one) without denying the natural rhythms and boundaries of nature (which teaches us to rest and honour cycles of night and day, rather than always being 'on').

In this healing work you can grow into your own power. It will enable you to boldly and courageously act, to live your higher consciousness in the world and to help manifest humanity's future as a consciously loving, powerful and wise species creating a world of beauty and peace together.

SOUL HEALING PROCESS FOR CLEARING FEAR AND STEPPING INTO YOUR POWER

You will need a cushion or blanket to sit upon, or a chair, four white candles (or tea lights) and a lighter or matches, and a piece of Quartz. If you do not have a piece of Quartz, a small vase or a glass with some clean water in it would suffice. You may also like to have the book open to page 17, which features the Clear Quartz Crystal Angel Mandala in full colour.

Find a quiet place to sit where you will not be disturbed and place the four candles around you in four directions so that you have created a sacred diamond shape around you. Place one in front of you, behind you, to the left and the right. Place your cushion or blanket (or chair) in the centre of the diamond and the Quartz or glass with water in front of you.

Light your four white candles saying the invocation below:

"I call upon Archangel Metatron, divine archangel of peace and power, I call upon the Angel of Clear Quartz in your unconditional love, light and power. I call upon my own higher self, my own soul, and the beings that love me unconditionally. Be with me now as I heal my soul."

When you have lit the candles and repeated the invocation, sit comfortably on your cushion, blanket or chair and gaze at the Quartz or glass before you. Place your right hand above the object and your left palm open, resting on your leg and facing upwards.

Repeat this statement, "Archangel Metatron and the Angel of Clear Quartz now cleanse this sacred object thoroughly, that it be free from fear and negativity, and filled with love."

Close your eyes and focus on breathing and drawing in cleansing light and love through your left palm, and releasing it out of your right palm on the exhalation, releasing into and through the sacred object of your Quartz or water glass. Repeat this cleansing breath seven times.

Keep your right hand slightly above the crystal or glass and place your left hand over your heart, repeating this statement, "I choose now of my own free will to release my soul from fear of power and authority, to forgive and release all memories of abuse of authority by myself or others, from this or any lifetime, that I may be free to bring new awareness of loving power into my life and onto this planet now. I call on the Angel of Clear Quartz and Archangel Metatron, help me draw this fear from my soul and release it now with grace and mercy. So be it!"

Close your eyes and breathe deeply, imagining as you breathe in, there is the presence of

Archangel Metatron completely enveloping you and as you breathe out, there is a magnetic pull of the crystal (or glass) from your right hand, drawing out old toxins of fear from deep within your soul. You may feel emotions releasing. Just stay with the breath for at least forty-four long slow breaths in and out, with focus on the angelic light around you and the crystal drawing old energy out of you from the palm of your hand. Your arm may feel dirty or heavy as this is happening. Just remain focused and breathe.

When you have completed your forty-four breaths and feel ready to move on, place your hands in prayer position in front of your heart and quietly say, "Thank you". Place your hands in your lap and rest for a moment. If you want to meditate a little you can. Just stay with the breath and relax.

When you are ready, place your right hand above the object and your left palm open, resting on your leg and facing upwards and repeat this statement, "Archangel Metatron and the Angel of Clear Quartz now cleanse this sacred object thoroughly, that it be free from fear and negativity, and filled with love."

Close your eyes and focus on breathing in cleansing light and love through your left palm, and releasing it out through your right palm on the exhalation, through the sacred object of your Quartz or water glass. Repeat this cleansing breath seven times.

Then open your eyes and place your left hand on the sacred object and your right hand on your chest, over your heart centre.

Repeat this statement, "I draw to me, through the unconditional love, light and grace of the Angel of Clear Quartz and the power, presence and love of the Archangel Metatron, what I need to heal my soul relationship with power now, that I may live my soul light fully and completely on this Earth, free from fear and anchored in love. Help me now beloved ones, through unconditional love and divine grace, to surrender into complete transformation of my relationship to power. I choose to honour myself as a powerful being, spiritually and in all ways. I choose to feel safe and secure in this power, to always know that you are with me, guiding me and that I choose to be powerful in a wise and compassionate way. Through the grace of the Divine, so be it!"

Close your eyes and focus on the breath. Allow yourself to draw in angelic light through the crystal (or water), the power of Clear Quartz amplifying the grace and blessings of Archangel Metatron, as it flows into all levels of your being. Visualise breathing in the light through your left hand, into your heart, and the light flowing down into your belly and then all the way down to your feet and into the Earth. At the same time, imagine that light flowing up from your heart all the way up to your head and out through your crown. Picture or intend that you are filled with light until it seeps out through your skin and fills the room that you are in. Imagine it filling your entire home, then your suburb, your country, your planet and radiating out into the universe. Keep relaxed and breathe in and out for at least forty-four breaths.

When you are ready, simply withdraw your hands from the crystal and place them in your lap, resting and holding awareness of this power of light within you and all around you.

Remain in a restful pose for as long as you like and when you are ready, place your hands in prayer position in front of your chest and bow your head slightly, closing your eyes if you wish to and just saying, "Thank you".

Rest for a moment then get up, extinguish your candles and place your crystal where it can remind you of your changing relationship to power. If you wish to dispose of the water, lovingly surrender it to the Earth in a garden or house plant.

You have completed your soul healing ritual and now is the time to be open to positive changes in your own thoughts, feelings and behaviour as you get used to living with more power. You will get used to it – just give yourself time to adapt. You will become more comfortable with power and more skilled at using it. Simply have faith in yourself and let it happen.

PSYCHOLOGICAL-EMOTIONAL HEALING WITH CLEAR QUARTZ AND THE ARCHANGEL METATRON: RELEASING POWER ADDICTION AND BECOMING GENUINELY EMPOWERED

Addiction to power is rampant in contemporary culture. The lure of it can cast even the most spiritually committed individual into a trance. We may lust for spiritual power, physical power, financial or emotional power or some combination of these. We might forget that the power of the Divine is greater than any other power we could possible imagine. This power is within us, waiting to be awoken with love.

In spiritual traditions in particular, where power is often considered a dirty word, the desire to be powerful can also be tainted with shame and guilt. This doesn't make our healthy and natural need to explore our power go away. It just makes us more inclined to judge it as unspiritual, as belonging to the ego. We can attempt to hide our quest for power from others, and even from our own conscious awareness. This makes it even harder to be free from judgements about the desire or need for power. Being upfront about this desire and need however is what helps us cultivate a healthier relationship to power and a wise and playful expression of it spiritually, emotionally and physically in the world.

At the heart of any obsession with power is a deep, subconscious feeling of helplessness, powerlessness, abandonment and rejection. Combine this with the often limited definitions of power in contemporary Western society (such as having a lot of money or a certain profession as a form of status) and it is easy to see that healing, transformation and a more 'empowering' definition(!) of power is greatly needed.

When we are in touch with our power in a healthy way, we feel more trusting of ourselves and of life, less helpless and more able to act when needed. We are able to live our intuitions and visions in the physical world. We fear less and resist the flow of life less (because we trust where it is leading us) and so our creative expressions can happen quite quickly. We are less subject to how others may think things should be done, and more able to just be and do according to our own inner wisdom. We can be more playful in life. This is not a way to try to avoid suffering. It is more about engaging with life from a position of feeling empowered to do something with what is occurring. When we feel empowered, we feel more able to creatively work with a situation, rather than only having to either endure it or be broken by it.

Being empowered is not about controlling others but rather offering an inspirational alternative about how to live on this planet through positive choice and intention. For many of us, this is a completely new idea. We might not have many role models (if any) for living an empowered life, so we may need some help in really 'getting' this idea of power and how to live it. The Archangel Metatron and the Angel of Clear Quartz are willing to bless you with what you need to get this flowing in your life.

HOW DO I KNOW IF I NEED HEALING IN THIS WAY AND AT THIS LEVEL OF MY BEING?

If you have dreams within that just do not seem to be manifesting – no matter how much you try or how hard you work, then somewhere within you there may be a subconscious block preventing you from actualising the divine power that is already within you. If you find that you are more powerful in your inner world, in your visions or fantasies, than in your day-to-day experience of your manifestation ability, then it may be time for you to take the healing journey to step out of a denial or addiction to your power (and perhaps fear of failure, shame and being hurt) and begin to really live into your own power and experience it.

If you haven't had any well-functioning role models for healthy power based in love, this healing may really be a leap of trust for you – and very exciting too. It won't always be easy but this healing will help support you to reach beyond what you have known into a more satisfying way of being. If you are prepared to be uncomfortable at times as you grow, you'll find the whole experience more enjoyable and profoundly changing. You have the power of the Divine within you. Its true nature is love. It is time for you to access it, become one with it and to live your spiritual potential now, in this lifetime.

The healing process below will prepare you to receive and manifest what you need including an adjustment in your intentions, beliefs and emotions, so you can attract uplifting people, situations and opportunities through which to express your powerful self. It is so much more fun, more exciting, and more vulnerable, real and refreshing to live in this way. Once you realise that trying to control life circumstances and situations is about an addiction to power that covers up distrust and feelings of helplessness, you can begin to experience genuine power instead. Genuine power is not about control. It is a responsiveness and playfulness that become possible when you fundamentally trust in life.

Surrendering the addiction to false power and stepping into real power is where you stop trying to control life and really start living it. I remember when I first began healing my own experience with power addiction. I craved being alive, to surrender into the unknown and to live in a less controlled way, with more freedom to really let go and just be me!

Yet at the same time I was so scared to step outside of what I knew and to let go of my attempts to keep myself hidden away and 'safe'. The forms of addiction that I used to support myself and attempt to control my life were so familiar to me.

At the time I really couldn't imagine ever living without them. It was a long and difficult road, with many stops and starts along the way, and I have since learned it can be much quicker and easier with the grace of divine healing. I had to learn how to take risks and trust in life – to not try to avoid getting hurt, but to realise that I had enough spiritual power within me to live in a less defended way. I had to learn that my power could guide me into some interesting adventures, and that in the end, I would be even better than OK!

Divine healing helped me let go of my fear and learn to trust, to awaken enough to realise that I had power within me, and it was alright to practice using it to support myself as I grew spiritually mature enough to allow the divine to support me!

You can choose to be open to receive that grace now beloved. You have been drawn to this chapter to receive it. Once you start really living in your power, it will be so interesting, so full of adventure and unexpected (and joyful) twists and turns, you'll never want to stop. Have faith and know that this process will help you step out of the past and into a new way of being.

PSYCHOLOGICAL-EMOTIONAL HEALING PROCESS FOR RELEASING POWER ADDICTION AND BECOMING GENUINELY EMPOWERED

For this exercise, you will need to find a comfortable place to sit where you can write comfortably and won't be disturbed, preferably somewhere private where you can speak aloud and not be concerned about being overheard. You will also need two pieces of paper and a pen.

Sit quietly and say the following, "I call upon the healing power of my own soul, and upon the Angel of Clear Quartz and the Archangel Metatron. I ask for healing, assistance and protection now, so be it!".

Close your eyes and focus on your breath. Visualise or intend that the space around you is filled with clear light, and know that the Angel of Clear Quartz is with you. Then focus on the energy around you and imagine it becoming very refined and pure, strong and powerful, flooded with light. Know that the Archangel Metatron is also now with you.

Sense or feel these two angelic energies blending into one beautiful light all around you. Breathe this light in and relax for a few moments. Imagine this energy flowing in on your breath, and descending deeply into your belly, down through your legs and into the Earth. Then imagine the energy flowing into you again on your next inhalation and rising up through the heart, all the way up and out through the top of your head.

When you are ready open your eyes and pick up your pen.

On the first piece of paper, write down how you feel, what you believe and what you think about the people in your life (or in general) who are powerful. This may include people in positions of authority, who have a lot of influence in your life, people who are wealthy or successful or even how you imagine yourself to be during the times when you express your power. What do you think or feel about these people? What are your attitudes towards them?

Notice if these are generally positive or negative emotions, attitudes and beliefs, or a mixture of both positive and negative responses.

When you have finished writing this first list, say the following statement, aloud if possible, "I now choose to forgive and release all the negative role-models of power from my body, mind and energy field. I no longer choose to keep these as my reference for how to be powerful because they do not resonate with my heart's truth. I now choose, of my own free will, to call upon the Angel of Clear Quartz and Archangel Metatron to assist me in generating new models of power, to live my power as fully from the heart and soul of my being as possible. Through divine grace, so be it."

Pick up your second piece of paper ready for the next part of this healing exercise. Now focus your attention on a figure who is powerful in an extremely positive way – either in your life or that you have heard about (such as a political or spiritual figure whom you may admire). If you cannot think of a real person that you have been exposed to, then choose to create an imaginary figure, imbuing him or her with all the personality and soul traits that you imagine would make a positively empowered being. Write down as many qualities and descriptions as you can about this powerful figure and how that power manifests in a positive way. You may write descriptions, draw imagery or write words or feelings. Whatever feels right for you. If you find yourself struggling to do this, perhaps because your exposure to power has been primarily negative and very traumatic, do not worry. The presence of Archangel Metatron will be with you and heal you as you do as much, or as little, of this exercise as you can.

When you have finished writing this list, repeat the following statement, "I forgive myself for any time I have not stepped into my power, was not ready, willing or able to do so, or just didn't know that I had the choice at the time! I forgive myself for all of this now, and release any old shame or self-criticism or judgement from my body, mind and energy field. I acknowledge that I have always done the best that I could and I now choose, of my own free will, to begin to experience myself as an empowered being, with wisdom, inner strength, a willingness to trust myself and to trust life. I know that everything that happens is an opportunity to grow. This is my true power, my ability to grow spiritually and rely on the love and peace that is within me. Through divine grace, I call upon all the relationships, situations and opportunities that can mercifully and lovingly bring me into more power, optimism and self-expression now. Through my own free will so be it!"

When you are ready, crumple up your first piece of paper in your hands and say, "I release you now with complete forgiveness and acceptance. Go in peace." Toss that piece of paper away into a rubbish bin. Take your second piece of paper and place it somewhere that will help remind you of this positive vision of power and help it seep into your subconscious mind throughout the day. You may choose to keep it pinned to your mirror or the back of your bedroom door. I suggest keeping it near you for at least the next four weeks as you grow into this new expression of yourself. Do not give up. You WILL get there. Have faith and know you are being helped. In fact, the process has already started.

PHYSICAL HEALING WITH CLEAR QUARTZ AND THE ARCHANGEL METATRON: CLEARING CONFUSION AND CHOOSING STRENGTH

Sometimes our power issues show up in a physical manner. Our difficulty in being clear, concise and direct in our energy mentally and emotionally can filter down into fatigue in our bodies. We can have all sorts of anxieties and ailments, such as immune and digestive problems and headaches, and feelings of physical weakness that arise which are actually more about us forgetting our strength than something being wrong with our body!

Lack of clarity and forgetting that we have great inner strength that can flow into our bodies when we need it can cast us into overwhelm and lead us into fatigue. There are times when we need to rest and that is important. There are also times when we will gain the replenishment and energy that we need from an empowering physical practice such as yoga or the physical healing practice shared below.

HOW DO I KNOW IF I NEED THIS PHYSICAL HEALING PRACTICE?

If you tune in with your body as you read the practice outline, you will know if your body wants to do it! If you are not feeling so in tune with your body, but you have any of the following physical symptoms then you may like to give this practice a try anyway – tiredness, fatigue, overwhelm, headaches, digestive or immune depletion (feeling like your digestion is slow and heavy or feeling a bit sick or run down).

PHYSICAL HEALING PRACTICE FOR CLEARING CONFUSION AND CHOOSING STRENGTH

Pick a space where you can stand comfortably and not feel crowded, where you can speak aloud and not be concerned about being overheard and where you will not be disturbed for the next five to ten minutes.

Start by saying the following, "Of my own free will, I now choose to liberate my body from confusion and liberate my inner strength, releasing it into my body. I choose to do this through unconditional love and grace of the Angel of Clear Quartz and Archangel Metatron, so be it!"

Stand up with both your feet about hip width apart and your arms resting by your sides. Keep your joints, including your knees, slightly bent and comfortable.

Focus on your feet. Rock slightly backwards and forwards until you find your balance between the front and back of your feet. Shift your weight slightly from left to right and back as you find your sense of connecting all four sides of the feet with the earth.

Then focus on your belly and imagine that you can feel a cord of light from your feet rising up to your belly, igniting the inside of your belly. Imagine that a fire is growing in your belly as you rock slightly back on your heels, bouncing up and down lightly on your heels (without your feet leaving the ground). The more you rock on your heels, the more the cord of light reaches up to your belly and inside your belly a fire grows.

Imagine this fire growing until it feels natural for you to open your mouth, stick out your tongue and breath out with an "ahhhhhh" sound. Repeat this several times, imagining that each time you do it, you are releasing confusion, debility and fatigue. Then stop and close your eyes, standing still for one long slow deep breath in and out.

When you are ready, begin tightening every single muscle in your body – your face, your arms, your shoulders, back, abdominals, buttocks, legs and even your feet. Pull every muscle tight as you breathe in for one breath, then let go and as you breathe out, become relaxed.

Be aware of the energy moving in your body, the strength that is awakening. Repeat this contraction on an in-breath one more time, breathing in, tightening and holding in the breath for a moment, while contracting all your muscles, then letting go and relaxing on the out-breath, feeling the awakening of strength in your body.

When you are ready say the following sentence at least three times. "I am clear and strong, and I honour myself. I am powerful in body, mind and spirit."

When you are ready, take a deep breath in, exhale naturally and open your eyes.

PRAYER – AFFIRMATION

To invoke the healing power of Clear Quartz and Archangel Metatron at any time, you can repeat the following affirmation quietly in your mind, or aloud.

"The Clear Divine Light Ignites The Loving Power Within Me."

2.

ARAGONITE (Sacred Rest)
and ARCHANGEL REMIEL (Carer of the Soul)

THE GIFT OF REST

SPIRITUAL GUIDANCE FROM THE ANGEL OF ARAGONITE
AND THE ARCHANGEL REMIEL

With so much to do and so many dreams to manifest, your precious heart also needs rest in order to grow. You cannot do it all at once. It would not be so much fun if there was nothing left to do or learn anyway. What we offer you now is permission to be just as you are right now. Know that you are doing well. Know that it is all happening in perfect time. Know that there is no need to rush. Know that you are loved, accepted and cherished. And so now beloved soul we ask if you will receive our gift. Will you open your heart to receive the gift of rest and allow all else to happen naturally? You do not need to turn the planets or make the stars shine. It all happens naturally and so too does your divine path unfold without you having to make it so. Rest now. Let us hold you near. It is in rest that the healing occurs and then you are ready to play once more.

PICTURING ARAGONITE

Aragonite takes several different forms. It can look like sparkling white coral. It can also look like dark orange-brown sputnik-shapes, round with cylindrical shaped 'arms' poking out. It can also look like a soft smooth fan shape, white in colour with beige tinges.

The energies of Aragonite are inviting and warm no matter what the shape. They have their own personalities, as I believe all crystals do, but there is a supportive energy in all the different forms of Aragonite which is the same. There is perhaps a little hint here from the Angel of Aragonite about how rest can come in different forms too – physical, emotional or mental, depending on what is needed, through stillness or nourishing activity .

HEALING PROPERTIES

Aragonite is a grounding, comforting crystal that helps us access the quality of sacred rest. It helps anchor us to our lower chakras so we can connect to the Earth. If we have a lot of mental power and often force ourselves to accomplish tasks without taking into account the needs of the body and mind to replenish, then Aragonite can help us reconnect and rebalance. If we are very task-oriented with an endless 'to do' list, Aragonite helps us learn that balance is ultimately more productive than endurance that stretches us beyond limits in an unhealthy way. Burn out takes a lot longer to heal and repair than taking timely breaks to replenish ourselves.

Aragonite helps strengthen our nervous system and it helps us learn how to draw in to ourselves, to conserve and build energy. If we have a tendency to give more out than we take in, emotionally, financially, energetically or otherwise, then this stone helps us learn to find more balance in our giving and receiving energies. Aragonite helps heal the wounding that keep us in the pattern of giving away more than we take in.

Aragonite also helps us find the spiritual presence within our own physical bodies. It assists us to not only turn our awareness to the heavens in seeking divine connection, but to recognise that there is within our body a sacred divine presence. There is a feminine wisdom within the body which teaches the productivity of rest, of how essential it is in a culture plagued by symptoms of imbalance due to overemphasis on activity. Aragonite supports healing of those symptoms (such as disease, depression and addiction) whilst helping prevent the imbalance in the first place by calling us back to rest when needed.

ABOUT THE ARCHANGEL REMIEL

Archangel Remiel has a sacred task of caring for souls. He is associated with the qualities of mercy and compassion which are essential for being able to rest. Without kindness and compassion there is no recognition of limitation and the need to honour it.

Remiel is an archangel of transitions, helping souls move from one phase of life into the next natural phase. In any transition, there is a moment that requires patience and surrender, to let go and allow the process to happen. Sometimes this involves uncertainty or confusion as the old way of being is released and the new way has not yet been firmly established. Remiel is with us as we go through these transitions. His love and protection allows us to feel safe and rest patiently as we await the new phase to come into being.

I had a personal encounter with Remiel during the writing of this book. I had scheduled a month to complete the task, which is not very long at all, but I had an overseas teaching program to prepare, for dates that were already booked, and I couldn't afford much more time than that one month to complete the book if I was to be able to honour my other obligations. To stay on schedule, I needed to write very quickly. When I was well rested, to write a chapter or sometimes even two in one day was attainable as information flowed quickly. However when mentally tired, writing anything was a challenge! On one such day I was worried that I would fall behind and wondered if I was utterly mad to set such a challenging pace for myself.

In response to my concern, Archangel Remiel spoke to me with a simple statement that took me straight into my heart and helped me to let go. He simply said, "come to me and rest". That statement helped me enormously. I did trust His loving guidance and I relaxed and took a break. As I switched off, my mental batteries could get recharged and the information began to flow again. Within a day I was writing again. The book was finished on time. I even had a few luxurious days to spare before charging into my next project.

SOUL HEALING WITH ARAGONITE AND THE ARCHANGEL REMIEL: NATURAL ALIGNMENT WITH YOUR SOUL

When we are aligned with our own higher self we feel connected to something much vaster than ourselves that is nourishing, loving and wise and capable of holding us when we cannot hold ourselves. During times of intense growth there can be inner tension and purging of old emotions as our being seeks to cleanse itself of old energies and open up to new light and life within. If you are surrendering at a deep level, there will be times when you don't feel that you are able to control the process, that you are being swept up in a flow of energy and you have no choice but to go with it, for it is too powerful for your conscious mind to restrain.

This can be challenging, and if you do not feel held by a loving, containing presence during such moments then it can be downright terrifying. It is the sacred presence of the soul or higher self, that spiritual part of us that is vaster than any of our fears or issues, that enables us to really let go without fear, even if we don't understand what is happening or why. Archangel Remiel and the Crystal Angel of Aragonite can help us connect with our soul, to really feel that we are loved and held, no matter what.

What brings us to this alignment with the soul and allows for deep growth to occur within a sense of security and trust? Actually, alignment with the soul is our most natural state. It is the innate balance of our being. What takes us out of the state is more of an issue – and that is overactivity and concern with having to make something happen. Rest is the natural healer of this unhelpful belief system. It takes us out of having to make something happen and into a state of surrender where the body naturally heals itself and aligns with the soul.

It is a little bit like those inflatable toy 'punching bags' that stand upright, and can be kicked or punched away from you and will then quickly snap back into an upright position. There is a weight at the bottom of the bag which keeps it connected to the ground and helps pull the bag back into an upright position after it has been hit. Our body is like the weight in the bottom of the inflatable toy and the upright position is like the natural alignment of the body and soul together. The more force we use, the more the bag moves out of alignment, but as soon as we stop, it naturally pops back into an upright position again. It is the weight that enables this to happen, it pulls it back into alignment instantly. This is what happens when we rest, dropping our awareness into the body. Our soul alignment snaps back into place and we feel reconnected.

HOW DO YOU KNOW IF YOU ARE HEALING AT A SOUL LEVEL IN THIS WAY?

You will know when you need to align with your soul because you will feel that your life is asking something of you that is greater than your current abilities, state of awareness and consciousness. You will have to grow in order to grasp what is happening from a higher perspective and to allow it to manifest through you.

You might be going through a period of confusion or doubt, lacking clarity about how you are supposed to handle a particular situation or repeating pattern in your life, or you may just feel unable to break out of a 'spiritual stalemate' into a new reality. You might be attempting to change your life experience in some profound way and in need of an influx of supportive energy to help you shift vibration. You may be searching for the courage to test out new, more empowering belief systems and ways of living and being in the world. Rest helps you recharge, replenish, restore and reprogram yourself into alignment with your own soul so that you can accomplish these tasks with more wisdom, inner power and less forceful struggle. Alignment with the soul is always helpful, but especially during such times.

SOUL ALIGNMENT PROCESS FOR DIVINE CONNECTION

For this process you will need a comfortable place where you can rest – preferably sitting on a chair or lounge with the spine upright, your back supported by cushions or a blanket, but you can lie down if you prefer. If you choose to lie down you may fall asleep but if this occurs then perhaps this is just the sort of rest that you needed.

You will also need to turn off your phone or computer, to create a peaceful and quiet space if you can, and one candle (a tea light is fine) lit in your space also. If you have a piece of Aragonite, then place that near your body or hold it lightly in your hand if you wish. If you do not have a piece of Aragonite, that is fine as we will be calling upon the spirit of the crystal to be with you for this healing process.

After you have lit your candle (making sure that there are no windows open near the candle that could cause something to ignite should you fall asleep during this exercise), place it where you can see it easily, sit or lie comfortably and say the invocation or prayer below:

"I call upon Archangel Remiel, divine archangel of rest and transition, and I call upon the Angel of Aragonite through unconditional love. I call upon my own higher self, my own soul, and the beings that love me unconditionally. Be with me now as I heal my soul."

Sitting (or lying) comfortably gaze at the candle and visualise or intend that the pure flame of the candle is burning within your heart chakra in the centre of your chest. Continue to gaze at the candle or close your eyes and imagine or intend that the flame grows brighter and stronger with each inhalation. With each exhalation the flame expands until your entire heart feels like a flame that is gentle, pure and yet also very strong.

Repeat this statement, "Archangel Remiel and the Angel of Aragonite, I call upon you now to bless me with the gift of sacred rest. I surrender all holding on, all tightness and stress, I surrender into divine peace and rest."

Focusing on your heart and the flame within, imagine that as you close your eyes, you can see inside the flame of your heart with your inner vision. Imagine that within your heart, a temple of light opens up and you can step within it. There is light around you, above you, behind you and before you. You feel your whole being melting into this beautiful bright and softly inviting light.

As you connect with that light it grows within you and you start to feel each of your cells pulsing with the energy of that soft warm light. You feel the energy drawing you towards the Earth beneath you. From beneath you, you sense an even brighter light opening up and a beautiful cradle of light forming in pure white and soft brown earthy tones. It is warm, nourishing and very strong. You can choose to rest into that cradle if you wish to do so, allowing your body to become heavy and relaxed, as you settle into the cradle of light, created by the Angel of Aragonite.

As you rest there, you become aware of a second source of angelic light filling the space. It descends as a column of light and then expands into the space. You may sense massive pure white wings with touches of earthy tones in each feather, and a sense of deep peace and trust fills your being. This is the presence of Archangel Remiel.

His energy wraps around the cradle of light with a feeling of a big hug. Imagine settling deeper, feeling peaceful and relaxed. You may find emotion arising as you let go and that is just fine. You may have thoughts or worries begin to rise. This is a sign of healing too. Just allow any emotions or thoughts to pass through you as you focus on the feeling of safety and peace, relaxing and resting.

When you are ready, repeat the declaration below. Say it quietly to yourself. Allow your voice to be peaceful and soothing. Speak slowly and really feel the words as you speak them. Allow the words to feel soft and take you deeper into the awareness of light in your heart.

"Through my own free will and the graceful healing of Archangel Remiel and the beautiful Angel of Aragonite, I give myself permission to rest. I surrender striving, fighting, forcing and struggling now from all levels of my being. Here and now, I choose to permit myself to feel safe, to trust and to rest. I trust and I rest. All unfolds freely and according to divine perfection. There is nothing to be done except to trust and to rest. I do so now with gratitude and contentment in my heart."

Keeping your awareness on the light, close your eyes again and just be. You might rest for a little while, fall asleep or just sit quietly and peacefully feeling the angelic presence that loves you and supports you so much.

Take as much time as you need and when you are ready, allow yourself to gradually bring your awareness back to the room. Take a moment to reconnect to the imagery or sensation of the candle flame within your heart, burning gently and strongly. Touch your heart lightly with your hands for a moment and bow your head honouring yourself and the importance of allowing yourself to rest.

When you are ready, extinguish your candle and ease back into your everyday life. Your soul alignment ritual is completed. You will be changed each time you do this process. Every time you choose consciously to rest, you are building a loving and respectful connection to your body and your soul and declaring that you are worthy. It is safe to trust that all things come at the right time and the right way without fear-driven strain. Rest is a statement of trust that you are doing just fine and all is well in your world.

PSYCHOLOGICAL-EMOTIONAL HEALING WITH ARAGONITE AND THE ARCHANGEL REMIEL: CALMING THE MIND

The mind is something like a sword. We can use it to cut through confusion and find clarity or we can lose control of it, likely causing much pain. The difficulty with the mind is that it tends to be worshipped in Western culture and most education from an early age onwards is geared towards orienting us in our minds. We are taught to think according to a strict set of rules and cultural programming rather than to feel our way through life. This means that the mind gets the job of doing more than it is equipped to do. The heart is supposed to lead us, the mind is meant to be utilised to put our inner guidance into action. Somehow we got this mixed up and learned that the heart is second to the logical mind, and we learned to trust our minds to lead us instead of our heart wisdom.

The result of this mix up is not so great. We can end up feeling overwhelmed, confused, tired and exhausted, not sure which way to turn or just feeling like we aren't doing a very good job of managing our lives. What is needed first in such cases, is compassion. Otherwise we aren't going to give ourselves the recognition that we need healing or the time of day to receive it. Secondly what is needed is a chance to empty out some of the content of our minds, giving space in which to rest. There is a spiritual teaching that a full cup cannot receive any more – and so it is with the mind. When it is full of thoughts, lists, worries and anxieties, there is hardly any space to receive the clear guidance that would help us navigate life far less stressfully and more effectively. Calling on guidance to help us is very easy to do. The key is to have enough space to receive the impulses that flow instantly from our guidance to us when we ask for help.

So much mental agitation is based on a lack of trust. Without trust, our mind is easily filled with endless worries. Anxiety can develop as we push others away and try to handle our inner stress on our own. A kind of pain-based independence is created and the mind has to do more than it should. It tries to handle every detail rather than softening and expecting that life will present us with the help that we need for our projects and relationships to be successful.

HOW DO I KNOW IF I NEED HEALING IN THIS WAY AND AT THIS LEVEL OF MY BEING?

If you feel trapped in patterns of procrastination or you are trying to work but cannot summon the energy to do it, if you are having difficulty sleeping or meditating because your mind just will not stop reeling with ideas and thoughts, if you feel depressed, if you are suffering from anxiety or fear (even if you cannot quite articulate what the anxiety or fear may be about) or if you feel that you are the only person that you can rely on to manifest your dreams or create the success you desire, then you are in need (or soon will be) of a mental healing that empties and calms the mind. It is time to open to accurate guidance, fresh energy and healthy nourishment through your relationships.

This might seem like a lot to ask of a simple healing practice like the one outlined below. However it can be reassuring to realise that the only thing that stands between us feeling supported in our dreams, nourished by our relationships and supported by life – able to let go of mental striving and perfectionism to live with more pleasure, spontaneity and creative productivity – is an emptying out of our minds. When we do this, we open to new and more desirable thought patterns that become the template for improved life experiences, filling some of the space created by releasing outmoded thought patterns. We can always choose to leave a little mental space within, so that guidance and wisdom can 'pop in' whenever they choose!

PSYCHOLOGICAL-EMOTIONAL HEALING PROCESS
FOR CALMING THE MIND

This is a simple healing exercise that is effective and can take from a few minutes to over twenty minutes if you need it. The most important preparation for this exercise is to find a version of the posture that you will assume for the healing that is comfortable for you. You can choose to do this in a variety of ways depending on your flexibility. You will be in this posture for several minutes so it needs to be comfortable. You will also need to wear enough layers to stay warm as you will cool down as you start to relax into this pose.

Please note if you have low blood pressure, then it is recommended that you speak to your health care practitioner before doing any deep relaxation work or forward folding yoga poses like the one described here. You may choose to do this exercise simply seated comfortably instead of assuming a posture.

The original version of the posture is called "child's pose" in Hatha Yoga. The basis of this posture is to kneel with the tops of your feet resting flat on the floor, then sit your buttocks down on to your heels, when you are ready, then leaning forward, resting your forehead on the floor, or if you cannot reach the floor, then rest your forehead on your fists, gently balancing on each other and resting on the floor to provide a prop for your forehead.

A variation of child's pose, is to have the arms extended by your head, resting the hands, palms down on the floor. Another variation is to have the arms resting down by your sides, with the tops of the arms and backs of the hands resting on the floor, palms facing upwards, beside your feet.

The tops of your feet will be resting on the floor, toes touching and knees can either be together or apart. If you find it uncomfortable or claustrophobic to have your knees together under your chest as you curl over, your forehead towards the floor, the knees can be widened as you work slowly towards laying your forehead on your fists or on the ground, with your buttocks working towards resting on your heels.

If you don't feel comfortable in this yoga pose, don't force it. The pose of the child is a resting pose and this healing exercise is based on assuming a physically calming and restful posture. The benefit of a forward folding posture like the child's pose where you are bending at the waist and compressing the front of the body slightly, lowering the head, is that it activates the parasympathetic nervous system which calms you down and eventually empties and stills the mind.

So if you need another option for a comfortable posture for this exercise, you may like to try sitting on a cushion on the floor and resting your arms and forehead on a lounge seat, or sitting at a table and placing your arms on the table, lowering your head and resting them on your hands on the table.

Just follow the basic principles of the posture – you are bending forwards somewhat from the waist and you are placing your head lower than if you were sitting upright, resting your forehead either on a cushion or other surface such as your hands or fists on the table or floor. The key is to be comfortable and be able to hold the pose for several minutes at least. Your body and mind need time to unwind and connect with peace, especially if you are wound up tight with inner stress and mental tension based on overwork.

Once you have experimented with some postures and found what feels comfortable for you at this particular time, prepare yourself to take the posture and before you do so, repeat the following statement of intention, "I call upon the grace and healing of Archangel Remiel, please hold me safe as I release mental stress and open to peace. I call upon the healing regeneration and practical reorganisation of the Angel of Aragonite, please help me through unconditional love to empty and reorganise my mind so that it supports the graceful manifestation of the true desires of my heart. I surrender and rest now to allow this to happen effortlessly and with grace and mercy. Through my own free will, so be it."

Assume your posture and focus on the breath. Allow yourself to sense what is happening in your body as you rest. Bring your awareness to your joints and to your spine as you bend forward, allowing your forehead to rest on the floor or your hands. Become aware of the breath and allow it to flow deeply in and out. Be patient and allow yourself to gently draw your belly button in towards your spine. Notice as you do this, that the spine naturally responds by lengthening, allowing you more easily to place your forehead on your hands or on the floor, and your buttocks (if you are in traditional child's pose) can reach your heels more fully and settle. Focus on the breath and allow the spine to elongate and relax.

Imagine your forehead discharging any excess energy, either straight into the floor or through the cushion or your hands, straight into the Earth. Imagine a slight pulling effect as the Earth draws out old energy from your mind. If fear or other emotions come up as you let go, this is a good sign that it is working for you. Try not to shy away from the process. Let the emotion go along with the thoughts and patterning, straight into the Earth. After you have been with this process for a period of time that feels emptying enough for you, stay for at least another three deep slow breaths.

Next, imagine that instead of pulling energy out, the beautiful earth energy of peace is rising up into your mind from the Earth. Imagine breathing it up through any part of your body that is contact with the Earth – your forehead, your arms or hands, your feet, your knees and lower legs, or if you are sitting on the floor, imagine breathing up through the base of your spine. Let that earth energy of peace fill you. Imagine that there is a vast space opening up inside of your body and mind as you breath and then just follow the breath and forget about releasing or drawing in energy. Just focus on the breath, stay in the posture and let it happen. You are being helped by the crystal angels and the healing will happen naturally.

When you have had enough, very slowly curl up to a seated position, bringing your head up last. Rest here for as long as it feels good or simply fall asleep if you are doing this as a cure for insomnia. When you are ready, slowly begin to move your body and bring your awareness back into the room, ready to move on with your daily activities.

If you are going through a particularly challenging, demanding or stressful period in your life, you can repeat this exercise as a form of daily meditation. If suffering from insomnia, you can practice just before retiring each evening. You can also use this practice to come into your body and ground your mind first thing in the morning upon rising. It can be a lovely way to greet the day with love and a more peaceful mind!

Depending on what you needs are, this practice can be effective over time, gradually discharging old programs and opening you up to more supportive and nourishing mental states of peace, or a powerful calming practice when needed from time to time.

PHYSICAL HEALING WITH ARAGONITE AND THE ARCHANGEL REMIEL: HEALING THROUGH PEACEFUL CONNECTION TO THE EARTH

Often we don't really know how to rest. We may try to give ourselves a break by going on a holiday and then getting incredibly stressed over how to take care of our animals, plants and business whilst away, or by oversleeping, overeating, drinking too much, exercising too much or emotionally medicating ourselves through other various addictions like sex, shopping or endless television watching! I once worked in a management consultancy business where some of the executives were so stressed by the thought of leaving the control that they had over their career to go on holiday with their family that their blood pressure would rise until they could finally go back to their demanding jobs again! Who knew 'taking a break' could actually create more stress?

In such instances, the result of trying to take a break is often frustrating and not genuinely restorative if what we really need is rest, rather than some temporary thrills (as fun as they may be at times) or obligations to 'go away on holiday'.

If we haven't been taught as children how to naturally listen to and respond to the needs of our body for rest (that would be a rare and precious lesson in a contemporary Western culture) then we might actively avoid rest, trying to distract ourselves rather than simply letting go and allowing the body the peace that it needs to restore itself.

I remember once hearing a farmer talk of nature as being able to heal herself, as having her own wisdom and rhythms but just needing time and patience to repair herself. If we respected Her in this way, he said, She could handle over-farming from time to time, provided that she was allowed to recover and repair. The body is much the same. It has an amazing ability to self-heal if allowed to do so, even after periods of great imbalance, but we must be prepared to give back to ourselves, not just constantly take until we end up unwell.

HOW DO I KNOW IF I NEED THIS
PHYSICAL HEALING PRACTICE?

Physical fatigue can become such a way of life that we often have no idea exactly how exhausted we are until we stop to rest. I suspect that we intuitively recognise this and that is why many of us are afraid to actually stop. It is when we stop that we become more present to our situation. We might suddenly realise that we are very tired and worry that we can't take the time to rest because of all our responsibilities. We may have to say 'no' to certain people or obligations in order to take care of ourselves. That may cause tension that could actually help heal a relationship but this may be difficult to accept at first. The whole situation might be challenging – and so we stay busy to avoid having to deal with it. Eventually however we will need to accept the responsibility for self-care if we are to continue living a healthy and productive life.

Yet the longer we leave it, the greater the task of healing will be. If we remember that small conscious steps can be enjoyable and lead to great gains, then the prospect of actually stopping and letting ourselves rest can be less confronting.

I see this often in yoga classes when a portion of the class will always leave at the end of the physical practices but before the final resting pose and meditation which is often only a few minutes in Western classes anyway. We are still learning the productive value of rest. Or perhaps it is fear that prompts those premature departures from the classroom, fear of what may arise in the rest. We do need courage to allow ourselves to rest when the culture around us may not see its value or even actively despise it as self-indulgent or lazy.

Yet rest brings us many productive gifts. Rest helps us become clearer and more focused, as we relax and feel more open to creative solutions. It can help us tap into the endless stream of divine assistance that is always reaching to us. It enables us to switch off from a problem to gain a better perspective when we return to it. Many modern health issues such as sleep disorders and eating disorders (especially over-eating and digestive complaints) are symptoms of insufficient rest. Often we only rest when our body forces us by becoming sick, but if you learn to honour your needs for physical rest, sickness will become something that happens far less frequently, ultimately saving you time, money and discomfort, and helping you feel more in tune with yourself. It is quite simply, a far more pleasant way to live.

PHYSICAL HEALING PRACTICE FOR PEACEFUL
CONNECTION TO THE EARTH

For this healing practice, you will need somewhere you can lie comfortably on your back, feeling warm and comfortable, with your head and knees flat on the ground or slightly elevated with a folded towel or small cushion to support your lower back if needs be. You will be relaxing so you will likely become more cool and may need additional layers of clothing or a blanket over you.

Disconnect your phone and if you wish to play peaceful healing music, you can do so, or you may prefer silence. You can do this practice lying in nature or at the beach if you are able to feel that you are safe to completely let go of your awareness of your surroundings (perhaps if you are with a supportive friend). If not, choose to do this practice indoors in a safe environment where you are unlikely to be disturbed for around twenty minutes at least.

The yoga pose we will use to support us in our healing process as we make peaceful connection to the Earth is called Savasana or dead man's pose (or corpse pose). It seems simple enough, lying on your back and not doing anything in particular. Yet I remember a yoga teacher saying once that the teacher of her particular school of yoga, whom hundreds of Western students had excitedly gone to see speak at a yoga conference, yelled at them and made them all lie in Savasana for ages because none of them could do it properly! It was an amusing thought – many super-fit and powerful yoga teachers being forced to lie still until they could 'master the pose' that so many Westerners would dismiss as nothing at all.

I found this intriguing. See for yourself if this conscious choice to rest comes easily to you or is difficult in this healing process below. If you are mentally struggling to let your body relax, you may like to start with the healing process before this one and then move on to this practice to complete your healing session.

Start by saying the following, "Of my own free will, I now consciously choose to give my body permission to completely relax and heal. I choose to do this through the unconditional love and grace of the Angel of Aragonite and Archangel Remiel, so be it!"

Then your job is to get warm and comfortable lying on your back with your eyes lightly closed. Imagine that they can roll back slightly in their sockets as you relax. Let your breathing slowly and naturally flow. Allow your feet to be wider than your hips and your legs to roll open slightly resting on the floor and your arms to be extended, as far away from your body as feels comfortable, also resting on the floor.

You may like to intend to tense and then relax every part of your body from your toes up to the top of your head, or simply to imagine that each muscle becomes soft, falls away from the bones and relaxes.

Take at least ten deep slow breaths in and out and allow yourself to lightly focus on letting go. You may like to breathe in the word "let", and breathe out the word "go", repeating it silently in your mind. When you are ready, imagine that any stress is melting out of your body and into the Earth underneath you, that your body is heavy and connected to the Earth through its weight.

Imagine or intend that the back of your body becomes soft and fuzzy so it becomes hard to tell where the Earth starts and stops and where your body starts and stops. Imagine that your breath and heartbeat mirrors the breath and heart beat of the Earth herself. Imagine that the water of her rivers is the blood in your veins, the oxygen flowing out of the trees is the same breath that you are inhaling. Imagine that her fire-filled volcanoes are the warmth in your body and blood and then just let go.

Stay there in peaceful rest for as long as needs be. If you are doing this to rest before bed time then simply roll over on to your side and drift off to sleep.

Or if you are doing this practice and need to awaken again to move on with your day, when you are ready, begin to move your fingers and toes slowly. Then you may like to draw your knees up to your chest, hugging them lightly before rolling on to your right side and slowly coming up to a seated position. When you are ready, take a deep breath in and exhale naturally and open your eyes.

PRAYER – AFFIRMATION

To invoke the healing power of Aragonite and Archangel Remiel at any time, you can repeat the following affirmation quietly in your mind, or aloud.

"In this moment I rest in the peace of grace and am restored."

3.

PINK CALCITE (Unconditional Acceptance) and ARCHANGEL ANAEL (Angel of the Heart)

THE GIFT OF UNCONDITIONAL ACCEPTANCE

SPIRITUAL GUIDANCE FROM THE ANGEL OF PINK CALCITE AND THE ARCHANGEL ANAEL

In acceptance there is no defeat but an opening to success! We wish for you to honour your ability to create love, wealth, wellbeing and more. We can assist you best when you do not put us to the test, asking why this or why that, closing your heart or stepping back. Instead allowing life to flow with acceptance is how you spiritually grow and learn to put the past behind you, opening your heart that love may now find you. Unconditional acceptance frees you to trust and you can leave the rest up to us! Open your heart to acceptance and peace, and the past you shall forever release. You are now open, trusting and free. Our grace is received by you easily, and we help you see how much easier your life is meant to be.

PICTURING PINK CALCITE

Also called Mangano Calcite, Pink Calcite isn't partially translucent like other calcites tend to be, but a smooth opaque symphony of soft baby pink tones appearing as bands of colour, blending naturally into the slightly deeper candy-pink tones of the crystal.

I have only ever found it as a tumbled stone – sometimes quite large. This is the other distinguishing feature of Pink Calcite from the other, more typically harder edged or geometrically shaped calcites. Pink Calcite is usually a smooth edged organic or rounded shape that sits comfortably in the hand, which is a perfect way to bring that energy straight to the heart.

HEALING PROPERTIES

Pink Calcite is a heart healer. It softens aggression, bitterness and despair, opening the heart up to acceptance and peace which then clears and frees you to have new experiences. This stone is a bit like the 'iron fist in velvet glove' in the sense that it is a very powerful healer, but does so in a gentle, softly inviting way.

To even look or just hold a piece of Pink Calcite it soothing and gently opens the heart to softness and peace. It is a tonic to a heart that has suffered many disappointments or much sadness and grief. Pink Calcite gently wears away the old residue of emotional suffering, helping you find acceptance to enable you to let it go. In freeing yourself from the past, you will also free yourself from expectations of future disappointment or suffering that create a fear to really open up and let your life happen.

Pink Calcite is a gentle but powerful healer on its own, but it also combines well with other crystals to amplify healing results. It soothes the nervous system and is even helpful for children (or inner children in adult bodies) who are going through times of bullying, great personal challenge (combine with Tigers Eye) or nightmares (combine with Black Tourmaline).

Pink Calcite is a hopeful stone that helps one let go and be open to a new life experience with greater peace, trust and harmony within the self.

ABOUT THE ARCHANGEL ANAEL

Archangel Anael is associated with the wisdom of the planet Venus. Venus is sometimes referred to as the Star of Love and Venusian qualities include love, affection, wealth, pleasure, sexuality, harmony in relationships and within the self, and general wellbeing, as well as career success and recognition. These are all rather attractive qualities (another

Venusian domain – attractiveness!) and so as you can imagine, Anael is much loved and called upon as an angelic healer (more Venusian energy – popularity!).

Calling upon Anael floods you with a cacophony of 'good feelings'. You could just sit quietly and call upon her to enter your heart and a few minutes later feel rather more amazing, attractive and magnetic than you did only moments ago.

However the meaning of the name of Anael takes us more deeply into what this divine being truly offers our soul. Anael means "the Grace of God" and this is the gift of unconditional acceptance.

Acceptance without condition opens us up to divine grace, which is the energy that takes us beyond our own efforts or capacities into a more blessed state of divine intervention and solution! This is what working with Anael feels like – our world becomes somehow more beautiful, a bit like feeling in love with life, and we become more capable of experiencing some of that golden, feel-good factor of life. The gift of divine grace helps us move out of suffering and into peace. And the pathway to that peace? Unconditional acceptance of all that has been and is yet to be. After all, you cannot have the sweetness of lemonade without some tart lemons!

SOUL HEALING WITH PINK CALCITE AND THE ARCHANGEL ANAEL: FROM DENIAL TO DIVINE GRACE

Many old souls are Healers. They have an interest, passion and deep commitment to self-healing and to be a vessel of healing on this planet. This is an intuitive recognition of their soul purpose and also their wounding. All healer souls, at some point, will have learned that the wounding is where the light comes through. It is the wounding that teaches compassion and allows for great wisdom to be developed in the healing process.

There is however a time when focus on the wounding needs to shift so that the wound can finally heal and the gift can then be utilised – be it compassion, wisdom, understanding and so on – without the wound having to remain alive, stimulating unconscious behaviour and repetitive patterns of suffering and disappointment.

You could compare it to a groove that, over time, becomes worn into the road as many cars drive over it. When you drive along that road, the tyre of your car can so easily slip into the groove, wearing it in even more. Progressively it becomes harder and harder to get out of that groove, unless a more powerful force begins to take over the steering of your vehicle consistently enough that a new groove begins to form and the old one can eventually be softened through rain and will even out, eventually disappearing.

The grooves in the soul are karmic patterning that gets repeated and repeated until a lesson is learned. Sometimes however, especially for an old soul, the patterns are so deep after so many lifetimes, that it is hard for the soul to lift itself out of the karmic weight of a repeating pattern. Sometimes it just needs a divine hand up so it can get new bearings and move on. This is what divine grace provides. It flows willingly and readily if we are able to receive it. We receive when we are able to acknowledge and unconditionally accept where we are – and perhaps also where we would like to go – say for example from chronic disappointment in your visions not manifesting in the way you would like to a place where you gratefully feel blessed that your visions are manifesting so divinely!

To get from disappointment to fulfilment, the soul needs to conquer denial, and become truthfully and unconditionally accepting of the situation it is in. It must allow itself to receive the divine help that wants to assist. It's self-defeating to say, "No, no, I'm fine" and turning away divine help when you actually are in need. To accept our humanity, which means we can often (or perhaps always!) happily benefit from divine assistance, means unconditionally accepting that we are not here to live a life on our own, but in flow with the rest of life. We can take any burdens of super-independence and 'having-to-do-it-all' off our shoulders and accept our need for help. Then the blessings of Anael, of divine grace, become available to the soul and life moves on, often with head-spinning speed!

HOW DO YOU KNOW IF YOU ARE HEALING AT A SOUL LEVEL IN THIS WAY?

Sometimes we can believe that we are in total acceptance of a situation – and perhaps at one level (most likely mentally) we are. Yet perhaps whilst we speak the right words of acceptance, underneath we haven't quite let go of an experience yet, and still wonder if perhaps we could have played it differently or better. Unconditional acceptance takes us to a deeper level that allows for completion of an experience, freeing us to learn from experience and freeing us also to move on.

Your soul has come to this planet to manifest a particular spiritual destiny. Sometimes this is called your life path or purpose, and essentially your soul purpose is to be yourself as wholly and completely as you can possibly be. Then opportunities and experience flow to you in divine perfection, easily and gracefully. It is total acceptance of yourself – which comes from deep in the soul, through the heart, not just in the logical mind – that allows for this fluidity and grace to occur. That means you don't need to compare yourself to another, nor do you believe that others should be compared to you – for better or worse. You accept that all divine creatures are as they are meant to be – even if some are a bit too spiky for your liking. They are just different faces of the divine and when you know that you are just as you are meant to be, it is much easier to accept that others are likewise. Then life flows as it should.

So this is how you know if you are in need of soul healing around unconditional acceptance. You can simply ask yourself if it is possible that you could open up to life for a smoother, swifter and more graceful manifestation of your spiritual destiny this lifetime.

For probably most of us, that answer is going to be a "yes" at some point or other in our path. This is why the Angel of Pink Calcite and Archangel Anael have come to you now. They sense what you need to more fully be your soul on this planet, at this time, and want to give this to you. The question for you is, can you give yourself permission to surrender into this process and allow yourself to receive, even if that means facing and feeling some pain before you can accept and then release it? You would not be offered this gift at this time if you were not ready and capable of this healing. Sometimes we just need to take an act of faith and believe in ourselves.

SOUL HEALING PROCESS – FROM DENIAL TO DIVINE GRACE

Find a quiet place to lie comfortably where you will not be disturbed. If you have any Pink Calcite, have it available to hold or rest on your chest if comfortable, during this soul healing. If you do not have any, don't worry, as we will invoke the Angel of Pink Calcite and the healing presence of the stone will still be with you during your meditation. You may also like to have the book open during this process to page 19, which features the full colour Crystal Angel Mandala for Pink Calcite. You will need a cushion or blanket so that you can lie flat on your back with your body comfortable and your arms and legs uncrossed and resting on the floor or other surface, if you are lying on a bed or massage table for example.

Start by saying the following invocation.

"I call upon Archangel Anael and the Angel of Pink Calcite through unconditional love now. Be with me dear ones and help me heal my heart and soul. I now choose, of my own free will, to surrender any lack of acceptance of myself, of any other, of any situation or experience that I have had, whether I consciously recall it or understand it or not. I now choose to unconditionally accept all that I have ever done, experienced and been. I lovingly and unconditionally accept myself now. This has all been learning. It has all been for the growth of my own soul and I choose to be at peace with my life experiences from this and all lifetimes now. I forgive myself. I forgive all beings. I choose to let go of old disappointment, fear, anger, regret, grief, sadness and despair. I choose to let go of my attachment to the past and any expectation that old pain must repeat itself. I choose to accept all that has been so that I am now free of it, opening up to new light and new life. Through the Divine Grace of Anael and the healing support of the Angel of Pink Calcite, so be it."

Your role is to now simply relax and allow your healing to happen. Allow your arms and legs to rest at a comfortable distance from your body, and prepare to relax. Focus on your breathing and allow your eyes to close lightly. Imagine that you can feel the weight of your body on the surface supporting you and begin to let go.

You may find that it is hard to relax, or easy, that you have visions or feelings that come to you, or you may not feel much is happening at all. Whatever is taking place, in whatever way it is taking place is perfect for you at this particular time. The soul healing may or may not be felt, but it will be unfolding to the extent that is right for you dear one.

Relax. Trust. Focus on the breath and imagine that there is a soft golden pink light around you and that you are being held in this light. Imagine, visualise or intend that this light and the edges of your being become blurry and hard to distinguish what is you and what is the light. The more you can dissolve into this softly golden-pink healing light, the more you are allowing the supportive presence of the crystal angels to help you release and let go, unconditionally, to open up to a new future, a healed experience for your soul to shine even more brightly in the world.

Stay in this place of golden-pink light for as long as you wish, and ideally for at least forty-four long, slow, deep breaths in and out.

If any feelings, thoughts or emotions arise for you during this time, any memories or resistance, anger or frustration, know that this is your soul releasing. You may even find yourself thinking, "This exercise isn't working for me" or "I'm not doing this right." These thoughts are often simply manifestations of the ego as it does its best to protect itself from truth which might bring temporary pain. If you find it too hard to let those energies release and pass, then simply intend or imagine sending soft golden-pink light to the feeling or memory and helping it to be released.

When you are ready, wiggle your fingers and toes, slowly and carefully making your way up to a seated position, bringing your hands into prayer position in front of your chest, and just say, "thank you".

You have completed your soul healing process.

You can call back that soft golden-pink light at any time you find yourself resisting or struggling to unconditionally accept an experience in your life, simply by touching your heart and closing your eyes for a moment and thinking pink! You'll call back the healing energy that your soul has now taken in through this healing process and spread it through your life, clearing your energy from past pains and opening you up to more in the present moment.

PSYCHOLOGICAL-EMOTIONAL HEALING WITH PINK CALCITE AND THE ARCHANGEL ANAEL: HONOURING THE WISDOM OF UNCONDITIONAL ACCEPTANCE

Part of the conditioning in much of human culture, particularly in the West, is that it is seen as a weakness to be accepting and that we have to fight and dominate circumstances or situations that we perceive as obstacles to eventually triumph in life. The gift that Pink Calcite offers us is a different wisdom. Its teaching is about using our will, our inner strength, to accept what is presented and to expect that within all situations there is something helpful, no matter how challenging it may be at that exact moment. Pink Calcite encourages us to not see acceptance as weakness, but to come to understand it as a spiritual strength that is based on trust in the divine genius lurking in all situations, just waiting to be unveiled.

There can be various reasons why this is hard for us to do. To start with, it is often the exact opposite of what we are taught as children and conditioned to do in our culture. We are generally taught that it is a 'dog eat dog' kind of world where we must fight and force our way through life or risk becoming a downtrodden victim or martyr to the needs of others. To accept is often seen as submissive or weak, rather than wise and empowered. Within this framework, the path of acceptance as a way to be still and present with something that is causing pain – to find the healing gift in it and move through it, more powerful for the experience – is a foreign notion.

If we have internalised this programming, which is rife in Western culture, even in spiritual circles where one wouldn't perhaps expect it to be, then it takes conscious recognition of the belief system operating within us before we can then choose to say, "Well, it's not so much fun with these beliefs – I am not particularly enjoying the life experiences that they create, and I would like to do a healing and try out some other belief systems instead".

The other resistance we can encounter to unconditional acceptance is that it tends to show the truth of our own pain in a situation. We are often confronted with a realisation of our own contribution to a situation which has been hidden from our awareness up until now. It might be a part of our personality that we have found hard to love, that was judged or that we believed was not worthy of love. The moment we say, "OK, here is something that is happening now, I can't pretend that it is not" is the moment that we are faced with the pain that is within us, trying to get our attention and be freed. That pain is the divine in disguise, seeking more of our soul to come to life. But until we give ourselves permission to accept what is happening, our behaviour, even the behaviour of others that we don't like, to just say, "Yes, this is happening and I will be present to it now," the disguise will remain in place and we'll just be running from avoidance to despair, which is not so much fun at all. The more sensitive that you are, the more in tune with truth you are, and the more this avoidance will really feel harmful to you.

What is required is often just recognition of why we have subconsciously withheld permission from ourselves to unconditionally accept everything in our lives and a decision to give ourselves permission to give it a whirl anyway, with a view to releasing the situation, and allowing it to heal. There is a saying that what you resist persists, and now you also know that what you accept, doesn't remain, but is freed and heals.

HOW DO I KNOW IF I NEED HEALING IN THIS WAY AND AT THIS LEVEL OF MY BEING?

You'll know when you need this healing because there will be something that is still not sitting right with you. It might be a conversation that you keep replaying in your head, a situation or encounter that you had where you felt that you weren't able to be really heard or didn't get the opportunity to genuinely express yourself. You might still be thinking, days, weeks, months or years later of what you wished you had of said or how you could have handled a situation differently. It might be a situation that feels incredibly unfair and unjust, or it could even be something that you hardly dare admit, that just seems to be so stuck – a relationship, a financial issue, a health issue, anything that is holding you in a position where you cannot seem to flow and let go, to move on, no matter how much you try to convince yourself that it is OK to move on, that you are ready, it just doesn't seem to be happening.

This process is about letting it be. Accepting all that has happened and softening into experiencing and being able to release through graceful divine assistance whatever it is that you have unconsciously been avoiding. It is to allow yourself to see, "What is it in me that brought this situation to bear? What is it in me that I need to unconditionally accept to be free here and now of this past struggle?".

If there is anything within you that is niggling at your conscience or your soul, then this is the sign that this gift of grace is coming to you at the psychological and emotional level to bring you healing now. You deserve peace, beloved. There is nothing that you have done or anything that you have been that is anywhere near as bad, shameful or unworthy of love as your deepest fears would have you believe. You are a beautiful soul having some interesting experiences! This healing process is an opportunity to find the freedom to turn past experiences that are stuck into wisdom now.

PSYCHOLOGICAL-EMOTIONAL HEALING PROCESS FOR HONOURING THE WISDOM OF UNCONDITIONAL ACCEPTANCE

You will need to find a comfortable place to sit where you can write comfortably and won't be disturbed, preferably somewhere private where you can speak aloud and not be concerned about being overheard. You will also need a sheet of paper (or your journal) and a pen.

Sit quietly and say the following, "I call upon the healing power of my own soul, and upon the Angel of Pink Calcite and the Archangel Anael. I ask for healing, assistance and courage now. Bless me with the gifts of truth, acknowledgment and unconditional acceptance now, so be it!"

Close your eyes and focus on your breath as you become aware that the crystal angels, the spirit of the stone and the archangel connected to that stone grow visible or palpable in your space. Imagine that the space around you becomes full with their healing presence. Imagine or intend that there is a light of golden-pink that begins to enter your heart from that healing presence around you. Allow the heart to become light and strong with this golden-pink energy and when you are ready, touch your hand to your heart and say the following statement of healing empowerment:

"I love and honour myself and all that I have been. I accept that I am worthy of healing and that life loves and honours me too, and all that has been presented in my life has been given to me as a gift of love that I may grow, release old pain and be free to just be me. I now choose to acknowledge the truth of my experiences and the courage that I have within my heart to not judge myself for it. I choose to unconditionally accept all of my choices and my experiences now. I choose to be open to let go of past pain and to find the love, sometimes hidden at first, in everything that is or ever has been in my life. I free myself from guilt or shame and realise that I am just loved. Through my own free will, so be it."

When you are ready, begin to write a list of any quality in yourself, any situation in your life, or any quality or situation you see in the life of another person (if this helps you get started), that you cannot accept. There is no need to censor or edit yourself. Let yourself be surprised by what comes up if need be. There is no judgement in this space, only curiosity and openness so that one can heal and grow. Write your list of people, circumstances, situations or memories, encounters or fears and when you have finished, place your pen down and rest the paper on your lap or a table where you can easily reach it.

Become aware of your breath and say the following healing declaration:

"I call upon the Angel of Pink Calcite and the Archangel Anael, please help me see the divine healing that is hidden in these challenges that I have not accepted as yet. Help me accept them now to see beyond the illusion that keeps me in pain and into the truth that would heal me and help me grow in peace and light. Help me open my heart beloveds, that this may happen now. Through my own free will, with divine grace and compassion, so be it!"

Gently place your right hand on the paper and your left hand on your heart and be aware of the golden-pink light all around you in the room, flowing in to your heart as you breathe in. As you breathe out, the golden pink light flows into the piece of paper and every situation and person and circumstance that you have written down. Let the light flow as powerfully as you can and know that healing will happen energetically beyond the confines of time and space. The mind is not anchored by time, nor are the emotions. They exist beyond the physical reality of time and space, so the healing can happen now – whether your list involved past, present or future people, situations or events.

When you are ready, pick up your pen and next to each item on your list, see if you can sense, or feel what the divine lesson or learning could be for you. Be patient, don't struggle. Simply say at each point, "I accept you unconditionally. What are you teaching me?". Then write down the answer. It doesn't matter if the answer doesn't make immediate sense to you or doesn't come straight away. Your wisdom will flow simply because you have asked for it to do so. All you have to do is trust it. Allow it to express itself now if it does so, and if not, have patience and faith. The answers are already within you and now they are making their way up to the surface of your conscious awareness. If an answer has been buried deep it may need some more time to become obvious to you and that is just fine. It may happen days or weeks from now when you least expect it. Suddenly the point of the lesson will become obvious, you will take it on board and finally let it go.

When you have had enough of your writing, and you feel ready to draw your session to a close, just take a few moments to read aloud any comments that you have written about what your learning or lessons may be. If you haven't connected yet with consciously recognising a lesson in a situation, that is fine. Trust it will come at the right time. Now it is time to say your closing prayer:

"I give thanks to the Angel of Pink Calcite and Archangel Anael for your healing presence and ask that it continues until I have learned this lesson of unconditional acceptance and am in flow with the divine wisdom that reaches for me everyday. May I be blessed with compassion and assistance as I learn to accept rather than reject my life in any way. I choose to experience peaceful trust and to honour all my emotional experiences without judging myself. I choose to love and accept all of me unconditionally now and through all time and space. Through my own free will, this is so."

When you are ready you can either keep your piece of paper somewhere that feels healing, such as under a piece of Pink Calcite in your healing space or bedroom, or return it to your journal, or if it feels right you may like to carefully burn that piece of paper and scatter the ashes in a garden, intending to release the energy as you do so.

Well done. You have completed your deep psychological and emotional healing process.

PHYSICAL HEALING WITH PINK CALCITE AND THE ARCHANGEL ANAEL: UNCONDITIONAL ACCEPTANCE OF YOUR BODY

Our bodies are often the set for waging war against ourselves. We push, punish, judge and condemn ourselves via picking fault or fearing the humanity of our bodies. Yet they stay with us, doing their best to keep up and honour us.

I vividly remember once, not so long ago, seeing a man walking his dog on the street whilst I was driving to a dance class. The man was quite tall and fit-looking, striding off down the street and whilst his small white dog tried to keep up with him, his little legs powering along, with an expression of what I could only call adoration and devotion on his tiny furry face. I could tell that the dog was also quite old and tired, but it was so determined to keep up with his master.

I had an incredibly emotional and painful moment as I witnessed this vignette. There was something about the unconditional love, devotion and loyalty that this dog had for his master even whilst the owner was striving off at a pace that the dog could hardly keep up with. It did more than pluck at a heart string. My heart heaved in my chest as I saw it.

In that moment, my own inner story was projected onto that dog and his master. The story of how I had related to my own body and how loyal it was to me in response to my striving off down the road of life at a pace that my body could barely sustain.

Watching that interplay between dog and owner brought to my own conscious awareness a very painful heart reality for me. I realised that I had been denied the permission I so desperately needed to just love, honour and accept my body, to be so grateful for its devotion to me, to all that my spirit wanted to do and be in this world. I had to consciously recognise how much my body had been a key to my spiritual path this lifetime. It had adapted and grown, healed itself, put up with my carelessness and ignorance, and still when treated with even the smallest degree of kindness would respond with love and appreciation, warm feeling and happiness. It was quite a moment, confronting decades of disconnection and abuse and feeling the emotional recognition of this, a deep love for this body that moved me to tears.

It can be a challenge to get beyond the obsession over how we look or how many miles we can run. It takes bravery to find a more holistic approach to fitness and wellness that doesn't involve punishing ourselves. In Western culture you will be challenged greatly in this, by those that want to manipulate you with advertising more often than not, as you 'rebelliously' learn to just love and accept your body.

To help yourself with this process, you may wish to choose friends that are interested in listening to their body and honouring its wisdom, rather than dominating it. Friendships can be a great support to the following healing process, which helps us heal a history of abuse towards our body – whether conscious or unconscious. This abuse may come in the form of mental hatred, lack of acceptance, constant judgement and assessment, or pushing and ignoring needs for healing and rest. If we treated someone else like this, we would be labelled an absolute tyrant. It is time that we heal our relation to our bodies, and in doing so, our relationship to the feminine wisdom, to the Earth and her gifts will heal as well, allowing for more peace and prosperity for all. But for now – let's start with the body and building acceptance for this precious animal that loves us so. From that place of love, such wellbeing and contentment, peace of mind and soul can unfold.

HOW DO I KNOW IF I NEED THIS PHYSICAL HEALING PRACTICE?

If you have ever struggled with accepting your body, how it looks, what it can or cannot do, with being a man or a woman, or with any aspect of physical reality – including aging, being sick or needing rest, being judged for your skin colour, size or weight, gender or even sexual preference. Even if you didn't judge yourself but were subjected to the judgements of others, then this healing will be of benefit to you and your body.

Apart from that, to just be loved doesn't even require a reason. It will be of benefit no matter what level of acceptance you are currently holding for your body.

PHYSICAL HEALING PRACTICE FOR UNCONDITIONAL ACCEPTANCE OF YOUR BODY

This simple and powerful practice requires that you sit where you can be comfortable and speak aloud without having your privacy disturbed.

Start by saying the following healing declaration:

"I call upon the golden-pink light of the Angel of Pink Calcite. I call upon the golden consciousness of Archangel Anael and I open my heart, body and soul to receive your gifts of unconditional acceptance, love and healing now. With kindness, mercy and compassion, so be it."

Close your eyes and focus on your breath. Imagine that the light of the crystal angels is with you now, filling the space around you and entering your heart, flowing down through your arms and legs and warming your entire body gently from the inside.

Say aloud, "My beloved body, how grateful I am for you and how sorry I am for my inability to really care for you the way I would have liked to at all times. Please forgive me dear one. I am so appreciative of your loving devotion. You are beautiful and precious and I am so happy to have you with me. Thank you! I ask you to receive the gift of this healing from the crystal angels and from me now, in appreciation as I learn how to have a better relationship with you. Thank you for your service to my soul. Thank you beloved one. Thank you."

When you are ready, imagine that the energy of soft golden-pink light that is flowing into your heart from the space around you begins to powerfully flow through both of your hands.

Gently touch your head with your hands and let the light flow in, filling all parts of your head

Say, "I accept you unconditionally. Thank you".

Gently touch your throat, front and back, with your hands and let the light flow in.

Say, "I accept you unconditionally. Thank you".

Gently touch your chest with both hands, intend that the light flows in.

Say, "I accept you unconditionally. Thank you".

Touch your shoulders and let the light flow.

Say, "I accept you unconditionally. Thank you".

Touch your abdominal area. Some people find this hard to do. If this is you, keep your touch gentle and light and make sure that you keep breathing in and out and take your time.

Say, "I accept you unconditionally. Thank you".

If there is anywhere in this process where you are struggling to really let the words feel meaningful, stay in that area. Keep your hands there, let the light grow and let the words be repeated. Don't force it, be patient.

It can be hard to receive love when it has been withheld and replaced by criticism or judgement and your body may struggle to receive the love you are offering, the acceptance may be a bit of a change and so it may take some getting used to! This is a good sign that change is initiated. Be patient and be loving. It may be years of harsh relating that you are healing. Give your body time to receive.

If you feel in any part of your body that it wants more light, take your time with that area and let the light flow. If you feel energy releasing or emotion arising, thoughts or memories, just keep letting the light flow and be there for yourself by staying connected to your breathing and knowing that the crystal angels are with you in the light that is flowing.

Touch your lower belly, above the pubic bone and let there be light there.

Say, "I accept you unconditionally. Thank you".

Rest your hands on your genital area at the base of your spine.

Say, "I accept you unconditionally. Thank you".

Keep your hands near the base of your spine and let the light flow all the way up the back of your body, your lower, middle and upper back.

Say, "I accept you unconditionally. Thank you".

Rest your hands at your upper legs, letting the light reach there, front and back of your thighs and hip joints.

Say, "I accept you unconditionally. Thank you".

Rest your hands at your knees, letting light fill your knee joints, front and back.

Say, "I accept you unconditionally. Thank you".

Rest your hands at your lower legs, letting light touch the front and back of the lower legs.

Say, "I accept you unconditionally. Thank you".

Rest your hands at your ankles, letting light be in the ankles, within them and all around.

Say, "I accept you unconditionally. Thank you".

Rest your hands at your feet, letting the light fill all the parts of the feet. Toes, heels, arches and tops of feet.

Say, "I accept you unconditionally. Thank you".

When you are ready, take a deep breath in and out, drawing your hands into prayer position at your chest.

Say, "I accept you unconditionally. Thank you".

When you are ready, just open your eyes.

Well done. If you are recovering from abuse in any form, you may like to repeat this exercise every day for the next three to twenty one days. You will find it deeply healing.

PRAYER – AFFIRMATION

To invoke the healing power of Pink Calcite and Archangel Anael at any time, you can repeat the following affirmation quietly in your mind, or aloud.

"I AM one with the Golden – Pink Light of Unconditional Acceptance. I AM."

4.

SELENITE (Peace)
and ARCHANGEL MELCHIZEDEK (Angel of Peace)

THE GIFT OF DIVINE PERFECTION

SPIRITUAL GUIDANCE FROM THE ANGEL OF SELENITE
AND THE ARCHANGEL MELCHIZEDEK

We bring you the peace of higher consciousness, the recognition of divine perfection at play in your life now. We offer you the peace of remembering the truth of your being and the divine essence of who you are – so much more than you could imagine yourself to be! We lift you from fear into peace, we help you expand from doubt into knowing, we touch you with grace and open you up to the gentle remembrance that you are safe and free, held in the perfect blossoming of your inner divinity. Let us be with you now. We guide you to remember that you are loved completely. There is no need to fight or resist what is. Even within the greatest storm, there is an eye of stillness and in that place you cannot be harmed. Come with us now, into the still temple within and allow us to bless you with peace. Then you shall relax and see, the perfection of your unfolding divinity.

PICTURING SELENITE

Selenite comes in various formations but perhaps the most familiar is the white satin spar formation. This serene stone looks like pure white translucent light turned into form. It can be polished and shaped into eggs, tumbled stones, large pillars and wands, and even beautiful statues. I was blessed to encounter a large Selenite Kuan Yin statue recently, with a very peaceful vibration. Selenite can be partially sheer, or very sheer, depending on how much it has been polished. In its more raw state, it can seem white and softly flaking on the outside, but the energy is just the same – utterly serene.

Another form of this pure white Selenite is Fishtail Selenite, sometimes called angel wing Selenite due to the formation of the stone, which fans out like fishtails (or angel wings!). There is also blue and green Selenite, and the stone also varies in form to manifest in orange and brown tones, with a grainer, almost sand-like texture. The latter is often called Desert Rose Selenite and is a soft brown with white edging, formed as small rosette-shaped balls, joined together.

HEALING PROPERTIES

Selenite is peace in crystalline form. It is calming to hold and those that recognise higher vibrations will often feel the presence of angels simply through being physically near the crystal. It is a great crystal to have in the home or work place to raise the vibration of the environment. Selenite is quite common to find and usually inexpensive. Despite its high vibration, it provides an emanation which is very accessible, even if you haven't developed your sensitivity to crystals as yet.

It can work powerfully on all levels of our being, helping us let go of tension and open up the crown chakra to divine connection, to attune more effortlessly with our Higher Guidance and our own divine soul. Selenite helps the soul talents express through the physical body, including the awakening and strengthening of telepathic ability, talents for healing and channelling and an enhanced capacity to receive and manifest inspirational energy.

Fishtail Selenite is particularly effective for healing the nervous system and helping it adjust to higher frequencies when one has been calling in higher guidance and growing in the ability to hold and emanate higher frequencies energies (for example, in one's healing practice or after a period of intense inner work that has allowed for more soul presence to manifest in the body).

Blue Selenite works with the throat and third eye chakras, opening them up to clearer and more soul-attuned expression and is especially helpful for those who channel through writing or speaking. Green Selenite opens the heart and helps attune it to receiving angelic contact in the physical body and emanating it to the environment in which one lives. Desert Rose Selenite helps clear old programming that has become outmoded (especially in all practical matters including business and financial matters) and supports the grounding of new affirmations and new, higher-vibrational realities into the physical world.

You can probably sense from this description that Selenite is a truly spiritual stone. It is equally connected to the spirit and to the spirit in form in the physical world and it assists us in anchoring soul presence through all the different aspects of our lives, from the most esoteric practices that we may do in meditation to the most ordinary 'day-to-day' activities.

ABOUT THE ARCHANGEL MELCHIZEDEK

Archangel Melchizedek makes me giggle. He is a stupendously powerful and massive being of light. He radiates peace. In some spiritual traditions he is considered to be the teacher for angels as the Christ Consciousness is for humanity – the inspirational teacher that we may aspire to be like as we grow spiritually. His spiritual magnificence is so great that it is challenging to accurately express it with mere words.

What I find humorous about Melchizedek is how he has confounded humanity over thousands of years with shifting identity. He weaves such mystery! His name pops up in a number of spiritual traditions, always described very differently. He has been called the saviour of the world, a teacher, a high priest, a king and of course, an archangel. He has been one of the spiritual rocks upon which the evolution of this world and beyond rests. He is a being of such magnitude and he makes me giggle because we still really don't know who or what he is and he doesn't seem to mind in the slightest!

If he wasn't so vastly important and loving to the evolution of humanity, you might imagine he was a spiritual trickster having a laugh. But actually, the diversity in explanations of who and what Melchizedek actually is says more about humanity – we are learning to accept that the divine doesn't always come in a form that we understand. So whilst those around him have many opinions about who or what he is, this angelic master just gets on with his spiritual job of being peace. This mysterious figure is not affected by any of this debate. His feathers unruffled, he just gets on with the task at hand.

Melchizedek helps humanity on many levels, but one form of support in particular is that he helps those of us who do not comfortably fit into one particular stereotype or human-defined category. He empowers us to not get caught up in needing to define ourselves and instead to delight in the process of just being our light, even if those around us are baffled and want to know – what are you? Are you this or are you that? Melchizedek teaches us that it doesn't matter. You can complete your soul path whether you are defined and understood or not. Phew! In fact, stimulating those questions in others and challenging the need to define in order to accept, might be part of your soul legacy. So we can call on Melchizedek and just be.

SOUL HEALING WITH SELENITE AND THE ARCHANGEL MELCHIZEDEK: THE PEACE OF DIVINE PERFECTION

Within many old souls there is a subconscious, or sometimes very conscious, sense of a task or mission to complete this lifetime. There is a recognition at an inner level that you have incarnated, taken form in a body, in order to do something on this planet. It might be to learn a particular lesson or master a certain wisdom. It might be to live a balanced life and get better at loving others or it might be to deeply transform yourself, master the path of divine enlightenment and then be a guiding light for others treading that path. It may be anything and everything in between! The best and highest path you can walk is your own path – whatever that may be.

This sense of a stirring within, an impulse to get on with your life path or soul purpose can range from a gentle nudge to be a better person to a deep, uncomfortable sense that there is something that you are really supposed to be doing, even if you are not exactly sure what that is. This can be accompanied by some anxiety and frustration, as it may feel really important, whatever it is that you are supposed to be doing, and you wish you could work it out! It's like a much bigger and more spiritually uncomfortable version of "I feel like there was something else on my shopping list that I forgot to write down, but now I am in the supermarket, I can't remember what it is!".

For old souls in particular, there is a sense usually that there is quite a bit to get done this lifetime. Older souls are like the big brothers and sisters of the spiritual playground. They help guide others and provide places for others to find comfort, assistance, protection and even sometimes offer much needed (and compassionately shared) truths. Old souls are just capable of taking on a little more spiritual responsibility and this usually means that they have at least a few spiritual lessons to learn this lifetime and quite a bit of Earth school to master.

This sense of spiritual tasks to be completed can be a source of inner drive, taking one deeply into a path of self-healing and spiritual exploration, but also a source of great worry and urgency, sometimes quite overwhelmingly so, leading to fear and anxiety. It can be stressful to drive to get things happening without being sure how to do so or exactly what those things should be. Sometimes our desire to do so many things at once can be overwhelming and so we fall into procrastination and fear because it is too much for our energy system to handle. Depression can also result where the inner task desired by the soul is being blocked by a physical reality that impedes the learning, as though the souls world and the world of the body are not meshing well. This can happen when the soul and body are learning to be as one with each other. Just like any relationship, there can be hiccups before the two parties learn to tolerate, then perhaps like, love and respect each other so that a successful sacred marriage occurs.

The soul healing that is needed in any of these scenarios is the same. It is a stepping out of identification with the chaos of the apparent drama and the sense of urgency, pushing, striving, and consequent depression or anxiety, and a stepping into the higher consciousness of divine perfection. Something truly miraculous occurs when we are able to do this – we realise that everything is just as it is meant to be and there is nothing to worry about! Then something else happens, we drop into peace. In peace, we let go and we let God, so to speak. We allow life to happen and we allow the Universe to unfold. We are a part of that creation, not separate from it. As it unfolds, so do we.

In having faith and eventually recognising the divine perfection at play in our lives, we realise that what we want does want us, and the timing of it happening is perfect too. We will be ready when the world is ready and the world will be ready when we are – it is all perfect. Often times this awareness is gained through hindsight. I have seen my deepest life concerns and anxieties fall away with the passing of years and the growth of my own insight. Suddenly that which once was a perplexing and disturbing question became a situation through which such grace had been delivered, I couldn't help but weep and say, "thank you!" from the depths of my being to the unseen kindness that kept me on my path, even whilst I struggled to understand why it was thus at the time. Calling on the divine perfection unfolding to take us into peace protects us from so much unnecessary suffering. We may need to wait two decades (or lifetimes) to genuinely 'get it' but sometimes we can be gifted with experience of peace in the here and now, transcending the need for deeper struggle to find out 'why' and instead trusting, flowing and knowing that all is revealed in perfect divine timing. The purpose of this soul healing is to take you into that peace now.

HOW DO YOU KNOW IF YOU ARE HEALING AT A SOUL LEVEL IN THIS WAY?

If there is any part of you that is not sure about your path, about whether or not you are doing what you are meant to be doing, if you are chasing some pursuits and wondering if they are a key part of your journey or a distraction, or even if you are on the path strongly and with great clarity, but would simply be open to receiving an awareness of a bigger piece of the divine puzzle of which you are a part, then this is for you.

This soul healing is also for those that are struggling to understand why things are happening the way that they are in their lives. Even if they can accept it, they may like to experience the even deeper peace that comes from an experience, a revelation, of the divine perfection of a particular situation or life phase, which will shed some light on why they have been lead into it and for what purpose it has been created. This awareness may happen during the healing or in the days, weeks or months following the healing. The process of revelation will be kick-started by this healing practice. The way it unfolds will, of course, be divinely perfect for you.

SOUL HEALING PROCESS – THE PEACE OF RECOGNISING DIVINE PERFECTION

Find a quiet place to sit or lie comfortably where you will not be disturbed. If you have any Selenite, have it available to hold or rest near your body, preferably around the top of your head, resting on a pillow if you are choosing to lie down during this soul healing. If you do not have any, don't worry, as we will invoke the Angel of Selenite and the healing presence of the stone will still be with you anyway. During this process, you may choose to open this book to page 20, which features the full colour Crystal Angel Mandala for Selenite.

You will need a cushion or blanket so that you can lie flat on your back with your body comfortable and your arms and legs uncrossed and resting on the floor or other surface, if you are lying on a bed or massage table for example. Or you can sit comfortably, with spine relatively straight, on a comfortable and supportive chair.

Start by saying the following invocation:

"I call upon Archangel Melchizedek and the Angel of Selenite, Crystal Angels of Peace be with me now. I call upon the peace within, I call upon the peace within, I call upon the peace within. Lift me higher into the peaceful recognition of divine perfection. May I see, know, hear and feel the divine perfection in all that is taking place in my life and beyond. May I know this without any doubt to be more real than any anxiety, fear or distress. In deepest peace I now choose to surrender and be blessed. Through my own free will, so be it."

Close your eyes and focus on your breathing. Allow yourself to take your awareness beyond the day-to-day world and follow your breath to a place deep within yourself that is open, vast and peaceful. Perceive that peaceful place within as growing vaster with each breath in and out.

You become aware within that peaceful place of a fountain of light. It glows pure white and is built out of Selenite crystal, shining white and pure, soft and luminous. In the fountain there is pure clean water and pure sound of angels. You may hear it with your inner hearing or simply know that it is there. The sound will bring you more peacefulness even if you do not physically register it.

As you move closer to that fountain, you become aware that the pure bright light that surrounds it is actually the heart chakra of a very large archangel. The fountain of Selenite, flooded with crystal clear water, with light and pure tones of angelic sound, lies within the heart chakra of Melchizedek.

You may sense his face, or simply feel yourself in his presence now. You may feel tears flowing as your heart opens. Allow waves of light to emanate from this fountain within his heart, down through the crown of your head, pulsating slowly down through your entire body, peaceful waves of divine light and love from the great archangel. These light and sound waves fill your body with a sense of peace. Just receive. Allow yourself to surrender into these peaceful waves of sound and light, which you hear or see, or simply be open to receiving.

As you receive these waves of peace you begin to realise that they are familiar, that they are YOU, the truth of your being, your own divine soul. This peaceful, powerful light and sound is your inner nature.

Perceive or imagine that you are at the centre of this peace, with Melchizedek and the Angel of Selenite sending pure light to your soul, strengthening the peace within your centre until you begin to feel that you simply are peace.

Take your time and just be with it.

Finally allow yourself to perceive that around this centre of peace, you can see the physical forms of your life – your body in this lifetime, perhaps in others, your relationships, your work, your thoughts and feelings, all around the edges of this massive centre of peaceful energy, a bit like the edges have been dipped in coloured glitter and are shining back at you in different colours. Notice how the edges of this peaceful cloud of divine power that you are emanating fan out into all these different expressions in the physical world, at its edges, and yet is pure divine peace, waves of light and sound, at its core.

Stay with this for a moment, identifying with the peace that you are and allowing the edges of this massive soul chakra that you are in, with its peaceful light and sound, to simply be a tiny part of this huge soul self. See, sense or feel how the peace from the centre extends into the very edges. They may look as though they are different glittering colours, but the energy of which they are comprised is this same peaceful divine energy that exists in the centre of your soul.

Finally take in a slow deep inhalation and then slowly exhale and intend to spread the peace from the centre of your soul all the way out to the glittery edges even more than it already is. Repeat this breathing pattern a few times. Allow the glittery edges of your soul to be infused with the same intensity of peace as exists at the centre of your soul chakra.

When you are ready, say the following:

"I open to the peace of divine perfection. Everything is in order within my soul and within my world and the divine plan is unfolding exactly as it should, no need to be concerned. Instead I feel the peace of my own being and I am bathed in it constantly. I am the pure light and sound of peace. Peace reigns within me and all around me. Divine perfection reveals itself always and I feel deep peace and trust in this process now. So it is."

When you are ready just take a few long slow and deep inhalations and exhalations as you bring your awareness back to your physical body in the room. If you have been lying down, roll to one side then slowly sit up. If you are seated, begin to move your hands and feet and gently, when you are ready, plant your feet on the floor to ground yourself and place your hands in front of your heart centre in prayer position and say, "Thank you."

You have completed your soul healing process.

PSYCHOLOGICAL-EMOTIONAL HEALING WITH SELENITE AND THE ARCHANGEL MELCHIZEDEK: PEACE THROUGH DETACHMENT

Cultural conditioning, which is a primary force shaping our belief systems and life experiences, often includes the notion that if you let go of something, you'll lose it. In fact fear can make us hold on to the point that we inhibit rather than encourage our manifestation. Most of us who have done some inner work know that to let go is to allow energy to flow, but the practice of it can still be challenging at times. Sometimes it might feel like you have to stop wanting something before what you once wanted can come to you! However letting go, detaching, isn't actually about not wanting anymore. It's about trusting that what you want will come to you and it's just a question of allowing the divine perfection work out the timing and method for its delivery.

It's a bit like ordering a new stove, a new cooking set of professional-grade pots and pans, and a new set of kitchen cupboards for your kitchen. It's all very exciting and we might be thrilled about the new cooking set, dreaming of the dishes we will create. But the Divine knows, in its ever-so-practical perfection, that if the kitchen cupboards don't arrive first, there will be nowhere to place the cooking set. The stove will also be difficult to install if the cupboards aren't in place to receive it.

Detachment isn't necessarily about saying, "Oh well, I guess I don't really have to want what I want after all". Often it is more about accepting that you can have what you want, but you are going to have to let go and allow it to come to you in its own way. That is a peaceful recognition of divine perfection. You might be so excited about your cooking set that you don't think about where you are going to put it, but the Divine knows you need those cupboards first to hold what you want in place.

When you allow life to unfold with detachment, you can trust that the genius of divine perfection will sort it all out for you. I have experienced this in my own life so many times, on a daily basis in fact, that I now know that detachment is not only about making the waiting less painful for us, but allowing divine perfection to take care of the details so that it all unfolds just so. I have lost count of the number of times I have thought, "Well, how perfect is it that it worked out that way!" after some series of 'coincidences' happened according to a sequence of timing that 'just happened' and worked out perfectly (but differently than I had planned). And those are the times that I had the consciousness to see it in the moment. I also have enough awareness to understand that there are levels of divine perfection unfolding that are beyond my own consciousness and to trust this is to honour that higher intelligence and let it do its job.

Of course as we start to do this, many blocks to accepting higher consciousness can come up for us. Self-worth (do we matter enough to be taken care of by the Divine?), trust (I have been abandoned, rejected and betrayed before, will the Divine do the same thing to me?) and fear (if I am not in control, I don't know what will happen or how and I don't like that!) are just a few. To be present to those arising feelings and to send them peace will help allow detachment to manifest and our life experience to flow with even more ease and less resistance to the divine perfection unfolding in every life at this time. The healing process below will help too.

HOW DO I KNOW IF I NEED HEALING IN THIS WAY AND AT THIS LEVEL OF MY BEING?

If you feel like you have placed 'an order' (a desire, a wish, a dream) with the universe for something to manifest, and you feel like it is delayed, held up or you wonder if it has been heard and responded to, or even wondering if it is going to happen at all, then this process is for you!

PSYCHOLOGICAL-EMOTIONAL HEALING PROCESS FOR PRACTICING DETACHMENT

You will need a place to stand comfortably where you won't be disturbed, preferably somewhere private where you can speak aloud and not be concerned about being seen or overheard.

Stand quietly and say the following, "I call upon the healing power of my own soul, and upon the Angel of Selenite and the Archangel Melchizedek. I ask for healing now that I may experience the true peace of detachment, the true peace of knowing that my soul light and dreams are manifesting now. I ask to experience the true peace of joyful trust in divine genius and perfection. Please bless me with healing now beloved crystal angels. So be it!".

Close your eyes and focus on your breath as you raise your arms open above your head and tilt your forehead to the heavens. Imagine that you have magnets in your palms that draw in heavenly energy. Using softly focused intention, draw down light with your palms from above the crown of your head, alongside your body, until your arms are resting by your sides and your palms facing the Earth, sending that energy of light deep into the Earth.

Say, "I draw the peace of heaven down to Earth through my body, mind and soul."

Then do the reverse, drawing the palms of your hands from the Earth, with magnetic pull, up along side your body, sending it up and out to the heavens above, opening your arms above your head, and tilting your forehead slightly to the heavens.

Say, "I draw the peace of Earth up to heaven through my body, and soul."

Place your hands in prayer position in front of your chest and say, "I now choose to trust, to let go, to surrender and detach from all that has held me back from true peace. So be it".

Stay with your breath and allow the magnetism in your palms to become stronger before gently moving your hands in front of your chest, palms facing outwards. Intend to breathe in and exhale out through your palms, letting go. Repeat the process again, breathing in and letting go as you 'exhale' through your palms, releasing. Continue this process several times as you relax.

Place your hands back in prayer position, this time with your thumbs resting gently on your forehead, slightly above the centre of your eyebrows, and make the following statement, "I now choose to detach from my own self-created struggles, with compassion and joyful freedom. I don't have to struggle for my desires to manifest. I choose to allow them to unfold in the best and most joyful way that the Divine can imagine for me! I trust. I detach. I allow and my dreams to flow into reality so much faster now. Through divine grace, perfection, and my own free will, so be it!"

Breathe in and as you exhale, imagine you can breathe out through your forehead and your palms, letting go of any old energy and attachment. Repeat this breath process several times, taking your time and focusing on letting go as you start to relax.

When you are ready, either continue standing or sit quietly and comfortably and make the following healing declaration:

"I call upon the Angel of Selenite and the Archangel Melchizedek, I call upon my own divine wisdom and my own power of free will. To these holy witnesses I now declare that I detach with love in my heart and allow myself, my true destiny and my highest healing to manifest. All situations, circumstances, relationships and opportunities in my life are now blessed by divine perfection and grace and are peacefully in accord with all that is meant to be for the highest spiritual destiny I can live. I detach, I accept, and with gratitude I thank you for your assistance now, restoring me to peace and my life to Divine flow and perfection. So it is."

When you are ready, either sit or continue standing and close your eyes for several slow peaceful breaths as you allow the power of your declaration to shine out to the Universe and reverberate through your soul.

When you are ready simply open your eyes and you have completed your healing task. Congratulations!

PHYSICAL HEALING WITH SELENITE AND THE ARCHANGEL MELCHIZEDEK: HEALING THE NERVOUS SYSTEM

The nervous system is fundamental to an enjoyable body-soul connection. It is hard to connect to our spiritual guidance and inner peace at increasingly high levels if our nervous system is struggling to hold the voltage of it. Some nervous systems, particularly of those with an ability to bring through healing energy or channel divine guidance, are quite sensitive. This sensitivity allows them to register very pure and high level vibrations, which others that have tougher nervous systems may not register in quite the same way, if at all. The tricky part is that the sensitivity means that their nervous systems will need a little more care and attention than most others.

Once you know how to manage the needs of your nervous system, becoming more attuned to your own sacred biology and how to care for it, you will be able to enjoy the benefits of your sensitivity, including a capacity for uplifting and sublime states of exquisite connection with the spiritual worlds. As you learn to care for your own nervous system, you will be able to avoid becoming overwrought and exhausted while doing spiritual or healing work on yourself and others (where you can otherwise be quite energetically stretched..

As the nervous system heals, you may find all sorts of 'gremlins' emerging in the course of the healing practice itself or in the hours, days or even weeks following your practice. This is the body ridding itself of old energy that it no longer needs. A somewhat graphic (but helpful) comparison could be if you have food poisoning and you regurgitate what you have eaten, you 'encounter' whatever toxin you took in again as it comes out. So it is with toxic energy. It doesn't just get taken in, it needs to be released as well. Now it will either be concretised in the body over time and experienced in the release as illness or disease, or if you catch and release the energy before that happens, you will experience it as either an emotion, memory or feeling as it is released, or even just as energy moving and releasing. All this is fine, to be expected and just a natural part of being a human and doing energetic healing work. You don't have to analyse or attach to anything that is leaving. It is enough to notice it and perhaps even to have the momentary awareness that you are feeling this way because your healing practice stirred up some energy and is clearing out your body. It is a sign of something working, even though the effects sometimes leave us feeling a little worse before we feel a lot better. Have patience and trust.

HOW DO I KNOW IF I NEED THIS PHYSICAL HEALING PRACTICE?

If you are tired, worn out, or on the other hand over-energised and so full of beans that you can hardly keep up with yourself, then it is likely that this practice will support you in coming into healthier overall balance with your body.

Yes, you can have too much of a good thing and you'll know this if you are becoming imbalanced in your emotional life or physical wellbeing from your spiritual practice. It isn't common to do too much (as opposed to too little) meditation in Western culture, but it can happen that a burst of enthusiasm for the practice leaves you feeling spacey, cranky or out-of-sorts at first.

You may need to slow down and temper your practice, while giving your nervous system some care. As it purifies itself, using the spiritual energy that you have drawn in through your meditation or inner work, sometimes it's necessary to let that run its course before you call in even more. If you have been doing a lot of healing work on yourself or others, then your nervous system is highly likely to need some tender loving care to restore it from activity into peacefulness. This practice will support you with this also.

If you have come through a major transition, physical, emotional or spiritual, if you are in process of recovering from an addiction or trauma or some description or if you are quite simply in need of a holiday from a vey busy lifestyle, then this is for you.

PHYSICAL HEALING PRACTICE FOR
HEALING THE NERVOUS SYSTEM

This simple and powerful practice requires that you sit where you can be comfortable and speak aloud without having your privacy disturbed. If you have a Fishtail Selenite, please have it resting in contact with your body wherever it feels best.

Start by saying the following healing declaration:

"I call upon the Angel of Fishtail Selenite and ask for your healing blessings and assistance now. Restore my nervous system with your gentle and powerful healing energy. Archangel Melchizedek, please oversee and confirm this process. So be it."

Close your eyes and focus on your breath. Imagine that the light of the crystal angels is with you now, filling the space around you and entering the top of your head, flowing down your spinal column and flowing as a gentle, soft, but powerful energy of light and sound along your spine. Imagine that the light and sound, whether you see it or hear it, or not, is exactly the right intensity for your body.

Say aloud, "My beloved body, how much I love you and wish to honour your now with this healing. It is safe for you to receive this healing and let go. Trust me now as I honour you with loving peace. I choose to release from my nervous system now any attachments, beings or implants of any description that are not based in unconditional love. I choose to release from my nervous system now any damage or fatigue. I choose to receive perfect healing for my nervous system through karmic grace and unconditional love. So be it."

When you are ready, imagine that the energy of Fishtail Selenite – soft, pure, pulsing and peaceful – is vibrating within your nervous system, all along your spine and fanning out like large soft angelic wings to include either side and the front and back of your body.

Be aware of your breath and just rest here with this energy for at least forty-four long, slow deep inhalations and exhalations, and as long as it feels right to do so after that.

If you lose count or lose focus, just come back to the breath, pick any number and start again. Don't worry. It will be perfect for you.

When you are ready, say, "Thank you for the healing," and open your eyes.

Well done.

PRAYER – AFFIRMATION

To invoke the healing power of Selenite and Archangel Melchizedek, at any time, you can repeat the following affirmation quietly in your mind, or aloud.

"I AM peace, endless and profound.
I AM divine perfection, it is everywhere, all around."

5.

LABRADORITE (Uniqueness) and ARCHANGEL IAHEL (Angel of Solitude)

THE GIFT OF INDIVIDUALITY

SPIRITUAL GUIDANCE FROM THE ANGEL OF LABRADORITE AND THE ARCHANGEL IAHEL

We come to you who are in this world but not of this world, who wish to establish higher truths and live according to love rather than fear. We come to you who do not fit the mould, who choose to live uniqueness and authenticity, who are not afraid to rebel against what is expected in order to be yourself. We gently guide and protect you, as you seek your own truths within, as you create ideas for a new world of peace and plenty, as you walk the path that has never before been walked, entirely new and from the heart of you! We come to you now dear individual beings of light, for you are unique but never alone, and we help you in your sacred task of honouring your differences whilst remaining connected with love to the world that you choose to serve with your light.

PICTURING LABRADORITE

Labradorite is a soft grey stone with luminescent flashes of brilliant colour that only becomes visible when it is turned towards a source of light. Then this apparently subtle and soft stone becomes vivid, bright and striking, with flashes of yellow, orange and vibrant blue emanating from the crystal. There is also a more rare yellow Labradorite which is mostly white with yellow tones. The iridescence of Labradorite has always reminded me of the beauty of peacock plumes. The colours seem to come alive as you hold the stone and direct it towards light. They also have an otherworldly quality, a mystical feeling, as they seem to appear and disappear depending on where the light hits the stone.

This crystal often features in jewellery, carvings and in tumbled stones.

HEALING PROPERTIES

Labradorite is a stone for seekers, for those drawn to other worlds – both in terms of other forms of intelligent life around our Universe (believing this Universe to be rather too big a divine playground for humans alone) and other planes of reality within our own minds, endless and yet to be explored and experienced. It is a stone for those who are not completely of this world, although they are here in service and have chosen at a soul level to be here. These types of souls don't fit into the stereotypes of human personality and often need energetic support to remain true to who they are. There can be much pressure in society to 'fit in' and conform. Pressure to conform rather than be one's own true self can make life more difficult than it needs to be, and Labradorite can help minimise the effect of such social pressures on the individual.

Labradorite serves these kind of souls well, and also those who want to know more of who they are as individual and unique beings, perhaps having had enough of playing it safe and following the rules of society, wondering deep within if there could be more to them than what they had come to believe.

Labradorite deflects unwanted energy from the aura and helps mend any tears in the auric field, allowing for a naturally protective energetic shield to form around the person working with the stone. This creates much needed space to find one's own thoughts and feelings. Without that energetic space within which to connect with our own truths, we may feel bombarded or confused by the energies of other people. We can easily pick up and gather the thoughts and feelings of others. If we feel confused, overwhelmed or uncertain, then it is likely that this has occurred. Labradorite can help us avoid this psychic sponging from happening in the first place. Obviously the more naturally psychic, sensitive or empathic you are, the more helpful this is.

Labradorite is also a stone of strength, helping the wearer connect with Universal energies, and their own higher self. It helps to bring the talents and uniqueness of that higher self into more powerful connection with the physical body. This enables your gifts and talents to flow, empowering you to step beyond the expectations of others and begin to live more of your own spiritual destiny.

Labradorite also clears fear and disappointment from this or other lifetimes which could otherwise undermine your faith in yourself or the Universe. It calms the mind, enhances your ability to meditate and encourages you to trust and rely upon yourself, knowing that you have much wisdom and strength within you.

ABOUT THE ARCHANGEL IAHEL

Archangel Iahel is an Archangel with a specific task of caring for those who are hermits, philosophers and those that require separation from the world to tend to their inner tasks for a while.

This separation could be on a very simple level – just a need to get away from everyone else's opinions about something happening in your life, to collect your own thoughts and get in touch with your own sense of truth about how to deal with a situation.

Or the need for some type of separation could be on a more dramatic and life changing level. It might be the decision to leave a relationship or to move to another country. It could be the need of a person grieving the passing of a loved one to withdraw from their usual social life and spend some private time acknowledging their loss. We even enter into a type of separation when we read a book like this one, turning our attention inward to our own journey, leaving the external world and its demands behind. We withdraw inwards when we do inner work such as writing in a journal, meditating, or sitting in nature as we focus on tapping into the inner guidance of the heart. Archangel Iahel helps us find the strength to take these steps and to stay with our experience, to be focused rather than distracted by external demands for our time, attention or energy.

It can be difficult to really honour the inner work and still be engaged in the world as we normally are. At times, we will need to let go of our more social ways to go within and connect with a truth that lays beneath the surface of our everyday awareness. The inner world can sometimes call for absolute attention, deep focus and concentration that we may unravel an inner mystery and resolve it within. Then we can emerge and reconnect with the outer world again. Iahel is like our spiritual tour guide on this process, safely heralding us out of the daily grind and into the inner temple of our soul.

This may take an hour. It may take seven years, a lifetime or more depending on our own soul path. If we do not honour our needs for 'time out', we may end up being drawn away from the world unconsciously through depression, illness or anxiety disorders. These are a way for us to enter the inner terrain, but it can be much less stressful to simply honour the need when it is there and do it, rather than resist and be 'forced' into it by our own unconscious mind manifesting in uncomfortable symptoms.

The Archangel Iahel helps us enter into a period of temporary withdrawal from the world with more grace and less suffering. He helps us to recognise when we need such time to ourselves, and to have the strength to act on that recognition. This may mean cutting back on social time for a while, or engaging in more creative pursuits that connect you with yourself such as meditation, dance, art or writing. It might mean pausing before making a decision on an important matter.

When I first called upon Archangel Iahel, I didn't really know what to expect as he was not an Archangel with whom I was familiar. However being a bit of a hermit myself at times, loving my own solitude, I was looking forward to feeling his presence. What I felt was waves of descending sweetness, cascading down through the crown of my head all the way to my feet and then into the Earth. I felt him before me as I bent my head, my hands in prayer at my brow, and heard him whisper to me that he knew me well and had been with me for lifetimes. He bent his head to mine and I sensed that he held a scroll. As I opened to receive the wisdom in that scroll, he guided me to change my focus for this section of the book and to include reference to the need for healing solitude as a way to really know who one is. I felt sweetness and peace so strongly that all I could do was just sit and be with it.

It is his sweetness that helps us let go of all the glamour and attachment to the world for a time. It is the sweet relief of peace and quiet after so much noise. Sometimes we need this in order to feel centred enough to jump back into the fray! All play and no peace makes for an overstimulated and cluttered mind.

SOUL HEALING WITH LABRADORITE AND THE ARCHANGEL IAHEL: FROM REBELLION TO UNIQUENESS

Part of the task of an old soul is to be strong and self-loving enough to be the true spiritual self in a culture where that self is not necessarily understood, accepted or honoured by others. Sometimes an old soul can spend lifetimes setting themselves apart from typical culture and beliefs, radiating an alternative consciousness, a different way of believing and being in the world. They do this out of service. They can eventually become a spiritual role model for those ready to evolve beyond the established norms. For this to happen, an old soul needs to recognise, accept and even appreciate what makes them different, rather than judging or trying to hide those qualities. This often requires plenty of time spent in personal reflection and exploration, integrating experiences of not quite fitting in (or not fitting in at all) with the culture around them. From that place of peace within, such souls can then comfortably share the beautiful and precious healing gift of themselves with the world. By celebrating their uniqueness, they give others permission to also find their own unique essence without judgement or fear holding them back from exploring and discovering who they truly are.

Uniqueness, with all its difference, helps heal. It offers opportunities for greater love, tolerance, acceptance and wholeness. It can bring more fun, interest and variety to life, as well as more balance, providing a vision and experience of what has been lacking. It can teach us to love more unconditionally. When we are confronted with that which we do not consciously identify as being 'normal', we can choose to become more accepting and comfortable with that which makes us different, rather than judging it from a place of fear. We have plenty that makes us similar, finding our differences doesn't lead to disharmony, it actually can create more freedom to live and let live.

Uniqueness is not only a gift however, it is also a challenge. The world we live in can be so rigid – oftentimes something has to be able to be 'categorised' or fit into a mould in order for it to be valued. So, it can taken a boldness of the spirit and a great deal of courage in the heart, as well as a certain rebellious quality in the mind and an unwillingness to conform to others' expectations in order to be simply be one's own person.

There is a point however, where the hold of society and the need to rebel in anger or fear begins to loosen. Anger and fear are helpers at that time, supporting you in breaking free from lies you have believed about yourself and the social conditioning that has been imposed upon you. To break with mass conditioning in favour of living your own life, at times requires the liberating and healing force of rage. It is not comfortable but it can be necessary for a time. However once you are free enough from the interference of others within your own energy field, something that these crystal angels can assist you with, then the stronghold of yourself becomes more powerful and the expectations of others matters much, much less. You no longer have to fight for your individuality. You can just know it and live it.

If we are rebelling constantly, rather than as part of a process, then it is possible that we are still in the grip of that which we are fighting against. Rebellion is a healthy part of the spiritual path but it is meant to lead us to freedom, not remain constant. To rebel is an expression of anger and rejection of values that don't resonate with us. Once we are strongly established in our own values, having released those that do not resonate with us completely, we are free. For a soul that has come to be unique and inspirational to others, a rebellious nature can be supportive of the soul path. That soul has to be strong enough to stand apart from the consciousness of the collective in order to offer an alternative frequency of ideas, beliefs and ways of being in the world. That soul has to be at a different vibration to the unconsciousness of mainstream culture. It is the rebel within that grants the permission needed to be true to yourself, even if this means not conforming to expectations of society. Eventually however, that rebellion serves its purpose and instead of pulling away from society to distil our own values, we already know what we are about. We can then simply choose to radiate our vibration and live our values, often becoming an inspiration for others.

This soul healing process will support you in making this grand leap. If you have already made it, it will help take you deeper into your uniqueness, and create even more peace within you, and peace with your world. This will enable you to be a more powerful healing agent for global healing than ever before.

HOW DO YOU KNOW IF YOU ARE HEALING
AT A SOUL LEVEL IN THIS WAY?

If you have ever felt that you have had to fight for your right to be you, then the learning and wisdom of Archangel Iahel and the Angel of Labradorite is part of your soul path this lifetime.

If you are searching for your uniqueness, if you want to know what it is about you that sets you apart from the crowd and you are more interested in being your true self than in gaining the approval of others, then this soul healing is happening within you.

If you believe that there is more to you than what you have been told you are and you are open to discovering who you are even if parts of you do not fit within the expectations of others, then this soul healing is happening for you.

If you sense that deep within there is a part of you that just HAS to be lived no matter what, even if it ruffles feathers or makes you feel different from the world around you, even if you might be concerned about being misunderstood, ridiculed or judged for it, but you just have to be YOU anyway, then this soul healing is happening for you.

If you feel you are meant to be a little different (or a lot different) from society, then this healing is for you too. You are one of the souls who have the spiritual task of helping heal the world through balance, tolerance and wholeness. May you be blessed now in your task, beloved.

SOUL HEALING PROCESS – FROM REBELLION TO UNIQUENESS

Please light one candle (a tea light is fine) and make sure that it is in a safe glass container so you don't have to worry about the flame. Place it where you can sit and gaze at it comfortably. Find a quiet place to sit where you will not be disturbed. If you have some Labradorite, place it near your body as you sit. If you do not have any, don't worry, as we will invoke the Angel of Labradorite and the healing presence of the stone will be with you.

Start by saying the following invocation:

"I call upon Archangel Iahel and the Angel of Labradorite. I gratefully receive your blessings now. Thank you for assisting me in stepping out of what I have known and into my truth of my being. Thank you for protecting this sacred space that I have created. Please assist me now in transitioning from the spiritual lesson of rebellion into the spiritual lesson of uniqueness. Thank you. Through my own free will, so be it."

Focus on your breathing and allow yourself to direct a soft gaze to the candlelight flickering. Breathe in and allow your focus to dwell upon the candle flame. Breathe out and allow your focus to deepen, as though you are looking into the flame, seeing deeper within it. Let your gaze be soft as your breath flows and either remain focusing on the candle light or close your eyes and imagine the flame with your inner vision.

Imagine that you are sitting around a campfire and the flame burns steadily. Gazing at it you become aware that you are sitting in another world, a sacred world, around this campfire. There are mountains of Labradorite around you and a massive Archangel holds his wings around the campfire. You sense that you are safe and protected and nothing at all can harm or disturb you.

You become aware that sitting around the campfire with you are a circle of beings. They belong to different tribes and you are in this circle with them to release sacred contracts you have made and establish new ones.

Say aloud to these beings, "I welcome you, brothers and sisters of tribes from afar, and I thank you for the learning we have provided each other. I now choose of my own free will to release any contract or vow I have ever made with you to rebel against you, to fight for my individuality or to struggle to gain your acceptance or rightful acknowledgement. I forgive myself for any time I have asked this of you. I now choose to release all such agreements through all layers of my being and through all time and space. I release these agreements now and I forgive you, I forgive myself and I release any unresolved suffering or karmic energy from these agreements into the fire. Through the grace of the Angel of Labradorite and the Archangel Iahel, so be it."

Focus on your breath and allow yourself to breathe in the light of the crystal angels and breathe out into the fire, letting it grow brighter and more intense as you exhale. Allow any old energy that has kept you trapped in patterns of rebellion to be exhaled on the out-breath. Repeat this breathing process at least three times or for as long as feels appropriate for you.

You may find that all the beings around the campfire willingly acknowledge you as you do this and as you release on the breath, they leave the campfire. You may find that one or two remain and you need to repeat the statement again, adding this to it, "As a sovereign being of light, in a free will zone, I now make this choice for myself and acknowledge you that are bound to honour it, go in peace beloved, I no longer hold you here to me in conflict."

Once you are alone at the campfire, or as alone as you feel you will be at this time, allow the Archangel Iahel to approach you, with sweet, powerful waves of energy and guide you away from the campfire to a place of deep peaceful solitude in the mountains of Labradorite that surround you. Just you and the crystal angels now. Imagine a sun or moon in the sky, or a bright pure light that glows down onto the mountains of Labradorite, casting light and causing the crystal mountains to shine brightly with luminescent blue, orange and yellow. Feel the beauty and perfection of the crystal as it shines its energy upon you. Simply bathe in it.

When you are ready, make this declaration of intention:

"I now choose to renew and update my soul contract and state the following of my own free will. I am at peace with my differences and my individuality. My uniqueness brings great gifts of healing to the world, and I accept my differences absolutely and completely. The responses of others to my uniqueness is a reflection of their own ability to love themselves unconditionally. I help them by loving myself unconditionally. I choose to be open to learning and knowing more of my own unique soul light. I choose to love and honour what I discover, with gratitude, an open heart and open mind, knowing that all that I am is perfectly created for my divine purpose this lifetime. There is no mistake or error in me, I am perfectly just as I need to be. I open to receive me! So be it."

When you are ready, take a few long, slow, deep inhalations and exhalations as you bask in the energy of this declaration. Imagine this energy reverberating off the mountains of luminescent Labradorite, growing stronger and more powerful, until it eventually wraps around you as a beautiful blanket of luminescent light, flashing shades of many colours. A unique living light show surrounds you. You realise that this is part of your own soul.

Let this living light wrap around you and move through you, as you just breathe with it, noticing that it flows with your inhalation and your exhalation. It is you. Without losing connection with that light, allow your awareness to now include your physical body. Notice how the light is around your physical body from the top of your head to the soles of your feet. Notice how your physical breath and the light are connected as one, flowing with each other in and out.

When you are ready, place your hands in prayer in front of your heart centre and say aloud, "I honour the uniqueness that I am and I empower the Angel of Labradorite and Archangel Iahel to assist me in knowing that self and sharing it lovingly with the world from a place of truth, peace and empowerment, and unconditional love. So be it."

When you are ready, just open your eyes. You have completed your soul healing process.

PSYCHOLOGICAL-EMOTIONAL HEALING WITH LABRADORITE AND THE ARCHANGEL IAHEL: THE GIFT OF SOLITUDE

Those of us that naturally love and relish moments of solitude are often in the minority in Western culture, where extroversion and 'getting out amongst it' are the norm. But spending time in solitude is a prerequisite to knowing oneself. It can be hard to hear the voice of our own feelings and intuitions if we are bombarded with the feelings and opinions of others.

Solitude gives us a chance to sort through what belongs to us energetically, what is an expression of our own truths from our own centre, and what is just psychic debris, in the form of thoughts, feelings and impressions, that we have subconsciously picked up from others along the course of our day. This is particularly helpful for natural psychics or empaths that tend to feel the feelings of others and even think the thoughts of others quite naturally, often without being consciously aware of it.

Solitude helps these souls to sort through and release what doesn't belong to them, reducing stress and increasing general wellbeing. It also can help give a real sense of who they are, which can feel so 'right' and replenishing after the confusion of swimming around in the thoughts and feelings of others.

Solitude is a way of spiritual cleansing and it can help us emerge more clear about who we are, how we feel and what we need or want, in connection with our own inner guidance and therefore more at peace.

It takes courage for many of us to be able to go into solitude. If you have already done quite a bit of inner work or have a natural tendency to enjoy your own company, being more of an introverted personality, this task will feel easy and enjoyable for you. If you are like the majority however and find that without external stimulation and social contact you feel uncomfortable, then it will be a new experience for you to learn how to connect with yourself, to find yourself beyond all that distraction. It will be worth the initial discomfort You'll find answers and inner knowing comes to awareness much more easily either during periods of solitude or a short time afterwards.

Solitude does not have to become your only way of life in order for it to be effective. I often struggled in my earlier years with my need for solitude, believing that I could either have that or be in the world, but not both. It took me many years to learn that sometimes the healing for me would come from socialising and sometimes I just needed solitude to restore myself.

The gift of solitude is there for us when we need it. At times, it may mean learning how to withdraw into yourself and find peace whilst in a situation where you have no privacy. Solitude is ultimately an inner peace that it is far more than a product of a physical situation. It is a mental state of withdrawal and immersion into the self for healing and replenishment. You can be alone and still refuse to go into yourself, or you can be surrounded by people and still feel the nourishment of solitude.

Once you have truly experienced solitude, you won't resist it in future but will come to love and embrace it. Even if your needs for solitude are less than mine, for example, you'll learn to get as much of it as you need, as often as you need. Then your time out and about in the world will have so much more of YOU in it, so much more of your truth and uniqueness, that you will find that fulfilling too. That is the wonder of solitude. It enriches us and in doing so, enriches all our relationships.

HOW DO I KNOW IF I NEED HEALING IN THIS WAY AND AT THIS LEVEL OF MY BEING?

If you are struggling to really know what you think or what you feel about a certain situation in your life or if you feel overwhelmed by the thoughts, feelings or opinions of others, then it time for you to reconnect and spend some quality time with yourself.

If you can't remember the last time you actually did something just for you or if you seem to spend all your time managing the needs, wants, expectations or demands of others, more than you tend to yourself, then this is an appropriate healing practice for you.

PSYCHOLOGICAL-EMOTIONAL HEALING PROCESS – THE GIFT OF SOLITUDE

You will need a place to sit comfortably where you won't be disturbed, preferably somewhere private. Make sure you switch off any computers and your mobile phone and shut the door. If you have a 'do not disturb' sign, hang it up!

Say the following, "I call upon the healing power of my own soul, and upon the Angel of Labradorite and the Archangel Iahel. Lift me out of the chaos of the external world and into the peaceful revelation of my inner sanctuary now beloved ones. Thank you."

Close your eyes and focus on your breath. Give yourself permission to let go of your daily thoughts or activities, of the cords that connect you to others, and imagine that you can place them on a shelf to one side. You can always pick them up again after you finish this process if you feel that you need to do so.

Imagine that you can withdraw your attention inside, to your breath and feel warm, cosy and peaceful within yourself. You may imagine that within your heart there is a beautiful room that you have entered and it is filled with objects that you love. It has light and space and is a safe, relaxing place for you to be.

Take some time to explore that room, knowing that it is just your space, laid out exactly as you would like it to be and only you go there.

Imagine that there is a beautiful large book in this sacred inner room that holds all the answers to any question you could possibly ever ask! Notice the colour of this book and on the front cover it says "The Book of Solitude". Imagine that this book is there whenever you need it and you can read it in different ways. You could read it like words on a page, but you can also open it up and step into it, crossing over into a peaceful inner world where your answers can come to you intuitively and without having to work through drama or analysis to receive your guidance.

When you are ready, you can either relax and remain in this space, feeling cosy for as long as you wish, or you can open up the book and step into it, moving into another world – an open, vast and peaceful world. Let yourself float in this world, almost as if you were floating on a cosmic ocean. You may sense the movement of water beneath you and find yourself floating in tropical waters. You may sense stars and planets around you as you float to the outer edges of our Universe. Perhaps you sense yourself held in light, floating in the loving energy of the crystal angels. Just let yourself be held and intend that one by one, all energetic cords that feed the energy of others into you fall away. The ones that need to be there will naturally re-attach after your process, so don't worry if you feel you are separating from loved ones. Your soul will still be connected, you are letting go at another level and it is safe to do this.

Even if you don't see them or know exactly who or what is on the other side of these cords of energy, imagine them snapping off and falling away. You feel surprisingly light and clean. You feel your energy relaxing even more as it released old thoughts and feelings. You don't know what they all are and it doesn't matter. You just feel more yourself than you have done in a long time and it feels good. Peaceful. You are safe and you are completely with yourself. You are enough. You are complete within yourself.

Imagine that you are handed a beautiful chalice or vessel filled with sacred pure water that glistens with flashes of beautiful light. Drink from it. Drink as much as you want and be cleansed and nourished by it. Imagine that the light in the water begins to glow within you and radiates out through the pores of your skin, until you are resting in glowing light. Just you. Utter bliss and peace emanates from you.

Say, "I give myself permission to completely receive myself now. I give myself permission to just be with myself and to enjoy receiving my own light and wisdom."

Staying with your breath, allow yourself to rest in the light of your own being for however long feels good, but at least forty four breaths. Breathe slowly, without rushing.

When you are ready say the following invocation:

"I call upon the Angel of Labradorite and the Archangel Iahel, and the gift of solitude. I call upon my own divine wisdom now and ask that any question or doubt that I have be answered through divine love and divine grace. I receive it effortlessly now. So be it."

Allow the light to change colour or grow stronger if it needs to do so, and let it be alive within you and all around you. Just be in that light, trusting that it energetically holds the answers, information, guidance and instruction that you need. You may sense issues coming to light that you didn't realise were bothering you. You may feel an awareness of something that you need to express that you didn't realise you wanted to say. You might just be aware of the light, or you may feel emotions and thoughts arising and leaving. Just be at peace and trust your own process.

When you are ready, feel yourself being drawn back towards your "Book of Solitude", popping through it, back into your inner room. When you are ready, become aware of yourself sitting comfortably in that inner room. How do you feel?

Imagine that shelf with all the people, thoughts and feelings, cords and connections that you released before doing this exercise. Is there anything there that you need to pick up again or can you leave it be now? If you do choose to pick something back up again, stay connected to the memory of you just being with yourself too. You can go back into the world changed for your experience, with more of yourself to share with, rather than give away to, others.

Become aware of the breath flowing in your body and of you in your physical body.

When you are ready simply open your eyes and you have completed your healing task. Congratulations. Remember to repeat it whenever you need to reconnect with yourself beyond the noise and distraction of the material world.

PHYSICAL HEALING WITH LABRADORITE AND ARCHANGEL IAHEL: BEING IN THE WORLD, NOT OF THE WORLD

Being in the world, rather than of the world is a question of balance. If we get the balance right, we are able to take care of ourselves – soul and body – in a way that really works for us. This allows us time out without disconnecting from the world in a way that would deprive us of the energy, fun, connection, playfulness, stimulation and excitement that it can offer. This balance gives us opportunities for spiritual growth and allows us to be of service to the greater good, both of which are vital to our wellbeing.

To remain connected but not overwhelmed, to be present and engaged, but not distracted from our truths, is a tricky question of balance. We get better at maintaining the balance by learning how to tell when we are out of balance (perhaps not caring as much as usual or feeling snappy, cranky or drained) and developing different techniques for bringing ourselves back into balance again.

If you are learning this particular talent for how to be in balance, well done, you are engaged in an advanced Earth school class for the soul.

HOW DO I KNOW IF I NEED THIS PHYSICAL HEALING PRACTICE?

The hardest part of this practice is recognising that you need it. As a culture in the West, there is a tendency to live from the head down. The head decides if the body needs exercise, when and how much. The head decides if the body needs to change appearance or weight, needs to be fitter, stronger or more flexible. It often does this by comparing us to others. In this way of being, the body gets told what it should be or not be and is hardly listened to at all. The pursuit of fitness can become punitive and the body can be subjected to all sorts of domination and abuse quite simply because our head is leading the way instead of listening to the body. It seems so silly when we really think about it because most of us know that the body holds its own wisdom and we can be healthier and happier if we work with our body, rather than try to control it and dominate it into wellbeing.

I remember training with a group from my local gym in my late twenties. I eventually realised I was training excessively. The entire group trained excessively. I was running up sand hills, along beaches, doing boot camps, weight training and boxing. I often trained twice in the one day. I was told to push harder, to fight limitation and to keep going – that it was all mind over matter. I became exceptionally fit in the sense that I could endure hours of intense physical activity without getting puffed out. I was very thin. I looked like a picture of health, until a couple of years into the training, when I developed chronic fatigue. My energy was so low that my work began to fail as I didn't have the energy available to attract clients to my healing practice. My body was so exhausted from being pushed in an imbalanced way, that it actually took me years to recover.

I began to realise I had been seduced into the glamour of fitness rather than a reality of wellbeing. Fortunately the Divine soon took over and created situations that took me out of the training group I was in and into gentler scenarios, one step at a time. It happened very gracefully and I was incredibly lucky to find two incredible Chi Gung masters, a gifted healer and massage therapist, as well as a wonderful counsellor, who helped me recover from the experience that I had chosen to put myself through. It was a powerful lesson and it changed me.

The healing process was hard for me because I knew that I needed to become more balanced, but because I had been so far out of balance, I had to swing back in the opposite direction for a while before I could eventually walk a more moderate path. I had to give up my addiction to exercise based on adrenaline highs for quite a while. My body became very tired even if I ran for short periods of time with 'sensible' breaks in between training sessions. If I started training hard again I would feel cold energy flooding my lower back as my kidneys became weak and drained. My body was no longer just putting up with my willpower. It was demanding that I listen to it.

As I did so, I found a completely different way to approach my health and wellbeing. I explored yoga and Chi Gung. I danced. My body wanted exercise that replenished it with vital energies rather than drained it of them. Eventually my body began to build up strength again and by that time I had lost all interest in punitive training. It seemed like madness to me because I had experienced first hand what imbalanced approaches to exercise could do to my wellbeing. I learned to gain strength and fitness in ways that were more nourishing and left me with more rather than less energy.

To find this balance for yourself takes courage, because what works for you and your body might be very different to what is currently being sprouted as conventional fitness wisdom by those that you admire. I have a spiritual teacher whom I love dearly who says everyone should be working out hard at the gym most days and eating a vegetarian diet. I disagree with this. I don't believe that there is only one path to wellness and I believe that if we try to follow someone else's path rather than discovering our own through experimenting with what suits our body and temperament, we may end up damaging rather than building our health.

Courage is needed because if you agree with what I am expressing here, then you will begin to place your own sense of your body above the instructions of your personal trainer or nutritionist for example, above the beliefs of contemporary medical practice and learn instead to get to know and trust your experience from within your body. Yes, you may need medical assistance and advice at different times in your life and you can learn from all sorts of health care providers and that is great. But what you are taking responsibility for here is the ultimate final decisions that you make about how you live in your body. What works for one will not necessarily work for another. In our uniqueness we discover different needs and different methods of healing ourselves and finding our own version of a balanced lifestyle.

If you relate to this journey of learning to honour the needs of your own body, then this healing practice is for you. Whether your experience was as dramatic as mine, leading to health complications that took years to heal, or are still healing, or whether it is subtly about you knowing when to exercise or not, then it is helpful for you. If you have ever been in a disordered relationship with eating or have been encouraged to push beyond your limits physically to the point where you are not sure where your limits are and you end up injured or exhausted, then this is for you.

PHYSICAL HEALING PRACTICE FOR BEING IN THE WORLD, NOT OF THE WORLD

This simple and powerful practice requires that you sit where you can be comfortable and speak aloud without having your privacy disturbed. If you have a piece of Labradorite, please have it resting in contact with your body wherever it feels best. If you don't have the crystal itself, you might like to leave this book open to page 21, which features the mandala for Labradorite in full colour.

Start by saying the following healing declaration:

"I call upon the healing power of Labradorite, I call upon the Angel of Labradorite and ask for your healing blessings and assistance now. Please cleanse, purify and strengthen my conscious loving connection to my own physical body now. Archangel Iahel, please help me disconnect from the drives and opinions of others that I may find my own truthful, loving and wise body-soul connection within me. So be it!"

Close your eyes and focus on your breath. Imagine that you are standing 'on top of the world' in a beautiful sacred space. This may be on a mountain, or even by the sea. Let it be somewhere in nature that feels high, peaceful and spacious. Imagine that you can hear your heartbeat and your breath more than anything else. Stay present in this place with yourself for at least ten breaths.

Visualise yourself with your hand on your heart or actually place your hand on your heart and repeat the following declaration:

"My body, I am connected to you with wisdom, love and respect. I honour your wisdom and receive your grace. Thank you for communicating to me and allowing me to hear you. I send you love now. May I serve you wisely and with compassion. So be it."

Give and receive love into your heart now. Just let love flow and know that you are connected to your body as this is happening.

Imagine then that there are suddenly millions of people around you, all with their own chatter, opinions and noise to make! But they do not diminish your connection to your body, to your heartbeat or your breath. Stay present and be aware that others are there, perhaps even choosing to send them love, but without being negatively effected by their presence. You stay in connection with your own heart, whilst gaining more energy in sending them love.

When you are ready, say, "Thank you for the healing. With deepest respect I now

commit myself to honour my own truths and live them with love." Then open your eyes.
Well done!

PRAYER – AFFIRMATION

To invoke the healing power of Labradorite and Archangel Iahel at any time, you can repeat the following affirmation quietly in your mind, or aloud.

"I AM me, I choose to be myself and I AM free!"

6.

BLUE OBSIDIAN (Clarity) and ANGEL AMITIEL (Angel of Truth)

THE GIFT OF CLARITY

SPIRITUAL GUIDANCE FROM THE ANGEL OF BLUE OBSIDIAN AND THE ANGEL AMITIEL

Deception creates confusion and truth brings release. We come to you now, offering this peace. Clarity awakens within you now, helping you find your way. We have heard your prayers for assistance and we respond without delay. There is nothing to fear in our revelation, nothing to resist or deny. There is no judgement or condemnation in seeing things as they are, only joy in being free from the lie. Take this opportunity to feel relief and to heal. We guide you now from what is false to what is real. No longer must you hide behind confusion. Accept clarity and let it be. Your clarity shows you the way forward. From confusion you are now free!

PICTURING BLUE OBSIDIAN

Blue Obsidian is volcanic glass. It was once molten lava that cooled and hardened quickly into a beautiful sheer glass-like crystal with a soft aqua-blue tint. Obsidian can come in other colours and degrees of translucency or opaqueness. Similar to Blue Obsidian is Green Obsidian. Apart from that, there is Black Obsidian which has a glassy, shiny black surface and Mahogany Obsidian and Golden Sheen Obsidian, which are not translucent at all, but contain a mixture of brown, black and luminous golden sheens respectively.

Obsidian often comes in rounded shapes such as spheres and large tumbled stones, and is often polished into wands, obelisks and pyramid forms. It can also be found in arrowhead formations which are usually in Black Obsidian, quite rough and raw around the edges, emanating a raw and powerful energy. I have also held free-form shapes, like small mountains, of Mahogany Obsidian – even the memory of this is so grounding and evokes a beautiful feeling of safety and peace – and a delightful Mayan-style carving of a tribal god in Golden Sheen Obsidian which my partner and I both enjoyed whilst strolling around the markets at Bondi Beach in Sydney one Sunday afternoon. Although I think my partner enjoyed watching me play with the carving and issue 'divine edicts' from it with a funny voice more than he enjoyed the crystal itself.

There is some debate about certain crystals and whether they are man-made or natural, and Blue Obsidian often arises in discussions of this nature. Interesting that this debate arises so fervently with a stone that is all about clarity, certainty and truth! I suspect this is part of the healing process that the Angel of Blue Obsidian is teaching humanity, for discernment is required to attain clarity.

If you are about to purchase Blue Obsidian, ask if it is natural or man-made. If you are not sure if the answer you have been given is correct, simply hold the piece in your hand (or tune into it energetically if you are purchasing online for example) and see how it feels. If you feel better for holding it, then it is helping you and would be good for you. Be grateful and work with it. Man-made stones have healing properties too. Certainly crystal-lovers often have a preference for completely natural stones, yet if a man-made piece has come to you, then trust that this particular piece can help you too – and perhaps you can help it by loving it and letting it do its job in healing.

HEALING PROPERTIES

Obsidian is a powerful stone, perhaps not for the faint-hearted. It does hold a raw energy and works powerfully and often emotionally in particular, in a cathartic way. It cuts through confusion and doubt and shows what is – sometimes with ruthless clarity, but ultimately in a way that is helpful in the long term (even if a shock in the short-term).

However I also find a soothing peace in its unwavering truthfulness – sort of like a friend that you know you can go to with any problem and they will give you their honest opinion, free from trying to manipulate you or get their way, or soothe your ego, they'll just give you honest feedback, which can be incredibly helpful in cutting through confusion and reaching clarity.

I place Blue Obsidian under my client's chair during a soul therapy session or divine healing on a regular basis. More often than not I place a mandala of different crystals according to my own intuition and higher guidance about what the client is in need of before they arrive for their consultation. Often their higher self or soul will call for a particular crystal. If a client has a look under their chair before sitting down for a consultation, they would see I've already been talking with their soul and the healing process began before they stepped into the room!

Blue Obsidian is one of the most recurring crystals 'called for' with many clients. I trust my guidance completely and I suspect that the frequent call for Blue Obsidian is testament to the fact that truth really does set one free – free to heal and to let go of the past, with higher understanding as a loving support in doing so.

This is what Blue Obsidian brings to the table (or under the chair!). It creates clarity, unveiling and revealing the truth of a situation. It peels back the emotional layers of pain that have led to confusion or deception (often as a way to subconsciously protect oneself or another) and shows you what you have denied yourself permission to see. It bestows the healing grace of clarity, without which healing can be elusive. If you don't know what you have done or what you are doing that may be holding you back, it can be tricky to consciously change your behaviour.

What I deeply appreciate about Obsidian is that it not only exposes the deceptions that have clogged energy flow within but it also helps to dislodge and dissolve the blockages. Unlike those people you may encounter in life who are quite happy to tell you all about how you should do this and that, but don't lift a finger to help you do it, Obsidian actually dives in with you and helps move the energy along to release. It has an incredible ability to actually shine a light on the truth hidden by lies, whilst also shattering the energetic structures (such as belief systems or fears) that have held the lie in place as a survival mechanism for so long. This ultimately brings great relief and clarity to us and any situation in our lives.

I have heard some crystal therapists say that Obsidian should be used with care, and perhaps this is true, but I also believe that if it has come to you or you are drawn to it, then you can trust that your soul knows what you are ready for. The power of truth is sometimes raw and confronting. It can be a bit of a shock to the system to be in clarity rather than confusion, for this brings us to a place of now needing to take responsibility and act. Life often moves extremely quickly from such a place, and yet with Obsidian by your side, you'll be helped to move past the shock and into the relief of feeling the truth of a situation and knowing what to do (or not do) next with relative ease. You won't be thrown into the river without a canoe (and a paddle)!

Because of its tendency to dissolve that which is impure or untrue, Obsidian is a stone without compare for blocking psychic attack and dissolving negative thoughts sent to you (intentionally or unconsciously) from another. Black Obsidian in particular is helpful for this process but Blue Obsidian will also help you recognise if there is a negative energy coming towards you or influencing you and will help you have the strength and clarity you need to say, "No thank you, go in peace".

Blue Obsidian is truly a detoxifying, clarifying and protective stone and genuinely helpful companion on the path for those that are learning what it is to be in one's truth this lifetime.

ABOUT THE ANGEL AMITIEL

The Angel Amitiel is known as the Angel of Truth. The human race is learning about truth spiritually at this time. We are learning that there are small truths and higher truths. For example, it might be true to one person that today is Wednesday and that might feel like an absolute truth, yet at the same time for another person in some other part of the world, the 'truth' could be that it's Thursday! So we can quickly see that the concept of 'truth' is quite relative and changeable. Our truths at the micro-level can change many times in one day. How we felt about something yesterday to what feels right at this particular moment can shift like the sands in the desert. We can recognise that a truth for us is not necessarily true for another – or 'one man's meat is another man's poison', as the old expression goes.

This spiritual learning about the flexibility of truth at a human level is teaching humanity how to love more unconditionally and find more tolerance for each other. We are learning how to respect our self and one another, even with great differences in belief. It is also teaching human beings how to be individuals with loving acceptance, giving permission to not have to fall into line with the opinions of others in order to be acceptable. These are important teachings and the Angel Amitiel helps us learn them.

However, there are higher truths. These are perennial, becoming more known to us as we grow. Forgiveness always leads to freedom is one example. It always applies. Then there are those truths that change us forever. A glimpse of one's own true spiritual nature is such a truth. The clarity that comes to us in such a moment – that we are a soul, or the entire universe, in fact, expressing itself as a human being for a time – can be enough to transform our perspective of who and what we are forever, freeing us from fear that has held us back, and allowing us to boldly live our truths with passion and purpose, once and for all!

In such a way, clarity can cast a death knell to the fear that we are not enough, which may lead us to miss opportunities and hide rather than reveal ourselves. If we subconsciously hide ourselves from Life, we can end up feeling very disconnected and lonely even though we may be trying to protect ourselves from being hurt through such choices. A glimpse of the genuine self – with its eternal innocence, purity and loveliness, is often enough to throw us irrevocably on the path to our own enlightenment, throwing our arms open to life and wondering what we were so afraid of after all. Doubts and concerns that once swayed us away from living our inner truth become as molehills instead of mountains and we simply ARE who we are without apology or shame. It is a beautiful spiritual awakening through a flash of clarity. This is the benevolent gift of Amitiel.

What I loved particularly about connecting with Amitiel was another truth that touched my heart, which is that the angels are with us all the time, whether we consciously recognise it or not.

How I came to clearly realise my long-standing (but previously unconscious) connection with Amitiel was because of a gesture that I often found myself assuming during divine healing sessions with individuals, usually during classes and workshops when the energy was quite strong. My body will assume certain gestures and postures. I don't think about it, it is like being moved by an invisible inner music and my body dances in a way. My hands take particular gestures and even my feet and eye gaze will be moved spontaneously and naturally. Mostly this displays itself in certain gestures with my palms and fingers touching in different ways – like an energetic dance of the hands. I trust the energy flow and my body, so I allow this to occur even though I do not always understand at the time what the particular significance might be. When channelling healing, I am in an altered state. I usually am conscious of what I am saying and doing but I am not always conscious of why. After experiencing the positive and powerful effect that this has on both myself and those I am working with, I have learned to trust and allow it to happen. I trust that my body-soul connection is strong and that wisdom is being expressed through my body. My role is to let it happen. Sometimes, if a particular gesture (these are sometimes called 'mudras') is happening repeatedly, I will research to see if I can find a meaning for it. Sometimes I find the answer, sometimes I don't, so I just choose to trust and carry on regardless.

Over the past couple of years, on a fairly recurring basis, I found my right hand assuming the gesture of index and middle finger raised together and the thumb holding the ring and little finger down on my palm, with my hand raised up to my head. When this gesture was assumed, I felt tremendous power pulsing through me and I knew that something sacred was taking place – I just didn't consciously understand what it was or why my body-soul was expressing it. It was not long into my research into Amitiel that I discovered this gesture is associated with this angel. It actually is the expression of this angel's energy!

This was a profound realisation. The revelation that this angel had been working through my body-soul was so deeply moving. I have often had clients say, "I can see your wings!" and I know that angelic energy is a part of what flows through my soul at certain times. This specific confirmation touched me deeply at a heart level. The fact that I didn't know consciously until just recently that this gesture was angelic, allows me to say to you, dear reader, that the angels are with you always, whether you know it or not! All you have to do is ask for their help and they are there. In fact given that you are reading this book, you can assume that they are already active in your life and helping you now. If you needed confirmation of this, consider it given!

SOUL HEALING WITH BLUE OBSIDIAN AND
THE ANGEL AMITIEL: SEEING WHO YOU ARE

It is my belief that old souls incarnate on this Earth to learn and grow through offering service to the greater healing of humanity and Mother Earth. There is so much love at the basis of such a decision, it is the Christ Consciousness in action. To me the Christ Consciousness is expressed not only through Jesus Christ, but through all beings that serve the Earth and humanity through unconditional love and divine service. This includes the Buddha, Ascended Masters, and other enlightened spiritual teachers who serve human evolution with compassion. Many old souls are learning how to embody this higher consciousness of divine love. This lifetime is their 'school' for doing so.

To choose to enter into the illusion of separation from the sweet wholeness of being at one with the Divine (which we do by incarnating into a human body) in order to find one's way back to wholeness and help others along the way is a profound spiritual decision. It is a choice that involves great bliss but also tremendous pain and suffering. It takes a courageous, confident heart which is absolutely clear and filled with compassion, willing to serve that others might be assisted, until all beings are enlightened and free.

One of the most important parts of this process is the shift from the pain and suffering of believing that we are separate from the Divine (which causes loneliness, anxiety, scarcity and fear), towards realising that we ARE divine, just in different clothing, so to speak. We can choose to experience the human condition without believing that we always have to get caught up in our suffering, creating stories about it, to try and make it make sense. Sometimes we will feel the need to try and make our suffering mean something or perhaps cast ourselves as the hero or the victim in a certain situation. Yet at other times as we grow spiritually we will be able to make a different choice, to observe our suffering and let it pass right through us, eventually just falling away into nothingness. As we experience being human, including experiences of pain, suffering, loss, and also, of course, sensual delights and falling in love, we can learn to change our perspective. We can begin to do this by imagining that we are the soul that is learning and growing through it all. We can be present in our experiences, but realise that they are all about spiritual growth and nothing more than that.

This process starts with the desire to know what you are learning from any situation and how you can grow and be free from the suffering that it has entailed, rather than falling into a victim position of wondering, 'Why is it happening to me?'. Once we are seeking the truth of a situation at the higher level of consciousness focused on finding the learning in a situation, we are starting to think more in terms of the soul. The soul doesn't really think, but as we think in particular ways this helps us connect with the higher consciousness of the soul.

When we focus more on what we are learning from a situation, rather than getting caught up in judgement, energy begins to move. Solutions and ways forward present themselves because instead of resisting, we are growing. Anything and everything that happens in our life is helping us to grow spiritually. Sometimes our spiritual growth will be through opportunities that lure us forward with great excitement. At other times our spiritual growth might be through a door slamming in our face and helping us to stay on the right path. We can choose at any moment to ask, "What am I learning here?". Just remember to be open to the answer coming to you through dreams, meditation and oftentimes when you least expect it because your attention is somewhere else and you are mentally relaxed. That might be when you are working in your garden, going for a walk or a yoga class, or dancing in your lounge room, lying in the sun or having a shower. I have received clear guidance whilst washing dishes! These 'ah-ha!' moments where we get a glimpse of the spiritual lesson we are learning through a particular life experience can be inspiring. When we realise that we aren't being punished, but rather are being asked to grow, perhaps to step into our power or be open to more unconditional love, it's easier to let go of fear and trust that our life is unfolding as it should. You can ask the question "Why me?" with a fearful heart and close off from your soul, or you can ask the same question with an open, trusting and curious heart and allow the soul to guide you through the challenge towards the solution.

HOW DO YOU KNOW IF YOU ARE
HEALING AT A SOUL LEVEL IN THIS WAY?

Every soul has a different path to awakening. For some, it is subtle and delicate, for others it's more extreme and sometimes quite abrupt. There are those that have no conscious clue that they are spiritual beings until a trauma or some meaningful event or life experience suddenly flicks the switch and there are those who are 'born with the lights on', that come into this world knowing who and what they are – a child of the Universe. And of course, there is every possibility in-between. No way is better than the other. Every situation and path serves the soul and brings it towards enlightenment via the route that suits it best.

There are times when we are more open than other times to receive a spiritual gift such as this, the gift of divine mirroring or realisation of who we are. Our realisation may happen in stages or as one sudden moment resulting from many phases of work in previous lifetimes, coming together in this one. Again, it matters not. The soul chooses everything – from the way we awaken to the timing of that awakening and its degree – with perfect wisdom.

Our job at the human level is to be as open as we can be to receiving those moments of grace where we see who we are – drink them in, take them into our hearts and let them penetrate our consciousness. You'll know when you need this kind of soul healing because there will be something in your life that isn't surrendered. It will be a situation, issue or difficulty that is just hanging on – perhaps coming up yet again to 'test' you, or perhaps a feeling that you just can't get a handle on a particular matter. There may be a fear or a doubt, or you may feel absolutely certain but feel like life isn't responding to you. You may just want reassurance to know that all is happening as is meant to be and you haven't 'got the wrong end of the stick' so to speak. This is when you need the gift of seeing yourself with clarity and accuracy. It helps restore faith and reconnect you with deep trust, surrender and peaceful, playful connection with life. You realise that you are love, and there is nothing to fear, no need to effect solutions, just to take intuitively-inspired action, to let go and trust.

If the awakening is sudden and powerful enough, it will shift you right then and there. However oftentimes there are a series of gentler awakenings on the path that guide us into moments of clarity, lifting us temporarily before we fall back into old patterns again for a while. We connect with the truth again, perhaps through a dream or meditation or moment of insight, and again we are lifted before once again falling. This can happen over and over, like gentle waves of consciousness, moving us moment-to-moment, deeper into an ocean of divine love, until we fully 'get' whatever it is that we are learning at this time.

I had a series of moments like this in my twenties regarding a relationship that I was in at the time. In many ways it was a deeply loving and spiritual relationship, but it also had its difficulties. Because it was my first serious relationship and I had very few healthy relationship experiences to draw from, I felt unsure and confused about the struggles I was having. I wrote down my feelings and dreams in journals over the years. One day, before I consciously began to deal with the reality that my relationship would need to end if I wanted to break out of the pattern that was stifling me, I decided to read through my journals.

Perhaps it was my own inner knowing or higher guidance that prompted me to do it, but I was utterly shocked by what I read.

Over the years I had already had many of the 'fresh insights' that had occurred to me more recently. A year ago, two years ago, three years ago, there they were, in ink, staring me in the face. I had already made the connection to the wisdom, honoured what was happening, but was as yet lacking the ability to really act on it, and so I had forgotten it, slipping into unconsciousness again as the old pattern had more power than the clear insight at that stage of my growth. Sometime later another wave of consciousness would lift me and I would again emerge with another insight. Not realising it was the same guidance reaching through to me over and over again, I would journal it and sit with it. This continued through the course of several years until enough insight had accumulated, enough growth had happened within me and I was ready to act on the guidance and leave the relationship. This was challenging because I truly did love my partner and had never imagined living without him. Yet I could finally reconcile the fact that I could love someone and not be able to grow within the relationship, that I could need time on my own, getting to know myself as an individual in a way that I never had been given the opportunity to do previously.

It is my belief that those gentle waves were more helpful for me at the time – helping me break through my own patterns in my own time. Anything more dramatic might have been too much for me to process at the time when I was not far enough along my path to be able to take the steps that would be asked of me by acting on my guidance. When I was ready to see it, take it on board and act on it, I did. That was my series of ocean waves.

Then there were other experiences which were unexpected, sudden and changed me. These were the experiences of receiving myself in a spiritual sense. They are so numinous, brief, and somehow also timeless, that they etched themselves into my being and remain as vivid years later as they did at the time of first experiencing them. What they asked of me seemed so subtle at the time – it wasn't about dramatic life changes but simply about realising more of what I truly was spiritually. The consequences of these subtle requests however, were far reaching and have taken me into spiritual states that I never even imagined I would be privy to this lifetime.

When you have precious moments like this,, they change you. Following such an encounter, there is a tendency to become extremely focused and confident on your path. There is a release of old fears, doubts or loneliness and an ability to be more decisive and simultaneously more surrendered into the unfolding of life rather than being attached to your own plans working out as you think that they should.

This soul healing may unfold for you as a gentle wave or a sharp insight. Whatever happens each time you engage with this healing process, it will be perfect for you.

SOUL HEALING PROCESS – SEEING YOUR SELF

You will need a quiet place to sit where you can be comfortable, warm, and not disturbed.

Start by saying the following invocation:

"I call upon Angel Amitiel and the Angel of Blue Obsidian. I call upon the highest truth available to me, upon a vision of divine clarity, with compassionate grace, kindness and mercy. May I be blessed with the revelation of the divine mirror. May I be blessed with the gift of divine witnessing. I call upon my own true, clear essence, my own soul. I love you and I wish to know myself as you with clarity. Please help me now. Help me know and realise the truth of my own being. Thank you. Through my own free will, so be it."

Focus on your breathing and allow yourself to close your eyes, letting the eyes either roll gently back or gently down, whatever happens naturally without force.

Follow your breath in and out, slowly and evenly. Allow your awareness to move away from the day-to-day world as you ride your breath deeper into the vast peaceful space opening up inside of you now.

As you move within, feel yourself travelling effortlessly on the breath until you are in an empty, open space that feels endless and safe.

Imagine that there is a crystal clear, aqua-blue tinted glass wall before you. As you approach the crystal wall you realise that the wall is not hard to touch, but actually made of living light. Allow yourself to step into that light and move through it in your own time, letting it strip away the false layers of your perceptions of yourself, conscious and unconscious, to the extent that is helpful for you now.

When you are ready, move beyond that wall of light, resting in an empty space of nothingness. There is silence. There is space. This is the Cosmic Void. It is utterly peaceful.

Into that Void, from within your own heart, imagine sending out the energy of this sound. Send it out and let it travel deep into the Void. Either aloud or silently in your mind, send the sound "I AM".

From the Void there is an instant response, a sound, light and energy, a consciousness and feeling that begins to build and grow. It is small at first and then more obvious and powerful. Let yourself notice the response from the Void.

What do you see, sense or feel? Be patient and be receptive. There may be colours, shapes, symbols or sounds. You may be taken on a journey or simply feel to be with the breath. Whatever happens for you, stay with it and trust that it is perfect for you at this time.

If you do not consciously register something, that is just fine! The intention will set a process in motion that will happen at a deeper level of consciousness regardless of what you observe. Stay present and complete forty-four breaths slowly in and out.

When you are ready, open your eyes.

You have completed this soul healing process.

PSYCHOLOGICAL-EMOTIONAL HEALING WITH BLUE OBSIDIAN AND THE ANGEL AMITIEL: THE GIFT OF INTUITION

Many souls that are drawn to healing this lifetime, be it to travel their own healing path or perhaps to share that gift of healing with others, will have had experiences where they were challenged to honour their own inner truths above the truths of those around them. Out of love or a subconscious (and important) need for acceptance, they may have discounted their own truths to make another more comfortable. They may have become internally confused as a result.

Tragically this often plays itself out in childhood, where a child senses a truth of what is happening, perhaps in reference to an anxiety held by a parent, and the parent cannot mirror the truth of that sense back to the child. There is no clarity in reflection, just murkiness and confusion for the child. Perhaps the parent believes that he or she should try and 'protect' the child from the truth, and whilst there is nobility in this intention, it isn't necessarily wise. This doesn't mean that the parent in question would have been better to have placed an inappropriate emotional burden on the child, discussing matters that are more for adults than children. It means that as a parent, you can acknowledge that you feel anxiety, but that you know that you are going to be okay and you don't want your child to have to worry about you. The fact that you want to take care of him or her instead, is real, truthful and helpful. To be truthful and acknowledge your stress in this way creates internal clarity for the child, where she learns that her inner truths are accurate and can be relied upon as an inner compass or guide.

This kind of honest mirroring, with maturity and sensitivity, encourages a child to continue to trust her instincts and intuition. If the parent believes they are supposed to be perfect or protect the child from realities of emotional experience, or even if the parent is just genuinely scared and doesn't know how to deal with their feelings of fear, then truthful mirroring becomes almost impossible. As a consequence, the child's internal intuition can become muddied with fear and self-doubt, confusion and distrust of his/her instincts.

In this case, the child most likely learns that what he or she feels is untrue, unreceived or unworthy of acknowledgment. This leads to insecurity as opposed to the inner security in one's own intuition that would have been present, had the truth been honoured. Or the child may learn that their parent cannot be trusted to be truthful, which can lead to even greater insecurity and despair. If a child does not feel safe with a primary caregiver, this can cause a level of inner distress that is too much to bear consciously, so it gets pushed within, along with the truthful sense of the parent's inadequacies.

This can be a sad state of affairs, but also an opportunity for a new pattern to be established and healed as the former child, perhaps now an adult or parent in his or her own right, chooses to develop and then reclaim the innate intuitive gifts and instincts that they once had to cast aside in order to survive. It takes bold faith to learn to hear, listen to and trust in their inner knowing, instincts and intuition. The old pattern of inner distrust is outgrown when intuition and instincts are applied to real life situations. Then one has to notice what happens when one fails to listen (usually a bit of a mess!), and noticing what happens when one does trust in one's intuition. Sometimes a lot of patience and trust is required, before receiving the confirmation that this is indeed the best way forward. At other times the proof the intuition is indeed wise and spot-on will be instant and trust will grow. This is the journey for many sensitive souls learning to believe in their own inner wisdom after growing up amongst many forces that discouraged it for various reasons.

HOW DO I KNOW IF I NEED HEALING IN THIS WAY AND AT THIS LEVEL OF MY BEING?

You will know that you need healing in this way if you feel that you spend more time looking outwards for guidance than inwards. If you tend to doubt what you sense about people and situations – only to be proven 'right' time and time again – then your connection to your intuition is an important part of your development and you deserve this opportunity to take it to a deeper, more respectful and trusting level.

If, as a child, you had many feelings, emotions, insights and knowings that your family or friends could not understand or accept (and you may have kept your intuitive gifts hidden because of this), then it could be time to rebuild them more than you have already.

Finally, if you have had a pattern of being enmeshed in relationships, where you put your own thoughts or feelings aside in favour of making another comfortable, perhaps taking on their viewpoints or beliefs and subsuming your own truths somewhere deep inside of you, then this healing will help you find a way to be yourself and be in relationship with others without losing connection to your own truths.

If you resonate deeply with this chapter however you may consider buying a piece of

Blue Obsidian and holding it for around a half hour or so every day, even if it is just whilst you are responding to your emails or reading a book.

PSYCHOLOGICAL-EMOTIONAL HEALING PROCESS – THE GIFT OF INTUITION

You will need a place to sit comfortably where you won't be disturbed and where you can speak aloud. If you have a piece of Blue Obsidian, please have it with you, touching your body, if not, we will call on the spirit of the stone anyway, so don't worry.

Say the following, "I call upon the healing power of my own soul, and upon the Angel of Blue Obsidian and the Angel Amitiel. I give you permission to help me restore my intuitive connection to myself thoroughly and completely now, with grace, mercy and unconditional love. May I be blessed with full connection to my intuition, according to my highest good. Thank you!"

Close your eyes and focus on your breath. Give yourself permission to let go of the day-to-day world and become more aware of your inner world as your attention drifts inwards on the breath.

Say aloud, "I release any fear of my intuition. I release any shame, guilt, judgement or blame, anger, misunderstanding, victimisation, hurt, torture, suffering or injustice that I have ever experienced, in this or any other lifetime as a result of my intuitive abilities. I now choose, of my own free will, to forgive myself and any other being involved in this distortion of my intuitive ability and I now free myself from the past. I have gratitude for the learning and I now choose to let the old patterning go. I now choose to honour and trust the voice within, each and every day, one step at a time. Through my own free will, so be it."

Imagine that within you, you sense a pale blue light. As you focus on this light it becomes stronger and more pure. It grows in size and intensity. You may notice dark spots or tears in this blue light, but as you peacefully allow yourself to focus on your breath and let your awareness dwell gently on the blue light, it heals itself, becoming more powerful. You may even notice a golden light or another colour flowing into the blue light.

As you sit with the blue light, allow yourself to really feel it. Notice its strength, its detachment and its knowing and any other sensations you feel. Imagine that blue light becoming crystal clear and sensing a clear powerful light behind it now shining through it. Stay for as long as you like with the sense or perception of the source of clear light shining through the crystal clear blue light, making it bright, radiant and alive with energy.

This blue light is your intuition and the clear light powerfully radiant behind it is your own soul. Stay peacefully connected and let any thoughts or feelings that come up in this process simply arise and fall away. It is part of your healing process that a cleansing of old energies happens. It is natural and nothing to be concerned about.

When you are ready, you can either relax and remain in this space, resting for as long as feels good, but at least for seven long, slow inhalations and exhalations.

When you are ready, say, "I trust myself. I give myself permission to completely receive my intuitive knowing and I feel peace and courage. I am so happy to be such an intuitive person and to be so guided by my inner voice. I am so grateful for the inner wisdom which I easily receive whenever I need it!"

Staying with your breath, allow yourself to rest with your soul light and the light of your intuition. When you feel ready to come back, breathe slowly and without rushing, gently open your eyes.

You have completed your healing task.

PHYSICAL HEALING WITH BLUE OBSIDIAN AND ANGEL AMITIEL: DANCE THE TRUTHS OF YOUR BODY

Your body is telling a story. When we don't know something consciously – either because it is too subtle to grasp or we are too busy, frightened or distracted to hear it, then the body tells it anyway. It may speak to us through somatic symptoms, illness or injury, random emotions that don't seem to logically relate to anything in particular happening in the moment, or even through dreams that may not make sense until we sit with them for a while. To take a moment to really just be with the body and receive its imagery through dreams, creative visualisation or meditation, is a wise and loving act. The wisdom is that the body doesn't lie. It can't. It can only ever tell us how we are feeling or what our experience was. It doesn't matter if another had a different experience to ours. Our experiences are our own, our own way of knowing and growing. We can trust them and find clarity if we so choose.

To get in touch with how we are feeling gives us an opportunity to delve deeper and make choices or take actions that are in alignment with our inner truths. They will serve us and others – even if others have a different truth, living your own truth serves the greater good. Knowing what is happening energetically in your own body is a way to be in touch with your own truths. Even if they are smaller day to day truths, they still have value and can help you live in a way that is conducive to greater wellbeing and fulfilment, calling your soul closer to you rather than pushing your divine self away through doubt or fear.

Sometimes the body will tell you a story about what is happening now. Often it will tell you a story that is unresolved from the past. When you do this body practice, if you are unsure whether it is a past or a present matter to contend with, you can follow the practice with the Gift of Intuition Healing (above).

HOW DO I KNOW IF I NEED THIS PHYSICAL HEALING PRACTICE?

One of the great wonders of the mind is that it is capable of seeing things from all different angles. This gives us a chance to find life and people quite interesting. But it can also lead to confusion if we try to navigate our way through life decisions and choices with our mind, as we are able to see things from many angles, and many different perspectives. This is especially true if you are quite an open-minded person! The body however, is much more anchored in this time-space reality and will tell you pretty honestly if something is for you or not at this time. Where the mind will tell you yes, but it could be just as valid another way, the body will just tell you how it is for you now.

Coming into the body is the best way to cure confusion, indecision and insecurity. Sometimes the body will present us with unexpected or confronting realisations, and we'll need to trust that if we are receiving that information, at some level we are ready for it. This happens naturally all the time as we outgrow our problems by not focusing on them too much and just dealing with what we can in each moment. In surrendering the mind-task of sorting everything through and just living our reality in the here and now, we let the body tell the story of our truth and we begin to outgrow the issue and grow into the solution – which is, more often than not, simply being present, letting something be, not engaging in the struggle and letting ourselves wait whilst we become bigger than the past pain and more capable of love in the present.

You'll know if this is for you because you'll find yourself thinking your way into circles and not necessarily getting anywhere. You'll want to drop the fatigue and stress of trying to work it all out, and just have it happen! Then you are in a place within where you are ready to connect with your body. If you aren't quite there yet, do the practice anyway. It will help you get there.

PHYSICAL HEALING PRACTICE – DANCE THE TRUTHS OF YOUR BODY

This simple and powerful practice requires that you have a private space with enough room to move a bit (or a lot if you feel you want to) and not be disturbed. You'll need to be able to close your eyes and move without having to worry about crashing into furniture, so you might need to clear a space or find some privacy in your garden. Or you can be inspired by a dear friend of mine who likes to dance on the beach. It genuinely doesn't concern her whether others will accept this or not. She likes it and just does it. We have danced, drummed and chanted together on the beach and there was no problem about being judged. The only problem was people wanted to stop and talk to us and/or join in! This was lovely because we were at play. If I was doing a personal healing however, I would choose to do this practice in a more private space. In that privacy you can allow emotion to come up if it wants to, to feel and to move without concern about being disturbed or assessed (or befriended!) by another.

You may or may not want to have music for this practice. If there is a piece of music that you feel you would like to dance to – then do so. You may find that it starts out feeling right and then you don't want to dance to it anymore, at which point allow yourself to turn it off and keep dancing or play something else. You can let yourself move by being as present as you can in your body and letting its energy move you rather than the music. This is how silence can work in this practice if you are inclined to try it.

Start by saying the following healing declaration:

"I call upon the healing power of Blue Obsidian, rising up from the volcanoes of Mother Earth, bring me your cleansing, beloved being of light. I call upon the Angel of Blue Obsidian, your light of clarity shines bright in my body and soul now. Angel Amitiel, dance with me beloved, the dance of honest and clear expression, that I may know more deeply how I feel, what I need, to be without thought, as I just allow movement to flow. So be it."

Play your music or be still in the silence.

Close your eyes and focus on your breath. Imagine that you are completely at one with your body, feeling your feet on the ground, your legs, hips and pelvis balancing on each other.

Then notice your spine, your ribs, arms and shoulders balancing and your head balancing on top of your spine. You are one whole being.

Let the heart become warm and feel the love and life in your body. When you are ready just say this declaration to your body, "I love you and I receive your communication beloved. Let us be together as you speak. I want to know your truths."

Allow yourself to move. Your movements may be small and delicate, hardly moving at all physically but perhaps noticing energy moving in your body. You may not feel a lot or you may feel a huge amount happening at a subtle level. You may feel that your body wants bigger movements and you may feel emotion arising and leaving. You may see imagery or feel, or not think much at all. Just let your body move you and let it happen. This is your dance of clarity and truthful expression. Allow yourself to just speak your truth through your body. If sounds come out, words, or just noises, if you want to sing or chant, hum or speak, let it happen but let it come from the body rather than the mind. Intend to let the body speak and lovingly accept what it has to say.

If you find yourself struggling to stay with the process, always come back to the breath flowing in and out. If you have judgement or criticism arising, it is trying to protect you from the truth, taking you out of the experience. Send love and go back to the breath and the body. You will experience what you are ready to experience, nothing more and nothing less.

When you are ready, stand peacefully and quietly and feel the energy in your body. Take four long, slow deep breaths in and out and when you are ready say, "Thank you. I love you. I respect you."

Then open your eyes. Well done.

PRAYER – AFFIRMATION

To invoke the healing power of Blue Obsidian and Angel Amitiel at any time, you can repeat the following affirmation quietly in your mind, or aloud.

"Clarity reveals my path always, it shines through me with love."

7.

POLYCHROME JASPER (Playfulness) and ANGEL CALIEL (Angel of Laughter)

THE GIFT OF DIVINE PLAY

SPIRITUAL GUIDANCE FROM THE ANGEL OF POLYCHROME JASPER AND THE ANGEL CALIEL

We bring you the gift of new perspective and fresh energy, lifting you from struggle into a place of lightness and glee. Laughter and play, each and every day, helps keep despair and boredom away! We have come to tell you that everything is alright. You do not have to worry nor do you need to fight. Let us reveal the humour reaching through the darkness of worry and doubt, that wishes to show you, there is nothing you are without! You have all that you need, you have all that you want, just waiting to be discovered, within you right now. When you relax and play, which we know takes great trust, we can help you on your way – why struggle when you can be lifted by us? Let us make your journey easier. Let us help you on your way. Come spend time with us beloved. Come enjoy divine play.

PICTURING POLYCHROME JASPER

There is a joke amongst some of my friends that I am a bit of a 'Jasper junkie'. It is true that I am frequently drawn to Jaspers and I find them to be greatly comforting and beautiful stones. Because they manifest in such diversity, they appeal to souls who are interested in variety. Jasper comes in endless spectrums of colour and pattern, which to my heart feels like a reflection of the diverse creative intelligence of the divine feminine Buddha, Gaia, herself.

What I love especially about Polychrome or Desert Jasper is that even within this one variety of Jasper, there is such diversity. No two pieces are alike. The patterning and colours range from dark browns and orange tones, to baby blues and soft creams. They will have tones of grey and yellow included at times also.

The Polychrome Jasper that I have been blessed to obtain is in freeform shapes large enough that I can't quite close both hands around them. I have seen it in smaller tumbled stones and in larger free form shapes. Many Jaspers, particularly Red Jasper, are shaped into wands and pyramids, whilst others, such as Ocean Jasper, are often shaped into spheres. These shapes all hold different energies – some are more directive (such as a wand or pyramid) and some emanate a field of energy more diffusely, such as the sphere. The free form shapes generate an energy field which is particularly useful to heal an environment as well as its inhabitant (so in a home, workplace or healing room for example). They have a free flowing, organic feel much like a child's drawing, which is quite liberating to the creative energies of those that behold them. Tumbled stones are a great option if you want to work with the stones for healing of the body. This allows the stones to be held or placed under a chair or on a desk, to do their job of rebalancing the energy field of the individual.

HEALING PROPERTIES

Polychrome Jasper is a colourful looking stone with comforting properties that both ground and bring energy to the body, whilst calming and balancing the chakras and energy field. They help nurture and protect and to me, are gifts directly from the Divine Mother to her divine children (that's you and me!).

Jasper supports us like lattice supports a rose bush. It helps us grow our soul light into full expression on Earth. It brings comfort to any emotional difficulty and any psychological struggle. It soothes the body when it is tired, balances it when it has been over-energised. It helps repair the energy field after much exertion, trauma or after a period of life where great endurance has been required. Polychrome Jasper in particular helps remind us of the amazing regenerative power of play. If we work hard, and have a tendency to become very focused on our goals, not spending enough time unplugged from work and in play time, life can become much harder than it needs to be, not to mention, much less fun.

Polychrome Jasper helps us learn to play in a constructive way. Many of us may subconsciously associate play as a destructive 'letting loose' activity involving addiction or indulgence that may give us temporary relief and leave us 'paying for it' the next day. If we don't really know how to play naturally, we might believe that these less helpful versions of play are the only way available to us. But this is not the case. Polychrome Jasper can help you learn how to play naturally and helpfully.

Natural play is an incredibly intelligent activity. It helps us gain new perspectives and fresh ideas. That is perhaps based on the notion that the best way to solve a problem is to step away and stop thinking about it! Yet there is more to it than that. Play is a way to tap into our divine nature which tends towards the creative rather than the logical. Strengthening conscious connection with our inner divinity always brings graceful solutions and blessings into our physical lives, as well as peace to our mind and heart.

Polychrome Jasper helps us find the strength of will that is required to step away from a project, problem or dilemma. It helps us to wrest our mind out of the quagmire and go dance barefoot on a beach, chase our pet around the local park, climb a tree. Polychrome Jasper inspires us to gather shells on the beach and make a beautiful design on the sand, allowing it to be washed out to sea again as a gift to Mother Nature. Or you might have the urge to wear a playful and colourful top – if you do this, you'll notice how much people are uplifted by the colour you have brought into their lives that day – you won't need to imagine it, they'll come up to you and tell you as much. If you need to learn new ways to play, this Jasper will help you find them. You'll just have an idea – and Polychrome Jasper will help you stir the daring to act on it.

Polychrome Jasper helps us become more present and aware of the moment we are in. This can help us release anxiety, which is often an emotional cue that we aren't paying attention to the truth of what is happening in the moment. We might be judging the past or fearing the future, and not really in the here and now which is the only place we can actually be effective with action!

It's a multi-level healing stone which works on all layers of our being – body, mind and soul, and helps us realise that having lightness in our being does not mean we are superficial. It simply means we know how to allow joy to have a place in our lives. It helps us heal any guilt we have about living in a more playful and flowing way which is helpful if we have been raised to believe that if we aren't working, we aren't being productive.

ABOUT THE ANGEL CALIEL

The Angel Caliel is the Angel of Laughter and Joy. He is also an angel that teaches presence. He says that with presence, joy and laughter become easier and more healing. When I called upon him, I felt a peaceful expansion in my heart and a gentle swaying of my body that was so delightful I just sat, open-mouthed (no doubt looking quite odd at that moment), and allowed his presence to have its effect. I felt a little like we were in an angelic version of a 'play fight' where he was pushing me about and it was fun – except the angelic version of the push in this experience was like being rocked on a heavenly wave.

As soon as I began writing this section, Caliel provided clear instructions for what he wanted to communicate. He said that he wanted to emphasise how important presence was to be able to gain healing from play. It is what distinguishes less helpful play (which might involve 'zoning out' or becoming less conscious through addiction or 'acting out' and then feeling perhaps ashamed or overly self-conscious later) from more helpful play (which brings a healing change in consciousness and much positive energy to us).

With presence, when you are really engaged with the 'game' that you are playing, with another or on your own with nature, your experience of time falls away. This is why you can be enjoying yourself and suddenly you wonder where the time has gone. He encourages you to become engaged in activities where you feel this way on a regular basis. You will know how often you need this – every day or every week for example.

Caliel says that when you move into a state where you forget time, when you are completely present in the moment and engaged rather than thinking or analysing, you then allow him, and the divine light that flows through him, to enter your energy field and bring you healing, replenishment and divine grace. The light of grace can flow into you more easily and you don't unnecessarily create negative energy by worry or complications by over-thinking. Then when you 'emerge' from your playful state, your answers, solutions and healing are right there within you, ready for you to become aware of them. The light of grace through Caliel simply brings them to the surface more readily. He says it is a little like the saying that a watched pot never boils. To step away and forget the issue allows the solution to come to you. He also asks that I explain that presence doesn't mean thinking during play, it means really experiencing it with all your senses. Like savouring a delicious meal, it is so much more enjoyable, and creates pleasant memories, when you really pay attention and thoroughly enjoy what you are eating. Without presence, that lovely meal might be a rushed affair where hours later you wonder if you actually ate dinner! Presence allows blessings and divine solutions to present themselves easily.

SOUL HEALING WITH POLYCHROME JASPER
AND THE ANGEL CALIEL: SOUL IN DIVINE PLAY

I have been blessed to work with some truly beautiful spiritual masters – many on the inner planes and some on the physical planes in a physical body as well, such as a Crystal Master called Raym and a Chi Gung master called Zhao. I also have my team of higher spiritual guidance and my own soul essence. What all of these beings have in common is a sense of humour. They are, put simply, very funny. I have lost count of the number of times a client (or others walking past my healing room) have commented on the amount of laughter that comes out of that room. Yet when we are in the space, there are often deep tears, much emotion, grief and plenty of darker states as well. Yet humour, joy, bliss and very often cheekiness – with great respect, and wit and with great harmlessness – are a part of Higher Level Guidance. You could think of the laughing Buddha or a joyful choir of angels singing, and this would be divine play. You could think of Mother Earth just delighting in her endless creative experiments – species of plants, animals and flowers – and feel her playfulness. Just witnessing a dog walking down the street – especially particularly quirky breeds where you can just feel Gaia saying, "Well, how about this one!" – can be enough to set me off in fits of giggles. The humour in creation, in experiencing the sometimes strange beauty of it, and just being able to love it and laugh with delight in it, brings us closer to the divine essence within.

Now, despite all of the above, I have to say here that one of my 'pet peeves' is the statement, "Ah, don't take yourself or your spirituality so seriously!", that expression might go further to include, "It means what you make it mean! It's all random!". I agree that learning to laugh at oneself (I do it quite often) and to realise that we attribute meaning to our experiences frequently can be helpful. I also accept that there is a dedication, commitment, discipline and sometimes tough love required from us to walk the spiritual path. Often on a daily basis. To deride this, to say, "Don't be so serious, put a smile on your face" can sometimes feel a bit fake to me. Yes, laugh, but also honour and respect the strength and commitment that is needed to do the inner work, to confront your fears and wounds, rather than just laughing it off and denying the pain within.

I feel it's important to mention this because divine play is meant to be a balance, to help us find that balance between commitment and joyful abandon. If you play too much and commit to little you may end up feeling restless and unsatisfied, unfulfilled and lacking in purpose. If you play too little and commit too much, you will lose the joy of your accomplishments and the fun of the journey may be lost in too much focus on the destination.

I honour the intent and the commitment required, and the hard work that comes with bringing our inspirations to life in the world. Yet I also honour the balancing effect of play that helps us live more of our divinity in this physical world, where it is needed most. It's really about finding the play and work balance that suits each one of us. Caliel will help you with this most pleasant spiritual homework if you ask him. He may appear to you, huge wings aglow, wearing a clown nose.

HOW DO YOU KNOW IF YOU ARE HEALING AT A SOUL LEVEL IN THIS WAY?

Some years ago I had slipped into a period of deep inner struggle. I was trying to break through a very old, very stubborn emotional pattern that was reaching a breaking point, but was so challenging that every day felt like a bit of a losing battle with this part of myself and the circumstances in my life that I believed reflected it. Not surprisingly perhaps, I had lost connection with my ability to really just let go and play, at a time when I needed it most.

I still have the tendency to want to get my work done before I really feel I have permission to play. I enjoy it more that way usually. Sort of like eating my main meal before my dessert. Yet sometimes my guidance and my own inner instincts do override this and I take some time out in the midst of a project to refresh and reorient myself and I find this extremely enjoyable and helpful. I also acknowledge the strength it takes for me to do this without feeling guilty about it and for me not to judge myself or believe that I have to apologise for the fact that I have worked on releasing enough fear that I can enjoy a nice life. I spent too many years with a lot to be grateful for, but so shackled by fear and anxiety that I genuinely couldn't relax enough to enjoy or play with any of it. It was long-lasting and painful enough that once I had moved through it, I would permit myself to play every day for the rest of my life if I wanted to do so! Thankfully I also love my work, so I want to do that too.

Yet not so many years ago, during that time of inner struggle, I had forgotten about this wisdom of play. I was so deep in the pain of the emotional struggle, that I hadn't been able to lift myself out and feel the lightness that I usually carried in my being. One afternoon I was driving home, sitting at a traffic light and I had an unusually dark and random thought. I wondered how I would feel if my life were to end at this moment. The instant, dramatic and surprising response flooded through my mind and body, crying out, "Oh, but this is so much FUN!".

"Fun!?", I huffed back in response, thinking of the years of deep inner struggle that felt so heavy, like I was getting nowhere fast, "Really?!". The feeling response of my soul poured through me again. "It's an ADVENTURE!"

Sitting at that traffic light, I could really feel my soul relishing the chance to take on the challenge of what I thought was an insolvable emotional problem. It loved it! It helped me step out of the unconscious victim-attitude I had slipped into, out of fatigue and the pattern of letting my own 'turkeys get me down', and allowed some playful soul energy to fill my heart.

This was also my first conscious realisation that my soul didn't choose life challenges under some duress or obligation to grow in spiritual power. It chose them because it loved the process! It was interesting, it was fresh, it was a challenge that it was absolutely going to win and it was going to enjoy the battle.

I just knew this was my soul in divine play – even in the darkness, in fact especially then, because it loved the spiritual challenge of it. All it took to recognise it, to live it, was to shift perspective away from the struggle and into the being behind all of it.

So my serene, comfort-loving smaller self, with its peaceful, quiet nature was meeting my adventure-loving, spiritual-warrior soul that loved to engage and fearlessly immerse itself in the experience of growth. It was quite a shock at the time. But it freed me up to let myself experience more consciously this adventurous part of me too. It rather dramatically changed my attitude to my life and helped me break through that pattern of struggle, embracing challenges not as things to be endured, but with a more enthusiastic sense of adventure that made my life much more vibrant again.

It was exactly the soul healing that I needed in that moment. To have that bold spiritual knowing that I would triumph, and the process of diving in and chasing the light through the darkness, was a grand adventure. It was to see life itself – the living of it, the journey, the experience – as fun. We all need reminding of this at times. If you feel like you may have forgotten this in your present circumstance in your life, or if you'd like more soul perspective to help lighten your heart and quickly resolve any challenges facing you at this time, beloved, then this soul healing is for you.

SOUL HEALING PROCESS – LIFE AS DIVINE PLAY

You will need a quiet place to sit where you can be comfortable, warm, and not disturbed. You will need space so that if you choose to stand or move your body as part of this process, you have a little bit of room to do so without crashing into a piece of furniture!

Start by sitting comfortably and saying the following invocation:

"I call upon Angel Caliel and the Angel of Polychrome Jasper. I call upon the playful humour of Gaia Mother Earth and the deep belly laughter of the Buddha of Joy. I call upon my own Highest Level Guidance and my own higher self. I call upon the joy that lies within the cells of this body divine and upon the playful dance of divine energy that fills our Universe. Please help me live the joy of my soul. Play with me, that I may have fun in my life and bring joy and laughter to others too. Welcome beloveds, through unconditional love, may we now play."

Focus on your breathing and allow yourself to close your eyes, letting the eyes either roll gently back or gently down, whatever happens naturally without force.

Follow your breath, in and out, slowly and evenly. Allow your awareness to move away from the day-to-day world as you ride your breath deeper within the vast peaceful space opening up for you now.

Become aware of a being before you – vast and large, a lovely Buddha-like being with a welcoming smile and loving energy. Move towards him and rest your head on his belly, if you wish, sitting on his massive lap like a child visiting a massive cosmic Santa Claus before Christmas.

Become aware of a sensation of movement. Feel it through your body and soul. You may hear, sense or feel a vibration, a trembling, a rumbling. It feels safe but powerful. Realise that the Buddha is laughing and feel the energy of it, the joy, shaking through your entire being. It isn't peaceful but it is safe and a bit of a thrill, not unlike being in a big inflatable jumping castle!

Let yourself just feel and be moved by his laughter, reverberating through his belly. You may feel like a cosmic child being tossed up in the air and landing softly on his big belly. You may imagine that you are in an ocean of joyful sound, rising and falling on the waves of it, merging with it.

Allow the energy of that deep belly laugh of the divine laughing Buddha to echo through you, tingling and buzzing into your being. Feel it becoming light within you and see, sense, feel or intend that light to travel with you, as you, now.

Imagine that you are that light and you are looking down at your body on Earth, at your life on Earth. Imagine sprinkling that light, that energy of the big laughing Buddha, down to your body and your life. You may send beams of light, sprinkles of glittering life force energy, as though you are releasing them from your fingers down to the Earth, like shimmering stardust.

You may sense the Angel Caliel with you helping you do this. You may sense beautiful buds of Polychrome Jasper rising up out of the Earth, as the Earth receives the stardust you sprinkle from your fingertips.

As you come closer to your body, beginning to connect body and soul consciously once more, stay present to the laughing vibration within your soul.

You may like to imagine your soul swooping, like a skilful bird, freefalling and diving, rising up again, flowing through your body and your life, enjoying the adventure of travelling on the Earth in your body and expressing itself through your life. Feel how confident your soul is in its task, how bright, how playful and how luminous. How it loves the experience. How there is so much help from the laughing Buddha, the Angel Caliel and the Angel of Polychrome Jasper through the Earth, if you ever need it.

Stay with your breath and if you wish to move, to stand up, to move your arms or legs, to let the soul energy of play move your body into dance for a few moments, please do so. Let yourself just be. The spontaneity can be great fun. Your movements may be small or large, and whatever you choose is perfect.

When you are ready, just open your eyes.

You have completed this soul healing process.

PSYCHOLOGICAL-EMOTIONAL HEALING WITH POLYCHROME JASPER AND THE ANGEL CALIEL: GETTING OUT OF A RUT

When you are a receptive and open being, sensitive to energy, which most of you reading this book will be, perhaps more than you realise, habit can be comforting. In fact in an age of so much uncertainty, helpful habits are essential! They can form the basis of what sustains and nourishes you, allowing you to then be spontaneous and unscripted in other areas of your life without feeling like you are rudderless or lacking in stability.

However sometimes we outgrow our habits and they get to be a bit stifling. If they have served their purpose but you are still caught up in the momentum of the habit and finding it a bit hard to break free, you may feel like your life is getting a bit stale and is in need of something fresh and new.

So perhaps there were external habits or practices that you used before you developed an ability to feel internally comforted. Now those external forms are unnecessary, much like outgrowing a teddy bear you had as a child. Or perhaps you just want to upgrade and revise some habits because you feel bored, lacking inspiration or in need of some fresh adventure in your life. Perhaps you just intuitively feel that you are restless, in a bit of a rut, and want to see what else life has to offer you.

To accept new possibilities in life, we have to be willing to surrender old patterns and be open to creating new habits. We might be even more radical and practice opening up to life less from habitual patterns and more from present-moment, spontaneous responses. If we want to have more genuine healing fun in our lives, we need to be able to be inspired and willing for that inspiration to shake up our world up a little! We need just enough rattling to dislodge old patterning. We can choose to create this for ourselves by letting go of how we have always done things. Some routine can be very helpful indeed, but a little spontaneity can also be very good for us!

We all vary in our ability to process change. We even vary in our ability to manage change at different times in our lives. This healing calls upon the wisdom of higher beings – the crystal angels and your own soul – to assist with calling in the change and opening you up to the change that will serve you best. To try to 'decide' what change is needed may be less helpful than receiving the change that happens through this healing process in a more organic, spiritually guided way. Another way to say this – change is what happens. It doesn't have to be forced, controlled or contrived. Change isn't about our will, it is about our response. You don't have to force your way through any of this process. You need instead to trust yourself and your ability to respond and grow.

HOW DO I KNOW IF I NEED HEALING IN THIS WAY AND AT THIS LEVEL OF MY BEING?

There are expressions that say variety is the spice of life, and that a change is as good as a holiday.

If you are open to some more spice in your life, a bit more stimulation or variety, or if you are open to breaking out of old habits, then this healing will serve you. If you have been stuck in a routine that you feel is not serving you, then this healing is for you. Also, if just want some more fun in your life, which requires an ability to be with the unknown with a sense of trust, then this healing will help you too.

If you resonate deeply with this chapter, you may consider buying a piece of Polychrome Jasper and keeping it in a room where you spend a lot of time. Jasper often works slowly and cumulatively over time. It is most healing to have it where you will be exposed to it for long periods of time on a regular basis.

PSYCHOLOGICAL-EMOTIONAL HEALING PROCESS – GETTING OUT OF A RUT

You will need a place to move comfortably where you won't be disturbed, where you can make some noise and not be heard or interrupted. If you have a piece of Polychrome Jasper, please have it with you, near your body. If not, we will call on the spirit of the stone anyway, so don't worry. You may also like to look at the Crystal Angel Mandala for Polychrome Jasper featured on page 23 in the full colour section of this book.

Say the following, "I call upon the healing power of my own soul, and upon the Angel of Polychrome Jasper and the Angel Caliel. I give you permission to help me connect with the energy of divine play, to break free from self-imposed limitations, from karmic momentum and habit, from that which no longer supports and now stifles the free flow of divine play through all levels of my being, including my mind. With grace, mercy and unconditional love, I ask for your divine assistance now. May I be blessed with the spirit of harmless play and the capacity for spontaneous action. According to my highest good, so be it. Thank you!"

Stand comfortably with your eyes softly gazing in the distance, on the floor ahead of you if it helps you balance or with your eyes closed if this is comfortable for you.

Focus on your breath. Give yourself permission to let go of the day-to-day world and become more aware of your inner world as your attention drifts inwards on the breath.

Say aloud, "I release any fear of becoming irresponsible or unproductive, I release any false notions of responsibility and maturity as being incompatible with playfulness, I release any false ideas that play is unproductive or unhelpful, and I release any shame about needing to nurture the child within through play. I now choose, of my own free will, to let the playful part of me express itself in healthy and helpful ways, in whatever way works for me! I accept that I don't have to laugh loudest to have much fun! I accept that this is not a competition or an obligation. This is just something I am doing for me. It is not about anyone else. I am gifting myself now with permission to play, to experience the freedom and joy of the big Buddha belly laugh that lives within me always, free from guilt and shame. So be it!"

Place your hands on your belly and softly bend your knees so you can rock lightly back and forwards on your feet, finding your natural balance. Let the breath move all the way down to your belly and if you have difficulty doing this, let your belly push out a little on the out breath, into your hands resting lightly there.

Take a few breaths and if you can, imagine that you can feel the big Buddha energy in your belly. You can even imagine a big Buddha living in your belly! It is laughing and joyful. You may like to think of something silly – antics of an animal, or a joke that you loved recently, or a memory of when you were a teen and laughed so hard your belly hurt. You may be able to do this easily, or you may not have a memory that easily comes to you. Either is fine. If you cannot recall something easily, imagine that the Buddha is in your belly and you can feel him laughing, the vibration of the laughter radiating outwards from your belly, reaching down to your feet and up to your heart.

When you are ready, make a sound that travels up from deep in your belly, through your heart and out of your throat! Let it just come out of your mouth. You might make a big "HA!" sound. You might feel like a bit of a fool then and giggle. That would be very good. Let your belly make some noises. You might say random words, you might just make noises. This may be easy and enjoyable for you. It might also be challenging, as the part of you that has tried to protect you from letting go in the past, for any number of previously relevant reasons, tries to tell you it's not OK to do this. But it IS OK for you to do this now. You are safe. Send a big inner hug, kiss or high five to that part of you and go back to your belly sounds.

Do at least seven belly sounds. They can be the same or different. Let them out.

When you are ready, say aloud, "Right now, if I was not human, but an animal, plant or natural object, what would I be?". Let the first thing that comes into your head, no matter how silly it may seem, be.

Then allow your body to play at being that being. Be the monkey, the tiger, or the tree. Be the rock, the candle or the crystal growing in the ground. Be the star in the sky. Be the table or the chair. Be the rubbish bin. Be the sun. It's all play. Just notice any thoughts that may arise, about how silly or unhelpful this is. Send them love and get on with being a porcupine or singing mermaid. Really go with it.

When you are ready, say, "I am me, in the here and now. I am _____ (say your name) and I am grounded in this reality, as _____ (say your name) and grateful for the energy of divine play. I surrender any worries or doubts about letting go of habits that no longer serve me as I open up to the new and unexpected. I am guided in unconditional love to that which serves me best. And I have fun along the way, even if it's just through laughing once a day! So be it!"

When you are ready, be aware of taking three long, slow deep inhalations and exhalations, then open your eyes!

You have completed your healing task. You've quite possibly been a little uncomfortable during the task but I hope you enjoyed yourself immensely.

PHYSICAL HEALING WITH POLYCHROME JASPER AND ANGEL CALIEL: BALANCING THE CHAKRAS IN YOUR BODY

The chakras in your physical body need balance through colour energy just like the physical body needs balance through certain nutrients and minerals. Polychrome Jasper has an abundant array of colour vibrations from which to draw nourishment for the chakras. And the Angel Caliel helps us relax through joy and laughter to allow for healing and balancing to happen very quickly.

This physical exercise helps the body rebalance through a playful healing activity.

I never really knew just how vital play was, until I adopted a cat. He would meow his various demands, and being quite an intuitive creature myself, it didn't take me too long to work out which meow went with which demand. Food was one (usually quite emphatic) meow, while clean my litter box, let me outside, give me fresh water, or I want a cuddle or some strokes, each had their own distinctive type of meow. I am just hanging out with you and feeling chatty was another. I am happy was another. I am cranky was a bite.

However there was one mysterious meow that I couldn't quite fathom at first. Eventually I realised, it was 'play with me!'. He wanted interaction, stimulation, games and fun. His antics were hilarious when that need was met and I would be laughing as he rushed, skidded on a carpet, slid across the floor and dived head first under a cabinet, so low he'd have to slide under with his legs almost flat out to either side. I got some play too, and when I would eventually return to whatever task I was engrossed in previously, I would do so with more energy. I really came to see how play is more than just a bit of fun – it's something that we actually need.

HOW DO I KNOW IF I NEED THIS PHYSICAL HEALING PRACTICE?

If you feel like your body currently holds more stress than relaxation, then you are probably due for a bout of playfulness. If you are tired, your body might need some help absorbing the bountiful energy around us always. Play can help you do this. Even for a short time as a prelude to rest or a type of active rest, play can help heal the body and even make other forms of healing more effective. Think about when your body repairs itself most actively – in deep relaxation of meditation or when you sleep. Play is a form of active rest that allows repair to occur too – repair and rebalancing of the body, mind and soul.

On another level this healing will help you in those times when you feel like you need some more colour in your life. This may be during winter or when you feel like you are emotionally in a 'winter' phase of your life, where your life is quieter and not much seems to be happening in your physical world.

PHYSICAL HEALING PRACTICE – ALL THE COLOURS OF THE RAINBOW

This simple and powerful practice requires that you have a private space with enough room to lie quietly or move a bit (or a lot if you feel you want to) and not be disturbed. You'll need to be able to close your eyes and move without having to worry about bumping into furniture, so you might need to clear a space or find some privacy in your garden.

Start by saying the following healing declaration:

"I call upon the healing power of Polychrome Jasper, of the Angel Caliel and of the Angels of Colour Vibrations on this planet and beyond. I call upon the healing vibrations of colour and sound through unconditional love. I call upon the Angel of Rainbows and I call upon my own soul. May my body-soul be blessed and infused with the healing colour vibrations that best serve me now. Thank you and so be it!"

Close your eyes and focus on your breath. Imagine that your entire body can breathe, in and out, through the pores of your skin. Your head is breathing. Your throat and chest. Your arms and torso can breathe in and out. The palms of your hands breathe and the tips of your fingers. The hips and legs breathe. Your knees can breathe. Your feet and toes.

Imagine you are swiftly moving deep into a rainbow of light, stepping into it, with colours red, orange, yellow, green, blue, indigo and violet fanning about before you. You can remain lying peacefully or gently stand up, letting your awareness remain in that rainbow symphony of light. The colours are all around you, like you are in the midst of a temple of light or in a sacred space with stained glass windows shining light as sunlight pours through them.

As you rest or move in those bands of light, notice how each one feels, sounds, tastes or looks to you. What is your response to each one? You may be very drawn to one colour or to all of them. Imagine that your body is completely open and takes in the colour or sounds that it wants. You don't even have to think about it, it just happens.

Ask yourself to move or just remain in these bands of light.

Take seven long, slow deep breaths in and out, and when you are ready, open your eyes.

Stand or sit peacefully for a moment and feel your body connected to the ground beneath you. Well done. You have finished your healing process.

PRAYER – AFFIRMATION

To invoke the healing power of Polychrome Jasper and Angel Caliel at any time, you can repeat the following affirmation quietly in your mind, or aloud (preferably whilst clapping your hands together in gleeful anticipation of fun, perhaps whilst jumping up and down on the spot).

"Colours of Life and Love, I AM at Play with You now!"

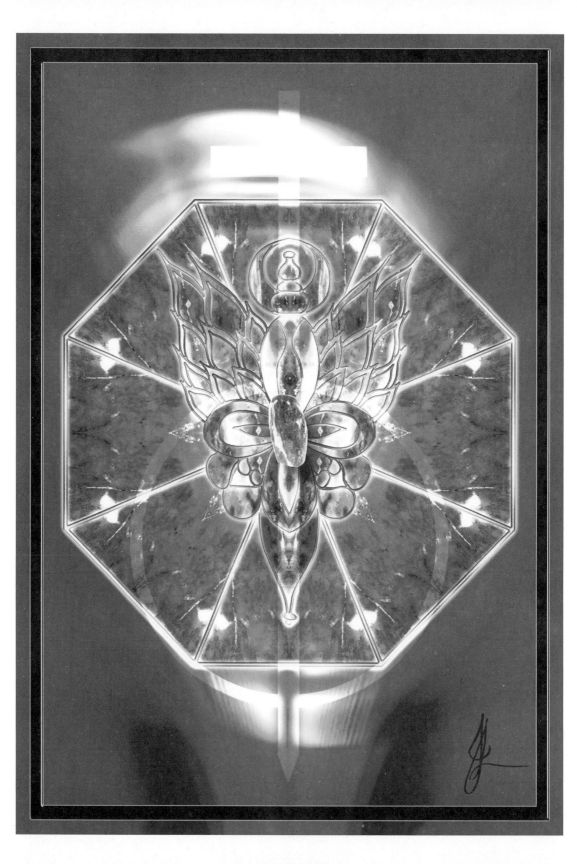

8.

LAPIS LAZULI (Insight)
and ARCHANGEL MICHAEL (Protection)

THE GIFT OF VISION

SPIRITUAL GUIDANCE FROM THE ANGEL OF LAPIS LAZULI
AND THE ARCHANGEL MICHAEL

We keep you safe from harm as you journey deep within to know the mysteries of the Universe, to understand the sacred teachings, to know the ancient wisdom. These gifts of divine vision are granted to those who are prepared to meet their fears and delve into their own darkness in order to find the light that dwells eternally within. Meeting the darkness opens you to the light. We keep you safe beloved, even through the darkest night. We free you from your fear, as you surrender into love, and your vision opens like sun light piercing through clouds above. All becomes clear, your path and purpose become known. Together we travel safely as your high destiny you now own.

PICTURING LAPIS LAZULI

Lapis Lazuli was prized in ancient civilisations like Egypt for its intense, vivid royal blue colour. Lapis is mined from around the world and is easily found and yet quite expensive. In fact the etymology of the name Lapis Lazuli is quite beautiful. In Latin, Lapis means "stone", and Lazuli was derived from an ancient Persian word for "Sky" or "Heaven". The translation therefore is Stone of the Sky, or Stone of the Heavens. The Lapis from Afghanistan in particular often has radiant flecks of gold pyrite within it which actually make it look like a star-laden night sky.

This crystal is often carved or used in jewellery although it is possible to buy tumbled stones and larger free form pieces. I was lucky enough to recently come into possession of a slab of Lapis Lazuli the width and length of my forearm. I had seen tiles made out of Lapis like this in a meditative vision of ancient Egypt, but it was only recently that I had seen slabs of the stone in the flesh, so to speak.

HEALING PROPERTIES

When I was a little girl, I used to lay on the grass in the back yard of my childhood home and gaze at the sky. There was something about its endlessness that felt more familiar to me than the apparent limitations of the physical world. Sometimes I would gaze at the soft blue sky during the day and just imagine what lay beyond the sky. I would get frustrated at the limitations of my mind and its inability to translate the rich feelings and impressions that flooded me as I gazed heavenwards. At other times, I would lay out there at night until my mother would call me inside. In those precious moments, I would gaze at the dark indigo blue sky dappled with stars, and feel something ancient, mysterious and unnameable stir within me. How I could feel such magic leap in my heart, and be so without words to capture and explain it? This is the stirring quality of Lapis. It has an ability to take us beyond the concrete mind into an abstract awareness of that which is beyond the capacity of language to explain. It is mystery dwelling in a stone.

Said to have been used in Cleopatra's eye shadow, and historically verified as being used in sacred objects and jewellery in ancient times, thousands of years before Christ, Lapis was loved and appreciated for its mystical beauty.

It has been my experience that many souls who are awakening past life talents or experiences from Egyptian or other ancient civilisations that prized Lapis Lazuli are very drawn to it at the time the soul is making that connection. The love affair may continue or wane, or reignite later on, when further delving into soul histories that have been associated with the stone.

The stone itself seems to establish stronger conscious connection between lifetimes and incarnations, beyond the matrix of time and space. I believe (not through any recorded history but through my own visions gained in altered states) that an elixir of the ground stone was used to facilitate inter-dimensional travel, but was dangerous and required great skill to use successfully so as to not poison the body. Lapis can assist with past life recall, not only of ancient civilisations where it featured as a part of the culture, but all lifetimes, particularly those that are anchored in the realms of the stars and not here on the Earth at all.

There is an energetic quality in Lapis that expands our vision, that broadens our perspective and viewpoint. An esoteric way of describing this would be to say that Lapis opens the third eye, the energetic gateway in the body (at the juncture where the brows meet, slightly above the centre of the two physical eyes) through which higher perception enters our consciousness and we become capable of clear sight. This clear sight has been called many things – clairvoyance, insight, inner vision, spiritual sight and the second sight. It is essentially an ability to see beyond the illusions of form and judgement and into the compassionate truth of a situation. True clairvoyance is drenched in love. It is not harsh in any way and yet is completely truthful. The highest visions are those based in love and Lapis helps open the inner vision of our heart and third eye – the inner sight or insight that we have – to the highest levels of attainment possible.

Lapis is protective against psychic attack, helping to raise our vibration to a place of detachment and love so that we can either deflect or release such attacks without fear but from a place of compassionate understanding. Its ability to undo the negative effects of psychic attack and clear us quickly and effectively is a real gift.

Psychic attack might seem like a lot of drama and whilst cases of severe psychic attack are actually very rare, psychic attack on a more mundane level is something many of us will experience at least once in our lives. If you are lucky enough to avoid such encounters, good for you! If part of your spiritual growth requires that you learn how to deal with psychic attack, the teachings in this chapter will guide you on how to deal with it.

I remember not so many years ago having the experience of singing in a spiritual centre where I spent about nine months learning different mantra and meditation techniques. One of the teachers in the centre, a self-aware and spiritually committed individual, who nonetheless had her own battles with jealousy, was sending quite a lot of negativity my way at the time. I knew it was because she wanted to sing and I had compassion because in the past I too had experienced the pain of feeling that what you wanted was being bestowed upon another, instead of you.

At the end of one particular singing session during a workshop, I stood up and began to walk out of the room when I had a painless, though very distinct sensation of a psychic dagger land right in my back. I had never consciously felt anything like it before, and psychic attack was not something that was often even a thought in my mind, so the clarity of the sensation and how easily I recognised what it was, as well as the experience itself, was quite a surprise to me. It did not hurt me though, I just noticed it without anger and let it go. I felt it drop out of my back as soon as I acknowledged what it was and also heard it land with a thick clang as it hit the floor. This was with my inner hearing or clairaudience, which was also quite a surprise at the time because it was so vivid. All of this happened in a few seconds. I then turned around and saw this particular teacher glaring at me, only a metre or so behind me, and I knew she had in a moment of deep inner struggle thrown this at me with her negative energy. I saw her hatred flash briefly through her eyes. Fortunately because I felt compassion and I did not fear or judge the attack, and luckily it had happened when my energy was extremely strong, having just been singing mantras in service to a large group of people, it didn't affect me negatively at all. It gave me an interesting experience and a learning about psychic attack and what kind of protection works.

The reason that I share this story with you is that Lapis helps to build the sort of energy field that naturally deflects psychic attacks with minimal harm and maximum learning. Whether those psychic attacks are done maliciously with intention to harm or unthinkingly, creating a 'curse-effect' through negative speech or apparently harmless gossip, it is very helpful to know that we can deal with these phenomena when need be. My wish for you is that you never have to deal with it, but if you do, you will be supported in doing so through Lapis and Archangel Michael helping you gather your own consciousness in a place of love to meet the challenge before you (or in my case, behind me!).

A situation actually arose with the same teacher some months beforehand. Someone that I didn't know at all sent me a message by email stating that he was a medicine man in Africa. He said that he had seen in a vision that I was being psychically attacked by someone near to me. I thanked him for his insight and sent him a blessing, politely declining his offer to slaughter chickens on my behalf. I explained that I had different methods of protection and while I very much appreciated his email, I would take it from there, so to speak. I did this with kindness and compassion, forgiveness and quite an energising bout of chanting! I realised during this process that it was this teacher from the organisation that I had been visiting.

The whole situation unravelled later that day. I encountered that teacher in a meditation gathering where she explained, with a great deal of humility, that she was envious of someone she had met in the centre. She said that she was jealous of that person's spiritual connection and was learning to find the connection within herself in order to outgrow the jealousy. She took responsibility for her emotions, and although she never approached me directly, after the class a friend approached me and said that she intuitively felt that the teacher was talking about me.

Fortunately, through the field of spiritual grace that was around me at the time, it was easily and swiftly resolved without any harm to myself. Lapis helps build the sort of grace through which psychic protection such as this can flow. We have the power within us to clear and manage our own energy but sometimes we don't always see what is happening. Perhaps we intuitively feel that someone is behaving badly towards us, or holds ill will towards us, whilst appearing not to do so. We may invalidate this truth because we want to see the best in people perhaps, rather than simply understanding that sometimes really lovely people struggle with getting a handle on darker emotions that are part of the human experience for all of us.

I remember my first spiritual teacher explaining that a negative thought in the spiritual worlds is like the equivalent of throwing a piece of furniture about the room in the physical world – so you can imagine the power of negatively directly energy from one who had a lot of power spiritually already. The situation with this woman could have escalated into something far more serious if I had of responded from my ego with anger or fear. Yet I never even considered that it could be an issue. Working with Lapis, in the way that it cuts through time and space, and operates on the spiritual planes, yet remains connected to the physical body, creates a field of protection around us much like the field of spiritual grace that protected me through these encounters. It is like there is enough goodwill to outweigh any negativity around us. It is just there when we need it. It is the power and grace of conscious protection. And it manifests however is needed – perhaps through a random email from an African shaman you have never met via Facebook, or via a dream time visitation by me telling you that you need to take care of yourself on a particular day or time (something which happened to a client of a colleague of mine a couple of weeks ago).

The grace field generated by Lapis Lazuli reveals the wisdom of the heavens to us. Sometimes it's a practical matter where our energy needs protection (a bit like an angel telling you that the spiritual door to your soul has a broken hinge and won't shut properly so it needs some repair). Sometimes it's a spiritual matter of realising a past life pattern so that it can be resolved in the here and now. This wisdom may come to you through meditation, dreams or in very tangible ways such as someone just telling you!

The energy of Lapis penetrates the physical body and helps rebalance and heal the throat and third eye chakras. It opens perception, balances energy, assists the regulation of hormone function, supports the wellbeing of the eyes and helps heal the hearing – both physical and spiritual hearing or clairaudience. Lapis strengthens and clarifies our sense of discernment on the spiritual level and increases our sense of smell on the physical level.

Lapis also brings peace and bestows spiritual confidence, which we all need from time to time when taking a leap into a new level of experience.

ABOUT THE ARCHANGEL MICHAEL

My first conscious encounter with Archangel Michael in this lifetime happened in a meditation with my first spiritual teacher many years ago. I don't even remember what the meditation was actually about. What I do remember is that I saw brilliant blue tones and I heard a voice that explained he was an angel, and his name was Michael.

I came out of the meditation and when it was my turn to give feedback in the group I asked if there was an angel called Michael. One of the other group members who knew far more about angels than I did piped up and explained that there was a great Archangel called Michael. Since then I learned that he is associated with various colours, including blue, and the blue ray of divine energy and will, is perhaps the most prominent.

Since then, he made various appearances in my visions and meditations and I learned more about him. His name means "He who is as God" which is a fairly powerful moniker! He is the Archangel that embodies the strength and power of the Divine and he is often pictured as a mighty spiritual warrior with massive wings and a brilliant sword (often in the midst of lopping the head off a demon – he isn't a fluffy angel, certainly).

One of my most funny memories of the Archangel Michael was not about him actually but about a group of women when I was teaching in the northern Australian state of Queensland earlier on in my spiritual career. I still have the recollection of Archangel Michael coming up in one woman's meditation. As soon as she shared it, a few of the other women became quite jealous, asserting that they too, felt a strong connection with Michael. I actually laughed out loud (I tend to do this a lot) and said that he had his harem in this room, which broke the tension and we could all see that this was actually quite an amusing situation. Seems that Archangel Michael is considered to be one mightily attractive angel. Personally I think part of that appeal is his divine masculine energy of protection.

I have had two powerful personal experiences of spiritual protection from Archangel Michael and both were quite different. They both occurred during a seven-year period where I was working very deeply with my own unconscious, learning its way through dreams and symbols, and taking an often arduous inner path of personal healing, finding my way through some incredibly challenging states of terror at times. I couldn't believe that my body could hold such intense emotions as the ones that arose during this period of intensive introspection and personal healing. At the time, my dreams were often very helpful and sometimes deeply disturbing. It is my belief that I would not have been consciously able to shed my ego defences to experience the levels of terror that I encountered in those dreams in a waking state. So the healing started with the dreams instead. It took many years to fully release and heal. There were levels in those dreams that related to me personally and those that related to the human condition as a whole. It was incredibly challenging to tackle these forces. The only way I seemed to be able to do so at that point in my development was through the dream state, which opened up a door into the unconscious realms and let me enter.

Working with unconscious material of dreams and visions is a dangerous task. It has been one of the most powerful healing agents in my journey, matched only by work with the superconsciousness of spiritual connection. It is not easy-going inner work however. There are times when you can question your sanity and if you are capable of containing the amount of negative energy that can arise during the journey. We require spiritual protection before descending into the realm of the unconscious, the dark place within us that holds our hidden divinity and brilliance, but also our deepest terrors and insecurities. As we delve into this part of us, we often find things that we wouldn't usually and consciously experience in our daily lives. Some are beautiful, such as our divine connection to all living beings. Some are exceptionally challenging to bring to consciousness, such as the self-destructive, death-wish urges that run rife in modern Western culture. Self-destructive urges can arise in less dramatic ways in daily life, such as through taking unhealthy risks, denying ourselves wellbeing through a healthy lifestyle, acting out through addiction or self-hating thoughts about our bodies. There is a much heavier expression of destructive, death-seeking energy that lies within the unconscious of all of humankind. It manifests itself in mass murders, terrorism and war, and in a glossier, but still highly destructive form, in advertising, which is often a vehicle for fearful cultural programming.

For those who are called to learn about the dark side of human nature as part of their journey spiritual protection through Archangel Michael will be a great ally. You'll know this is you if healing addiction, self-hatred, deep rage, eating disorders and/or depression are part of your personal healing journey this lifetime.

The first experience I had with psychic protection with Archangel Michael was during a dream whereby I was being threatened by a group of men that were threatening to attack me with bodily harm. I was surrounded and felt gripped by fear, unable to act. In terror, I called out to Michael and he appeared nearby. What happened however, surprised me. He didn't step in and protect me, instead he said very simply, "Fight!". The surprise of his edict jolted my awareness, and so I did. I turned on my would-be assailants, using their weapons against them and fought my way out. I awoke from the dream (more of a nightmare really) shaken with adrenaline pumping, but victorious.

In that instance, I trust that this was the best way. As it turns out, I was more than capable of protecting myself from the negative intention of these energies once I released my terror in witnessing their negative intentions towards me and focused instead on my strength.

The second situation, also in dream state, was very different. I dreamed that I was in a dark cavernous chamber in which there was a mad demonic assassin. She was inhuman and other worldly and extremely powerful. She was intent on destroying me and had no compunction about doing so immediately. The breathtaking element of the dream was how fast it all happened. As she flew through the air at me, her feet barely skimming the surface, she raised an axe over the crown of my head. I felt the terror of knowing she would destroy me at my crown, where I was most open. There was a terrible inevitability that I would die as she violently raised her axe and swung it down at the crown of my head. The horror of it was too much to bear, somehow I tore myself out of sleep with a gasp of sheer terror, jerking bolt upright in my bed just as a massive clanging sound of metal hitting metal pounded through my ears. I realised that her metal axe had rebounded off the sword of Archangel Michael, who had been there unbeknownst to me and at the critical moment had laid his sword flat across the crown of my head, deflecting her attack.

As I sat upright, still shaking with fear and drenched in sweat, my cat sensed my distress and ran into the room, jumping on the bed under my hand. I placed my hand on him, allowing his warm, furry presence to help anchor me in this physical reality once more.

The demon disappeared, never to return again. As I calmed down, I realised that Michael would never prevent me from growing in my own strength, but if there were ever a time when a threat was beyond my capacity to handle, he would be there. I didn't even have to call him. He knew in my heart that I loved and honoured him and wanted his assistance and he was dedicated to be my guardian angel this lifetime, and he would be there.

Some months later, I also found myself becoming freed of a negative and self-destructive pattern in me that I realised later was both represented by this dream assassin and fed by her within me too, as a deep terror was the emotion that lay hidden at the core of that self-defeating behaviour. Until I accessed and released the terror, I would never master the behaviour and be able to release it. I realised that what I had worked on in the dream not only related to that dream reality, but also to my daily life in this Earthly reality too.

SOUL HEALING WITH LAPIS LAZULI AND THE ARCHANGEL MICHAEL: VISIONING YOUR SOUL PURPOSE

One of the great gifts that comes with spiritual protection is an ability to 'enter the dungeon to retrieve the treasure' as my Guidance once put it. Around the pure power and purpose of the soul there can be a lot of 'gatekeepers'. These are a combination of actual testers, beings whose job it is to keep you from the truth until you are ready to wield the power that it will bring you with compassion and wisdom. This is not only so you won't harm others, but also so you won't harm yourself. Too much power before you realise the impact it has on you or another is a bit like learning to drive a new car with a far more powerful engine than your previous car. You might put your foot down only to find that a slight tap gives a huge acceleration. If you don't know how to handle it, you might end up in an accident before you even get the car out of the driveway, harming another or yourself in the process.

When you are given a glimpse of your soul purpose at the right time, you'll have enough power, experience and skill to know how to work with that purpose with wisdom. The vision can inspire rather than overwhelm or dishearten you, if you had received it before you were ready for it. Had I been shown what I know of my purpose this year, some years earlier, I wouldn't have had the personal growth under my belt to be excited and inspired by it, but quite possibly absolutely overwhelmed by the enormity of it. In still another year's time, this enormous task might seem very small indeed and I have no doubt that I shall be ready for another revelation, having been prepared and readied for the experience. This is just the way that spiritual revelation and vision unfolds. I have experienced it countless times in my life already.

Although encountering blocks to growth in the form of tester beings might seem intimidating, it is reassuring to remember that everything serves the Divine. Everything. Even the things that seem to push us away from what we seek are helping us grow smarter, stronger and wiser, to adapt and outgrow them to become one with what we seek until we are in a state of such awakening that we realise we can never be separated from what we seek, because we are what we are seeking!

Testers (and testing situations) help us grow. They challenge us and sometimes if they aren't of a particularly high level of consciousness, they may also seek to harm us. Now of course, this helps us grow too, but it helps to know how to either fight when necessary or to allow divine protection through Michael and Lapis, for example, to support us.

We have whatever protection that we may need available to us – often at our immediate disposal already. The most powerful protection you can ever have is walking your genuine soul path and aligning yourself with divine will. Divine will is sometimes seen as something separate from us, a force that tells us to do something we don't want to do! But divine will is actually a far more loving force. It is the truth that keeps us living an authentic path. To live in alignment with divine will is to live in alignment with our own heart. The divine will is that we be and blossom as who we are in this lifetime. It has the benefit of higher perspective than our more limited human consciousness as to how this can happen with the most joy and least unnecessary struggle. The only parts of us that would be threatened by this, are the wounded parts of us trapped in fear.

This soul healing is about accessing that protection through alignment with divine will and preparing to move beyond the dweller on the threshold of whatever new phase of spiritual growth we are currently moving towards.

HOW DO YOU KNOW IF YOU ARE HEALING AT A SOUL LEVEL IN THIS WAY?

If you are feeling like a big fish in a small pond, like you have abilities and talents that are not being utilised, then it is highly likely that you are at a threshold point in your spiritual growth. For whatever reason, and there will always be wise guidance behind any delay, you are waiting to cross. On the other side of the threshold you'll have the sense of suddenly being in a more powerful car, so to speak. You'll have the sense of being a newborn in some ways, learning how to operate in this wider field of experience and consciousness. It will feel stimulating and likely provide you with a fresh set of challenges to grow and develop.

If you feel that you are not quite over that threshold yet, then the grace of Michael and Lapis are here to help support your process (and perhaps even quicken it), seeing you safely through the transitional phase and into a new spiritual growth cycle.

If you are at a point in your life where you don't actually know or feel what is next for you, or you have a decision to make and you want to make the choice that most strongly aligns with your own heart and highest spiritual destiny (or in other words, divine will) then this healing process is timely for you now.

SOUL HEALING PROCESS – VISIONING YOUR SOUL PURPOSE

You will need a quiet place to lie down. If you have a piece of Lapis, whether as a stone or as a piece of jewellery, place it under the pillow behind your head, at the base of the skull where there is a small indentation between the two thick tendons at the top of your neck where it meets the base of the skull. You'll also need to be covered in case you get cold. You want your body to be comfortable and relaxed.

Start by saying the following invocation:

"I call upon Archangel Michael, Divine Warrior, and the Angel of Lapis Lazuli, Divine Seer, I call upon your vision, wisdom, protection and strength. I call upon your grace and healing now. I call upon the wisdom of Divine Will, that I may align my personal will with the love that is within my heart, that love being an expression of the will of the Creator. I call upon my own soul and team of unconditionally loving Higher Guidance. I call upon the Divine Blueprint of my own soul growth this lifetime and upon Divine Mercy and Grace. Reveal yourself to me now that I may be lifted through karmic grace and the benevolence of divine love, into the next phase of my soul growth and expression here on Earth. Through my own free will, so be it."

Focus on your breathing and allow yourself to close your eyes, letting the eyes either roll gently back or gently down, whatever happens naturally without force.

Follow your breath, in and out, slowly and evenly. Allow your awareness to move away from the day-to-day world as you ride your breath deeper within the vast peaceful space opening up for you now.

You see, sense or feel before you now a rich, vivid blue light. It is peaceful, powerful and pulsating before you. You may hear its energy or simply know that it is there.

Allow the light to beam forward into your third eye and forehead chakras, which are in the centre of your eyebrows, slightly above, and higher up in the centre of your forehead, and another right at the juncture of your hairline and the very edge of the top of your forehead. Let the light beam pulse into your forehead in a wash of deep blue light and peaceful energy.

Allow the light to stream down towards your heart where you notice a blue flame, growing in the heart, connected to the blue light beaming in and through your forehead.

This light holds information and that information will be downloaded into your subconscious mind through the light, and activated into conscious understanding through the blue flame growing in the heart. You do not have to have any impressions or understanding as this happens in order for the process to work effectively. Just allow the light to flow. The understanding will come as the flame in the heart burns and stimulates understanding as a soul knowing from deep within your own heart. In the coming weeks and months and years, you will just know what you need to know and at the right time.

Stay with the light and let it continue to pulsate into your forehead and down into the heart centre for as long as feels right but at least for forty-four breaths in and out.

When you are ready, gently place your hands on your heart and say, "This grace is within me now, and I am ready to take the next step. No tester shall deter me. With all the patience that is required, with loving gratitude, I embody this grace now. As each lotus petal of my soul unfolds in this body of light, one petal at a time, according to the perfection of divine timing and wisdom, the Plan unfolds and I know all that I need to know at the perfect time and in the perfect way. I align my will with the higher will of the Divine. So be it."

Be aware of the blue flame in the heart, and notice that it becomes a three-fold flame, of pink, blue and gold light. Feel this beautiful energy of peace and love in your heart.

When you are ready, place your hands in prayer, bow your head and then just open your eyes.

You have completed this soul healing process. Give it time to unfold and pay particular attention to your inner nudges, intuitions, synchronicities and dreams for the coming weeks.

PSYCHOLOGICAL-EMOTIONAL HEALING WITH ARCHANGEL MICHAEL AND LAPIS LAZULI: GENERATING THE FIELD OF GRACE FOR PROTECTION AND INSIGHT

This is a beautiful practice which I discovered quite by accident (if there were such thing as accidents!). I was originally thinking of my Chi Gung master, Zhao, who was away in China, meditating in a cave for months at a time (as enlightened Chi Gung Masters are prone to do). He is a powerful being and whilst I knew he would be fine, I still found myself feeling a maternal desire to nurture and protect him as he embarked on this deep spiritual challenge to serve through entering a deeply enlightened spiritual state.

Although the field of light around him that I could perceive on the inner planes suggested that I need not worry, I ended up praying on his behalf anyway, sending him angels and protectors. I had also had past life recollection of being killed whilst in a state of deep meditation, and this recollection created an awareness in me that one may still need a field of graceful protection even as a powerful spiritual being.

This practice of sending love to a spiritual teacher has developed further in relation to another spiritual teacher whom I love, the Dalai Lama. I have not yet met the Dalai Lama one-on-one. Perhaps I will one day, perhaps not. But I do have a profound love for his soul and the light that he bears on this planet that assists us all – Buddhists and non-Buddhists alike. This willingness to assist all that can be assisted, beyond the superficial differences of religious persuasion, is the sign of a very evolved being.

I was thinking of the Dalai Lama with love in my heart and I felt myself saying the blessings that I will guide you to say below. The response was a tremendous outpouring of love. Another sign of a genuinely evolved being is that you can think of them and send them love and their response to you will be instant, powerful and very loving. The grace that I was sending to him was returned to me multiplied. I realised that the field of grace is the essence of the Divine itself, it knows not of self and other. It just is. So when we send grace, we build it for ourselves too. This is the basis of the practice outlined below.

HOW DO I KNOW IF I NEED HEALING
IN THIS WAY AND AT THIS LEVEL OF MY BEING?

Building grace is not unlike saving money in your bank account. You might need it now, or you might save it for a rainy day (when apparently, according to this expression, one feels the urge to shop?) but either way, it's there for you.

There is never a time when grace will be wasted. It vests in your soul and can be used in healing for you and for others at any time. It is the empowering energy that allows for all manner of miracles and creativity, and in this instance, offers a field of intelligent divine vision, awareness and protection at any time it is needed. As you open to new levels of vision, you will grow. And sometimes as you grow, you'll encounter challenges and you'll need protection to get through them unharmed. Then you grow again and the process continues.

The field of grace generated in this simple practice can be called upon at any time you need to boost your field of grace, for any purpose that serves your highest good and helps you on your path.

PSYCHOLOGICAL-EMOTIONAL HEALING PROCESS –
GENERATING THE FIELD OF GRACE

You will need a place to sit comfortably where you won't be disturbed, where you can make some noise and not be heard or interrupted. If you have a piece of Lapis, have it with you. If you have a picture of a loved spiritual teacher, an angel or a being that you just love – which could be anyone from a religious leader to an historical religious figure or master, the Archangel Michael or even a planet or star that you particularly love, then have that with you too.

Sit comfortably with your picture if you have one, and your piece of Lapis if you have one, and say the following, "I call upon the healing power of my own soul, and upon the Angel of Lapis Lazuli and the Archangel Michael. I call upon the divine grace that emanates freely throughout the Universe, and I call upon the Spiritual Beings that love me unconditionally. May grace fill me and this space now, so be it."

Gaze softly at your picture, or close your eyes and allow yourself to see, sense or feel the presence of the spiritual being that you wish to send love and blessing to now. It may be your own soul or the divine soul of another being.

Take your awareness into your heart and imagine it growing strong and rising up to your throat, say aloud but gently and with love to your spiritual being of choice now, "May you be safe. May you be blessed. May you be filled with grace. May you prosper and may you thrive."

Repeat these words over and over again, gently and lovingly. Make up your own phrases if you wish to do so. Imagine sending a peaceful light of vivid blue with gold flecks from your mind to those beings, with the energy of peace held within it.

You may feel the energy of love and peace, blessing, protection, vision and grace returning to you multiplied. Stay with your vision and your practice for as long as it feels appropriate. If you have emotion or thoughts arising, don't attach, it is a cleansing, just let it be and continue with your practice.

When you are ready, say, "I am blessed in this field of grace. May those that serve be supported always. So be it."

When you are ready, be aware of taking three long, slow deep inhalations and exhalations and place your hands in prayer position in front of your third eye and bow your head to your thumbs. If you can be aware of the field of energy around you now, notice it. It will be stronger and your energy field will be more powerful. Make sure that your thoughts and words in the coming days especially are as loving as possible, and if negativity does erupt from you at times, that is OK of course, but ask for forgiveness as soon as possible, so as not to disturb the field of grace around you.

When you are ready, simply open your eyes. You have completed your healing task. You can do this simple and effective practice at any time you feel intuitively guided to do so.

PHYSICAL HEALING WITH LAPIS LAZULI AND ARCHANGEL MICHAEL: OPENING THE THIRD EYE

The third eye chakra has very physical significance to your body. It is called the master chakra because it regulates all the systems of the body. Your hormones, digestion, immune system, nervous system, regeneration and repair are all affected powerfully by your third eye chakra.

I remember a situation early in 2012 where I was with a group of women discussing our experiences with the third eye. I led a chant and we did a very short meditation, but mostly we just talked about our 'third eye' experiences and the wisdom of this chakra in our daily lives. The contents of this gathering were turned into a book called "Women of the Wise Earth" by Nicole Gruel. Even that focus for just a couple of hours on that chakra was profound. The next day I did a yoga class and it felt like my spine had elongated itself over night. The lines of my body in the asanas were longer and cleaner than I had ever experienced and I intuitively knew that this was as a result of the third eye work from the evening before.

HOW DO I KNOW IF I NEED THIS PHYSICAL HEALING PRACTICE?

If you feel that your body overall needs a bit of a tune up, if you have systemic difficulties or disorders to do with the immune, digestive or hormonal systems of your body, if you have been more stressed than you wish to be, or gone through trauma or grief or a period of prolonged illness or confusion in your life, if you want more movement and freedom in your body, and more acceptance and understanding of the patterns operating in your life, then this physical third eye healing is for you.

PHYSICAL HEALING PRACTICE – OPENING THE THIRD EYE

This simple and powerful practice will take you to the next level of third-eye opening and activation that is right for you. If you have a piece of Lapis that can rest on your third eye as you lie back comfortably, such as a small tumble stone or a piece of jewellery, then place it there, or also in the indentation at the base of the throat is fine too.

Start by saying the following healing declaration:

"I call upon the healing Angel of Lapis Lazuli and Archangel Michael. Please assist me as I open and activate my third eye chakra to the next level appropriate for me at this time. Of my own free will I choose to release any fears of seeing, any trauma from seeing in this or other lifetimes and any false responsibility for what I see from this or any lifetime. I release this now from my body, mind and soul. I ask for balance and healing of this chakra. So be it!"

Close your eyes and focus on your breath. Imagine around you there is a field of radiant blue light, peaceful, powerful, protective and wise. Sense your third eye, between your eyebrows, can perceive this light. The light enters your third eye, cleansing it, opening it gently and washing it out with a soft, lovely energy that feels relaxing and soothing.

Take at least forty-four long, slow deep breaths in and out, as this happens.

When you are ready say, "Thank you" and gently remove the stone from your forehead (or neck if you placed one there). Sit up slowly and in your own time, open your eyes.

Stand peacefully for a moment and feel your body connected to the ground beneath you. Imagine that you can send love from your heart down through the palms of your hands and rub them together briskly, creating some heat. Feel that love in your hands and place them in prayer position at your heart. Then raise them up until your index fingers reach your third eye, between your brows, with your head bent slightly.

Pause for a moment and then open your eyes again. You have finished your healing process.

PRAYER – AFFIRMATION

To invoke the healing power of Lapis Lazuli and Archangel Michael at any time, you can repeat the following affirmation quietly in your mind, or aloud.

"Blue Flame of Divine Will, Fill my heart with Gold."

9.

PICTURE JASPER (Earth Wisdom) and ARCHON BARBELO (Prosperity)

THE GIFT OF SUPPORT

SPIRITUAL GUIDANCE FROM THE ANGEL OF PICTURE JASPER AND THE ARCHON BARBELO

Remember that you are my child of divine light, and that whilst you are with me, I offer you endless support. There is nothing to fear, my beloved child. I provide means through methods vast and wise, with my great peace, wisdom and strength. There is nothing to hide from, no part of you that cannot receive, and nothing that must be earned from me. I ask only that you receive. Allow me to love you and bless you. I speak to you through the stones. I tell you truthfully that my creative resourcefulness is without end. All blessings flow through me, from my heart to yours, abundantly. I am your path to peace. I am your path to security. I am your support, unconditionally loving and wise. Heaven exists not just in the skies! Look beneath your feet and feel my love rising up towards your heart. Let yourself be blessed from below, as well as from above.

PICTURING PICTURE JASPER

Picture Jasper is sometimes referred to as a type of brown Jasper. By its markings, it looks very similar to sandstone, although it is not porous like sandstone. Even when only lightly finished rather than heavily polished, it is cool, firm and smooth to the touch. I have seen this Jasper as spheres and tumbled stones, small and large, as well as free form shapes. It often contains various shades of dark beiges, and browns, and sometimes red and grey tones are included along with black or very dark brown markings.

When you look into a Picture Jasper, it actually feels as though you are gazing into an ancient painting. The markings are ornate and swirl into the most beautiful forms you can imagine. Every piece is unique. The pieces that sit beside me as I am writing today look like a sandstorm, a desert sunrise, an exploding galaxy and light breaking through clouds. Mother Nature expresses her creative side in so many ways, and her artistic streak emerges through all Jaspers, but particularly Picture Jasper.

I remember having a client once who had adverse reactions to the colour brown. It is quite a vivid memory because I suspect at the time I may well have been wearing brown (!) given that I absolutely love earth-toned colours (even my finger nails are often painted a dark reddish chocolate brown). We discussed at the time that her aversion to the energy of the colour, which is so earthy and grounding, could be related to a difficulty in being really present on the Earth. This is probably the only situation I could imagine where there was an aversion to a Brown Jasper such as Picture Jasper, for it is a truly beautiful stone.

HEALING PROPERTIES

I first saw Picture Jasper many years ago just as I was beginning to fall in love with crystals again this lifetime. It was right at the beginning of my healing career and I had started working as a part-time psychic at the back of a crystal store. Between sessions I would wander out from the tiny healing room at the back of the store, and spend time in the front of the shop, where crystals were laid out in various shapes and sizes. Whole shelves were dedicated to various types of stones. It felt like heaven to me! I still have pieces of crystal that were given to me from time-to-time in exchange for my work at that store.

I didn't receive any Picture Jasper at the time, but it was probably the crystal that drew my attention more than any other. Every day I would walk over to it and pick it up for a while, just loving it. I still remember that particular piece. It was a free form small size mountain that fit comfortably in the palm of my hand, lightly polished at the tip whilst the rest was unpolished, smooth though, and slightly raw. The energy of it was incredible – soothing, beautiful and beyond words. I just wanted to hold it all the time, but strangely I never purchased it (even though it was relatively inexpensive at the time).

Looking back, I realise I was not quite ready for its energy at that time. Now as I sit at my laptop, with four large oval-shaped stones of Picture Jasper sitting around me for crystal companionship and channelling for the chapter, I have come to realise that this is an extremely powerful stone. It contains the energy of the Divine Mother in her emanation as Gaia or Mother Earth. This being is a vast and powerful Buddha and not a small energy to handle at all!

You wouldn't probably think it would be an issue to receive the energy of the Earth, after all we live in Her field day after day, and our bodies are a part of Her. Yet to receive the energy not just of the body of the Earth, but of the great soul that animates it, is to tap into an incredibly vast energy field. Consider the electricity required to animate a single light globe compared to the power surging through an entire city. Both scenarios utilise electricity, but the latter does so with more voltage. It is similar when we compare the spiritual intensity of the physical form of the Earth with her soul. When we connect with the Earth's soul, we are moving beyond her physical form and opening up to receive her spiritual light. Our nervous system is the human equivalent of electrical wiring to conduct the flow of spiritual electricity through our bodies. Just as electrical flow requires appropriate wiring to handle the voltage, our nervous system needs to be strong enough to handle the high spiritual voltage of the Earth's spiritual light. As we connect with the Earth's energy in this way, we often go through clearing of old energy that does not resonate at the same frequency as the Earth's higher level spiritual light. That might be old fear, old issues to do with mothering and nurturing, to name but a few. Connecting with the soul of the Earth, which is what Picture Jasper encourages and facilitates, happens when we are ready to let go of a lot of old blocks to having a healthy mother relationship.

Until we have done enough clearing, or are ready to do the clearing, we may sense the love and possibility of what life could be like in healthy surrender to the Divine Mother, but we won't be quite ready to go there. Once we are, however, Picture Jasper can fulfil its special destiny of sharing communications from Gaia, Mother Earth, to her divine children. This stone reveals truths and earth wisdoms in its imagery, helping us gain comfort from Gaia's teachings of patience, seasons and cycles, of life, death and rebirth. It helps bring to the surface any wound (from this or other lifetimes) that has been lodged in the subconscious or unconscious mind – specifically wounds of guilt, shame, envy, hate or fear. Picture Jasper helps release the energy of these feelings, transmuting the energetic charge into healthy energy that can be fuelled back into the body. This is another of the earth wisdom teachings – by allowing old energy to eventually fertilise new life, nothing is wasted or purposeless. That understanding frees us to forgive ourselves and others for what we might have considered to be mistakes, and to let ourselves learn and grow from the experiences. The stone teaches us about how our past experiences help us grow to be where we are today. Acceptance brings peace, forgiveness and helps us gain more energy as we let go of the past and bring more of ourselves into present time. This strengthens the kidneys and heals the immune system, generating more nourishing energy for our life in the here and now, while healing us from fear and exhaustion.

With this chapter calling to you now beloved reader, it is highly likely that you are ready to go deeper on this journey into oneness with the Divine Mother, healing your own relationship with Mother Earth, your biological mother and your own body, while opening to the energies of receptivity, nurturing and nourishment, all of which are aspects of healing the mother relationship within.

ABOUT THE ARCHON BARBELO

An Archon is essentially a great angel. Not technically an archangel in the traditions of angelology, Barbelo is known as a truly great being. She is a feminine emanation that is often said to be even beyond what we know as the Creator, but the cosmic womb from which the Creator emerged. She is known as the divine womb from which life emerged, sacred, holy and immortal. She is about as powerful and high as you can get for a divine being, whether feminine or masculine in energy (keeping in mind that angels generally have no real gender as we do, but our classification of masculine or feminine is a way to recognise their particular divine qualities).

To me, Barbelo is something of a combination of goddess and angel, of form and beyond form yet existing nonetheless. I love her dearly. Her beauty is so palpable and her generosity with good fortune and abundance bestowed through divine grace is so much more than wealth in the narrower sense. To connect with Mother Angel Barbelo, is to connect with the essence of the Universe in your heart, to open the doors of the heart to a divine love that is completely and utterly safe.

If you have struggled in any way, financially or emotionally with anxiety and fear (this will include most of the human race as fear is what we are healing as a species) then coming home to Barbelo is like stepping out of a noisy and chaotic shopping centre into the most beautiful, serene and idyllic Island paradise you can imagine and feeling emanations of deep relaxation pulse through you. She is, in a word, heaven.

As I write about her, I feel sublime waves of energy rippling through me from above the crown of my head, down through my feet, gathering around the lower chakras of my body, bringing the higher and lower centres into similar sublime frequencies. I see a golden sun with wings shining bright and alive through my third eye, and I feel how she watches over us, blesses us always and is the source from whence we came as souls. .

Barbelo helps us feel spiritually safe, protected and held in this life and beyond. It is from this place of inner safety that we are able to trust in the process of life and surrender into our highest divine destiny. Without this sense of inner security we will never have the internal foundation of trust required to let go of our attachment to feeling in control (which can make life much more difficult for us than it needs to be), nor will we have the strength to direct and manage our own energy from an internal foundation of self-worth and self-validation.

Barbelo teaches us the balance between holding and surrender, between letting go and dynamically allowing life to be created through us in many ways. It is through her high and expansive consciousness that we learn how to bring heaven and Earth together as one, to find heaven in the Earth and to see the wisdom of the Earth in heaven. She is a precious jewel of heaven.

SOUL HEALING WITH PICTURE JASPER AND THE ARCHON BARBELO

The soul is a light being of great, vast power and tremendous spiritual ability. Yet there are times when it too needs help with its growth and development. Especially for those souls enrolled in 'Earth school' where the vibration is so dense. For the soul, life on Earth is an advanced spiritual lesson, mastered over many lifetimes. The soul gradually builds its presence, learning how to illuminate its human vessel (our bodies and minds) with its spiritual light. The aim is to shine enough light that there may be sustainable spiritual development for the human being. Too much light too soon and we can become overwhelmed, shutting off from our own light out of fear or confusion. Yet too little light and we can lose conscious connection to the spiritual light within us, mistakenly believing that this world of forms is the reality and the inner spiritual worlds are not. In such cases we can end up making choices based on analysis rather than heart-felt intuition, because we don't have enough inner light shining to be able to see into our own hearts.

The soul is constantly seeking to strike the right balance, to shine the most appropriate amount of light, to stimulate the right amount of spiritual growth, and all this at the right time too. As you might imagine, it's a task that is not always easy and sometimes the soul can just use some help.

Connection with the Divine Mother through the combination of Archon Barbelo and Mother Earth (through the Angel of Picture Jasper) provides the soul with this much needed help. These energies offer the soul the wisdom it needs, and the assistance and instruction on the skills required to learn how to balance its light and manage its spiritual growth, with the loving Divine Mother ready to step in and help if the soul tends towards too little or too much as it learns to master the art of radiating its spiritual light in human form. It is an advanced classroom for the soul, and this soul healing to connect with the Divine Mother provides spiritual tutoring at the deep level of the soul, often beyond the conscious mind.

SOUL HEALING – SUPPORT OF THE DIVINE MOTHER

At time, it can seem counter-intuitive to move more deeply into the Earth (where there is so much fear and density on the physical level) in order to find the light! Why not just stay in the realms of light in the first place? Because there is a remarkable spiritual adventure and experiment taking place for souls incarnated into physical form. This grand spiritual adventure is to learn how to bring consciousness of apparent opposites, heaven and Earth, spiritual and physical, light and matter, into oneness. The light that is born of this union is golden Christ consciousness, a truly precious form of love.

We have already started making these advances, but the Divine Mother wants no less than complete spiritual awakening and reunion of heaven and Earth. Just as we are learning to bring the light of love and acceptance to all parts of our personal journey (especially those parts that can be more difficult to accept!), so to does the Universe need to bring all aspects of creation into the light of love.

This means that matter needs to be awakened and penetrated by spiritual energy, and spiritual energy needs to find the form. They belong together. Naturally they are one, but in the density of this earthly plane, they often appear to split. This is a bit like the contents of a cosmic sandwich splitting apart when it gets subjected to some pressure in your soul's backpack! When it's time for lunch, those apparently separate parts are all included in your sandwich, they just need to be put back together again as one!

Whilst in physical form, where the illusion of separation feels so compelling, we are learning bit by bit, to heal the split between light and matter. We are learning to bring them together in divine alchemy so that the body-soul becomes one living being, completely fused with each other. Eventually it will radiate a golden light of divine love, absolutely free from fear in all its forms. This is the cure – not the temporary fix – but the absolute cure for imbalance, for loneliness, poverty, struggle, suffering and disease – all the shadow side of life on this planet. Through this process of learning to love and be lovingly supported by life on Earth, the soul eventually becomes masterful of earth plane lessons such as transcending fear through the art of inner healing. This eventually naturally expresses itself as outer transformation, as a healed life, lived in service and spiritual fulfilment.

The soul that is keen to take this journey is an advanced soul, one that is learning to move beyond illusion into truth. At times this task is tricky to say the least. It is easy to feel weighed down, stuck and in need of 'emergency cleaning' to help lift one out of the stickiness of fear or scarcity, back into that energy of love and trust that comes from the Divine Mother.

In certain phases of our development, we may need the light of the Father in order to grow, so that we can learn at a soul level how to differentiate ourselves and find our own path in life. Instead of being trapped by the expectations and demands of others, we need to be able to discern and remain true to our own inner light.

Yet at other times in soul growth, we need to learn to bring that light into connection with the world. To learn how to remain true to that light we have found within and to grow strong enough to transform our experiences of life rather than have our experiences of life diminish our experience of our light.

This is where we need the safe cradle of the Divine Mother – to help us clear and release old fears that our light would be extinguished if we descend too deep into matter. We might be releasing fears that our spiritual growth will be tainted or confused by the ways of the body and the world. We might hold past life memories of times when we suffered greatly in attempting to bring our light to the world. Many healers hold unresolved memories of being punished, tortured and murdered because of their spiritual beliefs. The pain of being turned against by a society that you were trying to serve might be immense and yet still largely unconscious – but still powerful enough to subconsciously hold you back from really living your life with all its spiritual fullness and potential this lifetime.

Sometimes the soul just needs help to clear the momentum of these patterns. The soul is always bliss. That is its unchanging essential nature. But it still needs to become powerful enough to radiate through fear and old trauma, allowing it to dissolve in the light of love, rather than having its innate light dimmed or distorted by the veil of unresolved issues.

Connecting consciously with the healing support of the Divine Mother restores some power to the soul, allowing it to grow in the loving safety and security of her divine protection and guidance. She simply wants all beings to be spiritually awakened and free. Returning to her, allowing her to give to your soul, realising that oftentimes the spiritual learning is not in the struggle but in the surrender of it to a greater spiritual power. This allows you to change your experience of what it is to live on this Earth from one based in survival, competition, fear and anxiety to an experience based in love, freedom, creative flow and spiritual empowerment. This latter reality is one infused with the loving presence of the Divine Mother in a palpable way. It is the way of life that is emerging most strongly since 11/11/11 as a viable alternative to the increasingly outmoded realities of human life experience based in fear.

You don't need to worry about how the Divine Mother is going to help your soul now, you just need to trust her enough to allow it to happen. That is what this soul healing is for at this time.

HOW DO YOU KNOW IF YOU ARE HEALING AT A SOUL LEVEL IN THIS WAY?

Sometimes we reach the edge of our abilities to propel our own growth. We have done a lot of work by our own efforts and we need some assistance to move us forward. We may not even know that there is further to go, or we sense that there is but we just don't know what it looks like. There are also moments on the path when we feel ready for our life to be more graceful. We are done with the fight, done with thrashing about, done with taking directions from the smaller self, done worrying about small matters. We are ready for a different life experience, ready to live large from the heart, and excited that it could come to us in the form of loving support. So we let go and let our soul grow.

I remember an early moment in this phase of soul development many years ago, having a dream that I could hardly understand at the time, yet which makes much more sense to me now. In typical dream wisdom, it was showing me what lay ahead even though it would be years before I could begin to understand how the dream applied to me. I came to rely upon that dream as a guide and teacher in the years following. As I grew spiritually, so did my understanding of the teaching in the dream. It supported me as I began the arduous task of undoing my personal will so that it could serve my soul more than my ego. I needed the wisdom of that dream to help me through that challenging process. I was using all my strength to achieve based on what my ego thought I needed to achieve, rather than what my soul was interested in experiencing. The difficulty that the dream addressed was that I didn't know what my soul wanted me to do, which was essentially to learn how to be in my own feminine energy, rather than my more typical driven, masculine energy. I literally needed years of experience, often in the form of obstacles, to be able to get the message that the dream offered me.

In the dream, I was driving a little black and silver sports car up a steep hill, with Jesus sitting on the passenger side with me, sandals, white robe and all. I parked the car and we got out. I noticed on my left side, a very steep mountain with an almost vertical uphill ascent. There was a black and silver mountain bike there waiting for me. Part of me felt thrilled at the exhilarating challenge that was presented in that scene. But on my right side, Jesus had somehow found a beautiful chestnut-brown horse and was leading it gracefully through a very narrow incline in some rocks. The energy of Jesus leading the horse was so peaceful that I decided to follow him, but I panicked as I met the rocks. They were so dense, I felt claustrophobic and had a sense of intense revulsion towards the heavy muddy energy of the rock passageway. It almost stopped me in my tracks. Eventually I passed through the passageway and stepped into a wide opening of a sacred desert circle, surrounded by walls of rocks. In the centre stood a beautiful cathedral made of mud, and flooded with golden light. It was luminous, lit from within with a holy gold light. It was beautiful.

I believe that the guidance in this dream was not only for me. It became part of the key of my personal journey and eventually my spiritual teachings. It taught me about letting go of the thrilling addiction to mind-driven challenges so that I could learn how to be present to the wisdom of the body and grow spiritually through that process. This is a lesson that Western culture is learning as a whole.

The black and silver car and mountain bike were symbols of the body, of the feminine. Black represented the feminine wisdom of Yin in the Chinese spiritual tradition and silver represented the feminine lunar energy. The dream was telling me that I was treating my feminine energy – my body and my emotions – as machines to be forced to do my will, like climb mountains! The dream also revealed my previously unconscious belief that growth was always about going higher, represented by driving upwards and the thrilling possibility of riding up a mountain.

Years after this dream, I began to have experiences in meditation where I was actively blocked by my own guidance from expanding out through my crown chakra and leaving my body and forced instead to remain in my body. I realised fairly quickly that this was for my own growth and I turned my searching from out in the Universe to exploring instead the Universe within my own being. I immediately experienced my body as vast and spacious, a constantly moving energy that was truly blissful, open and wise. I began to experience my physicality as energy, experiencing sensations of being pure golden light in meditation. It made me wonder what had prevented me from doing this years earlier – until I recognised the amount of pain and karmic suffering that I had to clear before being present in my body could be a blissful experience, rather than an energetically blocked and painful place to be.

You'll know when you are called to this particular phase of spiritual growth because it will happen in prelude to a time when your soul light is needed more in the world.

Perhaps you are about to start working as a healer, or you are considering writing a book or creating a new healing modality. Perhaps you are thinking of studying and sharing what you learn, or just starting to make some small but important life changes to allow more time and energy to be dedicated to your spiritual path. This is an important phase of growth, that will bring aspects of your spiritual and physical lives into harmony and oneness with each other, You'll need some divine assistance, which the mother willingly provides.

SOUL HEALING PROCESS – IN THE CRADLE OF COMFORT WITH THE DIVINE MOTHER

Choose a quiet place to lie down and be warm and comfortable.

Start by saying the following invocation:

"I call upon Angel Mother Archon Barbelo, with her generosity, support, divine grace and abundant love, bless me beloved, I gladly receive your beautiful energy into my being now that I may grow more into my true nature – as your divine child of light! I call upon the Angel of Picture Jasper and the Earth Buddha Mother, Gaia, beloved ones, be with me now, bring me comfort and peace. Help me release old programs, beliefs, energetic imprints and karmic patterning that may keep me from fully receiving the vast extent of your sacred healing and divine grace. I surrender into your loving cradle of light now dear ones, with comfort in my heart, peace in my mind, and a deep gratitude in every cell of my being that renders me endlessly receptive to your serene grace. So be it."

Focus on your breathing and allow yourself to close your eyes, letting the eyes either roll gently back or gently down, whatever happens naturally without force.

Follow your breath, in and out, slowly and evenly. Allow your awareness to move away from the day-to-day world as you ride your breath deeper within the vast peaceful space opening up for you now. Imagine that you can feel a sense of warmth growing in your body, perhaps starting at your legs and feet, growing in your belly and your heart, flooding out around you. Imagine that the edges of the body begin to melt into the floor beneath you and the clothes and blanket covering you. The warmth is everywhere. Comfortable. Nourishing. Without limits.

Allow yourself to relax into this warmth, with every breath in and out, letting your body feel somehow heavy and yet filled with light, and your breath be slow and deep, unforced and unrushed. Imagine that there is a sense that the energy of your body begins to softly rock, ever so slightly in a comfortable, soothing way from side to side.

You become aware of golden light all around you as this happens and a feeling of being held. You have the combined energies of the crystal angels and Gaia wrapping you up in the arms of the Divine Mother, feeling loved, comforted and safe. You are at home here. Let go and allow the golden light of the Divine Mother to enter your heart and fill you with peace and healing. Notice what may arise for you – thoughts, distractions, feelings, then let them go and be aware of the breath, allowing yourself to go even more deeply into the experience of being held.

Stay here peacefully for at least forty-four breaths and when you are ready, slowly come back to the space and open your eyes. Say thank you with your hands in prayer before your heart and gently come back to your physical awareness by slowing moving your body and eventually standing up. Make sure you are deeply grounded by bouncing lightly on your feet a few times.

You have completed this soul healing process and its effects will reveal themselves over the coming months as the soul processes the healing. If you feel in approximately three days time that you need to do this technique again, please do so.

PSYCHOLOGICAL-EMOTIONAL HEALING WITH ARCHON BARBELO AND PICTURE JASPER: CLEARING BLOCKS TO RECEIVING

It is common for those that are drawn to healing to believe, even if they are not consciously aware of it, that they need to earn their way through the world, to earn everything that comes to them.

I remember being told by an astrologer once, many, many years ago that I would not have to work a day in my life, that my chart had a divine cradle in it and that was that. I thought it was such a ridiculous notion that I couldn't even understand how he could say such a thing! But it also intrigued me enough that the memory of the statement stayed with me decades on. I suspect now, that what he was trying to say was that part of my soul experience this lifetime would be that I was held by the cradle of the Divine Mother. Now that has always been in my chart, but it took me many years to even understand what he meant. Why? Because I had so many subconscious rules about receiving that I couldn't accept the prospect of anything coming to me that I hadn't specifically earned myself.

I often say to clients that the Universe provides us with what we need despite our efforts more often than because of them. This is because we often put effort and energy into making things happen, when it would be better to place that effort and energy into our own selves in being open to whatever happens from a place of trust. We act from our heart, let go and allow the outcomes to be what they will from a place of trust in the divine support that loves us so greatly. That is what I had to learn to gain access to the cosmic cradle. It is the ability to receive that is the issue – not whether there is something to be received.

So that is what the following psychological and emotional healing process will focus on. What can we release so we are more capable of receiving, of being cradled by the Divine Mother? I have added releases below that may or may not feel right for you. If not, feel free to say them anyway, as this will bring healing energy for others and earn you some karmic brownie points in the process. If there are other thoughts or intuitions that come up for you, where you realise a block or belief that you are ready to release, you may add those into your declaration at the beginning of the healing too. Enjoy.

HOW DO I KNOW IF I NEED HEALING IN THIS WAY AND AT THIS LEVEL OF MY BEING?

If you find life is more struggle than flow, then you need to learn to receive more. This healing will assist you in this process.

If you feel that life offers you plenty but you feel guilt or shame in accepting it completely, then this healing will help you.

If you feel like others are getting a bigger piece of the pie than you are, then this is for you too. If you feel like you need to keep an eagle eye on what others are getting (or not getting) and comparing what you are getting or not getting (emotionally, financially, energetically, romantically, professionally, personally) then you are coming from a place of lack and you need to learn to receive, to shift lack for abundance.

If you have a fear that if you have, others will want to take, so better not to have, then this is for you. If you fear that others will steal from you – ideas, romantic partners, money, possessions, anything that you believe is rightfully yours – then you need this too. These beliefs are wounded. Why have them unnecessarily manifest in experiences of theft when learning to receive might be a far more enjoyable way to heal the wound within? Perhaps it is time to claim the wisdom that what is truthfully and authentically yours can never be taken from you.

PSYCHOLOGICAL-EMOTIONAL HEALING PROCESS – CLEARING BLOCKS TO RECEIVING

Choose a place to sit comfortably where you won't be disturbed, where you can speak aloud and have some privacy without interruption or distraction.

Sit comfortably and declare aloud, "I call upon the healing power of my own soul, and upon the Angel of Picture Jasper and the Archon Barbelo. Help me in this healing beloveds, that I may be free to receive, to grow with grace and divine flow, and to let go of that which has held me in fear and held me back from truly feeling loved, protected and spiritually safe. If there is guidance for me, let me receive it consciously and clearly, with mercy and kindness. So be it."

Take your awareness into your heart and imagine it growing strong and rising up to your throat. Say aloud the following releases, adding any others that feel right for you. Don't worry about getting the wording perfect, just take your time and express yourself as best you can.

"I now choose of my own free will to release the following blocks from my mind, my body and my soul. I choose to release thoroughly and completely, through all time and space, all lifetimes and all energy fields. I choose to release any associated trauma or cellular memory now that would prevent me from receiving the full extent of divine grace possible into all areas of my life."

Be focused and say the following releases:

"I release any fear that I will be weak, helpless, abandoned and rejected if I ask to receive help. I release any fear that I have to do it all on my own or else I am a failure or inadequate. I release any fear that if I let go I will not be in control and will not be safe. I release guilt or shame in receiving. I release the belief that others suffer if I receive and they do not. I release the belief that I can cause suffering in others by having a happy and supported life. I release the belief that I should avoid hope now because I'll only be disappointed later on. I release the belief that in avoiding commitment to anyone or anything, I will avoid being hurt too. I release the belief that to be safe and held means I don't get to grow and be independent and resourceful. I release the belief that letting vaster beings help me is a sign of weakness. I release the belief that I am not important enough to be helped because there are others who are suffering more than I am. I release the belief that if I receive I will owe something and be bound by duty and responsibility not of my choosing. I release the belief or experience that in receiving I become entangled and weighed down."

Gently open your arms and spread your fingers with your palms facing upwards. Plant both feet on the ground. Imagine breathing in love and breathing out through your palms, fingers and soles of the feet. Release these old beliefs now into the Earth. Just let them go. Imagine energy releasing from the back of your neck where it meets the base of your skull. Imagine energy releasing on your exhalation out of the back of your head and out of your ears. Breathe in love and on the exhalation stick out your tongue and open your mouth wide, releasing out of your mouth.

Then sit quietly, breathing in love from the Divine Mother by placing a hand on your heart and feeling her warmth already within you, alive in your heartbeat. When you are ready, say the following:

"I choose to receive. I am worthy. I am free to choose and to be loved and supported now and I deserve it. With gratitude I say 'Yes!' and surrender into love."

Repeat these words over and over again, gently and lovingly. Say this last paragraph at least three times or until you really start to believe it to be true.

Sit quietly until you feel that peace and comfort or until you have completed forty-four breaths in and out with one hand on your heart, and perhaps one on your belly. Be peaceful and let Barbelo hold and bless you now.

When you are ready, say, "I am blessed in this field of her grace. I receive her divine assistance and love in all ways. So be it."

When you are ready, simply open your eyes and you have completed your healing task.

PHYSICAL HEALING WITH PICTURE JASPER AND ARCHON BARBELO: PREPARING FOR THE GOLDEN BODY

The golden body process is a beautiful awakening of light in matter. We prepare for it by purification and learning to receive from a place of safety and trust.

Purification has begun in the emotional – psychological healing practice above. Now it is time to let the body benefit from the clarity by programming it gently with an ability to trust and receive.

The body is an intelligent animal with cellular memory. It needs a chance to release that memory to be able to receive freely. Like a computer with more soul, the body needs to clear old programs and upgrade to new ones and this can be done simply and with subtle grace.

HOW DO I KNOW IF I NEED THIS PHYSICAL HEALING PRACTICE?

It is my firm belief that the Universe always offers us more than we can ever conceive of receiving. With that notion in mind, you can pretty much expect that this practice is helpful at any time and in any situation.

It is perhaps most helpful when you are experiencing a feeling of frustration or block and find yourself meeting closed doors rather than open windows and need some help getting back into divine flow (keeping in mind that sometimes the divine flows in a different direction than what you had anticipated).

PHYSICAL HEALING PRACTICE – PREPARING FOR THE GOLDEN BODY

This simple and powerful practice will take you to the next level of preparation for the golden body, or the sacred marriage of body and soul. Be patient and trust. It is subtle and powerful. It is not recommended as a practice more than once a week or once a month if you are very sensitive to energy and highly responsive to healing.

Sit or lie comfortably with a piece of Picture Jasper touching your body if you have one. If not, you can simply open this book to page 25, which features the Crystal Angel Mandala for Picture Jasper.

When you are ready, say the following:

"I call upon the healing power of Picture Jasper and Archon Barbelo. I honour with your help my golden body of light. So be it!"

Close your eyes and focus on your breath. Imagine around you there is a field of radiant golden light. It begins to hum and buzz not only around you, but entering into your being, through your skin and dancing in every cell.

Take at least forty-four long, slow deep breaths in and out, as this happens.

When you are ready, say thank you and gently remove the stone from your body.

Stand peacefully for a moment and feel your body connected to the ground beneath you. Imagine a magnetic bubble of golden energy building between the sole of each foot and the Earth. Imagine this bubble grows so big it fills you, rising up through your whole body and out through the crown of your head, spilling over each side of your crown like a fountain and tumbling down, pouring deep into the Earth.

Pause for a moment and then open your eyes again. You have finished your healing process.

PRAYER – AFFIRMATION

To invoke the healing power of Picture Jasper and Archon Barbelo at any time, you can repeat the following affirmation quietly in your mind, or aloud.

"I am the golden grace divine, supported perfectly at all times."

10.

CARNELIAN (Life Force)
and ANGEL ISDA (Food)

THE GIFT OF NOURISHMENT

SPIRITUAL GUIDANCE FROM THE ANGEL OF CARNELIAN
AND THE ANGEL ISDA

Here on the Earth there is great warmth, peace and abundance waiting for you. We know that you fear being empty sometimes. That you worry you will not have enough. Sometimes you take too much of what you don't really need. We know this is because you are confused, so we don't judge it as greed. Instead we help you learn how to be fed, on all levels, with what you really want and need. Food for the soul, food for the mind, food for the body, to nourish well and be kind. To have enough and to trust that there will be more when in need. We want you to feel safe and at home, within your body, so your soul can grow. Let us help you find the warmth, nourishment and peace, as poverty in all forms, we help you release. We bring you the pleasure of a warm, vital life, of nourished body, and of mind fed with peace, of soul nourished by experience, growing big and strong. Of a life happy, healthy and long.

PICTURING CARNELIAN

Often available in tumbled stones, but historically, tracing back over several thousand years before Christ, it used by the ancients in jewellery. It features in jewellery from the Middle East, India and the West. My partner's great, great grandfather from Canada had an engraved Carnelian signet ring and my mother-in-law purchased a Carnelian medallion from Afghanistan carved with the image of a horse for me as a Christmas gift one year. The stone is not rare or difficult to find, though to me it is always a treasure. .

Carnelian ranges from brown – dark red tones, to vibrant reds and oranges, to tones of pink, pale orange and even white markings. Carnelian can look like divine fire, like a warm invitation to life in a stone! It has endless variety in colourful markings and patterning of swirls, banded threads of colour and more. It is mostly opaque but can include segments of semi-translucent colourless stone as well.

HEALING PROPERTIES

Carnelian brings more life to the body and helps attract the soul into the body. My Chi Gung Master Zhao used to say that just like a person wouldn't be attracted to live in a dirty and disorderly house, one had to make the body beautiful and clean to invite the spirit to enter. Holding Carnelian, having it around your home and person, is a bit like lighting some lovely scented candles, throwing a beautiful throw rug over the sofa, stoking the fire and snuggling up into a beautiful, inviting room that you just want to relax into. It can also be like the vital pleasure of stepping barefoot onto cool sand at the beach, fresh salt air clearing your head and lifting your spirits as you hear the waves crashing in and feel the aliveness and power of the ocean! Carnelian is both snuggling up at the cosy fire and feeling the aliveness of dancing to your favourite music with wild abandon.

It nourishes the body, helps it absorb nutrients and helps strengthen the lower chakras, which enables the soul to have more 'oomph' or power in how it expresses itself in the physical world. You may have an exceptionally powerful spirit, but if the lower chakras in your being are under-nourished, the soul won't have much to work with in terms of getting out and about and mixing it up in the material world. Carnelian helps to balance this which is great for people who spend a lot of time doing intense mental work or tend to live in their heads, don't get enough social or play time or just need to share some of the energy of their minds, which can be strong, with their body, which may be weaker.

Carnelian helps the feminine sexual energy to rebalance and feel nourished. Women in their sexuality actually perform a healing service to the emotional growth of humanity, and particularly of their sexual partners. Women naturally draw in energy through sexual exchange and that which is negative or dirty gets processed through their inner fire or shakti, as the Vedic tradition would call it. Carnelian helps to strengthen the inner fire and balance it. If a woman is called upon (even without realising it) to process of a lot of negativity through her sexual energy, the inner fire can become imbalanced as it grows very strong to meet the demand to process negativity and as a result, it can overheat causing emotional and physical symptoms. Or the negativity might be too much for her energy, draining her and leaving her feeling cold and lifeless. The woman might feel depression, inflammation in the body, stiffness in the joints or even deep rage which can get stuck in the hips. She may feel debilitated and drained of life force. All of this may remain subconscious until waking one morning and finding that the hips are very stiff, or the woman just feels awful for no particular reason, or perhaps she heads off to her yoga class, doing hip-opening postures and apparently out of nowhere, rage emerges from the depths of her body, where she could quite easily punch her yoga instructor if she really let loose! It can be quite a shock in that Zen moment to suddenly feel intense anger releasing from your body, even if it is just the body healing itself.

If you have a tendency to think too much, daydream more than do, worry that you lack courage to follow your convictions or just need to learn to value yourself enough to meet your wants and needs with a little more commitment (perhaps rather than meeting the wants and needs of everyone else before you even vaguely think about yours), then Carnelian can help you too.

ABOUT THE ANGEL ISDA

To connect with Angel Isda feels like molten-honey rising up from the Earth and descending from the sky. Her energy is somehow simultaneously light and substantial, almost effervescent and slow burning all at once. I really noticed her so strongly around the lower half of my body, from the heart down, as a supportive, comforting presence, which feels warm, stable, present and very safe.

The Angel Isda is often known as the angel of food, but she is actually the angel of physical, emotional and spiritual nourishment. One of her key tasks is to help humanity learn how to give the self what is wanted and needed. This sounds simple perhaps, but if we haven't learned these fundamental skills from our care givers growing up (more than likely because they hadn't learned it from their care givers and so on, back through the generations), then learning how to attend to our wants and needs can be utterly baffling! You could say that it is a bit like knowing that you are hungry but not knowing what you are hungry for exactly, so you just eat and eat and end up overfed but not nourished with what you actually needed.

This is the sad plight of the 'poor little rich girl' where there is so much and yet what is needed genuinely is absent. It is the parent who works all the time, providing gifts but not presence to his or her child. It is the overeater who craves feeling full and safe but hasn't learned what to eat in order to provide for the body, mind and emotions, Instead he/she opts for quantity, but finds that this is a temporary help at best, and is left feeling unsatisfied again, soon after. It is the person who obsessively shops or hoards objects, unable to emotionally or psychologically (or even physically) let go of being surrounded by possessions. This is beyond attachment to the actual possession itself, it is a fear that if a sense of emptiness is not filled, there will be such horror that cannot be faced, the emptiness might be endless and one could disappear into it altogether – so that fear is buried under a weight of acquisitions.

This also relates to the person who cannot receive, who cannot eat, who cannot hold any weight in the body or hold any dream in the life long enough for it to manifest. To the person who cannot engage in genuine, warm, loving and nourishing relationship with others. It also applies to the person who forces herself to exist on too little food, never dresses warmly enough, or forces herself to live in a cold house, rather than switching on a heater. This person is starving – on all levels. She is learning about nourishment, but rather than from the position of overdoing the feeding, she is underfed. She is learning how to overcome denial and in turn to love the senses, honour the physical body, the physical and emotional world, as a place through which the spirit can grow strong and flourish.

The Angel Isda has a lot of people to help! Fortunately she is exceptionally well-versed in nourishment and so she has all the reserves and resources she needs to rise to her formidable challenge. She teaches us to do the same.

SOUL HEALING WITH CARNELIAN AND THE ANGEL ISDA

For those souls incarnating in the West in particular, learning that being in a body and being spiritual can be mutually enhancing experiences is not the easiest lesson. Such souls often need to clear conditioning of various religious traditions and cultural mores that labelled the body as sinful or inferior, and sexuality as unclean or dirty, as temptation or distraction from the purity of the spiritual path.

This is not to discount the validity of the celibate and monastic lifestyles as a path to spiritual attainment. My grandmother, raised Catholic and devoted to the Virgin Mary, used to say "all roads lead to Rome", which I took to mean that all paths lead to the same place. It is just a question of choosing the path that is right for us.

For many souls currently incarnated, especially those that are spiritually progressive and helping create a new culture on Earth, learning to honour the divine feminine in form, through healing conscious relationship to the body and to sexuality, is part of their soul task. Carnelian and the Angel Isda helps support that soul task by teaching the importance of nourishment of the body and the soul, and the skills necessarily to achieve these tasks.

Learning how to be present with the body, how to honour it without becoming obsessed with it, how to honour our sexual energy and how to heal distorted judgements about this part of our being, are all lessons that support us in becoming more receptive to nourishment of body, mind and soul. I believe that part of our cultural obsession with sexuality is actually an unconscious attempt to not throw the body out with the bathwater, as it were. Sometimes when the psyche is split, obsession is the only way we can hold on until we give ourselves permission to bring that which has been denied into our everyday lives with more acceptance and peace. For those who sense that sexuality holds a key to personal healing, but without a level of acceptance and integration that would enable this to unfold as yet, obsession is a way to remain in touch with this part of the self. If you are feeling obsessed with sexuality, consider that there is healing that is trying to occur but you are still preparing for it. Your obsession is a way to stay connected to your sexual energy until you are ready to face that which needs to be healed. It might be old feelings of shame or rejection about your body or your worth as a person that are wanting to be healed and are hiding under your sexual obsession. Most human beings are working through experiences of shame and rejection as a part of their emotional healing, learning to love themselves and each other with less condition. For some, issues of rejection or self-worth will be hiding behind obstacles to career success, for others in weight and body image issues and for others in issues to do with sexuality or relationship, for example.

If rejection, self-worth or simply questions about your sexuality are issues that you or another are facing, Carnelian can help. Whether it be from a certain type of upbringing that was uncomfortable with sexuality, or religious conditioning or social mores from this or other lifetimes, or as a result of trauma following abuse, Carnelian can help gently heal, protect and nourish the sexual energy back into flow, gently supporting the self in healing sexual issues as the flow opens and becomes more vibrant.

There is a warmth and aliveness in the body when it is touched and fused with the light of the soul that becomes golden. It is a type of bliss. Yes, there are states of bliss that are beyond the body and these hold spiritual value of course. Yet there is a particular sort of loving devotion in the souls of those who are here to learn to love and honour the bliss that is incarnate when body and soul unite and become as one. They have come to this planet to honour the divine feminine and help her find her place in a culture that, in the West in particular, has been closed off from her wisdom for thousands of years.

In this spiritual path of honouring the divine feminine, life in the physical body becomes less about the struggles of limitation provided by time and space, and more an opportunity to explore the abundance of the divine through a feminine journey. It is about bringing sacred marriage between spirit and matter until spirit shines through matter, with matter, including the body itself, radiating golden light of divine awakening. It is an extraordinary, beautiful and advanced spiritual task, only for those that dare to shed old guilt, shame and anger, and instead open up to the divine energy of the body and soul as one pure, innocent, wild and golden being.

SOUL HEALING – GROWING THROUGH LIFE

Many souls who have had incarnations in realms other than the Earth (I would call such souls "star children") go through phases of spiritual homesickness. This can make it difficult to really ground and connect with the life here on Earth for quite a while. Such souls are used to being able to live in higher realms, where time and space do not impose upon them and thought communication is natural. Telepathic ability and a swiftness in comprehension are quite typical talents of such souls, which can still be utilised whilst in a physical body once the soul gets used to living in a physical world and realises that they still have access to their soul light and talents even whilst living in a physical body.

However, the time when there is a reconnection consciously to the spiritual worlds and a realisation perhaps that one does not only belong here on Earth can be painful at first. Depression, suicidal thoughts, deep despair, anger and angst can arise during such realisations. These are normal human responses to a rather non-human situation – feeling that you perhaps belong on a star or planet other than this earthly planet.

Part of the discomfort of this remembrance of different types of soul experience is that they are often less challenging than Earth school, which is a fairly advanced classroom. Things often move slower here on Earth. We have to work through thicker veils of illusion, and even great gurus and teachers are often subject to these veils at times, all whilst teaching how to master them. It makes for a pretty interesting experience of life sometimes.

When we look at the violence and fear that is prevalent in our world, or the abuse that happens even in the most apparently spiritually advanced groups and organisations on our planet, the Earth might not seem so advanced. Yet this is what makes the spiritual task of incarnating here to remember our divinity more like a spiritual PhD than a preliminary spiritual lesson. It is easier to remember oneself as divine in the midst of peace and serenity, but how much more difficult this can be when the ego is thrashing about and you are perhaps in the midst of a struggle with your own dark nature? How much more difficult is it when you are choking in the thick veils of illusion, trying to cut through what you know is untruth yet feels so compelling anyway (perhaps judgement for example), in order to find your light and be it?! Now that is the stuff of spiritual heroism.

So whilst we may intuitively look to other civilisations for guidance on how to be more peace-loving and operate in greater oneness and constructive interdependence with each other and our environment, we must also realise that coming to this planet is the mark of a brave soul that wanted to reach the outposts of spiritual light. We came with a conviction that we would be able to find the light here, awakening the divine even in those situations or beings that seem anything but divine at the time! Like pioneers discovering a harsh and untamed land and loving the adventure enough to seek the beauty that lies hidden within it, such souls are compassionate, devoted to the enlightenment of all beings and hold great power.

As we start to realise this, there is a peace and acceptance that comes into the soul. It begins to not only accept that it is here, but it surrenders into its plan and purpose for incarnation. It begins to actively learn about the Earth and how to love her for what she is, not resist her for what she is not. The soul learns to play with the body, to help it purify and awaken, and the body, and life itself, actively and lovingly receives the light of the spirit. The two go from apparent divorce to sacred courtship and eventually holy marriage. That is what the Angel of Carnelian and Angel Isda help us access. A warm presence of spirit and body together, the attitude of the soul towards life as not a restriction to be borne, but as an opportunity to grow in loving warmth. To have successfully passed the most advanced spiritual testing, making a priceless contribution to the evolution of the great divine being that is our Universe.

Our souls then start to want to be her. We become excited and stimulated by the challenges of manifesting their light here on the planet, and can often be incredibly enthusiastic, taking on many opportunities to help and simply to be – really enjoying rather than enduring life. It is a complete reorientation where heaven is not reached for as something away in the skies, but lived as in the form of the body. This brings peace, commitment, engagement with the world and great spiritual success.

HOW DO YOU KNOW IF YOU ARE HEALING AT A SOUL LEVEL IN THIS WAY?

There were times in my early path when I really struggled to accept being on Earth. I knew that I loved her and I wanted to be here and yet at the same time I absolutely yearned to be free from what felt like the shackles of my body and the heaviness of earthly reality. I vividly remember moments when I didn't identify with my body at all, feeling that I was only my spirit. Yet I wanted to be alive and felt an unbearable, unbreakable attachment to the body that I so struggled to feel at home in. The contract that I had made to be here in a body felt like it was a heavy weight coming down on me. I struggled to accept it in those moments, when the pain of resistance to incarnation was so excruciating, that I couldn't bear it for more than a second. I would shut it off as quickly as I could, snapping shut a metal door in my heart that would prevent me from feeling it. I believe that this unresolved wound is behind suicidal urges. It can be so difficult to stay present to those moments where the spirit is reconciling itself to being in the body. Even for me, being quite a responsive and adaptable creature, it was very hard. For others, it may remain unconscious and emerge in depression, lack of engagement in life for a period of time, suicidal thoughts or fantasies. These are all clues that your soul is going through an incredibly important transition point after which engagement in the physical world will become more free, surrendered, warm and inviting. To get there however is not always easy.

If you relate to this process, or would quite simply just like to feel that your world is warmer and more inviting for your soul path, that your physical existence and your inner spiritual life operate more in harmony with each other, then this healing is for you.

SOUL HEALING PROCESS – REORIENTING THE SOUL TO LIFE

You will need a quiet place to lie down and be warm and comfortable. If you have some Carnelian, have it nearby, possibly touching your body, especially from the hips down to the feet.

Start by saying the following invocation:

"I call upon Angel Isda, and the Angel of Carnelian and the Earth Mother, Gaia. Beloved ones, be with me now. Bring me comfort and peace. Help me release old programs, beliefs, energetic imprints and karmic patterning that may keep me from bringing my soul to life with grace, acceptance, surrender and play. Help me make life easier on myself, help me find your way of wisdom that echoes deep within me. So be it."

Focus on your breathing and allow yourself to close your eyes, letting the eyes either roll gently back or gently down, whatever happens naturally without force. Take your awareness to the connection of your body with the surface beneath you. Let your awareness become soft and the distinction between your body and the surface supporting you become fuzzy. Imagine that you are sinking into the Earth a little, that your edges are blending and blurring with the edges of the Earth.

Allow yourself to relax into the Earth with every breath in and out, letting your body feel somehow heavy and filled with light, and your breath be slow and deep, unforced and unrushed.

You become aware of golden light from within the Earth, rising up and filling you from the outside in. It feels good. You become aware of a temple deep within this golden light, and you allow yourself to step into it. It is perfectly serene and beautiful, with proportions that feel just right for you. Your favourite colours, smells, plants or animals. Your favourite types of nature – mountains, trees, oceans, sand from the beach, rich forest floor, thick jungle canopy or raw powerful fires and volcanoes. You feel yourself in an awesome energy that is inspiring, energising and beautiful. Allow yourself to be filled with awe and appreciation.

You then become aware of endless swirling rich red, orange, brown and pink deposits of Carnelian, as though they breathe in and out, emitting a radiant golden light that fills your sacred temple with a warm glow.

From within this golden glow, the Angel Isda arrives. She bears plates of fruit and nuts, colourful and lush and she smiles at you. "You have been invited to a great feast," she says, "And the table has been laid out and your place set – will you come?".

If you feel to say "Yes", allow it to emanate from your heart, and say it aloud or in your own heart and mind. She smiles at you and golden light surrounds you, filling your body with gold.

Let yourself bathe in that golden light for at least forty-four breaths.

When you are ready, slowly come back to the space and open your eyes. Say, "Thank you." Gently touch the ground beneath you with your hands and say, "I honour the sacred task of living my light on the Earth. I accept this beautiful offer to thrive and grow into divine immortality through sacred play within this temple of the Divine Mother. May my soul be blessed with peace, surrender, inspiration and devotion. May my days here be filled with passion, purpose and joy. May I find the wisdom in all experiences and trust myself and my process, that I flourish and am nourished. So be it."

Sit quietly for a moment, feeling the effect of your words and when you are ready, simply stand up, move about for a few moments and stretch your arms and legs, preparing to go about your day.

You have completed this soul healing process and its effects will reveal themselves over the coming months as the soul processes the healing.

Be open to saying "yes" to that which feels soulful and is presented as an opportunity to you. Don't hesitate. Embrace life. A new way of being in the world is upon you beloved. Accept the grace of it.

PSYCHOLOGICAL-EMOTIONAL HEALING WITH ANGEL ISDA AND CARNELIAN: FROM GHOST LOVER TO EMBODIED RELATIONSHIP

A ghost lover is the fantasy of your perfect partner. He or she contains all the qualities and charm that you could want and is just perfect for you (in your own mind). The embodied relationship that the Universe delivers for you will actually be spiritually perfect for you and your growth but will often press buttons (otherwise known as growth-triggers!) and be challenging at times. You can endure it until you master the lessons, or you can choose to cast it aside as not living up to your 'list' of perfect partner traits, and rely upon the volume of people that you will meet in a lifetime to offer your lucky ticket to a better relationship.

The problem with a ghost lover is that he or she is a ghost. It is an ideal, not a real, living being and will never turn into a real person. They are perfect (again, in your own mind) because they are a figment of fantasy.

Some souls are raised in a ghost lover household, where generations of marriages suffer chronic unhappiness and disappointment because one partner (or both) deems the other inadequate and to be failing to measure up to the perfection of 'the one who got away' or some ideal 'one' who hasn't appeared as yet. The 'one who got away' might be a 'perfect' father who died young, or a lover who was tragically separated from you by forces beyond your control, or a romantic opportunity missed. The perfect ideal yet to appear might be a fantasy based on a movie or a book. These souls might learn more about fantasy bonding than actual flesh-and-blood relationships.

Fantasy relationships do not provide opportunities for real emotional and sexual maturation beyond basic limits, and so they deny us the spiritual growth that would arise from genuine human relationship.

So why do we create ghost lovers at all? The ghost lover is really not about a physical life partner at all. It is about us meeting and connecting with what the psychologist Jung would call our contra-sexual nature. In men, that is the feminine spirit and in women it is the inner masculine spirit. The ghost lover is a way that we can get to know our own selves in a much fuller and more spiritually mature fashion. The difficulty comes if we don't understand this and try to make it about a relationship with another human being instead.

In men, the feminine spirit is the part of his soul that allows him to experience love, tenderness, connection, bonding, feeling, emotion, creativity and its expression through art, music, dance or poetry. Men in connection with their feminine spirit can be very masculine men, quite strong and independent, and capable of enough self-esteem to allow themselves to grow beyond what a culturally dictated, alpha male man is supposed to be.

Women who are in touch with their inner masculine spirit are often highly independent, adventurous souls who love to create, who like to read, to write, to explore the worlds of the mind, of philosophy and spirituality. They won't necessarily like traditional feminine roles and may be quite keen on equality and mutual respect in relationship. They will often have a highly developed spirituality and be happy to go against the grain in favour of living an authentic life.

If we can remember this, and realise that the ghost lover is actually the hidden part of ourselves that we are meant to make conscious and integrate, rather than an ideal that a partner is supposed to fulfil, we will find that our personal growth can rocket along at a rapid rate, and our relationships will be sustained with less conflict and disappointment, and more acceptance and unconditional love.

This sounds simple, but the very nature of a ghost lover is that it doesn't appear to be who we are – it appears to be something outside of us. The nature of that which is unconscious and yet to be brought into the light of our awareness, eventually claimed as us and integrated as one of our inner resources, is that we first encounter it as 'not us'. So we see it projected on another, or experience it in a dream. It takes great awareness to not fall into a fantasy about that figure, and let our dreams interfere with really relating with another human being in the here and now. We are seeking the balance of not pushing the ghost lover aside as an impossible fantasy, but instead learning to relate to this part of ourselves claiming our attention and offering us the gift of our contra-sexual self – our inner masculine or feminine nature. If we can recognise when this is happening and not get swept up by fantasies, and at the same time, not give up on the promises of greater wholeness, resourcefulness, wellbeing and pleasure that the ghost lover can bring us through our own inner work, then our life can improve and our human relationships can improve too, rather than having to compete with a fantasy.

Many years ago I had a vision that I hardly understood at the time, but eventually that taught me these lessons and triggered my growth. I saw a woodsman lying on the forest floor. His arms and legs had been cut off and I stood with long flowing red hair nearby him. I knew I could heal him. I approached him, but he couldn't see me as he was transfixed by a softly white, floating blonde-haired princess in the distance. He wanted her but he couldn't reach her and she wasn't particularly interested or able to help him anyway.

I came out of this vision feeling shocked by its graphic violence and the hopelessness of it. I knew in time however, that it was just about my own masculine self-learning to receive healing from the vital (red haired) feminine part of me that was flesh and blood.

In other words, my body. The fantasy feminine, the perfect princess fantasy, wasn't going to help him at all! I had to learn to accept and be with my real self and that would be my healing. Which is exactly what happened. Giving up the fantasies in favour of a more embodied reality, where there was experience instead of just yearning was a painful, drawn-out process for me. I had to learn how to love the feminine, my body and being physically alive, not constantly retreating into my powerful mind and imagination where my rich fantasy life seemed to offer so much glitz, but actually kept me away from really being able to live and be productive and engaged in my life (i.e. living with my arms and legs attached!).

It took much inner work with dreams and much patience to come out of a strong orientation to the non-physical worlds and learn to love, trust and accept life on the material plane. Fortunately I had a sensual side to my nature, an appreciation for beauty and artistry, and a love of dance and music, as well as a passion for nature, that helped lure me into the physical world. This paved the way for a level of peace with my body that I had never experienced before. It was the beginning of a new level of freedom. One that came through engaging with the world rather than shying away from it, no longer opting for the fantasy of being a princess rather than accepting myself as a warm-blooded woman.

HOW DO I KNOW IF I NEED HEALING
IN THIS WAY AND AT THIS LEVEL OF MY BEING?

This healing will be helpful if you feel that your relationships (including your friendships) could be more nourishing. If you feel you could receive more nourishment from yourself, if you have ever battled with loving and accepting your body, if you would like to release disordered eating, addictive negative thoughts about your body, or the body or weight of another (such as a child), this healing will assist you. If you struggle to accept your sexuality, if you feel inhibited sexually with your partner, or if you act out sexually, without connecting to your heart, If you feel that your spiritual life is more active on the inner planes than the outer planes of the physical world, then this healing is for you.

PSYCHOLOGICAL-EMOTIONAL HEALING PROCESS – FROM GHOST LOVER TO EMBODIED RELATIONSHIP

If you have some Carnelian with you, place it on your body, or near your body, from the waist downwards to the feet at any point that intuitively seems appropriate. If you don't have one, you might like to open this book to page 26, which features the Carnelian Crystal Angel Mandala in full colour and leave it close by during this process.

Start by sitting or lying comfortably with one hand resting on your belly and one on your heart. Breathe in and out, letting the breath bring warmth to the body.

Say, "I call upon the healing angel of Carnelian."

Be aware of a warmly glowing energy appearing before you now. Notice her face, her warmth, her love. She is shades of red and orange, with radiant bright orange wings and a deep red robe, tied with a brown cord. She has long flowing chocolate brown hair and deep brown eyes. She raises her hands and sends waves of golden light all around you, which you can breathe in as deeply as you like.

Say, "I call upon the healing Angel Isda."

You see a beautiful angel with radiant red wings and golden robes, she has a warm smile and she opens her arms to embrace you. Allow yourself to receive her angelic hug if you wish, letting warmth and peace flood through your body.

Say, "I am so grateful to my body, to my home for my soul, for allowing me to experience the joy of connection in this physical world. I now choose of my own free will, to give myself permission, unconditionally, to enter into safe, warm, nourishing physical relationship and friendships. I call upon the souls that can help me have this experience this lifetime as I now choose to engage more fully with the physical world. May the blessings of feminine grace help me heal as I reach out and allow myself to receive and to give in nourishing connection through my physical self. So be it."

Let the energy of your words be saturated by the golden light around you. Stay with the breath for at least forty-four counts and when you are ready, simply open your eyes.

You have completed your healing process. Congratulations! Now prepare to enjoy more relationships in the physical world. Remember to take time for yourself when you need it and that you can choose to balance solitude and connection in whatever way feels nourishing for you.

PHYSICAL HEALING WITH CARNELIAN AND ANGEL ISDA: THE NOURISHED BODY

It is my belief that we are as a species healing consciousness of starvation and poverty. Many souls come to have the experience in an intense and dramatic way in physical form and we have a chance to honour their spiritual courage by donating time and money, for example, towards lessening their suffering and helping heal their consciousness by relieving the physical reality of it.

There are other expressions of starvation in more wealthy societies, from the more obvious eating disorders of under eating or dieting at one end of the spectrum to fully-fledged anorexia at the other end of the spectrum. We can also express the poverty and starvation consciousness in a need to consume more than we really want or need – be it food, clothing, possessions, collectibles, books, DVDs, shoes, cars, gadgets and more. These things are often an expression of a feeling of emptiness within, to counteract feelings of starvation on emotional levels. What we are starved of may well be fun, play or affection, and this may also relate to past life issues.

Recently I was offering clinical supervision for one of my teachers at The Shakti Temple in Sydney. She had a client who was struggling with being overweight. She just couldn't stop eating. Both my co-teacher and I had the same flash of intuition. This woman felt like she was starving and was ravenous for food as a result. When my colleague went back to the client and asked her if she felt she was starving for food, she answered with a resounding "yes!". The beginning of healing for her situation was then to not focus on dieting or willpower, but to focus on clearing the past life memories of starvation that had left cellular trauma in her body and were still being acted out in this sensitive individual in the current lifetime.

I believe that those memories are stored in the greater soul of humanity and we are all responsible for its healing. Starvation and poverty is not just something that affects those experiencing the more obvious physical expressions of it. It is part of collective human wounding and we can do more to heal the dramatic imbalance that we see in human existence – mass physical starvation on one end of the scale and extreme consumption of mass produced goods causing excessive landfill and ecological strain on the other. These are one expression of the wound of starvation and poverty in human consciousness. Together we can start by healing our own body and enjoying the peace and love that this brings us, and allow it to spread out into the world, healing the wound, one being at a time.

HOW DO I KNOW IF I NEED THIS LEVEL OF HEALING?

If you find that you are not satisfied physically or emotionally, if you eat and are full yet still feel hungry in some way, then you are crying out for nourishment. Not more substance necessarily, but more nutrition in all ways.

If you are battling with eating or food issues, with your weight or with compulsive collecting, hoarding or an anxiety about clearing out your cupboards or letting something go, even if you don't really use it or want it anymore, then this healing will help you.

If you feel moved by poverty in any of its forms – obvious in societies where starvation, squalor and poverty are rife, or less obvious in the inner poverty that leads to hoarding and greed, then you can do this healing as an offering to humanity too.

PHYSICAL HEALING PRACTICE –
CLEARING CELLULAR STARVATION TRAUMA

Sit or lie comfortably with a piece of Carnelian touching your body if you have one. Alternatively, you can leave this book open to page 26, which features the Crystal Angel Mandala for Carnelian.

When you are ready, say the following:

"I call upon the healing power of the Angel of Carnelian and Angel Isda. Please help me clear all cellular records of starvation and poverty consciousness through all time and space. Through all lifetimes and all levels of my being. Help me release this now that I may bring more peace to the human collective. May the healing within me inspire and empower healing in all of humankind. For the greatest good, and with great joy in my heart, so be it!"

Close your eyes and focus on your breath.

Let the energy of what you have declared create a golden-red spiral of light, starting beneath your feet and rising up, growing larger and more powerful as it spirals towards the top of your head. Let the spiral grow stronger and descend again, flowing up and down your being, inside your body and along your spine, outside your body, up and down your energy field. Breathe in the spirals of light and intend to let go and release on the out breath, allowing the light spirals to carry away anything you are releasing. Whether you know consciously what is being released or not does not matter.

Stay with this inhalation and exhalation in the red gold spirals of light for at least forty-four breaths.

Say, "I now accept the goodness, safety and abundance that nourishes me, mind, body and soul. I accept this with grace and in service to the greater good. May all of humanity thrive, through merciful grace, so be it."

When you are ready, say "thank you" and gently remove the stone from your body.

Stand peacefully for a moment and feel your body connected to the ground beneath you. Feel the golden red spirals descending through you into the Earth. Feel the Earth connection as nourishing and supportive. Close your eyes, and gently say, "yes" to the Earth and her gift to you.

Pause for a moment and then open your eyes again. You have finished your healing process.

PRAYER – AFFIRMATION

To invoke the healing power of Carnelian and Angel Isda at any time, you can repeat the following affirmation quietly in your mind, or aloud.

"Red Gold Abundance Nourishes me without limit, Mind, Body and Soul."

11.

TURQUOISE (Amulet)
and ARCHANGEL GABRIEL (Strength)

THE GIFT OF SPIRITUAL AUTHORITY

SPIRITUAL GUIDANCE FROM THE ANGEL OF TURQUOISE
AND THE ARCHANGEL GABRIEL

You have within you great spiritual truth and light. Within this world, you can shine so bright! You can help others to find their way too, just being yourself and living what feels true. We bring you gifts to release the past and to shed disappointment about failure or false starts. We cleanse you of agreements you once made, of things that you said and promises you gave, that no longer serve your highest truth within. We help you release all that would hold you back from the new phase that begins! Receive from us now the gift of hope and release, of strength, protection and awakening to see, that you too beloved, have divine inner authority. Live your truth. Let yourself shine bright. It is safe to be seen. You are held safe in our light. Now is the time to honour your divine right, to choose your way forward and live your light. You have now, and will always be, a being of divine will, of spiritual authority. You have been chosen to take spiritual initiation, to grow into your power and lead others with love. You have been given this task with blessings from above. With support from the Earth and guidance from within, your initiation into spiritual authority and leadership, does now begin.

PICTURING TURQUOISE

Turquoise has been prized by native cultures for thousands of years. It is available often in jewellery but also in tumbled stones. It varies from pale aqua to deeper blue shades, which tend to have more copper content, and even tends towards green tones (such as in Tibetan Turquoise) which will have formed through processes with more aluminium or iron content. The stone can have veining of brown or even black threads running through it which indicate different mineral constituents. Native American Indian tradition has a beautiful expression for these lines running through the stone, they say that they are cracks where the stone was protecting the wearer and 'took' the blow of a situation or circumstance for them.

I have seen even minty green Turquoise flecked with orange matrix. Some dyed Howlite is falsely marked as Turquoise. It has exceptionally vivid blue tone, almost garishly so, and has its own healing properties, but is not actual Turquoise.

Turquoise has much natural variety and although some softer grade Turquoise is treated with resin to make it more stable for jewellery, there is much beautiful, natural Turquoise available, though larger pieces can be quite expensive.

HEALING PROPERTIES

Turquoise has many beautiful properties – it is a stone of protection and truth, of good fortune and an affirmation of high spiritual destiny that is available to us. It bestows a vibration upon the bearer of alignment to flow and good fortune, and to strength and protection.

Turquoise is one of those stones that I can virtually always wear and feel better for it. Some stones have a definite time and place when they work and when they are not quite right for me, but Turquoise is an everyday stone, useful and healing in all situations that I find myself.

Turquoise strengthens the immune system on the physical level and provides great psychic protection on the emotional – energetic level. It helps one gather enough 'energetic distance and space' to discern what belongs to the self as a thought or energy and what actually originates from another. This distinction can help the wearer actually release energy back to Mother Earth to be transmuted into unconditional love or returned back to the source of the feeling or thought, with compassion and detachment, knowing this is a lesson that will help that soul to grow.

Turquoise helps empower the throat chakra by clearing it of old declarations (which can powerfully influence us at a subconscious level, even over the course of lifetimes, lodging vibrationally in our cells). It empowers us to realise responsibility for co-creating life on a day-to-day basis. This is our inner authority in action – our ability to choose, to honour our freedom and take responsibility for it. It supports us to let go of false notions of responsibility that would distract us from really living into our will, power, choice and freedom as human beings on this planet. The ability of Turquoise to connect us to our own inner spiritual authority, naturally awakening the path of spiritual leadership within us. This does not necessarily mean that we will take on spiritual responsibility for the path of another. Sometimes the most empowering leadership is that which leaves a person in touch with their own inner power simply by recognising that it is there. It does often mean that we become more visible to others, inspiring and assisting them by simply being who we are with strength and confidence. Living our truth can be an inspired, indirect form of spiritual leadership.

Turquoise doesn't just help us live and express our truths, it helps us to discern and realise what they are in the first place. For those that are sensitive and take in energy and thoughts of others without always consciously realising it, this is a very helpful stone. It helps to build the sense of self whilst offering respect, tolerance and recognition for the self and for others without minimising the self. It helps one recognise one's truth as being the right way for the self, and allowing others to find their way. A 'live and let live' approach to life will appeal to those souls who love freedom or who are learning to accept the freedom of each individual to live their own path, including the self.

It is when you acknowledge the authority of the divine in yourself that you are able to start recognising it in others. It becomes less frightening, less like something we try to project on to another, a teacher, guru or guide, and instead we can accept that helpers on the path are here to help, but we can still assume responsibility for our own lives and choices.

Turquoise helps us tune into our inner truths, to clear external distractions. It supports us to find this divine authority within and gain the strength and wisdom required to responsibly exercise that inner authority, that power of choice, in a constructive way. There is an energy of grace and divine love within Turquoise that seems to bestow special blessing upon those to whom it comes. It is like Mother Earth lends some of her protective power to those that wear it, helping them find refuge in her strength whilst supporting them as they exercise spiritual leadership and service through aligning their inner authority with divine will.

ABOUT THE ARCHANGEL GABRIEL

The name Gabriel means "God is my Strength". This Archangel helps us find strength through faith in the divine, through our own ability to know and speak our truths.

Perhaps Gabriel's most well known role is in the Christian tradition where it is taught that this Archangel was responsible for the Annunciation to the Virgin Mary that she was pregnant with the child Jesus. Although I heard this story as a child growing up and being educated in a Catholic primary school, I didn't really experience the Archangel Gabriel as anything other than a figure in a story until I was nearly twenty.

I was in a meditation class with my first spiritual teacher, when I encountered a silvery light in the form of a being, and I experienced a rite of baptism that I found quite extraordinary. I felt myself being lifted up, as though I was levitating in the middle of the sky. I saw a huge platinum chalice filled with sacred water being poured over my head, lifted by a massive being of light that I somehow knew to be the Archangel Gabriel. It felt as though a waterfall cascaded endlessly out of that chalice. It just poured and poured over me and through me, as though it was more light than water. I had flashes of Gabriel, who appeared as brilliant pure platinum light. I also witnessed myself being blessed in this meditative experience. It was so bright, there were flashes where I was blinded temporarily by the light, before the imagery would slip back into view for another few moments. I was confronted by how raw and ecstatic my body felt. For a young woman who was extremely controlled, the uncontrolled responses of my energy body, waving about in ecstatic bliss as this was taking place, was not a comfortable phenomena to witness. However I had enough sense to realise that this was outside of my conscious understanding and to just let it happen.

Years later, I became more comfortable with the encounter. With more experience I began to realise that the body responds to divine energy in these sorts of ways and it can actually be a confirmation that what is happening is genuine.

After that, it wasn't long before I began connecting more with the Archangels and their metaphysical associations, calling on them for sacred healing rituals. Gabriel and the element of water, of cleansing and blessing, became a standard angelic fixture in my healing room from then on.

What I didn't realise at the time, was that this meditative vision was an angelic gift. It was an initiation, a declaration that I was going to be blessed and assisted in my spiritual mastery of the water element this lifetime. The water element is traditionally considered the domain of the Archangel Gabriel and governs our emotions and creativity. The gift that this vision hinted at (though I didn't understand this until years later) was that my emotional and creative life would be keys through which I would grow spiritually. I felt a magnitude at the time of the experience that I couldn't articulate, and yet looking back, I realised that it set me on a healing path for the following eighteen or so years. Gabriel, associated with annunciation, baptism, blessing and the element of water were all combined in this experience. It was an annunciation without words, and a blessing, that would put me on a spiritual path of learning through the mysteries, challenges and gifts of the water element for a significant portion of time following.

The ecstatic responses of my energy body were signs of the blessing being received. The body responds to energy sometimes in a quite unnerving way. At least, it can be a bit of a shock for our minds to realise in that moment that the body is responding to something that we don't necessarily understand. I have had students that can surrender to this, arms waving in the air during a healing or blessing, having uncontrollable fits of laughter or even crying, and somehow it's all good fun even though they do not understand consciously exactly what is going on. Others however can become quite frightened by the sensations of their body responding (or not responding and becoming immobile, which is another possible response to high energy) without their conscious mind controlling the situation.

Our level of comfort depends on how much we trust. When we call on Turquoise and the Archangel Gabriel we can trust that it is safe to let go and let our body respond as it will, trusting that we are protected.

When the Archangel Gabriel appears, perhaps with divine trumpet poised for a blasting, it can be a divine call to explore the water nature – the feeling side, the heart, emotions, the unconscious mind and to open up to receiving the gifts within these parts of us and explore them. Gabriel's strength will help protect you on the journey, preventing you from feeling overwhelmed and allowing an easier process in finding your wisdom through your experiences and explorations of your water nature. Water has a huge amount of power – it sustains life and it moves mountains. It is good to have some protective wisdom with us when exploring such powerful forces, which is what Gabriel provides.

SOUL HEALING WITH TURQUOISE AND THE ARCHANGEL GABRIEL

There is a great story in the Jewish spiritual tradition that the Archangel Gabriel was ordered by God to destroy Israel, after becoming extremely annoyed, by pouring hot coals on them. Gabriel felt compassion for those that were incurring God's wrath, so ingeniously the Archangel requested that the slowest, laziest angel in heaven be the one to pass the hot coals on to him. This way they would be nearly cold by the time he threw them at the Earth, giving the Israelites a chance to escape certain death! God became cranky with Gabriel's defiance and Gabriel had an angelic demotion for a short time, until his astuteness won him back into divine favour and back into the upper echelons of the angelic hierarchy.

There are many elements that I love about this story. The idea of a lazy angel taking so long to pass hot coals that they become almost cold is quite amusing. Yet the part that appeals to me most is that the archangel followed his inner spiritual authority, defying the harsh power of God, and responding with compassion, even though it cost him some angelic prestige for a little while.

In the time I have spent in various spiritual communities over the years, several months here or a few days there, I have noticed a tendency that is quite compelling to many human beings to just follow those that they consider further along the spiritual path than they consider themselves to be. Yet any teacher that says, "You should just follow me," without encouraging that person to learn to heed their own inner knowing is going to create followers and dependents, rather than spiritually empowered human beings. We each have within us the divine spark, the guru – teacher – wise woman or wise man – and God and Goddess. That's quite a lot of divine authority within each one of us.

Whilst it is good to be receptive to suggestions of those that we trust, no living being can replace our own divine authority and responsibility for ourselves. We have been given the gift of free will. With that comes a responsibility to account for it, to learn from our choices and be OK with that. Perhaps we may choose to hand our power completely over to another, such as a spiritual teacher. Perhaps that will be a great learning experience, pleasantly or unpleasantly. The choice to do so, or not, rests with us.

The best that any wise soul can do is to help restore you to your own inner authority, creating a bridge to it until you are awakened to the point of realising all that you are. This is a journey of many lifetimes of preparation and we will have many loving teachers and helpers along the way, many of whom we may not fully recognise at the time. Sometimes we will feel that we are moving forward, sometimes we may worry that we are falling back. We will always be offered help to find our way to our ultimate truth, the realisation of the divine authority, the divine spark and truth that lies within us. It is to this inner divinity that we can surrender, safe in the knowledge that it will guide us in unconditional love.

Unlike angels, human beings were given free will and as a part of that divine gift is choice, authority and freedom. There is something about the courage, compassion and cleverness in the defiance of Gabriel in that story, that is inspiring to those of us that sense sometimes that all is not as it appears to be with teachers who may claim that we should surrender our inner authority to them. No matter what clever words, teachings or explanations may be summoned to justify such a request, when it all comes down to basics, each human being has free will and each human being has their own spiritual integrity and authority within that free will. Each human being is finding their way back to awakening that part of themselves and each being can be supported by enlightened beings along the way. Ultimately, every one of us has to accept the inner spiritual authority, and the spiritual responsibility for ourselves that this confers (along with spiritual freedom) for ourselves.

Learning to overcome self-doubt, to not confuse inner knowing with arrogance or an unwillingness to be receptive to the wisdom of others, is a way to tap into the spiritual authority within you. This part of you will let you know loud and clear when something serves and when it does not. It will help you make choices in your life that help you grow and become more radiant. It will be the part that says, "You know what, everyone else is freaking out about this situation in your life, but I am letting you know, this is just how it is meant to be right now – even though it makes no rational sense, it is OK, so stay with it and be patient." It is the inner spiritual authority that gives you the strength to live your truths, even in defiance of conventional 'wisdom' or those that you have empowered as authority figures in your life.

At some point, you will eventually become your own divine authority. You will learn to trust in your own surrendered divine connection, and have faith in yourself and your own relationship with life and the Divine. You may have great helpers, even gurus and beloved guides in spirit along the way, but the true path is always leading you to the divine within you. As this unfolds, more and more you realise that it is always you choosing how you are going to live, in accordance with your own truths or not. This is a level of soul development that takes you from enslavement to mass culture and social conditioning, into a place where you can join the co-creative forces of new culture. Here is where you become an agent of healing, liberation and creativity on this planet, stepping into spiritual leadership that is empowered and empowering to others.

SOUL HEALING – CLAIMING YOUR SPIRITUAL AUTHORITY

The souls who are pioneering new culture on this planet have the apparently paradoxical task of surrendering into divine will whilst becoming a spiritual authority unto themselves! Tricky? Not so much. These paths lead to the same final destination. What you will find as you journey within to your own heart, seeking out the truth and spiritual right of self-determination within you, is that this part IS one with divine will. You and the Divine are not separate. It is the same beat in your heart that inspires your passion and purpose that is the voice of the will of the Source. They are not at odds with each other.

I remember being taught by my first spiritual teacher that we had to learn to surrender the little will of our ego into higher will of the divine. At the time of that teaching, it seemed like I had to break my own will over and over again in order for this to happen. I ended up handing over a lot of spiritual power to my teacher as a result, not really trusting that I knew what was good for me. Whether she wanted it or not only she can know, but I had twisted myself into a mentally confused state where I distrusted myself out of fear of being in ego rather than soul. For a time I had unknowingly cast myself into what I could describe as a cult-like situation where I allowed another to do my thinking for me. Whilst I still have a lot of love and respect for that teacher, I knew that I had to break from her and reclaim my power and faith in my own self and my own choices. It was a painful process, difficult at times for all involved.

What I eventually discovered was that there was no conflict between my own truth and divine truth. What I wanted for myself the divine wanted also. What I needed to release was the false notion that I had to get it for myself – that I couldn't trust that the Universe was interested enough in me, and supportive enough of me, to hear what I yearned for and to deliver it in the most interesting, unique and perfectly wonderful way possible.

Once I softened in my erroneous view of essential conflict between higher and lower will (mostly through actual experiences of fighting myself to let go of desire and then having what was perfect for me arrive on my doorstep anyway), trust in my own inner spiritual authority began to grow rapidly.

Instead of looking outside of myself and asking "Should I do this?" or "Should I live here or be with this person or choose this course or this career?", I began to trust my own heart was guiding me and no-one could know more than the divine force within me what I was meant to do with my life. If another seemed to know more, then perhaps they were just listening more closely to my heart than I was, or they were full of hot air! You could say that I stopped tending to put my power outside of myself and began to take it within. I began realising that the divine was in my heart, operating through me and as me, just as much as it was growing stars and spinning planets.

The relief was enormous. Whilst some may find comfort in the notion of another guiding them in such a way that they hand over their power to them, I found it almost unbearably painful. It felt like such an untruth. I had to take the leap however of deciding to trust myself implicitly, and be willing to bear the responsibility if something didn't seem to work (which I also eventually realised just meant that my viewpoint was just too short-term, and I needed a little more patience and trust). It meant that I couldn't blame another if something didn't seem to be working, and nor could I turn to another to ask them to change something for me. I just had to trust that the divine loved me and was in me as much as any other being.

What happened in that shift was that my life became infinitely more interesting, more dynamic, freer and more fun. I had reclaimed my power of choice and my willingness to bear the uncertainty that comes with freedom and responsibility for our own spiritual life. Perhaps paradoxically enough I became more capable of genuine surrender into the divine love and power that lay within me and all of life. I wasn't handing power over to it, but I was feeling more connected, loved and supported by it as I made my choices and lived my life. Eventually the distinction between this sense of the divine and this sense of myself began to blend and merge.

HOW DO YOU KNOW IF YOU ARE HEALING
AT A SOUL LEVEL IN THIS WAY?

If you feel that others are holding you back, then you are holding yourself back. Why? Is it just that patience is needed as you grow and develop into being ready to be a vibrational match for what it is that you wish to create or receive? Or is it that you are letting old doubts in yourself about your ability to wisely handle power with responsibility and freedom stop you from really claiming the divine authority within you?

The truth is that we never really step into our divine power until we are ready, willing and able to do so. Others cannot bestow power upon us, much as we like to imagine that this is the case. It is like imagining a rabbit's foot brings us luck. It is our belief that makes it seem true, but it doesn't make it a truth. The most anyone can do is, as Khalil Gibran, the Lebanese mystic put it, "No man can reveal to you aught but that which already lay half asleep in the dawning of your own awakening".

If we allow life, the ultimate teacher, to impress upon us that which is needed to guide us into deeper connection with our own inner teacher, we will find the spiritual power and dignity within and move more swiftly towards the fullness of our being, inspiring others to do the same.

I have seen people rush from teacher to teacher, seeking, always seeking – looking for what is already within them. Rather than seeking support from the external teacher to find the teaching within, they seek the external teacher to be the divine for them. I accept that every phase of the path has something to offer us and serves divine purpose. As we move through this chapter, it may be that you are fast approaching, if not already mastering, the spiritual lesson of taking divine responsibility for yourself. You may find yourself awakening the depths of your own spiritual authority, strength and power as a result.

SOUL HEALING PROCESS –
THE DIVINE AUTHORITY WITHIN YOU

Choose a quiet place to sit comfortably, where you are able to speak without being disturbed.

Start by saying the following invocation:

"I call upon the Divine Angel of Turquoise and the Archangel Gabriel. I call upon the unconditional love, light and power of the Source that dwells within me, as I reclaim in purity my divine authority. Of my own free will, so be it!"

"I now choose, of my own free will to cut any ties to any spiritual authority figure that is holding me back from the next phase of my spiritual growth and development according to the highest good. I thank all such beings for their service and now choose to let go. I now dissolve and disintegrate any contract I ever made with such a being that they hold the projection of my divine authority for me. I now choose to accept my own spiritual power. With respect, I now release any such bind that has held the illusion of power over me. I choose to recognise and live into my own inner spiritual authority with unconditional love and acceptance. As a sovereign being of light, and through my own free will, so be it."

Close your eyes and focus on your breathing as you become aware of a beautiful angel with bright, wide wings emanating a soft Turquoise coloured light from his heart chakra. The light becomes more bright, clear and strong as you are drawn towards it. Allow the light to fill your own heart centre. As it rises naturally up towards your throat, imagine that your throat is shining bright, clear Turquoise light in all directions, as though you have a vibrant blue sun radiating in the centre of your throat chakra, crackling with energy.

Allow yourself to breathe in and out, releasing any old energy out of the throat in all directions. You may see, sense or feel old energies burning up in this bright blue sun, you may sense energies falling away or old cords snapping off. Just be patient and stay with the blue light and the breath for at least forty-four counts.

When you are ready, imagine that you can travel within that blue sun and you see within the powerful light of that inner sun, a very wise, spiritually advanced being. It may appear as a wizard, a wise woman, a shaman or simply as light.

This is an aspect of your own soul.

Allow yourself to spend some time just being with this soul aspect. Feel what it is like to trust in this being. Does this being have any messages for you? Do you feel certain feelings such as peace, trust, strength or self-confidence in the presence of this being?

This being will be unconditionally loving and you will feel that you have nothing to hide or be ashamed of or guilty about in the presence of this being. You will feel more of yourself and there will seem to be less problems and struggles in your life simply being in the presence of this aspect of your own divine essence.

Stay there and breathe until you begin to feel that you can blend with this being, becoming one together. Breathe for at least forty-four counts.

When you are ready say, "I choose to honour my own spiritual integrity and authority.

It is safe for me to be responsible for myself. I do not have to be perfect, I just need to trust. I trust myself! I trust life! I learn, I grow, I always know what I need to know, and if there is something that I do not understand, then I just need patience as I grow and then I will understand. I have all that I need deep within. It is safe for me to honour my own power and so now I begin."

Place your hands on your heart and then on your solar plexus chakra (around your abdominal area) and just relax for a moment as the bright blue light of the sun radiates through your entire body now. Breathe for another forty-four breaths, that bright, clear blue light radiant through your abdominal area and heart too, and flowing out on the exhalation through every part of your body, cleansing and empowering you in your own connection with divine power within you.

When you are ready, say "thank you" to yourself and touch your heart, knowing that you are not alone. You are in connection with the divine force that lies within, that unites you with all living things.

When you are ready, open your eyes. You have completed your soul healing session! Congratulations for taking such a brave step. Be kind and patient and enjoy your unfolding spiritual maturity. Well done, beloved.

PSYCHOLOGICAL-EMOTIONAL HEALING WITH ARCHANGEL GABRIEL AND THE ANGEL OF TURQUOISE: GABRIEL'S MOON CLEANSING

Often we don't think much of a psychic and emotional cleanse. Yet when we actually have one, we feel so amazing afterwards, so productive, flowing, happy and clear, we can wonder why we don't do it more often.

Perhaps this is because emotional and psychic dirt is cumulative. We might not notice anything is clogged or blocked until it becomes quite dramatic that we are not feeling so good. The more in tune we are with ourselves, the more we are used to feeling clear, the easier it is to sense when we need an energy clearing. In the same way that the body needs cleansing and we can feel better after a shower or a dip in the ocean, an emotional or psychic cleanse can help us feel more energised, well and happier within ourselves. It is also easy to do. It doesn't have to involve a trip to the ocean (though a swim in a relatively clean ocean is perhaps one of the best psychic and physical cleanses there is) and can actually be done in our own lounge room chair.

When you are attempting to outgrow a habit, whether that be a physical activity or a particular habit of thinking or belief, then you will need more rather than less cleansing. In such times, you are flushing the system out. You are attempting to clear the old and replace it with the new. Just as you would clean weeds out of a garden before planting new seeds, to ensure a stronger and healthier, faster growing plant, so too do you clean the system of the old energy before implanting new beliefs or behaviours for a better result.

When what you are reaching for is deeper connection and reliance upon your own spiritual authority there are going to be some layers of conditioning that you are best rid of, that will not be particularly helpful anymore. This cleansing is dedicated to that particular process.

HOW DO I KNOW IF I NEED HEALING IN THIS WAY AND AT THIS LEVEL OF MY BEING?

You may not consciously be aware that you are in the process of connecting with your own spiritual authority. You might not think in those terms. But you will know when this is happening if you find yourself asking for the opinions of other less and seeking out your own truths more. If you find that you are more interested in what you think or feel and less interested in the opinions that another may hold about your life, then you are taking this journey. If you are seeking your own creative voice, seeking to find your own style, your own lifestyle, what really ignites passion in you, then you are ready for this healing. If you are seeking your own personality or identity, your own vocation or life path, your own voice – literally in terms of how you express yourself, or symbolically in a style of writing, poetry, creative flair or even personal style – then you are taking this journey in some way.

The healing process below will help you on the journey. Do it as often as you instinctively feel you need it.

PSYCHOLOGICAL-EMOTIONAL HEALING PROCESS – GABRIEL'S MOON CLEANSING

If you have some Turquoise with you, place it on your body, or near your body, from the heart upwards to the crown of the head, or at any point that intuitively seems appropriate. If you don't have any Turquoise, you may like to open this book to page 27, which features the mandala for the crystal, and keep it close by while you complete this process.

Start by sitting or lying comfortably with both palms upwards, resting the backs of your hands on your knees or the floor if you are lying down.

Say, "I call upon the healing Angel of Turquoise."

Be aware of a radiant blue wave of light, rising up from the Earth and carrying you into an ocean of blue Turquoise energy. Allow yourself to swim in it, to bathe in it, to enjoy the healing energy and perceive that it is cleansing you on all levels, energetic and physical.

Say, "I call upon the healing Archangel Gabriel and the Power of the Moon."

You see a brightly glowing, massive angel with radiant white wings and luminous white robes, holding a massive full moon above his head. The energy of the angel and the moon shines down into the ocean of Turquoise energy, filling it with silvery flecks of pure light.

As you float on the Turquoise ocean, bath in the light of the angel and the moonlight dappling the surface. Let yourself be cleansed by the light.

Say, "I now choose to let go of any fear or doubt that surround my own inner authority. I choose to release any false responsibility for any lifetime where I believed I became too powerful or harmed others, or misled them, through use of my own spiritual authority. I forgive myself now and I respect the right of every living being to find their own power and make their own choices. I now choose, of my own free will, to surrender any guilt or shame I have ever held consciously or unconsciously about being powerful or spiritually authoritative in my own life. I now release any despair or doubt about my ability to be an authority in my life with wisdom and love. I allow myself to be guided by the All That Is that lies within my own heart and I accept that my own will, my own heart urging is the voice of the Divine expressing through me. I accept this inner guidance now. I release any block to that guidance from this or any lifetime, with forgiveness, grace and the power of choice. So be it!"

Let the energy of your words rise up into the moon above Gabriel's head, absorbing into them and turning it into a beautiful shade of blue. The blue light from the moon and the blue turquoise ocean create a soothing space where you feel accepting of yourself and your spiritual power and strength within.

Stay with the breath for at least forty-four counts as you are bathed in this blue world of peace and inner power, and when you are ready, simply open your eyes.

You have completed your healing process. Be patient and trusting as you take your journey into your own divine power, step by step.

PHYSICAL HEALING WITH TURQUOISE AND THE ARCHANGEL GABRIEL: HEALING THE EARS

What we are told, what we choose to hear or even not hear, but is spoken to us nonetheless, is recorded energetically in our ears. Over lifetimes our ear channels can become clogged with so much stuff that it is hard to hear our own inner voice.

I often describe to my students that hearing internal guidance is at times like learning to hear a soft triangle chiming amongst the cacophony of a loud rock band! What makes this easier is clearing out a lot of noise and the memory or records of noise that make it hard for us to hear clearly.

If we hear something negative about ourselves for long enough, it can be hard to even hear, let alone believe, a compliment that someone may give us on that same issue. Recently I was waiting to go into a yoga class when I struck up a conversation with a woman that I had recognised as a regular in the classes. We chatted for a moment before she said that both her and her mother came to the classes regularly and had labelled me as "the woman with the good body", not knowing my name. She complimented my shape, fitness, tone and 'right amount of curves'. I was so shocked, after having rather my fill of judgements about my body over the years that I honestly asked her if she was mistaken and perhaps talking about someone else! In a similar way, so too do we struggle to hear the reassuring voice of our internal divine guiding essence as it speaks to us lovingly on a daily basis when our ears are so used to hearing rough vibrations of doubt, fear, 'you can't', or 'you shouldn't', and shaming, angry, guilty or negative words around us, directed to us or to others. Just being in that energy can require a good cleaning out of the ears!

When the ears are energetically cleaner, it's easier to hear what is real. It is easier to hear our selves think and it's easier to think more consciously from a loving connection to our hearts than reacting from a place of negative habit.

HOW DO I KNOW IF I NEED THIS HEALING PRACTICE?

If you feel that you can't hear yourself think, that there is so much going on in your own head that you aren't even sure what you think or feel, then it is time to give those ears an inner cleanse.

Inner ear cleansing is helpful in many situations. If you have been in an abusive situation in short or long-term scenarios, such as a relationship, then you will benefit from an inner ear cleanse. Likewise if you have had any involvement in a cult or organisation that attempted to dictate your beliefs about people in the organisation or how you should behave, donate money, be or speak, then an inner ear cleanse will be of healing benefit. A more mundane yet still important example is when you have just had enough of television jingles repeating in your head, or you can't seem to get another person's comments about you out of your head, then you need a clearing. An inner ear spiritual cleanse will support you in that clearing process.

Also at other times, you will have the sense that it will just feel really good. At such moments, it is likely that your guidance really wants to talk to you and will be able to be heard by you much more accurately and easily if your inner ears are cleared out, as this is a prelude to clairaudience (or inner clear hearing, the faculty through which we hear our guidance speak) too.

So if you are feeling this, or hearing this, trust it and let yourself have some time with this simple and powerful cleansing process.

PHYSICAL HEALING PRACTICE – GABRIEL'S EAR CLEANSE

Lie comfortably with a piece of Turquoise (even if in jewellery) lying on the pillow beside each ear. It can touch your outer ear or just be near it. Make sure the piece is large enough that it won't fall into your ear. If you don't have a piece of Turquoise, open the book to page 27, which features the Turquoise Crystal Angel Mandala and have it next to you as you complete this process.

When you are ready, say the following:

"I call upon the healing power of the Angel of Turquoise and Archangel Gabriel's Trumpet of Peace. Please help me clear all cellular records and memories, energetic imprints and blocks that obstruct clear inner hearing of divine truth within my physical ears now. I ask for this with mercy and with kindness. So be it!"

Close your eyes and focus on your breath. Imagine that within your head there are two small angels with trumpets made of Turquoise. One in each ear. They may tingle a little!

The Turquoise trumpets make a soft sound of peace and send cleansing turquoise light out of each ear canal, sending gentle cleansing vibrations through each ear, the entire part of the inner ear, washing them out, with outwards flowing energy.

As you breathe in, try to hear your inhalation. Each inhalation is the tiny angel in each ear breathing in. As you exhale, the angels are blowing through their Turquoise trumpets, sending healing energy, sacred sound, and turquoise light out of your ears.

Let the energy of your ears become clearer and softer, more open and protected as the angels cleanse and create a sacred field of protection with Turquoise energy around your ears, allowing you to deflect negativity and release old trauma from the ears now.

Stay with this inhalation and exhalation, with the angels in your ears cleansing from a place of love, for at least forty-four breaths.

When you are ready, say "thank you" and gently remove the stones from your body.

Pause for a moment and then open your eyes. You have finished your healing process.

PRAYER – AFFIRMATION

To invoke the healing power of Turquoise and Archangel Gabriel at any time, you can repeat the following affirmation quietly in your mind, or aloud.

"I AM the Radiant Leading Light of Divine Truth, Love and Power."

12.

PIETERSITE (Knowledge)
and ANGEL RAZIEL (Mysteries)

THE GIFT OF HIGHER UNDERSTANDING

SPIRITUAL GUIDANCE FROM THE ANGEL OF PIETERSITE
AND THE ANGEL RAZIEL

What you see depends upon from where you look. That which seems chaotic or to be feared, through higher knowledge, becomes divine order, to be revered. We help you realise that in this divine game of life, all is an expression of the sacred divine name. You just need to know the rules by which to play, which will empower you with loving knowledge as you find your way. We share with you the sacred spiritual keys, to help you unlock the ancient mysteries. To see within the chaos the order, within the struggle, you'll find the peace, and your limited perceptions you can then release. To find the freedom that exists within you right now, to be all that you can be – we'll show you how! It all starts with correcting some thoughts in the mind, in order to get in touch with the heart and learn to be kind. Then taking a step in faith beyond what you think you know, you'll open your heart and grow. As we lead you to the truth that there is nowhere God is not, deep in the divine heart, you have never been forgot. We'll help you remember how to live your life and win, receive us now and let these teachings in! Together we will journey into worlds ancient and new, and you'll realise in your heart, everything that which you know to be true – that you are here on this Earth to grow and be free, to choose to surrender to your own divinity.

PICTURING PIETERSITE

Pietersite is one of the relatively newer discovered stones in the gem marketplace. It is my sense that we discover stones as a gift from Mother Earth when we are ready as a species to work with their power. Pietersite was reportedly discovered in the early 1990's and didn't go on the market until later in that decade.

Mined mostly from Namibia in Africa, recently mines of Pietersite have also been found in China. The stone ranges in colour tones from warm brown tones, sometimes with tinges of red, to blue and grey tones, though the latter is more rare. It can also include partially translucent white or colourless segments with a slightly milky opacity. Overall, Pietersite can have a rich golden sheen to it with a reflective quality known as chatoyance (or cat's eye). This is seen in other stones as well, like Tigers Eye. In Pietersite, rather than the more typical banding, there are swirls that make it feel like you are peering into an endless storm, or gazing at a distant planet, seeing the swirling, living atmosphere reflected back to you in the stone.

HEALING PROPERTIES

The appearance of holding a storm in a stone gives us a clue to Pietersite's power. It is sometimes called "The Tempest Stone" and associated with the storm element which brings radical change, activates and cleanses all the energy centres in the body and facilitates deep spiritual cleansing.

When I first saw this stone, I fell in love with it immediately. I was transfixed by its beauty and aliveness, and recognised its power. That being said, there are times when I cannot wear it for long periods of time without needing to remove it from my person, especially if I am feeling more sensitive on that day. It is a powerful stone and it can facilitate great change. If you are already open, responsive and an adaptable personality, with a lot of natural storm energy within you (and you'll know if this is the case because you will feel as though you are always transforming and changing within or you'll constantly have a lot of change or upheaval in your physical or emotional life) then Pietersite might feel too destabilising for you at certain times, and you'll want to monitor how much you use it. Trust yourself and your own body. You'll know when you don't want to wear something, because you'll keep just taking the stone off or will have difficulty placing the stone on in the first place, dropping it or being unable to do up the clasp of the necklace, for example. That just means you are receptive to that stone and you've had enough for now. There will be a time when you want to put it back on again and that's fine too.

Pietersite is said to be a shaman's companion stone, but you don't have to be a shaman in the traditional sense to benefit from the ability of the stone to help you enter altered states quickly and easily. This can be used to deepen meditation, to help you gain access to answers that you need through meditation and vision quests which we will explore in the healing practice section of this chapter.

Another healing quality of Pietersite is that it helps you live your truth. I am extremely passionate about embodying teachings. There are plenty of people who have a lot to say, and maybe even a lot to say about how they are already masters of their teachings. I remember one spiritual teacher saying that she was a 'student of her own teachings' which I thought was humble and realistic of her.

Pietersite helps you walk your talk. One of my students once said that we teach what we most need to learn. It has been my journey thus far that I learn so that I am empowered to teach. Pietersite helps keep us authentic as we embody what we learn. One of the greatest compliments that a student has ever given me was from a lovely young Czech woman, with a very kind and generous heart, who said that when she needed guidance, she didn't have to remember exactly what I had said to her at any given time, she would just think of me and the guidance would open up in her heart.

This is what Pietersite helps bestow upon our soul – the ability to be what it is that we are teaching or sharing with others – a word for it is authenticity. It isn't about being perfect, it's about being real and coming from our centre in how we live in the world. As a healer, as a mother or a father, brother, sister, friend or teacher, just as a person, Pietersite helps you really live your truth in a way that not only helps you, but touches and inspires others when they even just think of you.

One of the most beautiful healing properties of Pietersite is that it connects you to a loving source of spiritual guidance (there are levels of spiritual guidance and the more unconditionally loving guides belong to the higher levels, and more trustworthy levels I might add, of guidance for humanity). It helps us do this by shifting and dissolving conditioning that is inauthentic. This might be conditioning that we have subconsciously taken on by the media, advertising, cultural values that don't actually resonate with our inner spiritual truths and so on. So if you do begin to work with Pietersite, prepare to feel a little angry (or a lot of angry) as you shed those elements of conditioning from within your being and liberate some more space for your authentic soul presence and spiritual connection to move in to your body and your life.

ABOUT THE ANGEL RAZIEL

The name Raziel means "secret of God" and this angel has quite a lot of speculation surrounding him, concerning the Book of Raziel, a sacred text that he is said to have given to Adam to help him survive and flourish when he was cast out of the Garden of Eden. I believe that this is symbolic of Raziel's special gift to us – that of higher understanding.

This is needed when we are living in the density of the physical world where it can be easy to forget that we are divine souls having a human experience. Instead we slide into the sleepy state of consciousness where we judge ourselves and others, feel fear, anxiety and loneliness and we generally lose conscious awareness of our ability to create reality.

When I connected consciously with Raziel to write this chapter something unexpected happened. I suddenly felt clear guidance to go back and check for errors in two other chapters, which I did. I made changes, guided to the pages almost automatically and a theme that I wasn't sure was exactly on the money, so to speak, when I was writing it suddenly presented itself in a revised version that was spot on. It was just so clear and obvious. Insights started to pour through and I felt not like someone who had been working intensively and needed a delicate day, but instead I felt able to summon the energy to complete the tasks on my writing schedule because the information and understanding I needed was already in my mind.

This is how I feel a lot of the time, but there are days when I have been working very hard and I am in need of a break, but for some reason I cannot just step away and I need to find the energy to continue. Pietersite is said to be of benefit in such times, being a stone that supports a person who feels exhausted but cannot take a break right at that moment. Raziel provided a similar service to me the moment I called upon him. It was the gift of flow that comes with knowledge simply being available instantly. When one has a tired mind, and it is not perhaps practical to meditate or have a nap, this can be incredibly helpful.

The Angel Raziel is said to bring the understanding of the mysteries, of ancient secrets that most know not of, and to share them with those who ask from a place of unconditional love. There is a saying that knowledge is power. With power we can create or destroy. The greater the power, the more considerable its positive or negative effect can be – not just for others but for ourselves as karma will always ensure that we experience all sides of what it is that we create in the world. It is a wise and sensible practice when calling upon the power of knowledge from Raziel that you phrase it as a request not just for knowledge, but for higher understanding.

Higher understanding takes us beyond knowledge. It takes us towards wisdom, towards a place where we can utilise what we know for our soul to grow. When this happens we are turning whatever the situation was that required us to sort something out into a growth opportunity. It is more than just having knowledge, it is shifting our perspective beyond the level through which there was a problem to begin with! Albert Einstein has been credited with saying that you cannot solve problems with the same level of thinking that created them – and so it is with higher understanding. It takes us out of the playing field, into a broader perspective with a more helpful perception, out of problems and into solutions. We have to be ready to let go of what we think we know and how we have interpreted the situation (and the need to be 'right') but if we can do this, we won't end up in the same situation yet again with someone else in future. Instead we'll outgrow it and move onwards and upwards into far more pleasing and fulfilling life situations.

This is the gift of higher understanding from Raziel. It is knowledge that empowers growth. It is the difference between knowing that you are struggling with a person in your workplace, for example, because they struggle to accept your gentle nature, and realising that it is your own struggle with your gentle nature, your own need to find a way to honour your gentleness from a place of strength, that is the issue. As you find your own strength and protection, for that gentle part of you, without hardening yourself but without expecting that others take care of you because you are gentle at heart, the issue with your colleague falls away. You have used higher understanding to transform yourself and the situation.

Higher understanding as a gift from Raziel is empowerment to transform. That is the storm element of Pietersite with some added Angelic potency. Together they are an extraordinarily empowering and powerful combination for divine healing.

SOUL HEALING WITH PIETERSITE AND THE ANGEL RAZIEL

There is a certain ability that the soul possesses, which is to be the stillness at the centre of any transition. The transition may evoke great chaos and upheaval in our lives and yet still contain a peaceful wisdom deep within it. The peace is the order that is unfolding through the change, the divine will that is driving it, and the wisdom that is unfolding through the upheaval. Another way to describe it is the breakthrough that will be enabled as a result of a breakdown. As the old proverb goes, what the caterpillar calls the end of the world, the master calls the butterfly.

Connection with the soul in the midst of deep life transitions, especially those that are quite powerful, can be like stepping into the centre or the eye of the cyclone. All around you may be instability, structures that you have known and relied upon are being torn up or dislodged through a force so far beyond your control. So you may choose to give in and flow with it. You can enter into a peaceful zone where you are just letting go and letting God, as the expression goes.

At the time of writing, I have a client who is going through this process. She is a brave and articulate soul who has done an immense amount of inner work over many years, peeling back the layers of who she imagined herself to be and how she thought she had to be in the world to find out a deeper truth, a more pure experience of her true self. It is beautiful to witness. She becomes more radiantly herself with each passing month. It is excruciating at times to go through because whatever she held onto to define herself, she is allowing to be taken from her. Sometimes this happens by her own hand as she lets go of this situation or that belief about herself, and sometimes it happens by forces beyond her immediate, conscious control. She is, by her own description, happy for no good reason.

Even with the crazy upheaval of her once-cherished beliefs and life-circumstances flying around her head, whipped up and out of her life by the force of her own soul storm, healing transformation and spiritual cleansing, she is identified enough with her own soul presence that she can recognise a state of peaceful acceptance that is beyond her ego. She sees beyond that questioning part that is wondering what on Earth she is doing to let all this happen! Why? Why would you step out of so much that society accepts and applauds?

Yet this soul is on a quest for her own truth, her own highest destiny and is courageous enough to let the divine storm of the soul move through her life. It is only by learning to identify with our calm centre, whilst all else is thrashing wildly about, that we can find a peaceful way through – not only into calmer waters but eventually becoming the butterfly to our caterpillar, evolving through great (sometimes stormy) personal transformation to emerge in a new form of divine beauty.

Interestingly enough, it is within the strongest storms that the eye becomes clearest and most peaceful. It is the same with the soul. I believe this is why I can get in a huff about a relatively inconsequential matter (fortunately I usually get over it pretty quickly) and yet remain relatively peaceful during some of the most challenging life experiences. In these bigger moments I am able to find a centre within me to 'hang on my cross' until whatever needs to be outgrown is outgrown. It can be deeply painful for the ego, but liberating too, as the soul grows so strong that it becomes more powerful than our resistance or fear. We learn to surrender into our own divine healing process and trust more. This gives us access to the divine power of the storm element. This is what the soul healing in this chapter is about. Learning to centre ourselves in the eye of the storm, so we can dive into our transformational processes and benefit from them, whilst not feeling completely ravaged by the experience. the purpose of this healing is to be able to find peace within ourselves and our lives, even if everything is not always peaceful around us.

SOUL HEALING – HONOURING STORM WISDOM

Claiming a body on this planet is actually a pretty big deal. Mostly we probably don't think like that, but there is quite a high demand for a human body from those souls who want to 'go to Earth school' and live in human form. Those of us that have a body this time won the spiritual lottery. We tend to forget all this when we are dealing with the ups and downs (sometimes many downs in particularly challenging periods of growth) of daily life. Why would there be such a high demand for human incarnation, as opposed to other spiritual experiences? Well life on Earth is like the most elite spiritual boot camp the soul can enter into. To graduate from this school involves total mastery over the densest elements of existence, over fear itself in all of its forms. The skills that are developed through that process are extraordinary and the soul itself becomes exceptionally powerful through the journey to that spiritual attainment, becoming a beacon of light and hope for all other souls still taking the Earth school training, a bit like graduate tutors. Life also becomes much more fun in the process, which is a nice added bonus, if one were needed.

There is, I believe, a highly mistaken and dangerous notion that once you grow spiritually, life becomes an easy breezy existence. What is more true is that we become capable of operating in a different way. We may be presented with what, from the outside, may seem like bigger mountains to climb, or it may seem to others that our lives become effortless. Internally as the soul becomes more capable, it tends to assume more spiritual responsibility. It lifts more weight, so to speak, but with less effort because it is aligned with greater power, to live more in the centre of the storm, so there is peace, rather than so much suffering. There will still be wobbly moments perhaps, I have witnessed such humanity still alive and kicking in some of the most enlightened teachers I have been lucky enough to encounter in physical form, but there is another way of deep trust and the soul that has been gifted with storm wisdom, learns to rely more upon trust, claiming more peace in the process.

HOW DO YOU KNOW IF YOU ARE HEALING AT A SOUL LEVEL IN THIS WAY?

When I started a four-month intensive Chi Gung training process in early 2012, I was introduced to what was called 'hard style Chi Gung'. I had heard amazing things about the course from a friend of mine who had done the course and experienced great physical healing and spiritual growth as a result. As my friend explained what the course entailed, her enthusiasm grew, quite possibly in proportion to my growing doubts! We would be encouraged to abstain from various foods and practices for the duration of the course. No chocolate, sex, spicy food, coffee or wine (to mention just a few of the 'guidelines' that painted an aghast expression on my partner's face as I told him that I planned to do the course and asked if he felt inclined to join me). We would be required to do an hour-long daily practice without fail unless we were sick or menstruating. The exercises involved throwing oneself again brick walls, doing push ups on our fingertips and performing hand stands, to name a few rather intimidating prospects. At the end of the process we would spend a weekend with the master where we would get up every two hours for the first twenty-four hours and do Chi Gung exercises with him. After that we would demonstrate our new power by chopping through slabs of granite with our bare hands and snapping chopsticks by jamming them into our throats.

As you could perhaps imagine, a peace-loving, yoga and meditation devotee with a preference to love rather than fight found all this rather dazzling and more than a little intimidating. On top of this, my friend explained that our energy field would be opened up and we would become more sensitive than we already were (and I was already quite a lot of sensitive!). All our emotional rubbish would come pouring out – even if we had done lots of work on ourselves. Old bits would come out that we didn't even know where in there.

The plus side? Our energy would become more powerful. We would grow and replenish our Chi. Mine had been depleted over years and years of giving healings and placing mighty demands upon myself in various parts of my life. I knew that I needed to learn how to replenish my energy from someone who had mastered that level of skill, and I had not met anyone who understood what I needed to be able to do that. I would, in short, learn what no-one else had been able to teach me. I felt like I would get answers to questions that I had been asking, to no avail, for years on my path. That learning was worth facing all the insecurities that even just the description of the course brought up for me.

So I decided I would commit and throw myself in the deep end and just trust. Which I did and it was an amazing, challenging, life-changing and truly gracious experience. I learned so much through going through the process and I got the answers to my questions. I have no idea if the others who trained felt the same way about the course, but I do know many people repeat the training and if you ever have a chance to study with Master Zhao (at Tiandi Qigong) when he is in Sydney (he is at the time I am writing this chapter, in China, meditating in solitary confinement for months at a time, and I have to say, that whilst he is in deep meditation, hibernating like a bear, his soul is glowing like a radiant sun right now and it warms my heart) then seriously consider it.

For now, I want to share one element of that experience with you which will help you know if you need the Storm Wisdom Soul healing.

On the first weekend of the training program, we learned the twelve cycles – twelve different exercises that would clear and build our energy. The first exercise involved speaking a statement that translated roughly as "strong as a mountain, stable as a tower" whilst kneeling in a deep squat position with the arms held in a certain way. It was to build strength. A squat for thirty seconds or a minute when you exercise regularly is not too bad. Two minutes might be a bit of a wobble factor, but the recommended five minutes was something else. Zhao laughed at us as we all wondered if we could do that, saying that he had once done the pose for four hours with his master as a part of his training. I didn't doubt it for a moment.

What he taught us was that you didn't do these strength poses through typical Western approaches of just flogging yourself and using blunt willpower. Instead you learned to find the peace in the posture, not unlike a yoga practice. In this Chi Gung style there was an additional element which was learning to call in higher energy to support you. As Zhao taught us, you call in the energy of the master (which is unconditionally loving) and your body relaxes and the posture becomes easier. To be in that state of unity with the master energy, which is essentially the peace of the soul, is an amazing experience. You can feel the effect of it even in your physical strength. It is one of the quickest ways for me to know if I am divinely connected in a conscious way or still in my mind. It takes about three seconds to determine. If I am not in connection, that posture will feel like it is impossible and even a minute will just seem like so long. When I am in connection, I sink into a timeless space where there is so much peaceful pleasure in that posture, you almost don't want it to end, such is the feeling of peaceful expansion and strength without effort.

I used this exercise to get me through one of the most professionally and spiritually demanding times of my life early in 2012. I had so much happening there were times when my mind felt as if it could either snap or become instantly enlightened. Such was the pressure my ego was under to surrender and surrender and surrender again!

I had to continually surrender identification with the creative chaos and the huge energy that I felt pouring through me whilst I grew big enough to receive the energy I asked for that my visions could manifest. I had to find a place of peace from which I could allow great complexity to unfold without drowning in anxiety because I couldn't control it and didn't know how it would all turn out. This exercise helped me make conscious physical connection with the loving peace that would sustain me, taking me into the eye of the storm so to speak. It felt like a lifeline to me at times. I would stand in that centre of peace and all around me I could feel the Earth shaking (which is undoubtedly what my poor ego felt at the time, as it was forced to surrender into what felt like larger and larger leaps of trust). To attempt to take on that load without continual spiritual growth into surrender would have been a fast road to a big mental breakdown!

The connection is what takes it from striving to divine peace, what takes it from overload to allowing the flow. This is when you know you will benefit from soul healing through storm wisdom. The connection is the stepping into the centre of the storm, the peaceful centre where all struggle falls away and effort is surrendered. The doing still happens but it no longer feels like it is of your own will. You feel like the wave being moved by the ocean, so much power is pumping through you. There is no thought, just peacefulness. If you need more of this feeling in your life, to help you move through a phase, a project, a life lesson and so on, then yes, this soul healing process is for you.

SOUL HEALING PROCESS – HONOURING STORM WISDOM

Choose a quiet place to sit comfortably, where you are able to speak without being disturbed.

Start by saying the following invocation:

"I call upon my own divine soul, the Angel of Pietersite and the Angel Raziel. Namaste beloveds. With unconditional love, I call upon storm wisdom, and I call upon the peaceful centre of all that is. I choose to surrender into higher wisdom any situation that no longer serves my highest spiritual destiny on this planet. In this body, I surrender the painful struggle that I am having with this situation of (name anything you want to resolve in your life) ... Through unconditional love and divine wisdom, I invoke this now with mercy and grace. So be it!"

"I now choose, of my own free will to step into the peaceful centre that lays within all, to be more in oneness with my own divine soul and to receive the divine assistance of beloved Raziel and Pietersite to help me do this now, so be it."

Close your eyes and focus on your breathing.

Imagine drawing an inhalation right into your heart chakra in the centre of your chest. As you do so, become aware of the sense of a peaceful field of light growing around you, starting at your heart and blossoming outwards. There is silence and space in this room, with a light and airy atmosphere. It is very, very still now. Underneath any noise or distraction around you, there is stillness. And quiet. So quiet and still that you can feel your heart beat, all the way down to the soles of your feet. It is so quiet and still that you can hear or sense your own heart beat reverberating through your entire being, like a gentle drum beat echoing in an open quiet room.

Stay in this peaceful place, sensing that its edges extend to surround your body. Notice how large this field of peace is around you. Does it extend just beyond your skin, or does it fill the entire room that you are in? Just notice what feels truthful for you and stay there for at least seven breaths.

When you are ready, follow the breath into the heart, down through your body and out through the soles of your feet. Imagine that beneath your feet and just beyond the edges of your peaceful centre, there is a massive universe of stars and rich deep grey blue night opening up before you. It expands and unfolds, unwrapping itself in your awareness until it is all around the edges of your peaceful energy field. There is a cosmos there, swirling patterns of stars and comets creating trails of light and colour. It is alive with energy and passion! There is so much movement, energy and power.

Stay connected with your peaceful energy field whilst witnessing this, continuing to focus on the breath and remaining detached as you rest in peaceful stillness. Remain centred and quiet even whilst appreciating with some awe, the universal ballet happening beneath your feet and all around you. A melee of lights and stars in constant play with each other. As the stars and lights beneath your feet explode and create new stars and lights, you feel more and more peaceful and calm within your body. The more you relax, the more impressive and beautiful the cosmic energy becomes around you, growing in power but not disturbing you at all.

Stay with this sensation for seven breaths.

Become aware of a massive angelic being arising out of the swirling colours and stepping into the peaceful eye of the cosmic storm around you now. He inclines his head gracefully towards you and you feel a sense of great light entering your being, causing your closed eyes to roll back slightly in your head as energy flows upwards towards the crown chakra, resting at the top of your head. Allow the light to flow out through the top of your head forming a tunnel of light that extends from your crown, far and wide out into the universe.

Descending into this tunnel of light at the crown of your head now is your own divine soul energy, which you may see, sense or feel as a light, colour or sound, even as a geometric pattern, or organic shape. Raziel helps to guide your soul light into connection with your body, as it flows in through the top of your head, all the way down to your heart, and then down through your feet, into the Earth. Be aware of yourself as existing within a great tube of light now, fanning down from above your head and fanning out through the soles of your feet, with you in the centre of the tube of light, growing until it is wider than your body. Let the light flow and feel the presence of the Angel with you as you surrender your thoughts and simply bask in this light.

Stay here for at least forty-four breaths and when you are ready, say, "Thank you and so be it!" Become aware of your fingers and toes by moving them slightly, stretching your arms and legs. When you are ready, open your eyes.

You have completed your soul healing process. Let the effect of it continue to unfold at a deep, cellular level and be open to fresh perspectives, ideas and ways of looking at situations in your life. The more unusual or different that they are, the more that they suddenly just occur to you in the midst of living your day-to-day life, the more likely it is that these are impressions of your own soul gifting you with the fresh insight of higher understanding. You'll know this for sure when the insights you gain help you move out of resistance or struggle, into a place of peaceful acceptance. Often humour about the situation also helps you let go and feel free of the pain that once surrounded the situation.

PSYCHOLOGICAL-EMOTIONAL HEALING WITH ANGEL RAZIEL AND THE ANGEL OF PIETERSITE: INSIGHT THROUGH PIETERSITE

One of the first lessons that I learned from my very first spiritual teacher was that higher guidance can't impress itself upon a mind that is already made up. Learning to be mentally flexible is an essential step in your personal growth process if you want to establish a clearer conscious connection to your guidance and allow them to help you get out of your own way and make life a bit easier for yourself.

This perhaps doesn't sound so hard. The difficult part is often identifying the opinion that we have and realising that it is just an opinion, not a higher truth. Believing that a situation is the way it is, or has to be a problem or a struggle, has to be a burden, is simply an opinion. There is no higher truth in that opinion, it is just one way of believing something to be – and there are always alternative opinions to be found if we care to look for them. If we feel stuck in a situation, it is likely that we could use some fresh insight of higher perspective to help us get unstuck. What is required for this to happen is mental flexibility, a willingness to bear the uncertainty of letting go of what we think we know, in order to be open to seeing things in a different way.

I had an experience of this early on in 2012 with a woman who had asked me to sing mantra and teach chants at a dance class she was running. I love dance, having run divine dance classes of my own some years ago. I also love to chant. So even though I felt a distinct sense of foreboding being in this woman's presence, I decided (heroically or stupidly, or perhaps a bit of both) that I would treat this discomfort as solely my own shadow material and go ahead and work with her. I thought I could sort out whatever it was within me that was reacting to her with a desire to keep her at arm's length, and I knew I would grow from the experience.

As I am sure is not a surprise to you, it did turn out to be a great learning experience for me and I did grow. However, it wasn't the most pleasant growth experience. I experienced some extremely nasty energy coming at me from this woman towards the end of our involvement. At the time I knew I needed to step away from working with her. I found little joy in being around her and although I loved working with the students in the class, and made some quite profound connections with many of them, it didn't really feel like

I was with my tribe. Her behaviour towards me shouldn't have surprised me, as over the course of the five weeks that I had agreed to work with her, every other person that she invited to come and work with her she had spoken negatively about behind their back whilst being delightful to them in person. I was more than a little uncomfortable with this, and wondered if anyone else noticed this quality and found it disturbing. Still, when she turned on me, I was disappointed, and more than a little angry.

Eventually I realised that I was attracting this lack of integrity because I wasn't honouring my own integrity which would have had me step back from working with this woman in the first place. Not out of judgement of her, but out of respect for my own values which I sensed were very incompatible with this woman's vibration.

Not long after this I was offered another chance to combine dance and chant in a very different way, with a very different woman, whom I respect and connect with deeply. Together we have a lot of fun and the classes we have taught together have been a growth experience for me in a much more loving and joyful manner because to work with this particular colleague aligns with my integrity.

I do acknowledge the courage that I had in not shying away from that which felt uncomfortable to me because I wanted to be open to personal growth. Through the experience with the woman who originally asked me to guest teach in a series of her classes, I did reclaim a more extroverted side of my personality which I hadn't expressed since being a teenager. This was helpful as it led to much more emphasis on performance in my work, which helps me reach out to others who might not otherwise find me or my work. Yet I also needed to find the higher understanding that would help me forgive myself for being a bit naive in trusting this person and not choosing to grow in gentler ways.

What helped me was a gift from my higher guidance. It was a gift of higher perception that came in a split second, in a humorous way, and with some giggles. This is quite often how my higher guidance, which I see as connected to my own higher self or soul, helps me out. I asked, "What is my involvement with this soul at this stage in my spiritual development? How can I deal with this?"

My guidance responded with a flash of humour saying that our souls had 'played cowboys and indians together over many lifetimes' and showed me an image of two children in dress ups chasing each other around a yard.

It made me laugh.

I felt my seriousness and concern, my anger at the behaviour of this woman and my own naivety soften and I just laughed. Our souls were playing a game of growth, and that is all it was – a game of growth together. It had no more reality to it, despite how real it may have felt at the time, than an imaginary world created by two children playing dress ups.

This viewpoint helped me call my power back from judgement of her and myself. I let go of the view from where I had stood and looked from a much higher perspective, which afforded me a more liberating and playful view. As per usual with higher guidance, hours of self-analysis and reflection were trumped by a little levity laced with deep truth, which took about two seconds of Earth time to deliver.

This is the gift of insight. When it is genuine you will know it because it will transform you from the inside out. It changes things. Knowledge is one thing but the gift of higher understanding is something else altogether. As a result of this insight, I immediately cut off involvements with another group that had a similar vibration to this woman. I did it firmly and quickly but with respect. I instantly felt more energy available to me and I realised that this time I was mastering the lesson with more dignity, grace and respect. That is the gift of insight. It can uproot a deep psychological block in an instant and empower you to proceed differently. It's a bit like you suddenly 'get' the point of the particular game you are playing, learn the rules, and you are free to just go for it, rather than muddling around as you try to work it all out on your own.

HOW DO I KNOW IF I NEED HEALING IN THIS WAY AND AT THIS LEVEL OF MY BEING?

We may think that we are getting something, a learning or lesson, but if it keeps popping up – perhaps with different people or situations, but with the same feeling for us – then we can guarantee that a higher perspective could help.

Perhaps you feel like you aren't getting a particular learning at all! You may feel as though you are stuck in a rut, or having the same record repeating over and over again and you just seem to be spinning your wheels and not touching the ground with any traction, not getting anywhere. A flash of insight could be just what the divine doctor ordered to get your soul on the mend and your energy flowing in more constructive directions.

PSYCHOLOGICAL-EMOTIONAL HEALING PROCESS – INSIGHT WITH PIETERSITE

If you have some Pietersite with you, even in the form of jewellery, place it on your body, or near your body, at any point that intuitively seems appropriate. Alternatively, you can simply leave this book open to page 28, which features a Crystal Angel Mandala for Pietersite in full colour. You will also need a pen and paper (perhaps your journal if you have one). You are welcome to have coloured markers, crayons or pencils as well.

Start by sitting comfortably with both palms upwards, resting the backs of your hands on your knees or the floor if you are lying down.

Say, "I call upon the healing Angel of Pietersite and the wise Angel Raziel. Please be with me, beloved crystal angels, and bestow upon me the gift of insight, of higher understanding that liberates me from the grip of my ego and helps me resonate at the level of soul, that I may be free from attachment and struggle, and grow with less effort and more glee."

Close your eyes for at least seven breaths and focus on your heart. Imagine a storm raging in your heart which you walk through, towards the centre of your heart which is peaceful, open and clear. The crystal angels are helping you. Just step one foot after the other towards the calm centre of your heart. Take your time and you may get there quickly or it may be quite a struggle. You will get there! Let your crystal angels lift you there and place you right in the centre of the calm eye, right at the centre of your heart, if you cannot get there yourself.

Say, "I choose to reside in the clear eye of serenity, dwelling eternally in the centre of my heart. The home of my higher understanding and wisdom pure and true, I open myself to receive the insight I need. So be it."

Now pick up your pen and paper (or journal) and begin to write. Don't think or analyse. Just let the words flow, whether you understand them clearly or not right now does not matter. Like dreams, guidance can make more sense when you sit with it for the coming days or weeks, although often it can be immediately clear too. Just let it be as it is, knowing it is perfect for you.

Stay with your heart awareness and contemplate what you would like to receive insight about, then write a brief title for that relationship, person or situation. For example, it might be "situation with person X" or "my job".

Place both hands on that piece of paper now, and imagine breathing wisdom straight from the clear eye of your heart, out of your hands, into the page for at least three breaths.

Then pick up your pen and start to answer the following questions. If you have listed more than one situation for which you would like to receive insight, complete the list of questions for one situation, and then the next, until you have completed your session. You may choose to do one situation per session as working in this way uses a lot of psychic and mental energy and you may simply need to rest before your mind starts to wander or it becomes difficult to stay in the zone. This is usually just a sign that you are mentally or psychically tired and need to restore yourself before delving deeper.

When you are ready, read the questions aloud and answer by writing the first word, association, or sentence that pops into your head. You may also feel inspired to draw a diagram or to use colour. Sometimes insight comes to us as images and symbols or as colours that inspire feeling. Here are the questions.

What do I judge most about this situation (or person or circumstance)?
For example "This person seems narcissistic and wounded. It is painful to be around her."

What is the wisdom hiding behind the judgement that I hold?
For example – "You are picking up on her inner wound and the pain you feel around her is actually her own pain."

What is the positive quality that I am learning and growing within from this situation?
For example – "Trust in my own perception and my ability to grow easily and gracefully through following my own internal guidance."

What is the next step for me in healing this situation?

For example – "Trust your perceptions and terminate your professional involvement with this person."

What is my highest learning here (if I can know this now)?

For example – "When you trust your own perceptions, compassion becomes easy. If you are struggling to have compassion, you aren't trusting your own perceptions and acting on them. Do so and compassion will follow naturally, and then you'll feel in your centre and at peace."

Complete as much of an answer to these questions as you can and take your time when finished to say thank you to your guidance.

You may wish to read over your questions now or at a later date and review your answers. If you don't understand something right away, you will more than likely have an understanding in a different way as your internal guidance cooks inside of you and things will start to make more sense in the coming days or weeks. Be patient and know that you can do this. It's just practice and patience that gets the divine insight flowing.

PHYSICAL HEALING WITH PIETERSITE AND THE ANGEL RAZIEL: HEALING EXHAUSTION

I have encountered exhaustion at different times in my life. Having a highly adaptable energetic constitution with a lot of sensitivity is great for spiritual growth and being able to do the work that I do as a healer. In fact it is essential. It is this exquisite body that I have been lucky enough to be offered as a soul that enables the work that I do. However I have a very strong mind and it can run away like a steam train sometimes, with a determination to accomplish tasks with such a rapid rate that my publisher has commented on more than one occasion that perhaps I needed to be tested for creative steroids. If this happens too often, although my creative output becomes very high, my body can get tired and drained, my mind over-stimulated and far too focused as I disappear into my work. I can topple out of my balanced lifestyle, becoming exhausted rather than energised by my choices.

My friends have a nickname for me, Red, which refers to my temperament – passionate, purposeful, driven and determined. I tend to just dive in and get things done. Sometimes it's wonderful. Sometimes it is a bit over the top as I choose to record two or three meditation CDs at a time, instead of one, or write a book in a month instead of a year and so on. I rely on meditation, dance, yoga, chi gung and my spiritual connection to keep me balanced and I listen to my body (or my partner – whichever gets my attention at the time) to rest when necessary. My creative mantra is 'juggle and surrender'.

I consider myself one of the lucky ones. I am able to do work that mostly energises me. I have had times in my life where I have been just as driven but because it came from the ego rather than in service to the soul light, my accomplishments brought me little joy. Until we find what truly switches us on, and even then sometimes if we push rather than flow, we can live on the edge of exhaustion. If we have a powerful mind, it is even more likely. It seems to me sometimes that tiredness is a modern epidemic, cured only by learning to connect with and love the body, making its wellbeing more of a priority than we generally tend to do.

Part of the gift of Pietersite is that it helps us rest and replenish even whilst on the go. For a Westerner this can be paradise. Sometimes a big fat roadblock is a gift from your soul and is to be treasured rather than resented, as it prevents future catastrophe. Yet at other times we don't need to do much other than become more present to what we are doing and releasing fatigue can happen through bringing the presence of Pietersite and divine healing energy into our body. What I love about Pietersite is that it is efficient. Just like a storm. It can make big changes quickly. So this very simple, very quick practice can have big returns, especially if you were to use it as a 'five minutes a day' technique for the next week, for example, or for the next month if you are aiming for a deeper healing of the body from decades of being forced to live out of synch with instinctual rhythms and in an unnatural and sometimes quite robotic state of always doing.

HOW DO I KNOW IF I NEED THIS HEALING PRACTICE?

If you aren't comfortable in your body, it is likely that it is filled with old energies and needs a good restoration and repair job. This healing practice will help.

If you are at home in your body then you'll know if you need to give it some extra care and attention. Like any divine animal, it will thrive with even a little love. Nature knows how to restore herself. She often just needs a chance to do so. This healing is that chance.

PHYSICAL HEALING PRACTICE – RESPITE WITH PIETERSITE

Lie comfortably with a piece of Pietersite (even if in jewellery) on or near your body. Be warm and comfortable. If you don't have the stone, we'll call on the spirit anyway, so don't worry. As an alternative, you can open this book to page 28, which features a Crystal Angel Mandala for Pietersite in full colour.

When you are ready, say the following:

"I call upon the healing power of the Angel of Pietersite and Angel Raziel. I call upon my own body-soul and the love of Gaia Mother Earth. Please help me now clear all cellular records and memories, energetic imprints and distortions of my body that have been created through drive, exhaustion, punishment, obsession, self-hatred and self-harm (conscious or unconscious). I ask for this with mercy and with kindness. So be it!"

Close your eyes and focus on your breath. Let the breath flow in and out of the entire body, like you are in a wave. Let the body ride the wave of your breath, almost like it is being held and can relax entirely with each inhalation and exhalation. With each inhalation it is held, which each exhalation it relaxes. Over and over again. Deeper and deeper with each restorative breath cycle. Let there be a pause between each inhalation and exhalation. The pause after the exhalation is a moment of peace for the body, where healing happens.

Stay with this inhalation and exhalation, with the crystal angels bringing their healing presence to your body, for at least forty-four breaths.

When you are ready, say, "Thank you," and gently remove the stones from your body if you have them.

Pause for a moment, then open your eyes. You have finished your healing process.

PRAYER – AFFIRMATION

To invoke the healing power of Pietersite and Angel Raziel at any time, you can repeat the following affirmation quietly in your mind, or aloud.

"Storm of Wisdom, Energy and Light, You Are With Me Even in Darkest Night."

13.

TIGERS EYE (Courage)
and ANGEL ADNACHIEL (Adventure)

THE GIFT OF INDEPENDENCE

SPIRITUAL GUIDANCE FROM THE ANGEL OF TIGERS EYE AND THE ANGEL ADNACHIEL

You have within you great courage and light. You always have the choice to live your best life. To step away from an existence that is draining and poor, to choose to live always being open to more. No other person can keep you in lack, you can always choose not to be held back. You have strength and knowledge to live your own way. Take action on your dreams and do not delay. No other than you knows better as to how you should live. No other than you knows what is in your heart to give. Give up the old ways of fear and living small. Your spirit is not like that – it is brave and tall! Let your spirit guide you, we will help you too. There is so much adventure for you to live, so much for you to be and do. We help you live your life as a great adventure now. Don't worry so much about the when or the how. Instead we help you live one day at a time. Be bold, dream big, each day take a step – it'll all work out fine! Find your inner pride, healthy and warm, and together we adventure towards the new dawn. For there is always a new adventure that calls, opening the heart and breaking down walls. Letting you live more intimately with life. Becoming to the Divine, as husband and wife. Living together in harmony and peace. Any boredom or procrastination, you will now release. Instead you live brave, vibrant and true. Now you live the life that was always meant for you!

PICTURING TIGERS EYE

Tigers Eye is typically golden brown, like a yellow tiger, with bands and chatoyance (which means a reflective appearance) that shines with aliveness. There is also red tigers eye, which is a less dynamic, more stabilising version of the stone, and blue tigers eye, which is high-vibrational and calming.

The stone we connect with in this chapter is Golden or Yellow Tigers Eye, which has bands of brown, gold, and warm yellow through it. It is often tumbled and can also be found in carvings. I have bracelets of tigers eye that I often wear piled on my right arm when I feel that I need it. It brings strength to my body and can be fun to wear. We'll look at the healing properties of the stone in more depth below.

HEALING PROPERTIES

I have always loved tigers eye, but then I have always loved tigers too! Being born in the Chinese Year of the Tiger, I look to the tiger as one of my soul animals, drawing energy and wisdom from these beautiful and powerful animals. Tigers Eye stone holds much of the tiger spirit of independence, commitment, strength, courage and dignity within it. It is not an uncommon stone, but to me it is precious. If you love tiger energy, you will probably love this crystal too.

It warms the body and strengthens the solar plexus chakra – which is the centre through which action occurs through us. With a blocked solar plexus, or a solar plexus that is not strong enough to handle the divine inspiration that flows through us, our visions don't manifest and we can feel like we are full of great ideas but no follow through. It can be very frustrating! We might lack the commitment and discipline needed to see a project through to its completion and we can begin to feel like we are failing, or yet to succeed. We can make this solar plexus deficiency mean something that it doesn't – that there is something wrong with our ideas or with us – when in reality, we are fine and our ideas are great. Our solar plexus chakra just needs come cleaning up and strengthening. We'll look to this in our physical healing process during this chapter.

Tigers Eye helps us bring spiritual energy into the body and funnel it through into the lower chakras, grounding us into a doing (rather than dreaming) reality when the time is right for this to happen. If you tend towards being a bit on the dreamy side, even spacey or vague and indecisive at times, Tigers Eye helps you focus, become more present to your body and this physical reality. It helps get your soul energy flowing through your body, which is essential if your inner dreams are going to manifest in your physical reality.

Tigers Eye clears mistaken doubts about self-worth and helps us identify our talents with accurate perception. It helps strengthen instincts and psychic 'gut' knowing, unleashing certainty of action where in the past there may have been wavering or indecision. It helps strengthen and protect our energy field and can bring a boldness to an otherwise gentle soul who might feel empowered to say "NO!" with great ease for a change.

ABOUT THE ANGEL ADNACHIEL

"Life is too short not to be lived wild and free. It is an adventure, a chance to play, with a heart of divinity. To love, and be loved, is an adventure great. To share one's talents without fear or debate. To just be in the world and to know you are safe, to step outside what you have known, to explore another place, to become bigger in spirit than you ever thought you could be, that is what it is like to be guided by me! There is a new adventure around every turn, there is always something new and interesting to learn. Be a pioneer in your own unique way, and you too can make a difference every day. Bringing a fresh view, a new experience like a child at play. You can help others live life without fear getting in the way. You can be curious, you can explore and succeed. Belief in life and yourself is all that you need."

When I connected with Adnachiel to begin writing about him, he took over and wrote the message above immediately, which I feel reveals quite a bit about him. He just gets on with what needs to be done and does it. He acts. He doesn't analyse and think, but just responds to the flow of divine energy, letting it happen through him. As a result, he has a lot of life force, he is very energised and energising to be around. Because he is tall, athletic and gorgeous looking, he is very easy on the (third) eye too.

There is a less conscious and inspired version of this notion of 'acting now and thinking later' which isn't always so wise. Being a tiger-person, I have leapt first and thought about it later on a number of such occasions. Sometimes it has turned out wonderful, and at other times I wonder what on Earth I was thinking (answer – I wasn't so much!). There is a saying that fools leap in where angels fear to tread. Yet like the lucky tiger I am, I suppose, I have managed to get through most situations and learn something, grow a little wiser (though perhaps not much more restrained) and on I go.

There is also the other extreme, where we think too much, and consider all viewpoints, until we are so paralysed by indecision that we really don't know what we think! Procrastination, overwhelm, even depression and blocked creativity can arise and we feel stuck.

Adnachiel guides us to a consciousness between these two extremes, where we don't think about our options until we are so befuddled by our own arguments we get stuck, and we don't mindlessly jump into situations without consulting our inner instincts first.

Adnachiel helps us be in touch with our instinctive self and learn to trust it. When we know, we know and we act without fear or self-doubt. We don't act from a place of thinking, we act from an inner instinct and inspiration. We allow the action to happen through us, we don't retard it by analysis and we don't contrive it by over-thinking. We feel a sense of trust in taking the action and we let it happen.

The ease with which we can be productive with such an attitude is extraordinary. There is a saying that if you want to get something done, give it to a busy person. Productivity tends to breed productivity. Have you ever been creatively engrossed in a project and suddenly so many new ideas keep flowing through? Your channels are open and you are not blocking your flow – so your life happens more instantly. This is the fearless flow and presence in the now, where life actually happens, that Adnachiel helps us embody.

SOUL HEALING WITH TIGERS EYE
AND THE ANGEL ADNACHIEL

Recently I heard a crystal healing teacher describe tigers eye as a 'stone for teenage boys'. With a touch of dismissal, my tigerish nature was initially adamant that this stone could not be so narrowly summed up and cast aside – and so I did growl at this remark).

As I sit with her comment now, I can find a broader sense of truth in it. I don't feel it is literally only a stone for teenage boys, but I do feel it is a stone that supports the development of the masculine spirit in both men and women. The masculine spirit is that part of us that is interested in independence, in carving out a life of worth and value (according to what our own individual values may be), it is the part of us that honours freedom and also responsibility for that freedom, it honours the consequences of our choices and fights for what feels worth fighting for. The masculine spirit is the warrior and Tigers Eye is the stone for the spiritual warrior.

Even as peace-loving beings, we often need to have a bit of fight in us. I remember the first time I boxed with my personal trainer, many years ago before I developed my yoga practice and was boxing for fitness instead. He was quite shocked that a 'pacifist' (as he had labelled me) could have such a right hook! He paid me what I suspect may have been his biggest compliment which was that "I didn't punch like a girl".

I was quite amused by his surprise at the time, as I had always known myself to be a fighter in a different sense – in the internal sense that I would not let any obstacle get in my way. I would always seek to find a way around it or simply wait and outgrow it. Sometimes it would take years, but I would always get there eventually. However because most of this process was internal, and I was most often a gentle-natured person in how I chose to relate to others on the outside, I realised that people who didn't know me well might not recognise my strength. It didn't express itself in obvious ways – like attempting to dominate others or control them. I was always more interested in gaining internal mastery than external domination.

This is the way of the spiritual warrior. It is about internal strength that may or may not be recognised externally. Sometimes only you may realise exactly how much power you have had to develop in order to conquer a fear, take a new step or to learn to be kind with yourself and others, rather than harsh and demanding. You might have to have the strength of self-belief so that when others do not understand, validate or recognise what you have attained within, you will not belittle or deny it yourself. The most courageous acts are not those that others witness and praise, I believe, but those that you are willing to honour within yourself, often with silent recognition, and continue to go about living your life and loving your self. This is true spiritual courage.

The strength and the fight of the spiritual warrior is channelled in this way – into the courage, sometimes stubborn determination and commitment required to walk the inner path in an authentic way. Let us say that you had a passion for cooking and you were born into a family of lawyers. Cooking might have been something that was not particularly important to your family. They might not even like food that much and see it as a wasteful indulgence or dismiss it in some way as insignificant, lacking in prestige or social status, and even consider it a bit embarrassing to the family reputation. But your heart is set on cooking. It is how you feel most alive, how you create, how you express yourself and your emotions, what you think about, dream about, what you just love to do and would do whether you would be paid for it or not. You just are a cook!

The spiritual warrior is the part of you that has the guts to go ahead and live your dream. To stand up to those parts of yourself (sometimes reflected back to you by others, including family members or people who tell you that you can't possibly succeed) that question your right to do so, and claim your right to live life according to your own truth.

It is the spiritual warrior that accepts the gift of our life, that really receives it by letting it be what it is meant to be and not trying to force it to be something it is not. Otherwise it's like receiving a clock as a gift perhaps, and then trying to use it as a dinner plate! The gift is not being utilised for what it is and it just doesn't work so well. The spiritual warrior picks that clock out of the dinner plate cupboard and hangs it up on the wall. The spiritual warrior says that all must be what it truly is destined to be.

Adnachiel helps us with this process by demonstrating what it is to be healed by Tigers Eye, to live the truth of the spiritual warrior without any inner obstacle. This angel's immediacy, unwavering resolve, swiftness, clear intention and unquestioning belief in his worth and right to act allow him to be a powerful and clear channel for divine manifestation. Without the obstructions and delays caused by fear, doubt, confusion, unworthiness, insecurity, or an unwillingness to be interdependent with all that is, manifestation can happen very quickly. It is like the difference between swimming against a powerful current, and eventually getting to where it was moving you, but with more exhaustion and less enjoyment perhaps, and swimming with the current, combining your power with the greater force and enjoying the accelerated flow.

The spiritual warrior learns, and Adnachiel helps us with this, that he or she does not have to fight what is, but fight the resistance to it. It is not life that we are fighting against, but our own belief that we have to try and dominate life in order to survive, thrive and flourish on the Earth. As we let go of the unhelpful type of fighting, flow happens. The more our inner warrior stands up for what is true and enduring, the more we refuse to bow down to that which would seek to extinguish the inner fire – the voices of shame, fear, doubt, judgement, anxiety and despair – the more powerfully that flow moves through us. Then we become like a wave in the ocean, with much power, and great triumphs and adventure open up to us.

SOUL HEALING – AWAKENING AND EMPOWERING THE SPIRITUAL WARRIOR WITHIN

The spiritual warrior grows in power with each step we take on the spiritual path. Every time the soul needs to break from some pattern that is holding us back, we are able to do so because the warrior within is stronger than the old pattern. This holding back may have come out of fear or guilt, out of shame, self-doubt or unworthiness. It may come from fear of failure, fear of success or any number of other fears that we humans so creatively imagine.

To break through a holding back of some kind takes courage. We might subconsciously try to shelter ourselves against life with all its uncertainty because there are times when it doesn't feel safe, secure and familiar. If we don't have the spiritual warrior activated within us, we'll be missing that vital courage that helps us choose to participate rather than withdraw. We have to participate in the uncertainties of life if we are going to translate our inspirations and dreams into real-life experiences! Otherwise we may end up dreaming of living, instead of really living, or when it is time to die, realise that we are yet to really live. May we all avoid such a fate!

It is the spiritual warrior that is the part of us that is more powerful than any fear that could hold us back from just letting go and being ourselves in the world, discovering who we are and sharing it freely. The spiritual warrior doesn't think about living, it just lives.

HOW DO YOU KNOW IF YOU ARE HEALING AT A SOUL LEVEL IN THIS WAY?

The soul has a craving for aliveness. I remember a time when I too craved this. I was locked in a prison of my own creation – so weighed down by fears, thoughts, anxieties – and using addiction to support myself with a false sense of safety through habit. I was completely stifled. My own belief that I needed a safety blanket in life was beginning to suffocate me!

I distinctly remember one vivid emotional moment when I stepped outside the apartment I was living in at the time, and felt the sun on my face, the beautiful scent in the air from nearby trees and the basic aliveness of nature herself. I was overwhelmed with a feeling of deep desperation, of longing to just be alive! But I didn't know how to free this feeling at the time. I didn't even know exactly what to make of that painful yearning moment. I had to bear a period of many years existing with the knowledge that there was a more alive way of being, but I couldn't summon it from within me as yet. I just wasn't quite ready.

If you had have asked anyone around me at the time, they wouldn't have guessed this was going on inside of me. Most of the time I was doing OK and had a good life, but deep within there was a part of me that was being held back and longed to be free! It was the wild spirit in me. The part of me that was fearless, would tackle any adventure and as soon as triumph was assured, or even before. It would take on anything because life was to be lived, feasted upon and relished with great vigour and appreciation. I wanted to dance, to play, to share the feelings of freedom and exhilaration that were inside of me. The ways that I had found to do this at that point weren't very nourishing to me and I was lacking some good alternatives! In short, I didn't want keeping myself feeling safe to stop me from feeling alive, but I also didn't want to just be careless and put myself into emotionally unsatisfying situations in order to try and feel alive. I wanted to take soulful risk and connect with new people and new communities. I wanted a new way to live! I had a sort of spiritual cabin fever that I had ignored for too long, telling myself that my life was fine. Actually my life was fine, but I wanted it to be on fire with divine passion.

Over the next several years, with many emotional ups and downs, I began making choices to be very uncomfortable as I explored new communities, new talents within me, and nurtured my adventurous streak to be alive with me every day. Eventually I found myself quite unexpectedly in company of a group of kindred spirits called the Warehouse Collective, which gathered to drum together. Sometimes there would be singing (often by me!) and often there was dancing. There was a wild, child-like freedom, a feeling of abandon and non-judgement in the people that gathered there. There was a sense of welcoming (even though it was all a bit intimidating at first because I didn't know a soul there) and I felt like I had found a community of kindred spirits. We were all quite different in our own ways, but we shared a passion for freedom of the wild heart to express. This was just one of the healing answers to my prayers that was delivered to me as soon as I was ready to take the risks involved with receiving it.

I had to learn how to feel safe within myself even whilst taking emotional risks with others. Being a sensitive-to-energy type of person, as many of you readers will also be, putting myself into unknown environments with varying levels of consciousness was frequently a genuine emotional and physical challenge for me. I would often feel emotional and psychological negativity as if I had been physically struck or had ingested a food that had turned bad. My body and my energy field had to grow together, and I had to clear enormous amounts of fear. It took me many years before I was able to be in such environments while sustaining my own vibration and feeling like I could remain myself (or at least return quickly to myself and my own vibration afterwards if somehow I got lost in the mess of it all).

It took a lot of courage for me, as it does for all sensitives, to put myself out there, to expose myself to community energies. It wasn't until I really felt stable enough, that I could protect and honour my energy without having to keep people at bay that I was ready to risk venturing into new communities. When I was ready, the Warehouse, and other communities including those that I began building myself, were waiting for me.

Before long, I was approached by two of the men who ran the collective. Being musicians themselves, we formed an informal musical trio that became the inspiration for the Divine Circus, a sacred musical performance group that comes together for impromptu music and performance, and sometimes larger events, for divine play.

In the unfolding of the music collective with these men, I found the freedom I was seeking because we found that together, we didn't tend to rehearse but instead just jam. We would just start singing and whatever flowed, flowed. It was often so beautiful we would all just sit and stare at each other afterwards and go "Wow!". It was art that was alive and hard to pin down. You could just let it flow. When we all surrendered together, and the chemistry was there, it was intoxicating. It was what I had been searching for without having a name for it beyond a deep craving to be more alive.

What I realise now is that it was the desire, the restorative need, to be consciously 'out of my mind'. There are times when I sing now and phrases and melody emerge from my body with my mind going "ah, where is that coming from?". Of course it's coming from my body-soul. This is where the spiritual warrior takes us – past our self-imposed barriers to life, to that place beyond the mind, beyond analysis and beyond unconscious risk taking. The spiritual warrior takes us to a place where the divine fool, the conscious risk taker, is alive in us and we let life happen through us.

One of the musicians from the Divine Circus said to me recently that unless he was feeling a bit scared, he knew the creative magic wouldn't happen. I don't tend to feel scared when I perform (I am usually so in the moment, I just feel what is happening then and there), but I knew what he was expressing. Often when you are out of your own control (which can feel scary or exhilarating depending on your level of trust) you are in the divine zone where life happens.

If you can relate to this sense of needing to be wild, perhaps to find what that might be in a healthy way for you, then this healing is for you. If you aren't permitted to explore your wild nature, your spontaneous and instinctive side, then you might have no recourse but to act it out in destructive addictions. Or you may feel stifled by trying to avoid risk and play it safe. If you feel that your soul might actually want to guide you into a more extraordinary, ego-challenging, deeply satisfying and fulfilling way of life, then this healing is right for you too.

If you are abandoning yourself in unconscious rather than conscious ways, perhaps by letting opportunities go by or love go to waste, by not paying attention to yourself or selling yourself short, by giving your body or sexuality away without loving, holding and honouring the value of this gift, then this healing is for you.

If you are ready to live with more conscious risk and less fear for your own safety, if you are ready to feel stronger and more stable within – perhaps more resilient without losing the exquisite gift of your sensitivity – then yes, this healing can help you too.

May your spiritual warrior kick fear and doubt to the kerb and clear the way for you to live this gift of life with more passion and abandon than ever before.

SOUL HEALING PROCESS – AWAKENING AND EMPOWERING THE SPIRITUAL WARRIOR WITHIN

You will need a quiet place to sit comfortably and speak without having your privacy interrupted.

Begin the healing process by saying the following invocation:

"I call upon my own divine soul, the Angel of Tigers Eye and the Angel Adnachiel. I call on the energy of the spiritual warrior, through unconditional love, so be it!"

"I now choose, of my own free will to be open to new ways of living, to learn how to feel safe and secure in ways that do not stifle my need for freedom and adventure. I choose to let go of having to know in advance how everything will unfold before I trust. Instead I choose to trust and let life happen. I know it will be amazing and I am ready to receive the gift of greater aliveness, through compassionate mercy and divine grace. So be it."

Close your eyes and focus on your breathing. Allow your awareness to drift down to the solar plexus chakra, in your middle to lower abdominal area. As you breathe in and out at your own natural pace, let the breath become slower and longer, with a slight pause between each inhalation and exhalation. Notice that a heat begins to build in the solar plexus area. Stay with this for at least eight breaths in and out.

Imagine when you look at your own solar plexus chakra, you become aware of an angelic being, flooded with warm, golden-yellow light, gazing back at you. With topaz coloured eyes, shaped like a tigers eye, radiant golden-brown and luminous yellow-gold bands of energy radiate out from her, like a sun. Allow her to gaze at you and you sense her fearlessness and power. This is the Angel of Tigers Eye.

Allow her to fill your being with this golden warm light, pulsating with life force and energy, through your entire body, from your solar plexus all the way down to your toes, and all the way out to your fingertips, and all the way up to the crown of your head.

Say, "I am brave, I am strong, I am worthy and I accept myself unconditionally. I let go of any shame, doubt, fear, anxiety or judgement that I have held against myself now, consciously or unconsciously. I now choose to liberate myself from any way that I have held myself back. I now choose to release any blocks to feeling safe in being alive and taking healthy risks. I now choose, of my own free will, to live more, to receive more and to give more of myself. It is safe for me to do this and I do so with loving wisdom and courage. So be it!"

The tigress angel winks at you and she looks upwards, towards the crown of your head. As you follow her gaze you become aware of a great thundering of hooves above your crown chakra. You can almost feel the force of the great hooves bearing down and the energy of the powerful Angel Adnachiel. As you see him approaching, he has powerful wings and an bow and arrow poised, and he rides a magnificent horse, with flaming fire all around him.

"I will lead you true, true as the divine arrow always hits the mark!" he says and fires his arrow, which rips through time and space with clarity and certainty. As you watch the arrow flying through the air towards a beautiful temple in the distance, your own mind becomes focused and clear. As you and the great angel watch the divine arrow fly through the air, it changes shape and becomes a human being, running straight towards the temple, with speed and grace. It is you! Breeze flows through your hair, and your body feels strong and free as you edge closer and closer to that temple. You have never felt so free and strong your whole life! Nothing can get in your way! You, as the arrow, land dead centre at the temple entrance way.

You enter the Temple, where you see that within stands a great warrior. Strong and powerful. It may be a man or a woman. Deep in meditation and yet aware of your presence and all that is going on around them. This is a being of unconditional love and respect for all beings, with great physical and spiritual strength. As you approach this being, you are aware of the being returning your gaze now. It is like a fire is switched on in this being and instead of quiet meditation they become alight with energy and potent aliveness. As you stare deep into each others' eyes, you start to feel that you are in fact the same being, that this being exists within you.

See, sense or feel how this part of you is more powerful than fear and open to life, wherever it may lead. This part of you trusts that even amongst great uncertainty, that there is nothing to fear. See, sense or feel how this part of you feels safe and empowered always, when confronted with a situation that has not been encountered before, this part of you is curious, patient and relaxed. Feel the inner security that arises as you see, sense or feel more of this part of your own being.

If you are ready, say, "I trust the spiritual warrior within me now. I choose to allow you to guide me that I may life more fully and trust where I am being led."

Remain in the temple with this beautiful divine warrior self and be. Stay there for at least forty-four breaths and when you are ready, follow the breath back towards your physical body in the here and now. Take at least eight breaths noticing how your body feels now that the spiritual warrior energy has been awakened and activated within you. The changes may be subtle or very obvious. Whatever you do or do not notice will be perfect for you.

When you are ready, move your arms and legs and open your eyes.

You have completed your soul healing process.

Let the effect of this healing continue to unfold at a deep, cellular level. Be open to saying "yes" to new situations and opportunities where once you would have pushed it aside or delayed. Ride the edge of your own discomfort as you let the Spiritual Warrior within guide you. Remember, once you become familiar with what was once unknown, that too can become comfortable as you grow. Trust and live free.

PSYCHOLOGICAL-EMOTIONAL HEALING WITH ANGEL OF TIGERS EYE AND ANGEL ADNACHIEL: SPIRITUAL INDEPENDENCE

It is a truth that you cannot give what you do not have. I have worked with some clients over the past decade that have genuinely wanted to be guided by higher will. They didn't want to make the same mistakes repeatedly and they declared that they would quite happily live according to higher will, if they only knew what it was! "Where is my spiritual road map?" one particularly bright and funny young woman would say to me in her sessions. "If my guidance just gave me one, I promise I would follow it and none of this drama would need to happen anymore!"

The eagerness to find the divine pathway through the drama of life and into a more aligned state of being where unnecessary pain can be avoided is understandable. However desiring that guidance tell us exactly how to get through the experiences of our life, instead of helping us as we do the work of learning how to live well, is giving up our right of spiritual independence before we even claim it.

It is true that as the soul matures it becomes more willing to live according to its sense of a greater good and higher truth. Some may imagine that this means any power and responsibility for personal choice falls away as higher guidance begins to dictate what to do and when. But this is not the case at all. The spiritual independence of the soul remains intact throughout its entire existence. That essence of the soul trickles down into our human selves leaving us with one rather important spiritual lesson that all of humanity is learning to heal individually and as a group soul – the lesson of healthy independence.

In a culture like the West, where individuality is often seen as being 'cool', you would assume that independence is a comfortable part of our way of life. I have a friend who teaches both adults and children. She says that she loves teaching adults because (often unlike children) you can just tell them to do something and they do it. There is a dependency that we often don't want to admit that lurks in us and in our culture where we feel that we need to follow the rules.

Sometimes this is for social harmony and it's helpful. At other times we get so caught up in what we think is the right thing to do, based on the media we consume and the opinions of others that we choose to empower, that we toss our independence out the window and play it safe, play it familiar, and choose what is acceptable in our heads rather than what feels real to our hearts.

Until we recognise our own dependence on being accepted by others, we can't choose another way. We may pretend that it doesn't exist, or feel ashamed of it, but until we recognise that it is a part of who we are and that's OK, it will continue to lurk in the shadows and we won't be growing and living as powerfully as we could be.

For many years I eschewed dependency. I hated the very idea of it! I didn't want to work for another person, I only wanted to work for myself and the Divine. I didn't want to rely emotionally or financially on another person, I wanted to be self-sufficient and resourceful. I managed to live like this for many years, and although I wasn't particularly warm and connected, I did feel powerful and strong – until I realised that my vulnerable self wanted to be loved and accepted too! I wanted to feel what it was like to not have to hold myself up all the time. But instead of seeking another person to prop me up, which felt co-dependent and unhealthy to me, I began to trust life itself would meet my needs. I began to soften and surrender and become more vulnerable in life. I began to experience more support from the world around me in response to this. Although I didn't lose my independence, my sense of being a free, self-determining spirit, I did learn how to let people in, how to let life help me and how to make my own life much easier. You could say that I made peace with my dependency needs and felt more supported as a result. I, in turn, became more empowered to help others because I had even more energy and resources available to me. In this way, I began to experience interdependence – that flow between strength and vulnerability that occurs when we are in conscious connection with the world around us.

The gift of interdependence requires that we balance our dependent and independent sides, recognising that both are valuable. When we accept our dependent side, we become more open to connection with others. When we accept our independent side, we become open to exploring our individuality. To balance both allows us to give and receive in our relationships with others and the relationship we have with our own self.

HOW DO I KNOW IF I NEED HEALING
IN THIS WAY AND AT THIS LEVEL OF MY BEING?

There are three ways that you will know if you need this healing.

You may be struggling with your independence – your right to be a free spirit, to have your own responsibility and your own choices. Perhaps your family, friends or partner cannot accept this for you, always wanting to make your choices for you. Or perhaps you doubt yourself, and whether you are capable of taking care of yourself on all levels, including financially and emotionally.

The second option is that you may be struggling with your dependency. Either you feel stuck in it (and relate to the first option above) or you deny it completely, finding it shameful and feeling averse to it. Perhaps you feel like you are a child rather than an adult in some area of your life where you still feel as though you cannot function or live well without another. This is not truth. This is a trust issue. What you need, life will provide. We just have to get out of the way of receiving, which we do by trusting more and letting go of expectation about having life come to us in a particular way or form.

Thirdly and finally, it might be time for you to break into the balance of these two aspects of yourself (independence and dependence), into the realisation of interdependence. This is where you accept that 'no man is an island' and you come out of your splendid isolation or your belief in your inability to stand forth on your own, and strike a balance. You are ready to live your own life, but you are open to the help that life will provide to you along the way. You are willing to take an adventure in living, and you are going to do your part, but you don't expect that you have to do everyone else's part as well! Nor do you expect so little of yourself that you don't believe you could manage to hold up your end of the bargain, so to speak. You are ready to find the balance and live it.

PSYCHOLOGICAL- EMOTIONAL HEALING PROCESS – INDEPENDENCE, DEPENDENCE, INTERDEPENDENCE

If you have some Tigers Eye with you, even within a piece of jewellery, place it on or near your body, wherever feels intuitively right to you. As an alternative, you can simply have the book open to page 29 which features the Tigers Eye Crystal Angel Mandala in the full colour section, and keep it next to you during the process.

Start by sitting comfortably with both palms upwards, resting the backs of your hands on your knees or on the floor if you are lying down.

Say, "I call upon the healing Angel of Tigers Eye and the brave Angel Adnachiel. Please be with me, beloved crystal angels, and bestow upon me the gift of independence, of healthy dependency and of the ultimate balance of these two expressions in conscious interdependence. May I thrive and help others to thrive. Please help me now through divine grace and my own free will, so be it."

Close your eyes and focus on the breath.

Imagine that you can sense a vast, dark, open space inside of you that feels peaceful and wide. Imagine that within that space there is a golden child, giggling and gurgling perhaps. That child feels safe and held. Around the child is the Divine Mother in her nurturing and protective aspect. This helpless child is in bliss being held in her love and power. Sense the unbreakable bond between them if you can and feel the peace of this in your own being. Let it move down from your heart into your stomach and your belly.

It might be easy or difficult for you to sense those feelings. If you did not receive that safety as a child in this lifetime, it might give rise to anger, sadness or relief (or a combination of these feelings or others) to begin to connect with this reality now. However, you are safe here and you deserve this care, so you may choose to stay with it, allowing emotions or thoughts to simply come and go as you rest in this connection between Divine Mother and divine child.

When you are ready, say the following, changing any words that feel like they need adjusting to suit your feelings. "I am worthy of being loved and supported. I choose to believe that life wants to help and support me through many sources. I enjoy and feel good about receiving support and help. I enjoy being assisted and I can and do assist others too. I don't worry about helping others because I know I am helped too. I experience an easy flow in my life of help and support and I receive it with grace and gratitude. I now choose to release any energy from my body, mind and energy field that does not resonate with this. So be it."

Breathe in the golden light from that golden child and breathe out, letting the light and energy release from your entire body, front and back, from every pore of your skin. Repeat that releasing breath, perhaps noticing any energy that shifts as you do so, and when you have stayed here enough, bring your awareness back to the breath flowing in and out.

Become aware of the vast open space again and sense a strong mature presence of a hero, warrior or adventurer, with love in their heart and an open attitude to life. This being is resourceful and capable, curious and confident. The energy of this being is vibrant and glows bright like a sun. Feel the energy of this brave and confident explorer before you now.

When you are ready, say the following, "I choose to forgive myself for any past failures, and I now see that they were all learning experiences, valuable in their own way. I now acknowledge my strength. I am empowered. I am capable of caring for myself and finding my own way. If I don't know something, I can find the answer if I need to know it. I am interested and interesting. I am open to new experiences that allow my life to be enriched and to grow. I choose to live with trust in my self. I am trustworthy and reliable. I let go of old judgements of being a disappointment or letting others down. These things are not real! They are not who I am, they are simply experiences that I had. I now choose to accept my competence and my capabilities. It is safe for me to be brave. I enjoy the thrill of living my own unique path and I choose this for myself now. I let go of what has stood in my way and I accept my right to thrive. So be it."

Breathe in and allow the golden sun energy of this being to radiate into you through the breath. Let it fill your body until you overflow with it, until you too are radiant, glowing brightly!

Stay with it for as long as feels right, at least for eight breaths, and then when you are ready. Come back to the breath and the vast, open space before you.

See before you now a circle of golden beings with energy flowing between them. As the energy flows in all directions, each being giving and receiving, they all grow more brightly golden. Notice the feeling of goodwill, of help and support, of confidence and trust, each being independent and dependent, helping each other and living their own truths. Feel the community energy of this – it is very strong.

Notice the feelings of co-operation, of mutual care, of each person's unique path helping and supporting another person's path – even when the two don't seem to be connected at all! Notice the easy flow of energy, almost like that entire circle of golden beings is breathing in and out in harmony with each other. Feel peace instead of competition and allow yourself to relax into this feeling.

When you are ready, say the following aloud, changing any words to reflect your truth if you feel the need to do so. "I am worthy of healthy, loving and supportive community. I co-create honest, supportive relationships easily. I attract nourishing soul families from many walks of life. I am fed and I nourish others through my relationships. I accept the love of others, I give love to others and we all grow. I release old negativity, programming, fear and conditioning that would hold me back from stepping into communities that enhance my vibration now. I release old vows made to any community that no longer serves my highest good, in this or any lifetime. I free myself to accept all of life as my community, trusting what presents itself to me shall be what is perfect for me at that time, through my own free will, so be it."

Stay with the feeling of sacred interdependent community, the balance, the companionship, friendship and play. Notice that you may feel challenged or uncomfortable in connection with others sometimes and that this is healthy. You are empowered enough to choose to be who you are and also be loving and open to others. You can do this because you trust yourself. You also trust your relationships to be strong enough to cope with you being yourself! Let this feeling of self-trust and trust of others fill your heart and overflow into your entire being now.

Stay with the breath for at least nine counts and when you are ready, simply open your eyes.

Give yourself a chance to re-read this healing process at least once in the coming week to help ground the new awareness into your being. Even just reading the declarations of intention out loud will help you to anchor new consciousness as you let go of the past.

PHYSICAL HEALING WITH TIGERS EYE AND ANGEL ADNACHIEL: HEALING THE STOMACH

Our stomachs often need some care. They digest not only the physical food that we intake, but often emotions such as fear and anxiety as well. Perhaps you have heard the expression that one just 'can't stomach' something? Feeling sick, nauseated or not being able to stomach something or someone in your life is a sign that you need to give your tummy some loving care.

The stomach, when clear, is a way for us to be in touch with instincts. We can be scared of our own instincts if our primary caregivers were scared of them when we were children. Sometimes the searing honesty of an instinctual response can be frightening to the parts of us, or others, that want to be in control. Instinct however, cannot be controlled. It can either be honoured and allowed to express, or suppressed and denied, perhaps out of fear, and shoved into the body where it may eventually make its presence known as 'disease' of some sort or another.

We don't have to be afraid of instinct. In fact, to be in touch with our instincts is very energising. When we realise that the responses of our instincts are information that we can choose to respond to as we wish, it removes some of the fear. Instinct can arise as emotion, and to feel that emotion can help us make decisions that are helpful for us.

Once I was speaking to a relative of mine about an issue I was having in one of my relationships. My relative explained that the person in question had a traumatic past that I didn't know about and that would explain the behavioural problem that I was finding difficult. Instantly, I burst into tears and just sobbed. I knew exactly what was being said to be me was true and my body released the emotion of it even whilst my mind was still taking it in and wondering if it were really the case. It turned my view of the relationship on its head for a while, but was ultimately very helpful, allowing for more honesty and closeness to develop.

If I hadn't allowed my instinctual response to surface, the healing that unfolded over a rather painful afternoon may not have happened at all. Instinct cut through the mind-stuff and I followed that to the truth, bringing about a great healing.

Tigers Eye and the Amulet of Adnachiel helps to clear the stomach and open us up to our gut instincts. It helps us allow our instincts to rise up when we need them. So much trouble can be avoided when we just follow our gut instincts about situations. Sure sometimes we know we'll get burned and we want to have the experience because we sense there is something there to learn and we want to explore it. But sometimes the instinct alone is enough and we can quite happily let a situation slide right past us without getting caught up in avoidable drama, because we listened to our gut from the outset.

HOW DO I KNOW IF I NEED THIS HEALING PRACTICE?

On a physical level, this healing will help with digestive problems, anxiety and nightmares, as well as with experiences of doubt, confusion, overwhelm or uncertainty. It is particularly helpful with children's anxiety, which often manifests somatically as stomach aches. If there is something in your life that you feel you 'cannot stomach' this will help dislodge it and get the situation moving towards healing.

This healing also helps restore impaired instincts, clearing habits around not listening to them or fears of what they might reveal. If there has been a history in your family of hiding truths, often likely to be the case when there has been mental illness or sexual abuse in the family history, or anything that could have brought 'shame' socially upon the family (such as having a psychic in the family or an unwanted pregnancy), then it is highly likely that your instinctual knowing will be both very strong and very repressed.

Instinctual gut knowing is beyond the mind. It is a way to connect with the truths of the body which enable us to know for sure, without having to wonder. With instincts we just know. I once had a woman say that she instinctually felt that I wasn't being completely transparent with her about other projects that I was working on while we were also working together. She was absolutely right. Although these other projects didn't relate to her, her instinct that I was holding something back from her was actually correct. I was doing this consciously because I didn't trust her and didn't want to give her any opportunity to sabotage my work. Her instinctual feeling made me wonder why I wasn't honouring my own instincts and declining her requests that I work with her!

As she began some predictable actions to sabotage my other projects (which I fortunately enough was able to deflect with a few deft actions), I realised that I needed to value my instincts more highly, especially in circumstances where I sensed that people were not fully supportive of me. I am lucky to have many supportive friends, clients and colleagues and I can sometimes forget that there are those that can easily feel threatened and will choose to attack, rather than reflect, in such cases.

Staying in touch with my instinctual nature helps me avoid getting in too deep with people who may behave in this way. Avoiding unconscious drama is surely one of the best uses of instinctual wisdom. The next best use is perhaps to learn from it so as to avoid it the next time!

PHYSICAL HEALING PRACTICE – HEALING THE STOMACH WITH TIGERS EYE AND THE AMULET OF ADNACHIEL

Lie comfortably on your back with a piece of Tigers Eye on or near your body, preferably around the stomach/abdominal area. Be warm and comfortable. If you don't have the stone, we'll call on the spirit anyway, so don't worry. Another option is to open this book to page 29, which features a full colour mandala for the stone.

When you are ready, say the following:

"I call upon the healing power of the Angel of Tigers Eye and the healing protective Amulet of Angel Adnachiel. I call upon my own body-soul. Please help now beloved ones, to clear all cellular records and memories, energetic imprints and blockages to the energy of my stomach and my instinctual nature. Through divine mercy, kindness, peace and unconditional love, so be it!"

Close your eyes and focus on your breath. Let the breath flow in and out of the entire body.

With each inhalation and exhalation the breath becomes warmer and more golden, circulating healing energy in the entire abdominal area, all the way down to your belly. Imagine fresh energy entering on the breath, and old energy carried out on the exhalation.

Become aware of a beautiful spinning golden-brown stone above you. It is radiant and full of light, with golden wings on either side. Say, "I accept the healing of the Amulet of Adnachiel now, through unconditional love, through all levels of my being, all lifetimes and beyond time and space, so be it."

Allow light from this spinning amulet to pour light into your stomach, cleansing it. Know that it is clearing at a conscious and subconscious cellular level, that it is healing karmically as well. Stay with the breath for at least forty-four counts as this happens. Let any emotion, even if it makes no sense to you, and any instinct of fear or anger, any feeling of nausea arise and be released. This is just your body releasing and it is a good sign that you are very receptive to the healing. If your experience is more gentle and peaceful, then just trust that this is right for you.

When you are ready, say, "Thank you" and allow the stone spinning above you to create a shield of golden light with a cross at its centre, hovering a few inches in front of your abdominal area. Say, "I permit this shield to protect my energy field as I integrate this healing, for the next forty-four days or for however long serves my highest good. Through unconditional love, so be it".

Then gently remove the stone from your body, if you have them, and take your time sitting up.

You have finished your healing process. You may feel quite emotional in waves over the next days or weeks. This is a good sign that your body is releasing old energy. You may find that your intuition and instincts become more strong and powerful. Don't be scared. This is just a sign that you are present in the here and now, which is how we 'know' things instinctually. There is nothing to be frightened of, but if you do feel uncomfortable, feel free to repeat the physical healing process up to three times over the next three weeks if need be.

PRAYER – AFFIRMATION

To invoke the healing power of Tigers Eye and Angel Adnachiel at any time, you can repeat the following affirmation quietly in your mind, or aloud.

"I AM an Independent Spirit Bright, Walking with All of Life, within Divine Light."

14.

BLACK TOURMALINE (Cleansing) and ANGEL LAHABIEL (Protection)

THE GIFT OF PURIFICATION

SPIRITUAL GUIDANCE FROM THE ANGEL OF BLACK TOURMALINE AND THE ANGEL LAHABIEL

We help you release, through deepest peace. We help lift you out of the vibration of fear, and deflect negativity away from you, as we draw you near. Into our spectrum of darkness and peace, into which old energy you can now release. We'll help you cleanse, we'll help you let go, and become empty so that you can grow. You'll receive new light for all that you release. We'll clear any ill-wishing, delivering you peace. It is time to let go, of energies old and dense, of that which is fearful and makes you feel tense. You don't have to defend, to hold on or protect, with our loving presence, all negativity we deflect. Now you are ready to let go of the past, to let go of the things that you have outgrown at last. With us step up now, into cleansing of grace, stepping into new peacefulness, into your rightful place. As you become empty and clear, feeling cleansed and new, you become capable of attracting new life and abundance too. Let us prepare you now to get out of your own way. To remove obstacles to manifestation without further delay. It is time to receive happiness, to be cleansed from sadness, anger and pain. Let our energy purify you now, like sacred cleansing rain.

PICTURING BLACK TOURMALINE

Black Tourmaline can be polished as tumbled stones or jewellery. It can be quite robust, shiny and firm when polished, or delicate, flaking off easily, in its raw state of long striations forming various sized pieces. As I sit here writing, I have a piece thicker than my forearm, but I also have a couple of polished pieces that fit in the palm of my hand.

Black Tourmaline has a grey black appearance when unpolished, with some shining elements when held up to a light source. It appears opaque and dense. When polished the stone appears as more reflective and holds more shine. Both raw and polished pieces are beautiful but I actually love the raw stone. It is less glossy than a finished piece, but emanates power and peace so strongly.

HEALING PROPERTIES

As a sensitive, the negativity of other people and even my own negativity, can be a challenge at times. I generally choose to surround myself with people who are more positive when I can, but we do experience all polarities of life as a way to grow and there are times when negativity or ill-wishing, either from external sources or from within our own unconscious may arise in the form of attempted sabotage or hateful feelings.

Black tourmaline has an incredibly powerful and yet gentle capacity to deflect such energy and to absorb it. Holding a piece in your left hand (or right hand if that is your non-dominant and receiving hand) whilst chanting is one of my favourite and most immediately effective ways of cleansing my energy field. I find it very helpful when something is emerging that doesn't feel great and also doesn't feel like it consciously relates to anything that I can deal with in the present moment. Sometimes there is just 'stuff' that arises and it may not relate to anything other than the body releasing dense energy as it purifies, creating space to be able to receive more light. In such instances, analysis is unhelpful as there is nothing to analyse and we often just need to let it go. If it gets a bit stuck along the way, because what we are releasing is still a bit stuck to us (in that we haven't completely mastered the lesson to which it relates), then black tourmaline can help us dislodge it and get it moving. If we need awareness and understanding of what it is that we are releasing it will come. Black tourmaline will help us understand what we need to know. It will also just help us shift energy when we don't need to know, we just need to let it go.

Black tourmaline creates a field of highly protective and deflective energy around us. When we are going through purification we can feel vulnerable and unstable for a while, especially if we are releasing a lot of old energy. In such times, black tourmaline holds us safe. It is hard enough to get into our own stuff and let it go if it is painful or has been unconsciously held in for a long time. To be bombarded with external distraction during such times whilst needing to stay in our own process is probably a bit too much to ask of any soul. So black tourmaline is there to help us. I liken this process to giving birth. Purification or the healthy use of the death energy is one and the same with birthing or the renewal of the life energy. It just depends on how we look at it. Do we identify with the part that is dying or the part that is being born? Whichever way you look at it, the process is both inevitable and powerful and sometimes delicate. It can require intense focus from us for the important transitional moments. Just as you would perhaps not ask a mother in the midst of physical labour, about to bring a baby into the world, to deal with any other task than the one immediately requiring her full attention, so too is it best to let ourselves deal with the purification process with some withdrawal from external distractions, so that it may occur as easily, gracefully and swiftly as possible. The deflective qualities of black tourmaline help us take that time out for ourselves.

Black tourmaline protects against ill-wishing (sometimes called curses – which can be very conscious and intentional or unconscious and unintentional), psychic negativity including psychic attacks (which again can be unconscious, such as through gossiping and speaking negatively about someone right up to fully-fledged, fully-intended malicious attack). What empowers these phenomena is fear within us. We have at any moment the free will to refuse to take on the effects of these situations. The difficulty can be to step out of the vibration of fear through which such attacks thrive and step into compassionate presence through which we become capable of genuinely saying to those that would seek to harm us, "Hey, you're scared, angry and fearful, I am sorry that you feel that way and I hope you can forgive me for any harm I've caused you now or in the past, intentionally or unintentionally. I don't wish you any harm and I'd like to send you compassion, I don't judge you – we all have struggles and we all have suffered – but you don't have my permission to remain connected to me in this way. You have to leave my energy field and take your own energy with you. I forgive myself, I don't accept this attacking energy, I do not deserve it and I release it now through my own free will. I ask for the beings who love you unconditionally to assist you now, but I cannot any further, except by letting you go and giving myself permission to be free of your influence. Go in peace beloved. You cannot stay here and you cannot return without my consciously given permission. So be it."

Black tourmaline helps us to get to this space by helping us rise above the fear that would keep an attack active in our energy field. It helps us move beyond paranoia, suspicion, fear and defensiveness through which negativity can gain a stronghold, dislodging what it is within us that has brought us to that place. We could have attracted such a situation through any experience of helplessness, fear or anger in this or any lifetime. As we cleanse our body-soul, we become able to release such negativities often even without having to become consciously affected by them. It is a process and black tourmaline supports us as we learn to master the lesson that love is more powerful than fear, and we can fight most effectively through loving compassion than by aggression or power games. Black tourmaline helps us disable the part of us that wants to engage with vengeance and instead to grow in wisdom, to outgrow the conflict in the first place.

Black tourmaline also helps protect us at a physical-energetic level, which in a modern age where we are exposed to different types of radiation fairly constantly, can be helpful.

It is my belief that the consciousness of black tourmaline actually helps us learn how to absorb the radiation that can help us (such as the spiritual radiation from the sun which holds great divine power and the living radiation of the Earth, which provides us with a tremendous alchemical container through which spiritual transformation is possible). It deflects that which cannot (such as electromagnetic fields from computers and cell phones). It might not be possible to walk around with big chunks of black tourmaline placed around every source of electromagnetic radiation (ah, but we can dream it into reality yet!) but we can always carry a small piece with us or call upon the Angel of Black Tourmaline for help in this way.

Black tourmaline draws negative energy off the body, like a spiritual cleansing rag. It is especially good for removing energy, such as fear-based thought, that is not particularly comfortable with the light. Its dark black and peaceful strength can be comforting rather than confronting to such energies that may recoil from the light believing that they will be judged or punished (as they are yet to learn about unconditional love, still being trapped in the energy of shame and guilt for example).

This crystal helps boost the immune system and encourage the body-soul to eliminate negativity and promotes purification. Through this process, black tourmaline actually builds a field of positivity within and around the body and energy field. This happiness is grounded and realistic – as black tourmaline is a grounding and earth-aligning stone. Sometimes happiness in others can seem more based in fantasy and being on a high of addiction or as a defence against darker feelings. This kind of happiness can feel contrived, artificial or uncomfortable to be around. The happiness that black tourmaline helps us access is genuine, grounded, perhaps less dramatic and overt, but real, connected to the body and comforting nonetheless.

The optimism that this encourages in the body is very helpful for maintaining health and wellbeing in the body, boosting the immune system and building energetic and physical strength. I remember once hearing the wife of my Chi Gung master guiding one of the students in our class to find more strength (to chop through granite bare handed, as you do) by 'thinking of something that makes you happy. Happiness makes you stronger!'. This is one of the many gifts of black tourmaline, it helps to create a positive mental attitude which then empowers us in all areas of our lives, without denying the darkness or suffering – it just helps us process that and move back to our centre.

ABOUT THE ANGEL LAHABIEL

Lahabiel is an assisting angel to the Archangel Raphael. Lahabiel appears to me as an ancient being well-versed in magical practice and very experienced in dealing with all types of curses and ill-wishing, psychic attack and negativity. He appears within a dark cloak, concealed and yet filled with light and power. This cloak allows him to witness the details of any situation without the sender of the attack becoming aware of his presence and 'covering their tracks' to avoid being seen and foiled at their dark game. In this cloak of darkness he can perceive what is happening and then respond most effectively, appropriately and I also feel impelled to say 'creatively', which makes me wonder what he gets up to sometimes!

He is called upon to ward off evil in any form – whether spell, curse, evil eye or more. He is well-versed in all forms of magical protection and more than this, he has a consciousness that helps us access the consciousness within us that is ultimately the best sort of protection, which is compassionate awareness, presence and divine love.

These qualities do not lead to indulgence and acceptance of negative behaviour, in allowing it to continue or in denying its existence. They are based on healing rather than fighting. They help us learn that sometimes the way is to lead with love. As my grandmother used to say, "You get more flies with honey than vinegar".

In law school, I played with the idea of becoming a barrister. I could think on my feet and was rarely at a loss for words. I could read people reasonably well and manipulate situations without too much difficulty, leading people to where I wanted them to be. I use these gifts in a far more soulful way now, but back then, not so much. My ego thought being a barrister would be pretty interesting. I rocked on up to class one day for a mock trial, which was essentially a group of students running a faux-legal trial to learn about how the court process works and get some hands on experience. I had my 'witness' in the stand, for the opposing counsel, and I proceeded to verbally tear her testimony and credibility to shreds. I was relentless and my 'witness' did not enjoy the experience (understandably) at all. It was not my finest moment.

At the end of the process, with the poor volunteer student who was the 'witness' seething at me for having putting her through all that, the lawyer who was acting as our mock trial judge (a young woman with a regal nature) gave me some sobering feedback. She suggested that I pull back my aggression and accomplish the same result without the violence. I was suitably chastised and I called my inner pit-bull into check. It was a learning about power. She was teaching me about the iron fist in velvet glove, just as my grandmother had done earlier on in my life, and just as various masters on the inner planes have done since then. One doesn't have to try to dominate another in order to be powerful. In fact if anything it was my own insecurity about not getting the job done at the time that would have pushed me to such ruthlessness with another. It was a good learning for me to come to grips with my own power complex and learn to wield it effectively (and that meant that it served love) rather than unconsciously (where it served itself). As an aside I offer deep apologies to the man that I was 'cross-examining' at the time!

Lahabiel helps us grow the consciousness necessary to become more powerful than an attack, which is rarely through fighting force with force. In fact to do this as a powerful healer is likely to actually pour a lot of energy into a situation and cause it to escalate unnecessarily. Calling upon Lahabiel and allowing him to assist us in lifting ourselves into a place of higher consciousness is going to diffuse the situation more swiftly and offer an opportunity not just for protection but for the highest good, which is actually the healing of why that situation is there in the first place.

Sometimes negative energy is brought to us because we can help heal it for the other soul in question. Lahabiel and black tourmaline together, with our willingness to honour the divine wisdom that has delivered this situation to us and not become frightened that we cannot handle it, along with our divine team of helpers, can help it heal and be released permanently. This is a great spiritual service. It does NOT mean that you go out like a winged-crusader looking for negativity to heal. That is a foolish task and one that an advanced group of some of my students learned not to do twice (with the added bonus of a lecture from me) some years ago. What it does mean is that you can be present to what comes to you and offer your service to the negative energy in question. It will either accept your help or not, but you are always allowed to offer it with detachment and compassion.

Lahabiel's message is to call upon him and allow his wisdom and experience to do the work for you – you just need to align your consciousness with his, and allow his protection and expertise to assist you. This is spiritual intelligence in one of its forms – to allow yourself to align with greater beings and in doing so, receive the benefit of their divine intervention. He also says not to worry. For any source of negativity, no matter how harsh or how long it has been going on, there is a small, efficient and effective step that can be taken and he knows what that step is and how to get you to it. All you need do is ask for his help and it will be yours. If you are encountering a long, drawn-out and bitter family law proceeding, or other dysfunctional family or work situation, this message can be reassuring to say the least.

SOUL HEALING WITH BLACK TOURMALINE AND THE ANGEL LAHABIEL

I recently had an experience with a very powerful healer who has a lot of natural talent. We did a past life regression together and what came through for her was that she had been a powerful, fearless warrior in a previous lifetime.. This energy of courage, fearlessness and strength, and quite a masculine approach to life, is still very present in her now.

Along with energy work, she does massage, and one of her massage clients came to her with a problem. Her client had unintentionally caught the attention of a witch who was using her occult skills to send negative energy, curses and so forth towards this client. I might add here that I have known of other witches that do this, though fortunately I know many more who do not. As the attacks escalated, this client had become frightened for her wellbeing.

The healer did her best to teach the client how to protect herself with useful techniques such as deflective mirrors, crystals and also used her own skills to fend off the attack. I saw her a couple of weeks later, looking triumphant, claiming that she had defeated the witch, the attacks had stopped and everyone was happier (except perhaps the witch).

I held my tongue and waited. Within another few weeks, this powerful healer looked exhausted as the witch was back to her old tricks again, apparently with some new ones up her sleeve. Again the healer took to defence and the war was on. And so it will continue indefinitely, even across the course of many lifetimes, until there is resolution.

This is where Lahabiel and our own divine mastery can help us where a fighting mentality cannot. If you choose to remain within the field demarcated by one who wants to fight, then you have to fight or lose. It's a bit like that expression, don't fight with a pig, because you'll have to roll around in the mud, and the pig likes it! Of course, you may relish the fight too, in which case, you always have that choice to engage. If you choose however to change the playing field to that of divine love and healing, then you have a chance to free not only yourself, but also anyone else engaged in the karmic drama at hand. The choice is up to each individual but you'll earn some serious karmic brownie points in even just presenting an option for healing to others involved. The way this healing happens is by whomever it is that is drawn into the situation looking within to see how they can grow enough to heal within themselves.

Sometimes there won't be much you can do but make the suggestion and leave it up to each person to choose for themselves. For resolution to occur, the witch in this situation cannot simply be bound, banished or blocked. That may work temporarily but it will not bring final resolution. She, just like every soul, has the spiritual right to find her own divinity. Which means that the people involved in the situation with her will need to sort it out. This doesn't mean diving into her drama. It means going into their own hearts and finding a way to make peace within themselves in their relationship with her.

This could involve the client and even the client's new boyfriend (who happened to be the witch's ex-boyfriend – so you may see more of the picture now). Resolution may mean forgiving themselves for being indulging of her for so long, or for getting caught up in drama in the first place. It might even mean forgiving a completely different person – perhaps the mother of the boyfriend, for example, for perhaps being so manipulative emotionally with him that he was unconsciously attracted to a woman who would do the same thing with him, drawing him into this drama, until he could learn that he was worth genuine affection. Or perhaps he could have to forgive the witch herself, realising that she was acting out her pain of anger at rejection and not feeling loved, and have compassion, whilst stepping away from her, and letting the connection go.

Each person will need to find their own way, and their own truth. Lahabiel helps block the drama so we can think straight and find our way. Neither he nor black tourmaline will block the learning. So if we are in a situation where we need spiritual protection, call upon them, yes, but also look for what it is within you that could be asking for healing here, or if it is not personally about you, then ask how you can serve the situation. For the healer in this situation, it could have been her job to provide temporary defence, but it could have been to provide higher consciousness, to lead the client and her boyfriend towards resolution through forgiveness.

When you attend to the spiritual task at hand, even that presented by an apparently negative situation like ill-wishing towards you, you'll grow and heal, gaining energy and optimism for it. Eventually, over time, you'll attract less and less drama into your life, living more peacefully. You'll feel protected in the sense that whatever presents itself to you, even the challenges, will be signs that you are ready to grow in strength and power, which do not necessarily equate to force. You'll know you'll be supported as you find your way through and you'll learn to have the quiet inner confidence of someone who knows that ultimately, they can take care of themselves and that they don't have to live fearfully.

SOUL HEALING – CLEANSING FEAR: PURIFICATION FOR PROTECTION

In going through the process of learning to access genuine divine protection, you have to learn to change your relationship to fear and love. In doing so, you are cleansing your being of the grip that fear has held on you, which is what all humans are ultimately doing on this planet.

When I first started this practice, I was worried. I thought if I felt any fear at all (which is a pretty natural reaction if the ego feels a threat to its existence – even though it might be covered up almost immediately with anger or aggressiveness), I would be done for. That any being that wished to hook into my energy could do so and I wouldn't be able to protect myself, let alone facilitate a space for another to do so.

I pretty quickly realised that fear was not the issue. Fear could come and go and it can be a way for us to identify useful information. It might show us that we are surrendering more into trusting in a relationship and perhaps feeling a bit insecure, a bit fearful in that process. This isn't bad, it is an insight about what is happening in our relationship and for us individually. We might even be able to become conscious about a pattern of distrust or abandonment in the past and let that go, realising that it doesn't relate to the present moment, and assuaging our fear with a more present-moment response such as the truth that we won't abandon ourselves and everything is OK. Or perhaps we feel fear because we distractedly stepped behind a reversing car and need to jump back and get out of the way!

Fear itself is just an energy. It is our identification to it – either through resisting it and trying to ignore its message (which can lead to panic and anxiety) or collapsing into it and letting it take us over (which leads to terror and eventually adrenal exhaustion) that are the parts we need to outgrow. We do this through practice. We learn to cleanse ourselves so that over time we have less and less of the old fear pattern running through us. We find it easier to unplug from the social conditioning and ancient human memories that say we must be fearful in order to survive, and we come more into the present moment, where we have the option to recognise how much safety we have in our spiritual light. We see that safety is not to avoid experience or never get hurt (though the latter will perhaps happen less), but to know that everything that happens is love reaching to us and we can always choose to find that love through any experience and therefore be the better for it, even if there is an "ouch" factor along the way.

I remember studying psychology at university (until I realised there was no soul in the course, and hot-footed it out of there immediately!). There were studies done where those that had committed crimes against other people were shown images of people walking down the street and asked whom they were drawn to attack. Showing a rather animalistic response, time and time again, the interviewees picked those that looked fearful in their body language. Those that would pose less threat, those that would probably be an easier target.

In the same way we broadcast fear from our energy field. We tend to attract bullying situations with that fear. It isn't a judgement of us or a declaration that we are responsible for the unconsciousness of others. It is an empowerment. If our own energy can be so powerful as to attract that negative situation, then it can be so powerful as to attract an equally positive one. We can heal and cleanse our energy, and allow the creative power of attraction to work in our favour.

Yet there is a belief that I have noted in many spiritually-oriented people that the more visible, empowered and confident you are, the more you are asking to have your head lopped off, kind of like whatever sticks above the parapet of the castle will be blown off by a cannon!

You might have had experiences like this in childhood where any display of power was treated with fear or crushed mercilessly, so you learned to keep yourself hidden away and not share your truths or power with the world. Or perhaps you just have that cultural association more generally. In Australia we call this the "tall poppy syndrome" where someone who "loves themselves" will generally need to be "taken down a peg or two". It's a dark version of humbling someone.

Part of what we cleanse as we do this soul healing technique, is our associations with not being fearful. How do we feel about feeling powerful instead of afraid? Does it have to be an arrogant, domineering, unappealing quality that makes others feel inadequate? Or could it be an enabling quality, that actually gives you the capacity to help inspire others from a place of trust, to change their relationship to their own fears?

Over the years, I have changed my relationship to power. I went from being addicted to it in the old style sense of power, to denying it in an effort to become more centred and gentle in my heart. Eventually I decided to learn how to integrate it into my whole self that my work could become more effective. With a healthier relationship to my power, I feel I can do what I was born to do on this planet. What has happened is that I have been enabled to serve others more – which for me is the whole point of having access to greater levels of power. Just like having more money, it's not just the having, but what can be done with it that makes the having important. What will I choose to do with it, what could I do with it?

The power then becomes about what can be given rather than what can be gained, denied or dominated. This makes power a very safe energy for a heart-centred person to wield. There is no need to fear that you will be taken away from your soul (at least, not permanently, you may get dazzled for a little while and that's part of the journey then) for eventually your growing power, just like all parts of you, will be laid down in service to love.

This is where purification and protection, cleansing the energy field of fear, takes us. It is a beautiful state of great divine play and freedom. We each take a step more deeply into this place of divine grace as we grow spiritually.

HOW DO YOU KNOW IF YOU ARE HEALING AT A SOUL LEVEL IN THIS WAY?

At least in Australia, though perhaps far less so in other cultures, we can find it hard to admit that we are a big soul. In fact it is often the big souls that feel that way, whilst others may broadcast their fine abilities with great vigour and perhaps some over-confidence!

I have always felt that humility is a good quality to have when you feel that you are called to spiritual leadership in some way. However what can happen is that humility can become humiliation if we allow past experiences to distort our self-acceptance. Humiliation is where we don't feel we have power. We have that emotion arise in response to feelings of powerlessness when we are subjected to abuse and sometimes just the natural experiences of being a human being where we are not in control of greater forces (as much as we might like to imagine that we are to avoid the anxiety that accepting this may generate at first).

If you are acting from a wound of humiliation, then you will be blocking your true power. Either you'll be over the top or under-playing. Humiliation leads to distortion so it won't be authentically expressed and a part of you may sense that, leading you to push your sense of your power away even further. Yet to be powerful is a natural human need and power itself is really helpful on the spiritual path and in all of life. It is a neutral energy – like anything, it's what we choose to make of it that turns it into a positive or negative.

Rather than dealing with power itself, clearing humiliation from the energy field, restoring its natural dignity and allowing its natural reserves of power to flow without obstruction and distortion is going to bring much vivaciousness, energy and passion into your life, as well as more optimism, creative confidence and self-expression.

Without healthy connection to your power, living your soul light on this planet is like trying to run a three-legged race. It might be interesting for a little while, but eventually you are going to want to take off that leg tie and be free!

If you feel (perhaps only in your most private reflections) that you could be a great soul, that in fact you could have something truly special to offer, and you are not seeing that reflected back to you, then a soul cleanse could be just what you need. If you find that you hold back rather than put yourself forward, or that you force your way in rather than trusting that the way will open up for you with little effort, then you too will benefit from this cleansing. Power you see, is not an independent source of energy. It is what happens when we allow the Divine (which is the ultimate power source) to flow through us with less and less impediment, block or resistance on our part.

SOUL HEALING PROCESS –
CLEANSING THE ENERGY FIELD OF FEAR AND HUMILIATION

You will need a quiet place to sit comfortably be able to speak without having your privacy interrupted.

Begin the healing process by saying the following invocation:

"I call upon my own divine soul, the Angel of Black Tourmaline and the Angel Lahabiel, I call on the energy of divine protection and purification, through unconditional love, so be it!"

"I now choose, of my own free will to dissolve and disintegrate any tie, vow or contract that I have ever made with any being, consciously or unconsciously, that I shall be humiliated, punished or hated for stepping into my power, or that I shall humiliate, punish or cause another pain for doing so. I forgive myself for all misuses of power in this or any lifetime, accepting that it was a way to learn. I now choose to honour my power through unconditional love, accepting that as I become ready for it, power naturally opens up to me. I do not have to seek or force power. It is not outside of me, but unfolding inside of me, as my heart blossoms and my trust in myself grows. I now choose to release any memory, imprint or belief system from my body and energy field that is based in fear, humiliation, shame or judgement of power in myself or another. I choose to see it all as learning. I choose now to release the fear I have of loving, of saying "no" with compassion and respect, of letting my soul power flow freely. I know that I do not have to choose between love and power, that these are one and the same. I now choose of my own free will to surrender into the unconditionally loving healing, purification and divine protection of Angel Lahabiel and the Angel of Black Tourmaline, and my own soul. Through divine grace, mercy, kindness and love, so be it!"

Close your eyes and focus on your breathing. With each breath in and each breath out you move more deeply into a vast, open, dark space, filled with peaceful black light. This light feels absorbent, as though it can draw out of you any fear or negativity, any old contracts and any old doubts or fears. Allow yourself to surrender into the absorbent nature of this dark light, knowing that Lahabiel and the Angel of Black Tourmaline are with you, keeping you safe and protected. Stay there for at least forty-four breaths. Let energy, emotion, thought or sensation simply arise and fall, being drawn into the darkness when necessary.

When you are ready say, "I call upon karmic grace and higher guidance that loves me unconditionally. I ask that I be shown now or in the coming weeks, with loving kindness, what steps I need to take to complete this healing process and allow more grace to assist me in releasing fear. Please show me who can help or how I can help myself through helping others. Thank you beloved ones. I am open to receive this guidance through divine grace, so be it."

Stay with your breath for at least another seven breaths.

When you are ready, move your arms and legs and open your eyes.

You have completed your soul healing process.

Let the effect of it continue to unfold at a deep, cellular level and be open to any thoughts or feelings that come in the coming hours, days or weeks. These thoughts and feelings can be guidance, helping you on your way. If you are not sure if a thought is guidance or not, you can confirm that it is guidance by asking, "Does this thought come from unconditional love? If so, then it may repeat itself, if not, then it must leave and not repeat itself. Through my own free will, so be it." Also test if it feels loving and non-judgemental to your heart. True guidance is never judgemental and always unconditionally loving.

PSYCHOLOGICAL-EMOTIONAL HEALING WITH ANGEL OF BLACK TOURMALINE AND ANGEL LAHABIEL: PSYCHOLOGICAL AND EMOTIONAL PURIFICATION

There is a saying in Buddhism that an empty vessel is the most useful. Certainly in terms of our ability to receive – abundance, support, answers, energy, manifestation of a dream – this is true. You could imagine that as soon as you put a request out to the universe, your own divine creative energy has started the manifestation process. We are as God-Goddess in that sense. What we speak about will manifest. This is one rather significant reason why it is helpful to do our best to speak about what we would love to happen, about solutions, rather than dwelling excessively on problems or negative talk about ourselves or others.

Manifestation happens with swiftness that equals our receptivity. To some manifestations we will be very receptive. We say hello to our friend and our friend responds. We have manifested a conversation with our words and intention (or at least, the beginning of one).

Other manifestations will be a push for us to grow in receptivity towards. I'll use an example from my own life. I wanted to sing ever since I was a little girl. I loved it but I kept it hidden except for occasionally jumping on stage in a high school musical and then back it went again as I laboured to get the best grades possible so I could have a 'secure' life when I was an adult, with a good job. I sang on and off my whole life and yet the thought of singing being a part of my day-to-day work completely eluded me. I would feel such grief that this couldn't be the case, because all I could see were pop singers. Not exactly me!

Then one day I went to a gathering where kirtan was being played. The musicians sing chants, and the audience echoes it back. Instantly I knew that I would be sitting on that stage doing that. I was absolutely sure. Within months, through a series of synchronicities, it had happened. I was happy. That was what I wanted It was happening, end of story.

However, after those few promising opportunities to sing kirtan for the gatherings, I kept being blocked from singing. I wasn't far enough into the organisation that hosted these gatherings to be accepted for this task anymore – quite possibly because I showed no interest in following the spiritual path that they wanted me to take if I was to become one of their teachers. If I wanted to continue singing, I had to commit to moving deeper within the organisation. What was asked of me was to dedicate my life in service to the particular guru of the organisation. I felt that I already served the Divine and still do. So I did not feel that I could truthfully follow the path that was offered to me. In fact, it had a cult-like element of unconsciousness that I was deeply uncomfortable with. The further I travelled into the organisation, providing healings for a number of its members from time to time and bearing their confidences (they chose me, for some instinctive reason, to discuss all the darker aspects of their organisation's financial and psychological journey), the more uncomfortable I felt.

More than that, I felt something else blocking me. Although I struggled against this at first, ultimately I learned to identify it as divine protection and I accepted it. I eventually realised that I was trying to take what was shown to me and make it manifest, instead of allowing it to unfold. I had gone from being receptive, and moved, to being attached and directive, and as a result, the unfoldment was stalling. I wasn't getting ahead, I was being blocked. It was just the Divine saying, "This isn't your resonance, this isn't your community, you don't have to try and make yourself fit to meet your needs for creative expression, I have some other things in mind for you – let go and let me move you".

It wasn't long after this that I received very clear guidance in meditation that my involvement with this community, which had ended up being about eight or nine months in duration now, needed to be terminated completely, that it was becoming a distraction and no longer supported my path. In the days following this meditation I formally announced my intention to withdraw from my involvement and stepped away with great sadness in my heart, but also with a sense of freedom and joy.

Soon after this letting go, opportunity after opportunity began rolling in for me to make music. I didn't even need to ask for them as I was being asked first. I had got out of the way and become more receptive to allowing the manifestation of my own soul to continue. There have been challenges along the way as I learn and grow, but the relative ease of manifestation of something that I once thought was a mere fantasy into a real-life experience happened within a matter of months. What made it thus? A willingness to get out of my own way and allow the divine to flow.

HOW DO I KNOW IF I NEED HEALING IN THIS WAY AND AT THIS LEVEL OF MY BEING?

If you are nursing a dream and it is yet to unfold into physical form, then it may be that you are getting a little stuck along the way. Divine timing is always perfect, but we need to meet it too! We do our part to be moved with our destiny. Surrender doesn't equate to laziness. Being moved by the divine often requires some heavy lifting by us as we build the disciplines to keep ourselves aligned with higher vibrations. The lighter we are energetically, the easier it is for us to be moved. Soul cleansing like the one shared above and the following emotional and psychological cleanse are ways to lighten up and let divine flow happen more easily.

Apart from that, clearing out attachment and learning to trust more is always helpful, no matter where we are in our process of manifestation. The clearer we are, the more trust we hold. The less attached we are to the 'how', the easier the manifestation will occur. It is simple but not always easy for us to honour this. This healing will help you get there and can be done at any time you want to boost your divine flow and get out of your own way. It is a short simple practice that can even be done daily for the next three weeks or as a regular spiritual practice 1-3 times a week, to help keep you in your divine zone of creation.

PSYCHOLOGICAL-EMOTIONAL HEALING PROCESS: PURIFICATION

If you have some Black Tourmaline, please do have it placed on or near your body. If you don't have a piece of the crystal you can simply open the book to page 30 in the full colour section, which features a Crystal Angel Mandala for Black Tourmaline.

Start by sitting comfortably with both palms upwards, resting the backs of your hands on your knees, you may like to have the black tourmaline between your knees on your chair or resting on the palms of your upturned hands.

Say, "I call upon the healing Angel of Black Tourmaline and the Angel Lahabiel. Please be with me, beloved crystal angels, and bestow upon me the gift of purification that I may surrender and be moved. I now choose, of my own free will, to release into the loving black ray of highest consciousness that which I can safely release now, that which would tie me down or hold me back out of fear or attachment from being gracefully and lovingly moved by divine love towards my highest spiritual destiny. Of my own free will, so be it, through divine mercy, compassion and kindness."

Close your eyes and focus on the breath.

As you breathe in, draw in a beautiful rainbow light. It contains all colours. Your breath may draw in more blue in some inhalations, or more red, green, yellow, indigo, blue, or purple or orange in others. Some inhalations may be pure white light. Others may have a dark deep purplish light. Allow that inhalation and exhalation to be whatever colour feels right. You may not even be conscious of the colour and that is also fine.

As you breathe in, imagine that the colour washes in from at least twelve feet away – from all around you, above you, below you, behind you, before you and on either side of you. It rushes into your being, all the way to the centre of your cells. Then reversing and flowing out with the exhalation, carrying old energy being released from the cells all the way out through twelve feet around you on the out-breath, carried away by the light.

Repeat this breath at least forty-four times. With each breath you are lighter in mind, body and emotions. You may sense energy or emotion, thought or feeling, resistance or distraction and all this is part of the healing process. Just stay with your forty-four breaths.

When you are ready say, "I choose to forgive myself and the divine for any time I have been stuck. I now choose flow, easily, gracefully and with unconditional trust. May I have the courage to let go and let divine flow. May I even enjoy it! So be it."

Stay with the breath for at least another nine counts and when you are ready simply open your eyes.

PHYSICAL HEALING WITH BLACK TOURMALINE AND ANGEL LAHABIEL: ELIMINATION AND PURIFICATION

An amusing little quirk (which I am pretty sure he won't mind me sharing) is that my large, soft, plush orange cat called Leo prances like a spring lamb after he goes to the toilet in the morning. He seems so happy and playful as though he has dumped not only the dinner from the night before but released the weight of the world too!

This is possibly not exactly the paragraph you would expect to read in an angelic crystal healing guide (and certainly not one I ever thought I would write) but I do learn a lot from the animal world about the nature of the body. And the body is often in a lighter mood when it can eliminate old energy. It makes sense of course. It isn't much fun carrying around toxins – they can make us feel clogged and a bit hazy around the edges instead of clear and playful.

We live in a world, particularly in the West, where toxicity of all kinds abounds. We can either say "to hell with it" and dive on in, perhaps to regret it later, or become fearful of it and try and avoid everything. Neither are particularly wise or practical approaches. Somewhere in the middle, there is a moderate path where we can live, have fun and be well most of the time.

So whether it is our bowels, bladder (taking a cue from Leo), liver, lungs, brain, bloodstream, lymphatic or digestive system that could benefit from a cleanse, we can rely upon the innate intelligence of the Angel of Black Tourmaline and Angel Lahabiel to help our bodies release and repair. Mopping up the toxins so our body doesn't have to bear the load, these angelic beings are able to cope with the burden as if it were a drop in the ocean rather than a flood.

HOW DO I KNOW IF I NEED THIS HEALING PRACTICE?

Elimination and purification at a physical level brings us clarity and energy – eventually! We often feel a bit worse (or sometimes if the purification is deep, a lot worse) before we feel better. I often compare it to lifting the rug in the hallway and vacuuming under it for the first time. Initially there is dust flying everywhere, but once its done it doesn't have to gather there any more causing allergic reactions to members of your household.

Once that cleansing process has occurred, you will feel better for it. Even as you share the detoxification load with greater beings than your own body (and we call upon Mother Earth as well for this task for she has great mastery in utilising old energy as fertiliser for new life) you will still likely feel some of the burden of the process yourself. You might feel unwell, even a bit sick or emotional as energies release. Trust that you can get through it and you will feel so much better for it (and not just because the symptoms have finished).

Purification is the most effective way for more light to get in. We clean the dirty windows and the soul light pours through. We see more clearly, we feel more joyful and life seems brighter. It is worth the effort of the practice and even the hardest part, which is often the three or so days afterwards. If you are really struggling with after effects you have a choice to redo the practice or to slow down your meditation and take a break for a day or so. A salt bath or shower scrub, or even better a swim in the ocean, can help a lot.

Step by step, much like the story of the tortoise and the hare, is best with spiritual practice. You'll get where you want to go most quickly by taking steps that feel right and not trying to force. Your body knows what it is doing and this practice calls upon its natural intelligence, aligning it with spiritual helpers, to support your detoxification process and open you up to more energy and light within.

PHYSICAL HEALING PRACTICE – ELIMINATION AND PURIFICATION

Lie comfortably on your back with a piece of Black Tourmaline lying on or near your abdominal area, lower belly, souls of the feet and/or palms of the hands. Be warm and comfortable. If you don't have the stone, we'll call on the spirit anyway, so don't worry. As an alternative, you can keep this book open to page 30, which features a full colour mandala for Black Tourmaline, and leave it next to you during this healing practice.

When you are ready, say the following:

"I call upon the healing power of the Angel of Black Tourmaline and the healing presence of Angel Lahabiel. I call upon the natural healing ability of my own body-soul and the loving grace of Mother Earth. Please help now beloved ones, to detoxify and purify, to eliminate and restore my body and energy body. Through divine grace, kindness and mercy, so be it!"

Close your eyes and focus on your breath. Let the breath flow in and out of the entire body, as if the entire body could breathe.

Imagine that your feet can breathe, in and out through each toe and the sole of each foot. Imagine that the feet become open and connected to the Earth as though energy could be drawn out of them, into the Earth, by Mother Earth's own loving nature. Allow this to happen now, visualising black sludge or anything else that you see, sense or feel leaving your body and being drawn into her. She is a vast, powerful being. What is difficult for us is easy for her to process. Have gratitude in your heart and send her love whilst you release through your feet.

Whatever you feel or notice in terms of thoughts or feelings, just let them rise and fall, releasing into the Earth.

Stay with this process for at least forty-four breaths in and out. You can release through all time and space, from this lifetime and others. Just let your body do what it needs to do and don't worry. Instead let yourself relax each more with each breath. The more you switch off and rest, the more your body can go into detoxification and elimination mode.

Let yourself become surrounded by a rich black ray of light. From within it, the Angel of Black Tourmaline rises up and gathers you in her raven-black, shimmering wings. The Angel Lahabiel steps forward in a vast black robe, with glowing light visible underneath it, seeping through its edges. The angel sends sacred symbols around your body and into your cells, releasing any negative thought or word that anyone has ever said or thought about you, releasing the psychic knowing and recording of this from your body through all time and space. Let it all go out of your feet on the out breath, into Mother Earth.

When you are ready, say "thank you" and allow your body to be wrapped in a beautiful clear bubble of light. Take your time and open your eyes.

You have finished your healing process. You may feel quite emotional in waves over the next three days to three weeks. This is a good sign that your body is releasing old energy. You may find that you feel unwell or have a headache. Make sure you drink enough water and call upon the crystal angels to help you.

If you wish to repeat the healing process again after three days you can, but it is not recommended that you do it more than twice a week. Give your body time to adjust. If you find that you just feel clearer and more energised after the practice, with very little side effect, then you may wish to do this practice more regularly as your system is likely to be already quite clean. Trust yourself and listen to your body and you'll find the best way to benefit from this healing practice.

PRAYER – AFFIRMATION

To invoke the healing power of Black Tourmaline and Angel Lahabiel at any time, you can repeat the following affirmation quietly in your mind, or aloud.

"Divine Black Ray of Purification and Protection you now bring Peace to My Body and Soul."

15.

MALACHITE (Evolution)
and ARCHANGEL RAPHAEL (Healing)

THE GIFT OF ONENESS

SPIRITUAL GUIDANCE FROM THE ANGEL OF MALACHITE
AND THE ARCHANGEL RAPHAEL

Although we are not the gentlest of angels and stones, we are dedicated to bringing you home. Back to your heart, through the pain and the doubt, into life, ending the drought of defence and loneliness, survival and fear, as to the divine, we draw you so near. No more will you push parts of yourself away, no more will you feel that you have to delay, in accepting all of you, all of life, all of the world, finding the divine within all, as your heart does unfurl. Through darkness and light, exploring the ups and the downs, you'll realise you are safe, from your base chakra to your crown. It's all just a chance to grow powerful and wise. You've been taught you must fear, but that is a lie. There is nothing to resist, no other place you must be. Everything in your life reflects your own divinity. Perfect as is, even if it seems hard to understand, all you need is to trust in your own divine plan. All is unfolding exactly as it should, and everything, even darkness, serves the greatest good. We'll guide you now, to embrace the dark and the light, to realise stars shine brightest in the beauty of night.

PICTURING MALACHITE

Malachite is a rich dark emerald green stone, opaque and patterned with swirls and bands of varying shades of green from darkest green to pale shades of emerald. It is often seen in jewellery, tumbled stones and carvings, and sometimes in larger free form shapes. It isn't uncommon but it is a more expensive stone. It is highly toxic and is safest used when completely polished, rather than raw and unfinished. Malachite is often naturally formed with other blue-toned stones such as azurite and chrysocolla, which can create a stunning 'peacock' effect of blue and green tones, but even on its own, it is beautiful.

I have seen it as flat stones and as what can only be described as 'bubble' formations, where semi-spheres rise up and the surface looks like many bubbles have formed. What is probably the most beautiful aspect of Malachite is its markings. The patterning can be stunning. I am currently writing this chapter with a small tumbled stone sitting next to me, which has a natural heart-shaped pattern at one edge, fanning out into bands of various shades of emerald green.

HEALING PROPERTIES

Malachite teaches us that beauty doesn't necessarily translate into gentleness and healing doesn't necessarily mean that we are freed from the darker aspects of life. Malachite is a powerful stone and it amplifies energy – positive and negative. Whilst it absorbs negativity in a powerful way (you can feel better in a few minutes simply holding a piece of Malachite, especially if you place it at your solar plexus as it will draw out negative energy like a sponge), it also needs cleansing regularly, which running under cold water with intention to cleanse can accomplish easily enough (do not add salt as it can damage the surface of this stone). If you are going to use it, clean it before and after use.

Malachite absorbs even the densest toxins, including radiation and smog, both physical (in terms of physical pollution) and energetic (in terms of psychic pollution such as negativity). Malachite vibrates with the consciousness of Mother Earth and the natural world. In the same way that Mother Earth can cleanse by absorbing so much negativity, transforming it and releasing it though an earthquake, flood or volcano eruption, so too does Malachite absorb and trigger release of energy. Cleansing will help prevent negative energy that has been absorbed by the stone leeching back out again, but it will not prevent the clearing process from happening. This may involve your own personal volcano eruption (perhaps discovering some anger as it releases from your body), your own personal earthquake (as you perhaps shake your world by stepping out of a situation that no longer serves your growth) or your own personal flood (through releasing grief and an ocean of cleansing tears for example, or enhancing movement of blood and lymph through the body as toxins release and the water systems of the body consequently flow).

Malachite doesn't hide or gently dislodge as some other stones do. It is one of the bigger healing stones in the sense that it gets the job done, so to speak, without waiting for a chisel if a hammer or hacksaw will get the process moving! It may sound violent, but it is not unnecessarily so. If Malachite has come into your life or you are drawn to it, then you are capable of dealing with this tough love, blunt honesty and revelation. You've actually drawn this vibration to you because it is either what you are able to work with or what you need to work with. Perhaps you are still developing sensitivity to more refined stones or you need to feel the emotions and the release process in order to learn about it at a soul level. Perhaps this is part of your life training in the healing arts at this stage. Your soul is enrolling in the master class of oneness, learning to not label one experience, one reality, as heaven and its polarity as hell. You are commencing the mastery of oneness which means finding the divine energy that lurks within all of life.

This is often the fastest, though not always the gentlest, path to healing and spiritual evolution. It is the way to overcome fear, including the fear of death, as the journey is to experience the divine that exists hidden within all things, even those that seem the opposite to what you would expect the divine to be. This probably sounds like a good idea, quite freeing, but to get to that place of utter acceptance within can really challenge us. We need to open ourselves to that which we would resist instinctively. To do this with consciousness and wisdom is a highly advanced spiritual practice.

Malachite has a lot of strength and power though, and it is going to help you take this path for however long you are open to it or feel that you need it. It is a bit like a spiritual personal trainer that is going to push you to do what it knows you can do, even whilst you are doubting and perhaps even fearful that it is beyond your edge. Just like with the trainer, however, you always have the final responsibility for your own spirituality and you get to choose what you take from the lessons of Malachite and even how you may choose to intuitively combine it with other stones (such as Rose Quartz or Pink Calcite) to soften the journey and proceed in the most balanced way possible. Don't worry about whether or not this 'slows down' your spiritual growth. There is no time in the world of the soul. It only exists here in the physical world. The evolution of your soul is guaranteed. It will happen in its own unique way. It just so happens that in being drawn to this chapter, at least part of your divine unfolding will most likely happen through the wisdom of Malachite.

Malachite clears the chakras, allowing them to naturally activate as the energy channels, known as meridians or nadis, can draw more life force through the body. As this happens you will feel clearer and more energised, though possibly also experience some detoxification symptoms such as emotional or physical fatigue or congestion as the materials release from your being into the energy field of the stone.

Malachite tends to remove the soft gauzy filters that we may unconsciously place over life situations or even our own characteristics. I remember watching the television series "Moonlighting" with Cybill Shepherd and Bruce Willis when I was a young girl in the 1980s. Cybill's character, Maddie, always had this soft hazy glow about her. Later I read that it was because a sheer stocking was placed over the camera whenever they filmed her! It killed a bit of the magic for me, I have to say. Whether or not that was how the effect was created, I don't know. What I do know is that Malachite would rip the stocking off and put some surgical-intensity bright overhead lighting in its place. Not so flattering but definitely more revealing.

This is Malachite's gift, to show us truth. It might not be as soft and pretty but ultimately it will be beautiful in a different way. There are times when I see this divine beauty, it is life itself like poetry in motion. I see it in action and am in awe at how exquisite it is – not just the genius of it, but the beauty of grace in how all our life experiences so perfectly guide us back to the Source. It is as if each experience is a divine breadcrumb on the path, luring us moment to moment, leading us home.

When I am going through something challenging, I remember this. It doesn't necessarily ease the challenge – coming to consciousness is not always a gentle stroll in the park, sometimes it feels like mortal combat with our own inner fears and demons – but it does place it in proper perspective.

I have had countless times where I have sat listening to a client and been moved by the beauty of their journey. They might be telling me this story or that and wonder at my exclamation of how perfect or beautiful that situation is for the soul. I do know that it can be hard to find the divine beauty in a challenge, but it is always there and if we care to look for it, we'll find it. Often it is just easier to recognise in hindsight, when we have had the experience of where that challenge was taking us. We can then acknowledge its perfection.

Earlier this year I heard a colleague describe a situation with a friend of hers. She was listening to him speak and she had the overwhelming knowing just suddenly occur to her that he was going to have a very difficult situation arise that would be quite traumatic for him. So she wept. Not out of fear or sadness, she wept at the exquisiteness of it. She instinctively knew that this trauma would be what brought his soul to life, what would awaken him and what would bring him home to his own heart. In that moment, listening to her speak, I knew she just 'got it'. She understood the raw beauty of wild grace. To the ego it wasn't safe, but to the soul is was truth. She was willing and able to see beyond the light and the dark of ego assessment and step into divine beauty itself. That was such a powerful moment, it still transports my body into waves of blissful energy, near to tears, to even just write about it.

This is where Malachite transports us. It is beyond safety, it is beyond assurances. It appeals to an entirely different side of us. It awakens and nourishes the part of us that yearns to be wild, to be free, to not live in a safe little world where all is known and secure (in our minds at least). It appeals to the part of us that is naked and completely surrendered into life, that doesn't hold itself back from the divine, but is a completely open lover to the cosmic divine caress.

To live in this way can require shedding deep fears and ancient grief, as well as layers of societal conditioning about security and survival. To live in this way requires a willingness to be trusting of your wild spirit in such a way that others may consider you quite mad for a time (until you seem to be doing OK, and then they may consider that there could something in all this spiritual aliveness stuff after all).

Malachite is not an inner child comfort stone. Although there is nothing to fear with Malachite, if the inner child within you isn't sure how he or she feels about the stone, it may be best initially to combine it with Rose Quartz and Pink Calcite. Malachite will help you release old conditioning and learn to accept your more adventurous and risk-taking side in a conscious way, dissolving patterning that may have previously tainted risk-taking with self-destructiveness rather than self-expansiveness. What will please your inner child, and your soul, as you work with Malachite, is that you will learn to live more fearlessly from the heart. life will become more vivid as a result, and your dreams, connections to divine guidance, and your visions and meditations will be more lucid. I have always felt that the eye of God-Goddess lives in our hearts. Malachite helps give it a spiritual eye bath, washing it and allowing it to see clearly to the beauty that lays behind appearances.

Malachite itself is said to be still evolving, and this is a truly precious aspect of this stone. The energy of Malachite now compared to about ten years ago is different. It is as though its vibration has risen without losing its power and grip on the physical world. Crystals are of course living beings. They hold a spirit, an angel, a consciousness and can evolve. Malachite in particular however seems to be evolving in a quite concrete way and this is part of what it supports us to do – evolve and transform our spirit, mind and even our bodies.

ABOUT THE ARCHANGEL RAPHAEL

When I was in school, I quite passionately studied art. From classical painters to edgy performance art, I loved anything that would capture me emotionally and fuel my vivid imagination. I would venture off to the New South Wales Art Gallery from time to time and gaze in wonder at magnificent, huge canvases like "The Visit of the Queen of Sheba to King Solomon" by Edward John Poynter. I would study the details and just be transported into the world I saw within the canvas.

I also became somewhat obsessed with the works of fifteenth century Italian painter Raphael and his series of rich oil paintings of the Virgin Mary. This quite possibly explains why, in a meditation not so many years later, when I heard the name "Raphael" I thought I was connecting with an artist of the High Renaissance period! It didn't take long for me to work out that actually this was an Angel reaching out to me and the angelic kingdom revealed a little more of itself to me. I am quite sure that Archangel Raphael would consider my initial ignorance of his identity to be highly amusing.

My next conscious connection with Raphael came a year or so later when I decided to study Reiki energy healing. I had been doing readings for a little while and felt a strong inner nudge to offer energy healing too. I already knew that I would work with the chakras and energy fields, not necessarily the terrain of traditional Reiki, but I felt that Reiki would give me some confidence with 'something to fall back on' if I got into a healing situation and for some reason completely lost my intuitive perception and all channelling ability! It took me a while to trust that my spiritual abilities would not randomly desert me at inopportune moments, like a sort of spiritual abandonment, and that I could always trust that if I leapt into a healing with someone, they would rise up and catch me.

So I enrolled in a Reiki level one class, during which we learned hand positions for healing on the body and received an energy attunement from the Reiki Master that would open us up to channelling Reiki (or healing energy) through our hands. I went through my attunement process along with everyone else, and that was that.

All the other students reported feeling heat in their hands and this effect and that. I didn't feel any of that. My hands weren't hot. They were naturally cooler as a rule anyway, but they were even more cool if anything. I was a bit worried! Maybe my attunement hadn't worked?

After the attunement our teacher sat down on a chair and asked each one of us to come up to her, one at a time, and place our hands on her shoulders, sending Reiki through to her so that she could check our attunements.

Each student approached her and placed their hands on her shoulders. She would say, "Oh, that feels so great – you have so much heat coming out of your hands!" or "Your Reiki energy is so strong! My shoulders feel so warm and relaxed!" and so on as each student made their way to demonstrate their new abilities.

Finally, after waiting towards the back of the line, hoping that perhaps my Reiki was just a bit delayed in heating up, I approached her and put my hands on her shoulders. I felt the coolness pour out of my hands and the teacher twitched a little. "Oh!" is all she said.

To say that I felt like the black sheep of that class was probably putting it mildly. In true stubborn Alana-ness, however, I persisted and eventually trained myself to pump heat-based energy through my body. From time to time I would feel cold energy and I would switch channels until the heat was flowing and proceed with the healing.

After about a decade of professional healings using this method I had a breakthrough. I realised that I had certain expectations about how the Divine should flow through me, but now I had grown enough to realise that I need to allow it to come to me as it chose, to open up to even greater experience of divine grace and healing.

This is the oneness with the Divine, the acceptance of how it just is, that Archangel Raphael began teaching me at the time of my Reiki training, though it took me some years to take on the learning. There is not only one way, or even a best way. There are as many different paths and processes, healers and healing talents as there are rays of light in our Sun (Archangel Raphael is said to be the Regent of the Sun – so those drawn to the sun and solar based cultures – such as Ancient Egypt – will often have a strong spiritual connection with him).

As guardian of all guardian angels and as guardian angel of the world and humanity, Raphael is an extraordinary being of light that helps us learn how to remove self-imposed limitations on the divine and let it come alive in us as it wishes to, that this is the way to healing with the most happiness and wellbeing. His energy balances the strength of Malachite and helps us find our way past our subconscious blocks to allowing ourselves to live as one with the divine love, power and light within us.

So over a decade later (proving that there are none so blind as those that will not see!) I had finally got resolution to a question that I hadn't even asked – what was this cool energy and was it OK? What I thought was a problem, mirrored back to me by my teacher at the time who obviously hadn't experienced the phenomena as yet either, turned out to be divine after all. When I let go of trying to meet what my mind expected to have happen and instead searched for the truth, the truth was delivered to me. The truth of it was that the energy in my hands was a healing gift that was unusual and didn't fit the typical mould. Once I stopped fighting it, I could realise its worth and accept it. I had never really 'fit the mould' in any way during my life, that's just how the divine is, when it is playing at being me.

This is the gift of Archangel Raphael whose name means "God Heals". It is the experience of the divine in and as you. It is the perfect divine comedy of our lives revealing itself and bringing us to peace. It is divine grace, that divine light that heals without harm. He is the perfect Angelic balance to the power of Malachite. As they wish to say now, "together we reveal truth with grace, guiding you to a more beautiful state".

As I write these last two paragraphs I feel cool clear flames opening up in the palms of my hands and I pray that this energy reaches right into the depths of your being through beloved Archangel Raphael, as you read these words.

SOUL HEALING WITH MALACHITE AND ARCHANGEL RAPHAEL

The soul wants to feel alive. Safety as we often define it can feel like a prison to the soul. However, it isn't necessary to throw all caution to the wind and become completely irresponsible for your own wellbeing in order for your soul to feel alive (fortunately enough). We are here to learn balance. What is being asked of us is to allow ourselves to be breathed by life. To tap into that desire which can be so powerful that it pushes us to step out of our comfort zone into the learning zone, where there is risk, challenge and discomfort as we stretch and grow.

It can be hard to really tap into this place in us. We may normally try to stop it with addiction, numb it with exhaustion or tame it with routine. Especially if we have had to safeguard ourselves against the vicissitudes of life as a survival mechanism against childhood suffering, trauma throughout life, or the brain programming of fear-based survival mentality that still thrives in modern humanity.

Malachite, with its cleansing and revelation, strips back the comfortable lies that we may indulge in to manage life. It helps us reach into our yearning for aliveness within. Choosing aliveness over comfort can be a challenge sometimes. The hidden gift in such a challenge is that you have to rely more on faith to get through it. This is how you grow spiritually – you place your faith more in your soul than your ego (which prefers instead to ignore faith and stay with what is known in order to feel comfortable and in control). In fact, you may have been so caught up with the need to find a way to be safe in the world, perhaps after a childhood that was deprived of the emotional and physical sense of safety that you needed, that you don't even know you have a yearning to be more alive until Malachite comes into your life and gives you a loving but shoving divine awakening.

This desire to really be alive can show up in our lives in varied ways. It can be a restlessness, a desire for something that thrills you, though if you try to translate it into a relationship fling or a new dress or gadget, it fails to be truly satisfied. Even an adventure to another country is only a temporary fix. It isn't about what you do so much as how you are in the world that is at the heart of this desire to be alive.

Often our hunger for aliveness calls to us through our desire nature, our sexuality, our creative energy and our physicality. In our modern, mostly thought-oriented culture, the non-thinking (or perhaps more accurately "beyond-thinking") ways of being are where we find our hidden opposite – the part that will help us feel more alive and bring us into oneness, into being with all of life. You can't get much more alive than that!

It was a surprise to me that spiritual urges could feel so primal and instinctive, but of course your soul is all of you – body and lower chakras included. If you have lived a life primarily in your head, or even in your heart, there will be a part of you that yearns to live through your desire nature and body, to bring the soul to life even there.

For those that lived in their lower chakras for a long time, by comparison, the yearning for more aliveness will be quite differently experienced. It will feel as a desire to ascend, to experience the passionate surrender of devotion, of divine love, perhaps of inner vision and divine connection, to surrender into bliss, into something beyond the self. There might be a seemingly endless passion for self-help and spiritual material, which is an inner urge for spiritual growth and awakening, for the reality of the divine behind the imaginations and fears of the illusory world. It is a spiritual version of craving a really nutritious meal when you have eaten junk for too long!

Whatever you haven't got to as yet is what your soul will nudge you towards. You may find that your responses to those that seem to have already got there can be quite passionate. You might be passionately attracted, or passionately repulsed, jealous, envious, curious or confused about it all.

That's good. It's you bearing the discomfort of growth. You won't get stuck there. You'll just need to bear it for a while as Malachite does its work and then be lifted as Archangel Raphael helps you to find the treasure within yourself, to find the oneness within you with all things. Then as you find it is alive within you, as you learn to accept and live this part of yourself, you will no longer have the same reaction to those that you once perceived these qualities within. You may have no reaction to them anymore at all.

One evening I was singing at a gathering which was a bit like an open musical jam. There were guitarists, flute players, didgeridoos and drummers, along with vocalists, including me, and my beloved crystal singing bowls. There was a lot of energy in the room and along with the chanting and crystal bowls, everything felt magnified and intense. The raw instinctual energy that I felt pumping in that room was so wild and free, so completely not of the mind, that it triggered an intense yearning within me, even amongst all of that playfulness. It squeezed at my heart so intensely that I was surprised by it.

Later the next day I entered into meditation with a request for higher guidance. As I came out of meditation, I was guided to Malachite. I didn't particularly 'feel like' working with it but I trusted it and out came an entire story that I wasn't even aware of until that moment. It was held so deep in my body it took an uncomfortable emotional experience to really bring it to conscious awareness. It was that yearning to be alive in a more profound way that my body was communicating to me – the energy in the room, the wildness and freedom of it, the absence of mind and analysis, the presence and playfulness, the rawness and absence of self-consciousness. That is what my heart was yearning for, abandon of the self in a conscious playful way.

The message that Malachite clearly revealed, cutting through my confusion, was that I was seeking to live at yet another level of wild divine surrender, claiming the exhilaration of letting go and letting God. I had gone some way with this, and now it was time to go further.

I didn't know what this would look like, but I accepted it as a message from my soul. In the weeks following this experience I met a new spiritual teacher on the inner planes through dancing meditation and was given new instruction for my spiritual growth. I was told to let myself be even more detached to outcome and to act with even more courage and trust. My yearning had been given its divine answer, in fact I suspect that the answer was always coming to me and actually triggered the yearning so I would be open to it! Such is the divine. It provides answers that help us ask the right questions.

You may not be able to identify that you feel stifled or in need of a more alive way to be. I couldn't articulate this need for many, many years. Essentially it wasn't until I had cleared enough fear to even be able to contemplate living in this way that I began to recognise the hunger for it. And as one gets used to living with a certain degree of surrendered aliveness, there is a hunger for yet more of it, which is what arose for me in the situation I described above. It is the hunger that drives us to seek and find those spiritual breadcrumbs on the path, feeding us all the way home.

SOUL HEALING – COMING ALIVE BODY AND SOUL

My favourite Tarot writer, Nancy Garen, in "Tarot Made Easy" says it best. "Will you choose aliveness even if there are no safe spaces?"

This is the call of the soul to unite with the body, unlearning doing and coming to a place of being.

I believe that so much of the spiritual path involves us unlearning. We might be unlearning having to defend, prepare, know in advance, manipulate, manage, control and contrive. If we lived in a physically or emotionally unsafe environment where anxiety and fear were denied, vilified, ridiculed, judged or responded to with fear and anxiety from our primary caregivers, then we will likely have developed a complex defence mechanism in order to create some sense of safety about being in the world.

As we grow spiritually, these forms of safeguarding the self can get in the way of us growing. It's a bit like refusing to take off the training wheels on a bike that you no longer need and finding that you can't ride as far or fast because the more exciting path is too narrow to keep the training wheels on!

It is a wise and essential part of the path to learn how to care for ourselves emotionally and to learn how to provide a sense of safety for ourselves, to learn to be in the world with training wheels on when we need them. So we learn how to step back when we need to, to say no when we need to, to set boundaries and to leave situations that are toxic or harmful to us. We learn how to let go and move on.

Then as we gain a sense of self and of strength, we learn how to hold our centre, stay present and engage. Rather than walk away we may find that the soul asks us to go deeper. Is there something here that could be a tool in our own mastery? Is there a lesson that we can learn and grow stronger in the process of learning? Is there a hidden gift in the discomfort of being here? Once that is resolved there is no walking away required. Situations that no longer have any karmic glue or stick in our life just fall away and we grow into new situations. There is so much less to do in life than we may imagine!

This is the coming alive of the soul in the body. It is letting life happen. Being moved. Allowing. Not resisting but flowing with the energy of it. It is an advanced practice and it is NOT the same thing as being blown about in the winds of fate, without will or personal power. It takes great strength to surrender. Think about a skilled dancer with a powerful body. It takes so much strength to allow the spirit of the dance to be able to move through his body unimpeded.

So it is with the soul and the body. To hone the vehicle, to strip it of fear and doubt, to gently and lovingly nourish it with trust and acknowledgement whilst building sensitive receptiveness to life so we can flow without thinking our way into trouble – that is an art. It is not simply lolling about as a puppet on the end of a string connecting you to the soul! It is a living dance of conscious co-operation and co-creation between body and soul.

HOW DO YOU KNOW IF YOU ARE HEALING AT A SOUL LEVEL IN THIS WAY?

I once had a dream so vivid, that I could feel the emotion of it for days afterwards. It was many years ago, but even so, I still recall it clearly. I was dancing and doing gymnastics, leaping and flying about the air with utter grace and no bodily limitation at all. It was exhilarating! I awoke with the feeling of great joy.

At the time, in my physical life, I was struggling with fatigue and feeling very stuck in my life. The contrasting dream reality, the energetic freedom and joy of it was like a glimpse of a distant oasis in a dry, barren desert. How I longed for some of that dream energy to come into my waking life! Many years later I realised that it had. It was through music and dance, yoga and much of my own hard work that had helped me break free from the self-imposed patterns that held me exhausted and trapped in a prison of my own creation. Now it was not only in my dreams that I could let my body dance in its own way.

If there is a part of you that is yearning for something to come to life within you or around you, that thrills at hearing a diva singing centre stage, or is mesmerised by a dancer in graceful liberation, surrendered into the music. If there is a part of you that is energised by an Olympic athlete, or inspired by an artist or public figure, then there is something stirring within you, something calling you to it. As you surrender to it, you allow it day by day to manifest from within. This soul healing process will help you get there.

SOUL HEALING PROCESS – COMING ALIVE IN BODY AND SOUL

You will need some music that you feel in the mood to listen to – quiet or energetic music, whatever feels right for you at this time. You will need a place where you can dance or move with your eyes closed without bumping into furniture (or standing on your pet!). Preferably you will have the phone switched off and find a place where you can just be for at least twenty minutes without having your privacy interrupted. Set up your music so it is ready to play without any fussing about.

Close your eyes, feel your feet on the floor and notice your breathing. Let your knees be unlocked and perhaps slightly bent and take your awareness to all four corners of your feet. Let yourself rock slightly from front to back on your feet, feeling the weight on the balls of your feet and then in your heels. Then rock slightly from side to side until you again come back to centre, letting your body naturally align over your feet. Allow the feet to begin to draw energy up from the Earth, all the way from your feet to the top of your head.

Begin the healing process by saying the following invocation:

"I call upon my own divine soul, the Angel of Malachite and the Archangel Raphael. I call upon divine source and the flow of life itself. I call upon grace, compassion, play and wildness, upon freedom, kindness, wisdom and courage. I call upon the rainbow bridge of love that brings body and soul together, I dance this bridge now, with aliveness and grace. I surrender my resistance and my fear to the crystal angels and I ask for help that I may live my life with passion and play, with receptivity and trust. Through my own free will, so be it!"

Play your music. Close your eyes then and come back to connecting consciously with your breath and be with your body. Notice how your body wants to move and let it do so. Your movements may be small or large. Forget about how it looks and focus on how you feel.

Let yourself dance whatever colour or colours of the rainbow that you see, sense or feel in the music. You may dance blue, red, green, pink, violet, orange, yellow, gold, silver, white, black, violet or more.

You may not feel drawn to colour at all and just want to move. Let yourself be and let it happen.

Dance for as long as feels right, whether that is a few minutes, a few hours or somewhere in between. When you have finished, close your eyes again (if you have opened them) and focus again on your breathing.

Notice how your body feels. The energy. The breath. The movement and the aliveness. Just stay present to it and notice.

When you are ready say, "I call upon karmic grace that I may live my fullest life in wild surrender to divine beauty and peace. Through gentle compassion and my own free will, so be it."

Stay with your breath for at least another seven breaths and when you are ready, just open your eyes.

You have completed your soul healing process. Feel free to complete it again at any time you feel like you need help moving beyond anxiety or confusion, into the flow of life.

PSYCHOLOGICAL-EMOTIONAL HEALING WITH THE ANGEL OF MALACHITE AND ARCHANGEL RAPHAEL: REPROGRAMMING SAFETY

The mind can get a bad rap in spirituality. We may worship it as the highest power or vilify it as a barrier against the heart. Truth is, it's just part of us and it can be an ally on the path if we don't make it master and if we give it some good nourishment.

Giving an experience of divinity is my passion. My tendency to want to just dive on in to getting those bodies and souls connected through energy transmission, dance and meditation, and my impatience with giving much explanation (one reason for my nickname of Red, I believe) has not always worked in my favour. I learned that sometimes I have to feed the mind with preparation and information so it wouldn't freak out as the experience took it into new terrain.

As we take the healing journey with the Angel of Malachite and Archangel Raphael there will be times when you may feel as if you are being asked to get your mind to make a complete reversal in ways of thinking and responding that have been habits for most of this lifetime if not others as well. I believe that the mind is absolutely capable of this. As we grow in spiritual intelligence we do become exquisitely adaptable and able to unlearn and retrain our body, emotions and mind, delivering results that we may have once believed impossible to achieve. But everything is sweeter with love thrown in the mix. So this healing process is a way to nurture, guide and reprogram the mind so the spiritual and even physical journey with the Angel of Malachite and Archangel Raphael unfolds most gracefully.

HOW DO I KNOW IF I NEED HEALING IN THIS WAY AND AT THIS LEVEL OF MY BEING?

I'll be the first to say that learning to surrender attachment to our own safety and security in favour of letting the divine work it out felt like madness at first. It was a major test in trust, even with proof that I would be cared for by that which was beyond my control, over and over again, it was still a big 'ask'!

If your mind rebels at this notion of conscious abandonment into life, if it wonders whether it is actually mature or sane to attempt this inner work,, then I suggest that you try this reprogramming exercise.

Every healing process in my work is offered from a place of unconditional love and intent that it be for your highest good. It is offered from a position of trust in the divine and your own innate spiritual intelligence. This is a way to explain how I know that you will release what you are ready to release and take on that which serves you only.

PSYCHOLOGICAL-EMOTIONAL HEALING PROCESS – REPROGRAMMING SAFETY

If you have some Malachite, please place it on or near your body.

Start by sitting comfortably with both palms upwards, resting the backs of your hands on your knees. You may wish to have the Malachite nestled in the waistband of your clothing or resting on the palms of your upturned hands.

Say, "I call upon the healing Angel of Malachite and the Archangel Raphael. I call upon my own higher self and upon the divine feminine wisdom of neuroplasticity, the wisdom that allows the brain to adapt and change to new life situations. Please be with me, beloved ones, and bestow upon me the gift of reprogramming my mind, brain and belief patterning within my cellular memory and astral body, that it may more accurately reflect a relationship to safety that serves my soul expression on this planet in unconditional love, joy, peace, freedom, creativity, passion, connection and playfulness. I now choose, of my own free will, to release into the loving consciousness of the Angel of Malachite all that which would hold me back from redefining my relationship to safety and my concept of how I can be safe in the world. I ask that this be done now swiftly, gracefully and honestly. I surrender traumatic memory and imprint to you beloved. Ease the symptoms of detoxification please Archangel Raphael, and help this be a peaceful process. Through my own free will, so be it."

Close your eyes and focus on the breath. Become aware of a rich emerald green light that is all around you, that you can breathe deeply into your heart. Allow it to grow and radiate through your body and mind. Imagine it seeping into your brain, cleansing and upgrading its programs and beliefs, its synapse patterning. Imagine a cool soft light accompanying this process keeping you calm and detached as you allow the divine light to do its work.

Stay with the breath as this occurs, allowing for forty-four inhalations and exhalations.

Then say aloud, "I am safe. It is safe to trust the divine flow of life. I am supported. My survival is through thriving and I thrive and flourish in my life. I have love and support. My needs are anticipated and met often even before I know what they are. Life loves me and serves my growth. I am one with life. I am one with my own soul. I trust and grow. I take risks from my heart and I love and I live freely. I am passionate, creative, intelligent and wise. I am growing always and I am open to discovering myself anew each and every day. The divine loves and supports me in this all the way. Through my own free will, so be it."

Perceive, visualise or allow the green light to begin forming new pathways of vibrant emerald green light in your physical brain now. Imagine that light causing old pathways that may appear as dusty old roads, with dry cracked mud, to heal, growing over with thick new green grasslands and turning into unused fields, with new clean pathways filled with light and energy forming in their place.

Stay with forty-four breaths in and out, and in your own time, open your eyes.

If you can do a forward fold with your body leaning forward and your head reaching towards your knees, either sitting or standing, then do this for a few breaths, slowly coming back upright again. Gradually move your fingers and toes, and stand up in your time, grounding by bouncing up and down on your heels for at least four breaths, in and out.

You have finished your psychological and emotional healing process. If you wish to do an intensive reprogramming, you can complete this practice one to three times per week for three weeks. Once you start to feel enjoyment in the energy of the words you are speaking (and feel free to adapt the words to suit your own personal truths), know that healing is happening in a meaningful way for you. This may happen on the first go or after some repetition. Stay with it and trust whether it is right for you at this time to persist and go further. Remember there is nothing to fear here, only life to be lived as and when you are ready and willing to do so.

PHYSICAL HEALING WITH MALACHITE AND ARCHANGEL RAPHAEL: THE HEALING FIELD

Archangel Raphael once gave me a specific healing meditation for my own personal use. It had such a powerful effect on me that I decided to record it that same day and have it available for download on my website (which it still is). It is called "The Healing Field". I will share a short version of it here with you.

How do I know if I need this healing practice?

The Healing Field is about letting the intelligence that is in the body and soul heal itself. It's a bit like a spiritual cast for a broken bone, resetting and coming back into perfection, as it is held in a loving net. One thing I did learn from my polarity therapy teacher – the body knows how to heal itself and to mend a broken bone! Trust it.

You can use this healing practice at any time. It takes you back into oneness with your perfected self. It will never cause you harm.

The practice here has the energy of Angel of Malachite added to it.

PHYSICAL HEALING PRACTICE – THE HEALING FIELD

Lie comfortably on your back with a piece of Malachite (if you have it) on or near your abdominal area, heart, in the base of the throat or in the palms of the hands. Make sure you are warm and comfortable. If you don't have the stone, we'll call on the spirit anyway, so the practice will still be just as effective on you. If you like, you can open the book to page 31, which features a full colour Crystal Angel Mandala for Malachite, and leave it open next to you during this healing practice.

When you are ready, say the following:

"I call upon the healing power of the Angel of Malachite and the Healing Field of Archangel Raphael. I call upon the natural healing ability of my own body-soul. Please help now beloved ones, to cleanse, refresh and restore my body and soul according to the perfection of my divine templates now. Through divine grace, kindness and mercy, so be it!"

Close your eyes and focus on your breath. Let the breath flow in and out of the entire body, as if the entire body could breathe. Imagine that you are being held in a loving net of emerald green light, with huge mountains of rich green Malachite crystal holding each corner of the net, as it softly stretches and dips in the centre. Your body is held softly but firmly in this sacred matrix.

Notice beautiful green laser-like lights emanating from the peak of each Malachite mountain. Fanning out, they form beautiful webs of luminous green light which builds into a softly flowing ocean of green light that flows all around you, until the field of light is above you, below you, to the left and the right, before you and behind you.

Whatever you feel or notice in terms of thoughts or feelings, just let them arise and be swept away into this light, cleansed and returned to you as fresh energy.

Stay with this process for at least forty-four breaths in and out.

When you are ready, say "thank you" and allow your body to be wrapped in a beautiful emerald green bubble of light. Take your time and open your eyes.

You have finished your healing process.

You may feel energised after this process and notice a change in your desire to live in particular ways. Don't feel that you have to hold on to old habits for safety or familiarity. Trust your instincts as you create new habits. If you feel challenged by any detoxification that arises (there should be minimal detox as green is cleansing and this is a gentle healing practice), simply call upon Archangel Raphael to help you cleanse with the green light.

Give yourself time to adjust and do this practice again in another week's time if you feel it is needed. You may like to use it whenever you feel the need for some gentle cleansing and replenishment.

PRAYER – AFFIRMATION

To invoke the healing power of Malachite and Archangel Raphael at any time, you can repeat the following affirmation quietly in your mind, or aloud.

"My Emerald Green Heart is Alive with Love and Oneness with All."

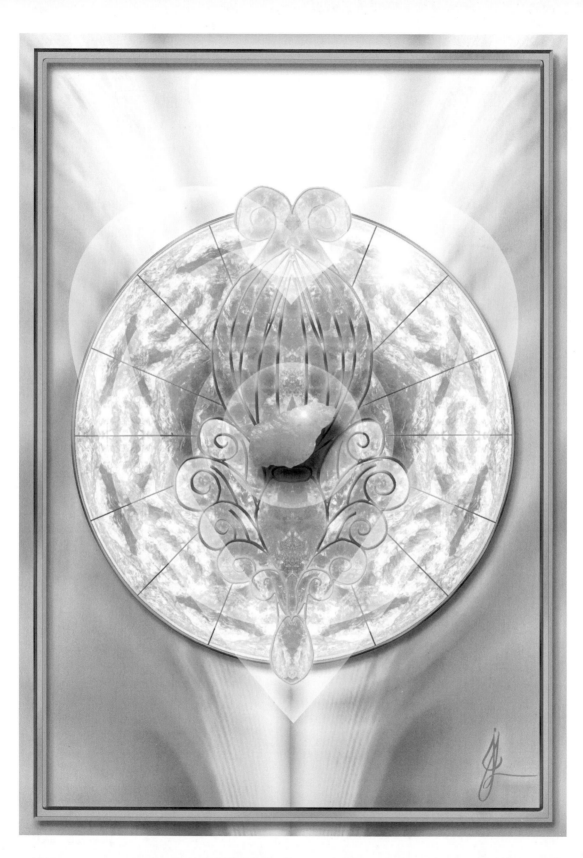

16.

ROSE QUARTZ (Unconditional Love) and ANGEL BALTHIEL (Healing Jealousy)

THE GIFT OF HEART HEALING

SPIRITUAL GUIDANCE FROM THE ANGEL OF ROSE QUARTZ AND THE ANGEL BALTHIEL

Gently we call you to your heart, to your soul home. The place within which dwells a sacred throne. A place upon which your consciousness can rest, where you can be at peace, beyond judgement or test. To enter this holy sanctuary within, some healing is now to begin. Such relief will come as you release sadness and grief. To let go of anger and jealousy brings you sweetness and peace. There is no need to hold on to suffering or pain. With softness and soothing, we help you reframe, that which you struggled with in the past, bringing you understanding, peace and freedom at last. We comfort the precious child within, we heal wounds that are old, we reveal your true value, more precious than gold. With reassurance and love, without condition or test, we help you realise that you are now blessed. To be who you are is sacred and pure. You don't need to be like another, that is for sure! And if you have had to let something or somebody go, don't worry, it's just helping your soul to grow. We'll help you surrender the loss you perceive, you'll then be ready to accept what you truly want and need. In fact, it is already on its way for your open heart to receive. There is so much love within you, endless in fact. We'll help you learn to take comfort in that. As you leave behind separation, loneliness and fear, and dwell happily in your heart-light, powerful and clear.

PICTURING ROSE QUARTZ

Think pink! Rose Quartz is one of the most commonly known crystals, second only perhaps to Quartz. Rose Quartz ranges from the palest whitish pink to deep dark rose tones. It is a blend of translucent and opaque finish and can contain soft white banding shaped in criss-cross overlays and straight lines running through the stone. Rose Quartz can contain rainbow inclusions. It can be raw or polished.

Rose Quartz has been used in jewellery and is often available in larger pieces as well as small tumbled stones. The first piece of crystal that I ever purchased was a large Rose Quartz sphere from my first spiritual teacher when she closed down her crystal shop in Hurstville, south of Sydney, and was selling leftover stock to her students. I remember it being quite an investment for me at the time, being a few hundred dollars. However a friend took one look at my smiling face when I held the crystal and promptly declared, "You must have it." I agreed, purchased it and have found it to be a soothing and gentle companion on my path of heart healing.

As I sit here writing this chapter, the sphere sits next to my computer. Another large polished free form shape sits on my lap. I must say it feels very much like being hugged. It is remarkably comforting. The free form is a particularly beautiful piece with many rainbows included in it and a criss-cross formation of white banding that forms a six pointed intersection. It looks like the inside of the six-pointed hexagram, which is a symbol for the heart chakra. It is a heart-balm in a stone.

HEALING PROPERTIES

Rose Quartz is the heart healer par excellence. It can be combined with any other crystal to bring softness and comfort and is a perfect stone to use with those that are sensitive as it will work on healing in an effective but non-confrontational and non-aggressive manner. This makes it perfect for inner child work or any kind of emotional healing where there is fear around the process of feeling the feelings and letting them go, or about the ability to feel the feelings. Rose Quartz creates a field of love and support, a comforting presence that creates a sense of safety and trust, of being held, which can make the fear lessen its closing grip around the heart, so it can open and shed old pain without resistance or struggle.

Rose Quartz is also a great stone to use with those that have a lot of anger or a violent nature, and have not yet truly received and learned to integrate the gifts of tenderness, gentleness, softness and love. These qualities can be repulsive to such people, who may fear them as weakness and a path to ridicule, shame or even death! There can be many experiences of trauma (in this lifetime and others) that give rise to such a belief system. This trauma can, over many lifetimes, become quite entrenched in the heart. The presence of Rose Quartz can help dissolve the trauma and release the suffering of the heart without pushing the person to a stronger and more cathartic emotional release which may not be tolerable for them. The gift of genuine and unconditional love is that it doesn't demand, it just gives. Rose Quartz holds this energy of allowing for emotional healing in one's own time. There is no push, just endless presence of gentle invitation to open the heart and receive.

Many souls who are on a healing journey were 'pushed' into it as a way to heal childhood wounds. Such souls may have grown up surrounded by grief or pain, perhaps in the emotional environment of broken family through death, divorce or infidelity. They may have been subjected to other emotionally challenging situations such as the financial and/or physical insecurity that accompanies poverty, sexual abuse or physical violence of any kind. Rose Quartz is an angel of comfort, helping to shed the cleansing tears and fiery rages that would naturally arise in response to such challenges. The Angel of Rose Quartz helps the heart to be free of the past and open to a completely different reality in the present moment, drawing in a healed future.

Rose Quartz also teaches one of the master healing lessons of the heart chakra which is forgiveness. Forgiveness is something that we can struggle with until we understand what it truly is. Forgiveness is not indulging bad behaviour, allowing abuse to continue or even letting someone 'get away with something'. Forgiveness is actually far less about the other person and far more about our own heart and our right to live a peaceful, healed existence. Forgiveness is the path, often the most effective path, to emotional and psychological freedom. We will explore this further in our emotional healing process below.

One of the gifts that we gain from forgiveness is more skill in being able to love with less condition. Mostly this is just practice! We can imagine that one must be born with an extraordinarily compassionate heart to be able to forgive, but our hearts are often far more capable than we realise – we just have to give them a chance to demonstrate their power to help us live life with a genuinely forgiving and therefore genuinely free and empowered attitude.

This doesn't just mean that others benefit, of course. To forgive ourselves for some of the terrible things that we think we have done, which very often is seen in a more understanding light when viewed through the eye of the heart, can bring us deep peace where we become much more tolerant of others and much more compassionate with the struggles of humans generally as we grow in consciousness. We can begin to truly love ourselves, to live with more kindness. It is a nicer way to be, and a relief after so much self-hatred that we may not even have been aware of – until Rose Quartz came into our lives and started helping us release it.

Self-hatred manifests in many ways that we often consider to be normal. Hating the self is what causes us to drive beyond our limits. It is behind feelings of unworthiness and addictions to self-harm – whether physically or through financial, professional and personal self-sabotage. Putting oneself into the care of others who are not up to the task and therefore end up harming us, is another expression of self-hatred. Disrespect for the environment and animals, disgust with our bodies, is another expression of self-hate. It can also be projected outwards and displaced onto various races, religions, animal species or body parts! So racism, religious persecution and sexism are other examples of deep self-hatred projected out onto the world. Self-hate fuels suspicion and distrust of others. Every abandonment or rejection can be interpreted subconsciously as a confirmation that we are hateful at our core, rather than being perceived as someone else's choice that has nothing to do with our value at all.

Hate is a dark shadow that many people find hard to access. To even admit that they feel hate can be hard for some to admit, like it is the worst thing in the world, yet it is just a feeling like any other. The less we are able to accept it and in doing so remove some of its power, the more it will be prevalent and active in an unconscious way in so much wounded human experience. If we cannot admit its existence then it is hard to become conscious of the damage it can do when left unchecked, let alone heal the original feeling to stop the trauma from repeating itself through unconscious patterning. Rose Quartz helps lift the veil we place between ourselves and our hatred. It helps us become conscious rather than scared of it. We can begin to merely witness that hate within, rather than deny it and unconsciously act it out. It can help us to find some love for that hating part of the self, to let it know that it is actually worthy of love, that it doesn't have to be angry or fearful and that we won't add negative fuel to the fire by casting it aside. Instead we can choose to call it into our hearts and help it find the peace that it needs; the peace that is given only through the soothing balm of unconditional love.

Sometimes in the course of healing work for a client in the room (or on the other end of a telephone call or email) I also do spiritual rescues. This involves the moving on of spirits that have become attached to people, places or things rather than crossing over into the light where their soul can complete its learning for the lifetime in question. It allows them to return to Source, rest, replenish and do what is needed before continuing on with their learning once more (which is most likely returning into incarnation to pick up the life lessons where they left off and progress with the soul growth process).

The core of this process is virtually always the same. It is to bring that being, which is often angry, frightened (in equal measure – there is usually a lot of fear under anger) and confused into connection with genuine love. This involves being firm, loving and compassionate, giving that being the ability to choose love. By calling in the beings that love them unconditionally and using the energy of Rose Quartz to bring that spirit of love into the space, we let them know that they will not be judged or condemned, no matter what they have been told. They are worthy of love and worthy to both give and ask for forgiveness.

This practice can free a spirit from a lifetime (or more) of suffering and help them find peace. The emotion in the room when a spirit release like this happens is proof of its veracity. It is an extraordinary moment, often highly emotional, and it feels very special.

Learning the lessons of Rose Quartz is also what empowers a healer to do this work and not be caught up in fear or anger themselves, wanting to 'fight fire with fire', which can happen easily enough if you have a lot of anger or fear directed at you and you tend towards being a responsive and passionate individual!

Rose Quartz helps us stay in the sanctity of the heart, where we know we are spiritually safe and of the most use to all beings. If you do feel drawn to do spiritual rescue work I would recommend that you undertake training (I can recommend a teacher whom I love and respect, Raym, in Byron Bay in Australia) and most of all, do the work with Rose Quartz on your own heart first. You will be on your way to being the clearest channel you can be. If you are meant to do healing work with others – either in physical form, in spirit, or both, then the work (and the training you will need) will find you. You don't have to go looking for it so much as being open to it finding you. Rose Quartz, and the open clear heart that it creates within you, will make you naturally magnetic and receptive to that which you need.

ABOUT THE ANGEL BALTHIAL

The Angel Balthial presented me with a spiritual gift when I began writing this chapter and calling upon him. It is a soft pink garland of celestial flowers that sits upon the crown of my head. If you were looking at me with your third eye at the moment, I would undoubtedly clairvoyantly appear as quite the modern-day techno hippie, typing at my laptop, surrounded by big chucks of Rose Quartz and a garland of celestial rose-coloured blooms resting atop my long, slightly wild, curly hair.

The garland itself feels quite beyond accurate description, which is a little confounding for a writer. The closest I can get to describing it is that it brings me an experience of comfort, grace, peace and love without limit. You'll feel it for yourself when we do our soul healing process below, which confirms my view that experience is often worth more than explanation.

Balthial helps us heal the heart – soothing grief, anger, fear, sadness and loss, despair and envy from the heart chakra. When the heart is open, we become aware of our own divine nature. We can see more clearly. I have said that I believe the true eye of God lays within the heart chakra. There is a lot of spiritual light that generates in the head when one meditates and does spiritual work, but it is only when that light joins with the light of the heart that one can radiate true compassion and see as God sees. Seeing without compassion can feel clinical and harsh to the one that is being 'seen' in such a way. These are the people who speak a truth that shreds and tears into us. To see with compassion is so much more than seeing. It is healing. To be seen in such a way can clear shame and guilt that has plagued someone for years, in a moment, and without a word being spoken.

It is my view that there is always another way. No matter where we think we are going or how we think we need to get there, there is always another way. So if we are getting blasted by truth, and it doesn't feel so helpful, in fact, it may feel harmful, then there is another way.

Balthial and the Angel of Rose Quartz bring us to the other way – the truth that is love, that is compassion. It is this truth that allows us to outgrow the old way of being with gentleness, simply letting it go. We can be flogged into an awareness or we can be loved and invited to step into it. Balthial invites us.

This angel helps us clear old density from the heart, whether from this or any lifetime, and helps the heart become vibrant and clear. We become capable of living from this more inviting place of love and support rather than punishment, self-flagellation and judgement. It is always our choice, but Balthial helps us heal the heart and develop compassion so we become more capable and ready to make the choice to live in a loving way.

What does this have to do with the garland upon my crown chakra? The crown chakra opens when the heart is empowered. The two are energetically intertwined, and they thrive when they can feed each other. Balthial helps us feed and nourish the heart and the crown, and through this, we open to deeper spiritual connection with higher guidance. We don't have to worry if something is genuine guidance or not when we feel the truth of it in the heart. This is where spirit and body work together. There is no question. You simply know it just as if you know if you were standing in a downpour of rain because you would be getting drenched, or you know if the sun is shining on your face because you feel its warmth. You just know.

Balthial is also known as the only angel that can conquer the genius of jealousy. Jealousy can be a tricky emotion for us to process. It's sister emotion, envy, can either inspire us to grow, to reach for that which we are projecting on to another and have not as yet found within ourselves. We can choose, through envy, to recognise that we need to nourish that part of us that feels lacking with more self-worth, and to grow into being able to have or be, in essence, what it is that we perceive in another. If we don't choose to do the work of bringing that disowned part of us into consciousness in our own unique way, then envy can drain our life force, sending power and energy to that person rather than to our own personal growth. It is up to us. Envy can be a call for personal growth, and a highly effective one, if we allow it to move us and call upon the crystal angels to help us grow consciously with self-love and kindness.

Jealousy, however is somewhat different. It arises in relationship and arises when we feel some aspect of our bond is threatened. It can be a vital instinct, telling us that something is up. But it can also be an unconscious expression of our own desire to own or possess another individual to prevent them from ever leaving us.

Or perhaps we feel jealous of another simply giving attention to someone else. I remember once feeling so jealous that a child of a friend of ours was getting what I considered undue attention from my partner. It was very early on in our relationship and I was very possessive of his attention and focus, (wanting it to be mostly on me!) without realising that I felt this way until this unexpected flash of jealousy overtook me.

My inner child didn't like it at all! I was shocked by the intensity of the emotion, which fortunately passed relatively quickly and didn't return when I was able to be kind to this part of me and accept that she really did want lots of love and attention from the men in her life. Even if it couldn't always happen in the way that she wanted, I would still be loving and attentive and completely accepting of her, and the men in her life didn't love her any less!

This helped cure the jealousy that I felt in that situation without me having to act it out in a ridiculous fight with my partner about his harmless attention to another person. This could have easily happened if my inner child feeling wasn't explored and responded to in a satisfactory manner – she certainly would have demanded some response and if I didn't give it, a fight with my partner would have most likely arisen.

Jealousy can be an expression of our insecurity or uncertainty within a bond of friendship or relationship. Jealousy is often an expression of our fear that the 'worst case scenario' is manifesting – that our partner or friend likes someone else more than us and may leave us for that person, leaving us alone and proving that we aren't so lovable, great or worth the commitment after all. Our minds are capable of producing beautiful dreams and also some horrific nightmares, and jealousy is an indicator that our minds are being tantalised by a night terror of some description, whether conscious or not.

During my early twenties, in my first serious relationship, I remember feeling jealousy arise over my partner's friendship with a new work colleague. It was painful for me to ask him about it, but I felt subconsciously that he was attracted to his co-worker. Although I knew he would not disrespect our relationship enough to act on anything he may feel, it was difficult for me to accept that this situation was occurring. I felt jealousy which let me know that there was a connection between them.

The learning was that my partner at the time could love me, be attracted to me and choose to be in a committed relationship with me, and part of this choice was choosing not to act on other attractions that he may feel from time to time. Jealousy was a good intuitive indicator, but I needed to work through it to get to what I was learning so that I would not be overcome by it, allowing it to poison my relationship or become more powerful than my own innate sense of self-worth and value.

Balthiel lovingly helps us with all these lessons. He provides us with the love and support, and the blessing of remembering our spiritual worth and beauty (the garland of celestial beauty upon the crown, that connects through the pink ray of divine love to the heart), which helps us learn the lessons hiding in an experience of jealousy, finding greater peace of heart.

SOUL HEALING WITH ROSE QUARTZ AND ANGEL BALTHIEL

There is a truth in the soul which, when accessed consciously, releases great peace through our being, healing a great variety of emotional and psychological issues through a singular moment of awakening. This truth is the revelation of innate worth.

In the midst of a human culture that is steeped in the belief system of needing to earn rather than simply receive, that there are no 'free lunches' and if something is given, you will be obliged to accept the responsibility for future help to return the favour, the notion of something being innate rather than acquired is a little out of the ordinary.

I remember my first spiritual teacher saying that we earned the right to spiritually progress and we earned the right to be gifted with a body this lifetime. Undoubtedly there is truth to this at a certain level of reality.

However, at another level of reality, beyond this immediate earthly world, there is a whole other truth which is that we have within us something that does not need to be developed, proven, controlled, or demonstrated, something that never requires validation or learning, does not need mastery or healing! It evades articulation or description and yet it is there, to be felt and recognised to the degree we are willing and capable of just accepting it. This mysterious aspect is the part of us that just is. It is innately worthy without any effort or reason or change. It could be called our essence, our divine core or spark, the centre of our soul, or the divine light within us, that life spark that just is. All else, every experience, every learning, every lesson, is just playful expression of that inner part of us through the many and varied levels of reality, of which this earthly world is one rather compelling example.

This is where the garland of the soul, the beautiful crowning glory of pink celestial blossoms that Balthiel gifted to me earlier today takes us. To dip into this place of connection with the worthy essence of what we are is a genuine heart opener. It is said in the Hindu tradition of the Guru and the Devotee that when the Devotee opens his heart, he finds the Guru there within. In Western spiritual traditions, such as Christianity we say that Christ lives in the heart. These are two different spiritual traditions, in their own way, revealing the same truth – through the heart we find the divine within us. Whether you personally define this as being Guru or Christ, or both, or neither, the divine is that part of you that is beyond this world of time and space. It is beyond any world. It just is. There is nothing to prove, nothing to do and nowhere to go. It is innately precious, beyond compare.

To connect with this part of us offers a peace-inducing sense of perspective! So much suffering in life is increased simply by limited perspective. We think the molehill is a mountain, and then we call forth higher consciousness only to find that it can be resolved and healed and sometimes quite quickly at that. What we once struggled with we no longer do and this gives us faith that perhaps current struggles may also resolve themselves in the near future. We find our perspective shifting from having to do it all alone in a quite despairing way, to enlisting help from divine forces and feeling more hope and trust in the process. We realise that we are a part of rather than apart from, the whole big divine mass of life within which we have our existence. It is, put mildly, a much more beautiful picture.

SOUL HEALING – CONNECTING WITH THE SOUL FOR PEACE AND RESOLUTION

There is not any situation that I can fathom which would not benefit from more soul. Soul in its pure and undistorted reflection gifts us with peace and love. These energies are a form of consciousness that help us find our way through the sometimes very believable illusions of this physical world into the truths that lie hidden in those appearances.

The suffering of being trapped in the illusion without understanding of its higher truths is a despairing and empty way to live, with temporary thrill at most. To live in connection with the peaceful light that dwells within allows your play in this physical world to be an expression of your essence, as though your whole life were the work of a great spiritual artist. Which it is! It is the ultimate shift in perspective – from identifying with the issue at hand to growing to identify with the source of light shining through it, once veiled, now revealed. This is the gift of Balthiel's Soul Garland of Peace.

HOW DO YOU KNOW IF YOU ARE HEALING AT A SOUL LEVEL IN THIS WAY?

There can be a hunger for more soul without knowing what it really is that you are hungry for. Sometimes in the midst of an inner struggle, we can be so focused on a "practical perspective" of what we logically think is needed to solve an issue (more money, a way to avoid ever having to deal with that work colleague ever again, losing weight or gaining power, for example), that we overlook what would lift us out of the struggle and into a divine solution, which is actually just more soul.

Connection with the soul brings us to a better place. It often presents us with a completely different way of looking at something and it can help us find a far more enjoyable solution to an even better outcome than we had once thought possible. It does require that we trust, however, and that we let go of our striving and ideas for solutions. We must become empty and receptive enough to receive new and improved approaches. It will happen if we allow it. This healing process takes you to that place to allow it to occur.

Whether it is a simple matter or a complex issue, nothing is too small or too great for the soul. It is alive in every part of you from the tip of your fingernail to the depths of your beating heart and restless mind, just waiting to bring you into the peace of your eternal and essential nature. It will accept anything that you genuinely surrender to it and bring healing. Without judgement or hesitation. This is the unconditional love of your soul.

SOUL HEALING PROCESS –
RECEIVING THE SOUL GARLAND OF PEACE

Find a peaceful place to sit comfortably with your spine relatively straight and your back supported. Place your palms upturned in your lap or on your knees, whatever feels comfortable and supports your posture. If you have any Rose Quartz, wear it or have it lightly touching your body. You can rest Quartz tumbled stones in your upturned hands if this feels comfortable for you. If you don't have any Rose Quartz, as an alternative, you can simply leave this book open at page 32, which features a full colour mandala for this crystal, and have it next to you as you complete the process.

Close your eyes, and become aware of the breath as you give yourself permission to journey within, leaving your day to day world of ideas, problems and solutions 'on the shelf'. You can pick them up when you return at the end of this process, with a different approach, if you need to do so.

Begin the healing process by saying the following invocation:

"I call upon my own divine soul, the Angel of Rose Quartz and the Angel Balthiel, I call upon Balthiel's Soul Garland of Peace, and of the true essence of my own divinity, through kindness, compassion and divine grace and unconditional love. I now surrender my attachment to how my life has been into the grace light of divine love, and ask that I be assisted by those beings that love me unconditionally to enter into the most receptive state possible to the healing that is flowing to me now. Through my own free will, so be it."

Close your eyes and relax. Follow the breath as it fills your chest and lungs on the inhalation, drawing your awareness into the centre of your chest and your heart chakra. As you exhale, let your awareness drop more deeply into your heart. Let this process continue for several moments, for as long as you need in order to feel that you are connecting with your heart.

Become aware of a softly glowing pink light within your heart. It feels really good to approach it, as it warmly invites you, and yet you may also feel some doubt, fear, hesitation or unworthiness, sadness, anger or grief as you approach it. Let these feelings arise and fall as they will, as you journey towards and into this pink light glowing deep within your own heart.

As you approach the light, it radiates higher and wider, expanding out until all that you can sense, all around you, is that softly glowing light. At its bright centre there is a beautiful angelic being, Balthiel with golden pink wings outstretched, golden robes and a warm gaze. As you approach him he smiles kindly at you and steps forward, holding a beautiful wreath of exquisite celestial flowers. They are in various shades of gold, pink and white, radiant with divine fragrance and very beautiful.

He raises the garland above your head and as it gently descends you may feel emotional as your heart responds. It gently and comfortably nestles upon your head now as the Angel Balthiel steps back slightly and holds his hands in blessing before you, sending you love, peace and healing.

Let yourself see, sense, perceive and simply receive (whether you feel it consciously or not) Balthiel's Soul Garland of Peace. Let its energy permeate your Crown and infuse your heart chakra with peace and love. Perceive or allow the light of this Garland to drip down into the very core of your heart chakra, gently awakening a divine eye that lays within it. You may see it as an inner eye, within a hexagram or a pyramid of light. You may see it as a flower opening or a spinning wheel of light – just let it be what it is. You may not see anything at all, which is also perfectly fine. Just trust and allow the process to happen. Let the light gently cleanse and open the inner eye of the heart. It may stir, blink or grow bright. Just let it happen as it will.

You may wish to remain here for however long feels right or for forty-four breaths.

When you are ready say, "I receive the divine blessing of my own soul, awakened in my heart. I see through the inner eye, through the eye of love, the eye of God, the eye of the Divine Mother, the eye of the heart. I receive the peaceful remembrance of who and what I am. I receive the shift in perspective and perception that this brings me and I open to the divine love that is me. So be it."

Stay with your breath for at least another seven breaths and when you are ready, open your eyes.

You have completed your soul healing process.

PSYCHOLOGICAL-EMOTIONAL HEALING WITH THE ANGEL OF ROSE QUARTZ AND ANGEL BALTHIEL: FORGIVENESS AND FREEDOM

To want to be over a situation or a person without forgiving them is like trying to walk away from someone whilst handcuffing yourself to them. The action and the desire are incompatible with each other!

Many people resist forgiveness because of what they think it is asking of them – to be made wrong, to be made weak, to not expect justice or to not be entitled to be heard, validated and acknowledged for the suffering they experienced.

In truth, forgiveness brings us quite the opposite. It delivers us with empowerment, higher understanding, compassion and resolution of suffering. Forgiveness is the action through which we say, "Hey, you did hurt me, but I choose to take my power back and be spiritually responsible for myself. I am now calling my spirit back from you and this situation, looking for the part I played in it with honesty and self-respect. When I find it, I'll forgive myself and let it go. I now choose to forgive you and be free from you and from this situation. I hope you can be free too."

Sometimes we may try to forgive, really genuinely want to – and just cannot. I believe that this is because we are putting the cart before the horse, so to speak. Forgiveness when we are ready, happens quite easily. It is a natural flow of energy that happens when we have accessed compassion. We just forgive – it is spontaneous, deeply and genuinely felt and permanent. We don't forgive one minute to be angry the next. If that is happening, then the forgiveness hasn't happened yet. That isn't bad, it just isn't complete. We want completion because it is what actually brings us freedom from needing to go another round with this person in a similar situation again, or with any other person in order to learn the same lesson.

Genuine forgiveness frees us. It is the lesson completed. It requires us to do the inner preparation first. That means feeling our feelings and giving our side of the story a voice. Letting ourselves be heard, validated and recognised for what we felt and experienced, without having to judge the other person or make them wrong or evil necessarily, but just with empathy, compassion and being 'in your own corner' as it were. You have to really accept and acknowledge what you experienced and be willing to feel and express the feelings it involved. You'll need a lot of self-respect to look for the part you played in the situation too, and to be strong enough to admit something about yourself that you may not like very much, but can learn to forgive anyway. This can take a little time. If you do this process and you aren't quite there yet, those feelings will come up for you before the forgiveness can kick in and that is part of the grace of the healing process. Try to accept it and know it may be uncomfortable but it is only the truth that can set you free.

After we have been truly and unconditionally heard, then we are in a position to manage the next step. We can learn to create an experience of being listened to unconditionally by and for ourselves too! Some examples are through journaling, talking to a good friend or having an out loud (but in private perhaps!) conversation with our angels. What matters is that we give ourselves permission to not judge what we have to express. So if we are venting and getting out our feelings to our angels, for example, or our best friend, we don't edit or judge it, we just express. When we choose not to judge ourselves, insight can follow. Compassion then often arises for ourselves and for others. If we are not feeling compassion then we just don't know the whole story. There is always a reason – even if it is very hidden – as to why anyone would act in a hurtful manner.

The other person may be struggling to learn, just as you are, and dealing with issues just as you are (although the issues may be quite different to yours, they will be struggling nonetheless). To realise and accept this is not to create excuses or permissions for bad behaviour but to develop compassion. This helps you distance yourself and detach yourself. Then their issue is not about you but about them. It is their struggle and their learning. If you are a sensitive and receptive being, especially if you are open to energy, and you tend to take in that which comes your way, learning to let go of accusations or feelings of guilt that have nothing to do with you, but are the accompaniment to another's unresolved issues is going to be essential for you to be able to forgive them. You have to hand back their energy to them and take any of your own spirit or power that you have handed over to them back into yourself.

This process of releasing energy that does not rightfully belong to you, and reclaiming energy that does, requires compassion. Otherwise, you will not be able to have the detachment needed to see what is the other person's issue and what is yours. It sounds complicated but it is not. When you are not judging another, you see them more clearly. You'll have to be prepared to see them more realistically. So they may not be the brutal bully or bitch from hell anymore. He may actually be a scared little boy in a grown man's body who is terrified of feeling the pain of rejection from his mother again if he becomes vulnerable with another woman. She may be a sensitive woman with a deep fear of abandonment, trying to seduce and charm all around her whilst preventing them from really connecting with her through walls of suspiciousness and manipulation, calling others to her with one hand whilst pushing them away with the other.

Compassion brings clarity. It brings peace and it brings release. It then frees us to be able to forgive. When you understand why people behave the way that they do, forgiveness becomes easier. You may not be gifted with precise understanding, and so part of your journey will be to trust. If you find that hard, then you can always rely on divine justice and karma! What this means to me is that all beings are in the custody of the divine, whether we see it being played out or not and you don't have to worry about how divine justice and fairness will evolve, it just will in its own way. It's not the same as genuine compassion, but it can help you learn to trust enough to approach compassion with less resistance if you are finding it difficult to get there. If you are still struggling to forgive, then there is an emotional truth within you that relates to the situation that is yet to be articulated, expressed and completely accepted within you. This healing process will help you with that.

HOW DO I KNOW IF I NEED HEALING
IN THIS WAY AND AT THIS LEVEL OF MY BEING?

When asked if we have some forgiveness that needs to happen, many of us will at first draw a blank.

I remember some years ago idly wondering if I needed some heart clearing in this regard. In a humorous reminder that what we put out of the Universe is always heard, my father arrived on my doorstep a day or two later with a box that he had 'suddenly felt he had to bring to me'. My father's inclinations to tidy up his collections of memorabilia are not common, so this was quite a significant action. The box he delivered contained many photographs that I had taken during my stint as a portrait photographer at university, which I used a source of income to help pay for law text books and the like.

I pretty much planned to throw all of the contents out as rubbish, but felt impelled to look through them first. It ended up taking me several hours to go through that box. I found images of people that I hadn't thought of for years, yet when I looked at the imagery I had emotions that I wouldn't have expected to have had. So I began a soul cleansing process where I sang the Hawaiian forgiveness prayer, which goes like this, "I'm sorry, please forgive me, thank you, I love you." As I went through each photograph, I could feel the energy of old emotion releasing and I knew that forgiveness of them and of myself for the imperfections of my interactions over the years, none of which were particularly conscious to me before I opened that box of photographs, was cleansing my heart.

At the end of the process I felt considerably different. I was tired but lighter and I put the contents into the rubbish bin knowing that it was well and truly done. It freed up much emotional energy that I didn't realise was still tied to the past and who I was then, allowing me to move on in my life. It was like releasing a burden that you were so used to carrying, you didn't realise how heavy it was until it was no longer with you. I was grateful that the Universe had responded so quickly and compassionately to my idle thought, and that it happened at a time when I had grown enough in the many years since university that I could relatively easily and quickly process any residual emotion from relationships from that time in my life.

The moral of this little story is that you may not know you have any forgiveness work to do until you are open to doing the work. Then the Universe will support you to do what you need to do to let the healing happen. It is never a wasted effort. As we open to greater forgiveness, it cleanses the heart and soul and brings more mental energy as well as emotional peace and satisfaction, improving our relationships in the present moment – especially our relationship with ourselves and with the divine.

PSYCHOLOGICAL-EMOTIONAL HEALING PROCESS – FORGIVENESS FOR FREEDOM

If you have some Rose Quartz, please place it on or near your body. You can use the mandala for Rose Quartz that appears on page 32 of this book as an alternative if you don't have the stone itself – just leave the book open to that page during the process.

Start by sitting comfortably with both palms upwards, resting the backs of your hands on your knees. You may like to have the Rose Quartz nestled in the pocket of your shirt, near your heart or resting on the palms of your upturned hands.

Say, "I call upon the healing Angel of Rose Quartz and the Angel Balthiel. I call upon my own higher self and upon the grace of compassionate wisdom, insight and detachment that allows forgiveness to flow easily. I ask for blessings that all relationships unresolved through lack of forgiveness can be blessed and healed now. I accept that I may or may not consciously perceive this healing and I accept that this will happen in the best way for my growth. I ask for divine empowerment that I may rise up to this level of forgiveness and call back my spirit to myself in wholeness, freedom and peace. May all beings be happy and free. Through my own free will, so be it."

Close your eyes and focus on the breath. Be aware of a beautiful pink ray of light that streams down from the heavens and up from the Earth towards your heart. It enters in through the soles of your feet and down through the crown of your head, meeting in the heart chakra at the centre of your chest, swirling and mixing with the love of the heart. Imagine your heart opening bright and clear. Any old energy is washed out of the body through these channels of pink light, carrying old pain and unforgiveness, judgement, fear, lack of understanding or need to express your pain out through either the crown of the head or soles of the feet. This pink ray has its own intelligence so just let it happen without trying to direct the process.

Stay with this process for at least nine long, slow breaths in and out, or for however long feels appropriate to you.

Then say aloud, "I forgive myself for my mistakes. I forgive myself for being human. I forgive myself for causing pain to others, intentionally or unintentionally. I forgive myself for not being perfect and for needing to grow. I forgive myself for not being able to forgive easily, for judging, for not understanding. I forgive myself for being in a position to be hurt by others and for allowing myself to be hurt in the past. I forgive myself as I forgive all beings now. May all beings be happy and free. May all beings be happy and free. May all beings be happy and free. So be it."

Perceive, visualise or allow the pink ray of light to continue to stir in the heart, carrying your prayer, "May all beings be happy and free," out of your crown chakra and out of the foot chakras at the soles of your feet. You can repeat this prayer aloud as a chant or under the breath quietly, or silently in your mind. Repeat it for as along as feels good. Know that the energy of this prayer registers in your body and your cells. It builds the freedom of forgiveness and generates good karmic energy in your heart. It brings you greater peace and happiness too, as you gift this energy to our beautiful planet. Keep repeating the prayer and let it be carried on the light to where it is most needed.

When you are ready, become silent, place your awareness in your heart and just receive. Stay with nine breaths in and out and in your own time just open your eyes.

You have finished your psychological and emotional healing process. You may notice thoughts of old relationships or past fights arising and falling in the coming days as your soul purges old energy through your heart. Just let it rise and fall and remember, it can just be 'stuff' leaving and may not mean anything beyond that!

PHYSICAL HEALING WITH ROSE QUARTZ AND ANGEL BALTHIEL: THE MEMORY OF THE HEART

I once saw a movie starring David Duchovny and Minnie Driver called "Return to Me". In this movie, David Duchovny's character, Bob, loses his wife in a car accident. She is an organ donor and her heart goes to a young woman, played by Minnie Driver, called Grace. The love story unfolds, with various amusing and awkward moments between Bob, struggling to let go of the memory of the wife he loved, and Grace, who is learning that she is worthy of a loving partnership and is drawn to the gentle humour and kindness of Bob.

It is not until well into their love affair that, in true Hollywood style, Bob accidentally discovers that the heart that beats in Grace's chest was the heart of his former wife. As one sassy character in the film puts it to her befuddled husband, "Grace has Bob's dead wife's heart!".

There is a poignant moment in the film where Grace, soon after her heart transplant, visits the zoo. Bob's deceased wife, Elizabeth, was a zoologist who was passionately committed to building a new gorilla enclosure at the zoo. She had a special bond with a gorilla named Sydney who was struggling with living in the zoo environment. The gorilla was socially withdrawn and becoming depressed.

Not knowing any of this, Grace visits the zoo, venturing into the gorilla enclosure. Sydney comes right up to her, seeking her out and ignoring the many other visitors. It is as if Sydney recognises Grace, though they have never seen each other before. The other characters with Grace think it is sweet. Yet it is only the audience that realises that Sydney has recognised and responded to the vibration of the heart in Grace's body. As Sydney and Grace gaze at each other and have a deep moment of connection through the thick glass wall, the living reality of the heart, and the vibration it holds, is revealed. It is an energetic imprint. It can be recognised.

I share this outline of a rather dramatic screenplay with you as it is a vivid way to explain the healing process for the physical heart below. The physical reality of the heart is that it carries energy. It can hold memories of heart attacks from ancestral lines and energy from other lifetimes. As the soul light infuses the heart, bringing it to life, it is capable of an intelligence and has a recorded history of experience that extends far beyond our immediate physical experiences this lifetime, in this particular body.

Cleaning out the heart not only benefits the heart itself, it improves our health and wellbeing, physically, energetically and emotionally. It benefits our children and those that we share our energy field with – which is be pretty much every living being on the planet!

HOW DO I KNOW IF I NEED THIS HEALING PRACTICE?

If you have a history of heart disease, grief or loss in your family, or other emotional suffering that you are aware of, or unaware of, this healing will serve you.

Each one of us carries heart issues from one incarnation or another. It is safe to say that whether you are aware of it consciously or not, this healing process will help benefit your heart.

PHYSICAL HEALING PRACTICE – HEART CLEARING

Lie comfortably on your back with a piece of Rose Quartz, if you have it, lying on or near your abdominal area or heart, or even at the base of the throat or at the palms of the hands. Be warm and comfortable. If you don't have the stone, we'll call on the spirit anyway of course, so the practice will still be just as effective for you.

When you are ready, say the following:

"I call upon the healing power of the Angel of Rose Quartz and the Angel Balthiel. I call upon the healing of the green ray and the forgiveness and compassion of the pink ray. I call upon the natural healing ability of my own body-soul. Please help now beloved ones, to cleanse my heart physical and etheric, through all time and space, through all lifetimes and all ancestral lines. Bring my heart into perfected health and wellness now. Through divine grace, kindness and mercy, so be it!"

Close your eyes and focus on your breath. Let the breath flow in and out of the entire body, as if the entire body could breathe. Then focus your awareness at your heart and allow swirling washes of green and pink light to alternate, with each inhalation and exhalation. First green light, then pink, repeating in and out for forty-four breaths. If you lose track of pink or green, don't worry, just surrender to the breath and let the process occur. If you prefer to think of a word rather than visualise a colour, you can repeat "healing" and "compassion" over and over again silently or aloud, as you breathe.

Whatever thoughts or feelings you notice coming up, just let them arise and be swept away into this light. They will be cleansed and returned to you as fresh energy.

Stay with this process for at least forty-four breaths, in and out.

When you are ready, say "thank you" and allow your body to be wrapped in a beautiful emerald green bubble of light, and around that a soft pink bubble of light. Take your time and open your eyes.

You have finished your healing process.

You may feel emotions and memories arising during and following this process, or a lot of emotion or intensity in your dreams. These are symptoms of your heart releasing. Be gentle with your body. Choose exercise that is kind to the heart and give yourself plenty of time to rest. If you are on medication for any heart or blood pressure related issue, the two or three weeks following this process is a good time to check your medication levels with your health care provider just to stay in tune with your body.

PRAYER – AFFIRMATION

To invoke the healing power of Rose Quartz and Angel Balthiel at any time, you can repeat the following affirmation quietly in your mind, or aloud.

"Pink Ray of Love Frees my Heart through Grace and Compassion."

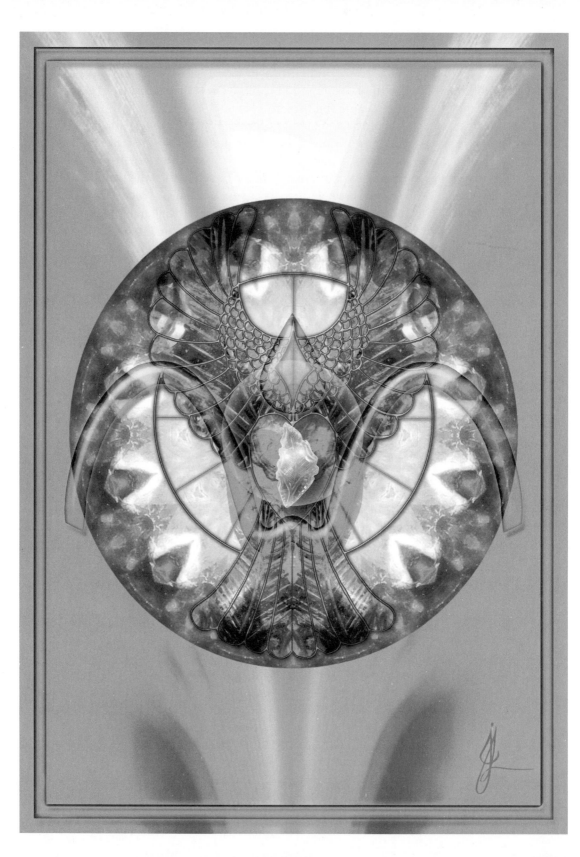

17.

AQUAMARINE (Expression) and ANGEL BATH KOL (Voice)

THE GIFT OF HIGHER CREATIVITY

SPIRITUAL GUIDANCE FROM THE ANGEL OF AQUAMARINE AND THE ANGEL BATH KOL

With your voice you can create worlds, define who you are and command the forces that once controlled you. You can speak, you can name, you can empower and defeat through the commanding presence of the soul in your voice. Within you dwells creativity and grace, the ability to heal this world and to rightfully take your place. As an emissary of light and an ambassador of peace, all this is possible when your power you release. Do not be fearful of the power within, of your voice rising up as you spread your own wings. For within you there is also great wisdom and love. You can bring forth the sweet grace of the Holy White Dove, blessing those that have struggled, offering premonitions of peace. All of this becomes possible as your voice does increase, vibrating in truth, power and light, realising that expressing yourself is your right. It can be done with kindness, even with silence or song, there is no need to worry, you can't get it wrong. There is no need to be perfect or without query or question, the power comes from expressing your truthful intention. Then from confusion or doubt you will be free. The truth shines light giving absolute clarity. No more will you wonder, 'Do I go this way or that?' The path reveals itself clearly, as a matter of fact. You will know which way to go, you will know what to say or do, because your inner truth will be the force that is now guiding you. All from your voice, setting the Universe in motion, as your manifestations emerge from the cosmic ocean. Your expression ignites divine creativity, it is your natural and wonderful soulful ability. It is just a matter of learning to be true, to all that you are, all that makes you just you!

PICTURING AQUAMARINE

Aquamarine is a stunning crystal varying from clear to opaque finishes in soft blue tones with some specimens displaying blue-green hues. It is often tumbled into stones or made into jewellery, but larger free form specimens of majestic rising columns of clear blue crystal can be found. Aquamarine is readily available though gem quality and larger specimens of Aquamarine can be moderately expensive.

HEALING PROPERTIES

Aquamarine feels soothing to hold and is beneficial to sensitive souls. It works equally well with those that are learning to develop and refine their sensitivity, helping them open up to the subtle energy worlds of spiritual presence, the chakras and aura, and energy fields, while learning to feel and know the subtleties of life more intimately.

When I connected with Aquamarine in order to write this section, what surprised me was that the energetic connection did not start with my throat chakra. It actually began deep in my solar plexus, rising up to my heart and then to my throat. I consider Aquamarine to be an excellent healer for the throat chakra. The stone helps us open up our ability to express and communicate, and to know and release our truths, our voice (in all its forms – creative, personal, emotional and professional) into the world. Yet the blue-green hues in some pieces, mirroring the blue of the throat and green of the heart, indicate that Aquamarine can heal blockages between the heart and throat as well.

The thymus chakra, between the heart and the throat, is the centre through which we 'go public', so to speak. It is the chakra that is blue-green in colour, and its health and wellbeing allows us to come out of the spiritual closet (as I call it) and let ourselves be known for who and what we are. It also helps us get our work published, release our creations into the world, and be publicly seen. This is an important part of the spiritual journey for numerous souls this lifetime – learning the art of holding one's spiritual centre and truths even in the face of powerful public projection. It requires a pure and unwavering knowledge of the self, otherwise the sense of public opinion can become overwhelming and distressing, or distracting, as the power of it pulls one out of self-awareness. Aquamarine can help reorient the self back to inner truth, without shutting off the world around us. It enables our communication to return to what is most authentic and truthful.

This can include healing fears of speaking up, anxiety about expressing yourself and an inability to really share what you are feeling, often for self-protective reasons due to unresolved past trauma. Sometimes very gifted communicators can find it hard to talk about what they are feeling inside. They might be able to express so much, with great intelligence and insight, and yet when it comes to expressing their own vulnerability or emotion, find themselves closing up or losing inner clarity and conviction. Healing the thymus chakra in its role as connector of the head and the heart, is a way to overcome this struggle and soothe the pathways, gently encouraging them to open (like putting some energetic WD40 on a creaky hinge), allowing the energy to flow. Aquamarine will support and encourage all of this.

As I explored the qualities of Aquamarine, I also sensed that the hidden yellow vibration in the stone (you may not see it physically but you can see it clairvoyantly and feel it energetically) was helping to clear and empower the solar plexus chakra, clearing out old energy stored there which may obstruct the natural energetic flow up from the Earth, towards the heart and then to the throat chakra.

Old experiences of fear, shame, self-doubt, unworthiness and anxiety can close down our flow of energy from inner knowing into outer expression. We think because the power isn't at the throat, that it is a problem with our ability to express. Yet that isn't the case. We can have a powerful throat chakra, with an evolved ability to express but no juice to fire it up because the energy is getting stuck lower in our bodies. This can get unconsciously misinterpreted as, "Oh, I can't sing. I don't have a good voice." Or, "I am not comfortable speaking in public or speaking up with others. I don't like confrontation." In reality those beliefs are not actually reflecting the truth of our situation.

To clear old shame and suffering from the solar plexus chakra, to release old fear from the heart, clears the pathways for the life force to flow and the voice to be connected to a source of power so it can emerge. Without access to our power, we have no genuine access to our true inner voice. We need access to our true inner voice to give expression to our inner power and create the reality we would like to experience through the old saying, 'what you speak about, you bring about'.

We will explore this now as we connect with the Divine and ancient Angel Goddess Bath Kol.

ABOUT THE ANGEL BATH KOL

I have known Bath Kol, without realising that she had a rather exotic sounding name, since before my birth. When my mother was pregnant with me, she became captivated by a painting in a store window that she passed when taking her daily walk. The painting featured a white dove descending through a stormy night. When my mother shared this story with me, I instinctively knew that what drew her to that painting was the call of my soul to her as I was preparing to be born into this physical world through her body. My mother and I have always shared a strong psychic tie to each other, and I know that this allowed her to instinctively recognise the call of my soul through that painting, out to her. She didn't have a lot of money at the time, but she deemed it important enough to save the funds and eventually purchase the painting, which now, nearly forty years later, hangs in my home. I always loved that painting as a child, long before I was old enough to hear and understand the story around how it came to belong to my mother, and eventually, to me. It brought me a sense of peace and connection as I would gaze at it. There was something about the purity of the dove descending, the whiteness of it against the dark grey and indigo sky that was beautiful and spoke to me at a level beyond words.

Some years ago, this painting seemed to come more alive for me, without conscious reason why. It was as if it was speaking to me yet again, carrying some message. My meditations became rich with experiences of such peace and grace. The experience somehow described itself to me as the Holy Spirit and ignited a clear flame above the crown of my head. The dove again was calling to me through my own soul. I had the imagery and the sensation of angelic wings at my back. I tried to dismiss as vivid imagination, and yet the reality of the experience was undeniable. Not quite sure what to do with all of this, I continued with my practice and just let it be, trusting that if it was helpful for me to know, the story would unfold for me. If not, then it was a beautiful experience and part of a greater mystery that obviously wasn't particularly necessary for me to understand consciously this lifetime in order to fulfil my soul destiny.

Around this time I was also bringing to life the use of sound healing in my work more fully. About a decade earlier, I had a vision of myself in a past life as a priestess in Atlantean times. I was singing into the bodies of patients lying on a bed of crystal in a crystal sound healing chamber. I wasn't using sound healing at the time I had that vision, or even working with crystals particularly, so again, I didn't quite know what to do with it, but accepted the beauty of the vision and how powerful it felt.

It was years later when that past life ability awakened into current life use. Chanting and singing, combined with the sound healing power of Quartz singing bowls and crystal layouts, I began to realise I was bringing to life again that which I had done previously – just in a more modern format. The principle of combining sound healing and crystal for powerful healing was exactly the same.

Eventually the pieces came together and found their way into one coherent pattern. The art of sound healing and the dove, the angelic energy that I felt within, often when I sang during healings. Then I was finally blessed with a conscious meeting of Bath Kol in meditation. She carries the energy of an ancient angel and the Holy Spirit or Grace aspect of the Divine itself. She is known as "heavenly voice" and "daughter of the voice".

I don't see her as much as hear her vibration, then feel her presence. This is unusual for me as I am highly visual, so I feel this is important as part of her divine quality. I believe that this is why she is symbolised rather than seen, as the white dove. She is divine sound and grace. She is experienced rather than witnessed. It is my intuitive sense that she has been emanating through my soul without me being completely aware of it for my entire life.

To connect with her was a discovery of more of the divine nature that is within and I believe her graceful presence can bring that gift to all who seek it from her.

SOUL HEALING WITH AQUAMARINE AND ANGEL BATH KOL

What Bath Kol through her consciousness as heavenly grace, and Aquamarine both assist us with is healing the issues that arise as we move more fully into our own divinity. It is often the case that when the external obstacles fall away that we begin to realise how much of our own struggle has been internal all along. We can empower another person or situation, a partner or an employment situation for example, with the 'crime' of holding us back from really living our truths, and yet when that partner is gone or we leave the job in question, we are left with ourselves and it is then that we meet the real holding back, which has been our own fear. In confronting the truth, where we in fact have been struggling internally, we are able to actually move through it. You cannot heal an issue by healing a symptom or blaming another. At some point if you really want something to shift, the core itself, within you, has to be healed.

As we approach our own divine enlightenment and the realisation of our own true divine nature, every issue, wall, block or doubt that we have ever had about being worthy and deserving of love, forgiveness, grace and compassion arises.

We often have no clue how resistant we are to the unconditional divine love that is within all of us, lying at the heart of our true nature, until we get close to it. Then the resistance we have suddenly becomes quite clear! The nearer the love, the more obvious our self-imposed barriers are to it. Whilst those barriers may make sense in terms of the history of our human wounding, they don't make sense in terms of the future of our soul unfoldment. So we need to get a grip with it and learn to let it resolve and let it go.

For many years, whenever I felt the kindness and lack of judgement of my own Higher Guidance – helping me debrief after teaching a class, doing a session with someone or working on my own life issues – I would end up crying. Not out of sadness, but out of deep pain releasing as I learned to accept and receive this gentle kindness, devotion and lack of judgement. I was overwhelmed by the willingness of my Higher Guidance to honour the best in me as truth, without ever punishing me for what I perceived to be the worst in me. I had enough awareness at the time to realise that this is what was happening. It wasn't confusing to me, but it was a little confronting to see that I, who knew Higher Guidance and their unconditional love so intimately, and had done for my entire life, could still have so much to release in order to reactivate my divine self-realisation again this lifetime.

Fortunately we have Bath Kol, who heals through grace and sound, and Aquamarine, who heals the entire system of self-expression. These two beings help us unravel this apparently obstacle-laden path to enlightenment, and lead us to the remembrance of our own divine purity and essence without objection, dismissal or incredulity!

SOUL HEALING – YOUR TRUTHFUL SOUL EXPRESSION

To allow your Soul to truthfully express itself is to open up to a revelation of who and what you are at a deeper level. There is a time in the path when we are ready for this. There is also much more time spent in preparation for such moments of divine self-revelation. Preparation time is where we work on healing the ego. It might be so that we are ready in several weeks, months or even years for a closer connection with our own soul without getting thrown into an utter tailspin. Why would we be in a tailspin? In such moments of deepening connection, we are increasingly exposed to divinity. Divinity is often experienced as chaos because it exists beyond our rational mind which would prefer to contain phenomena and make sense of things. Our ego has to be able to sustain experiences of chaos, of things not 'making sense' immediately, of mystery, to be able to connect more fully with the Divine and not become frightened and disconnect from it. This is what the preparation helps us develop.

In the same way that we don't just chuck the ingredients for a cake into a tin without mixing, shove it in the oven and expect a beautiful cake to emerge (or if you do, you are going to be disappointed), we have to allow the soul path to unfold according to a certain sensible order. Preparation is a key part of that. We don't have to consciously understand all this, we just need to trust that where we are at right now is perfect for us and when it is time for us to be on a different part of the path, we will be there.

I remember my first spiritual teacher saying once that she was talking to God in prayer and heard a voice say, "Who are you talking to?" as though there was no God, no 'thing' to talk to. She was sharing it as a moment of spiritual insight, however what I felt at the time (and I suspect by the group reaction, was felt also by the rest of my classmates) was that this was unhelpful to me! We all groaned! Most of the class members were just trying to get to a place where there was comfort in accepting insights from God with complete trust in the presence of guidance. Now she was saying that God didn't exist? It was too much, or not the right step at that particular time for us at least, and it was a very good learning for me that we have to honour exactly where we are our path at any given time.

Although since then I have had direct experience and insight into what she was sharing, I also have the awareness through personal experience that even the right thing at the wrong time isn't going to help us so much! We have to trust our timing, our process, and our path, and let it lead us, which if we don't squander our energy through excessive worry, we will find happens quite easily and even enjoyably.

I say this to you now so that you will allow this soul healing process to be what it is for you – as deep or as subtle as needs be. Accept it without judgement, without feeling disappointment or inflation as you feel you are either not enlightened enough or so utterly enlightened its a miracle that you are still in a body!

HOW DO YOU KNOW IF YOU ARE HEALING
AT A SOUL LEVEL IN THIS WAY?

There are times in your life where the roles you have played don't seem so exciting anymore. It might have been thrilling to play the lover, the teacher, the healer or the mother, or perhaps the adventurer, hero or addict, the villain, the romantic, the martyr or saviour, rescuer, visionary, leader, slave, family man or lightworker and so on.

These roles may have been helpful ways for your soul to express itself, and perhaps still are. Yet there will be a time when you realise that there is more to you than this. It is like wanting to go backstage after a performance to meet the actors themselves, rather than being satisfied just with the roles that they played.

It is that curiosity about the real person inside the character. What are they like? Is the character easy for them to play or the opposite of their natural way in the world? And what about the director? What was her vision for the unfolding drama? Did it turn out as planned? How much was her hand guiding the process? And so forth. We get a completely different sense of the drama, yet we have to surrender the fantasy of the roles being real too – and that was perhaps quite a lot of fun for a while. It is only when the fun becomes a bit 'funned out' and the mystery or magical promise of a role fades that we start to wonder what else there could be. It is then that we start moving beyond the ego level of reality and searching for more of our soul.

I remember when I started work as a clairvoyant in my early twenties. I was so incredibly excited to be actually starting to live a life that intrigued me and promised me such fulfilment through my work. I felt like I was stepping into the role that I was born to play (having a touch of the dramatic in my personality and dreaming of being an actress, amongst other things, when I was a child). I embraced the entire experience with gusto. I was SO ready to have a different life to the one that I had been living. I was sick of working in jobs that I was so underwhelmed by I ended up feeling bored and resentful, and even feeling lazy and irresponsible in my work, which was very out of character for me. Typically I would strive to become the very best, if I could.

Inspired by my first spiritual teacher and how she spoke of her life – free from so many constraints that I absolutely hated – I decided, with her encouragement and my own intuitive knowing, that the life of a spiritual healer was for me. It started off with my clairvoyant ability and in readings. I believed adopting this 'role' was my ticket into that life I desired. I was an old soul, but with a young and naive ego, and it was something of a shock to realise that the dream job wasn't going to be a dream after all.

I remember the crumbling of the fantasy vividly. I remember realising that the job wasn't the answer, that there was no answer presenting itself in that moment. It would take years and years of transformation before the answer would clearly reveal itself to me but I did ultimately discover that I was my 'true self' that I had been seeking all along, and lo and behold, I had begun to experience her more truthfully than I ever imagined possible. I plunged into deep depression, hopelessness and despair. I thought the role of clairvoyant and healer would be my way of out suffering. Looking back, it was an important first step that took courage and a lovely spirit of defiance, stepping away from a career in law in favour of a bohemian lifestyle that admittedly suited me a lot more but confounded my relations who didn't understand my choice. Yet it was not the fantasy that I had envisioned!

Rather than my life suddenly becoming easier, I was plunged deeper into my own healing journey. The more I chose to live from my heart, including doing clairvoyant work based on the inner vision of my heart, the more aware I became of unresolved emotions that were buried inside me. As my heart opened, what had been held within needed to be released! This required that I clear so much childhood grief that I cried intensely every evening for almost a year. It was physically exhausting and emotionally painful. I had learned in childhood, through my own sensitivity, to absorb the feelings of others. So those feelings had to come out too!

It took years of emotional purging and there were times when I genuinely feared that it would never end. Sometimes I felt as though I was drowning in suffering – of my own and of others. I had to learn how to be compassionate without getting caught up in the pain of others. I needed to be able to experience enough of it to relate to my clients, but not so much that I ended up drowning in it along with them. It was a challenging time for me personally, as I developed my healing skills, 'on the job'.

I had imagined that a change to a more heart-centred career would be what healed me. I just didn't realise that the healing wouldn't be a quick-fix by changing my life circumstances. What I learned was that there was no quick and easy way out, the only way out was through the pain, learning and gaining strength as I went. The path to a more healed consciousness was not an easy one, especially at that time. Suffice to say, there were quite a few spiritual temper tantrums that ensued.

The real change that I was seeking, the experience of fulfilment that I craved did come to me, but the stepping into a different role was only the first step, and it would be years later through painstaking inner work that I learned how to identify more with my soul. No matter what I manifested in my physical world, it was the soul that was the nourishing piece. It is like the ego is the shell of the food we eat, and the soul is the nutritional value. It is the soul that makes anything the ego does real, nourishing and fulfilling to us. If the soul is present, the ego at play in the world becomes a healing role in a spiritual drama unfolding. If not, we get caught up in the roles themselves, and they wear thin after a while.

As I began to heal the grief, disappointment, depression and frustration, with a lot of journaling, mentoring (with a talented and spiritually evolved therapist) and patience, I learned how to seek beyond the roles that I was playing. I began to dis-identify with these roles and realise more of my own divinity at work behind all of them.

It took many years and much inner work – confronting fear and anxiety, putting myself in situations outside of my comfort zone and letting myself be led by my own guidance – before I began to trust that part of me, knowing it was more real than the roles I had been playing. You could say that I had surrendered the fantasy of the role I was playing as a divine actor, and was now beginning to hang out behind the scenes (where all the really interesting stuff took place) with the director.

You'll know if this soul healing is for you because you will feel that you are outgrowing a role you have played, or you are happy (or not) within that role, and want to know what else there is of you to bring into your life. It may be other roles that present themselves in this soul healing, in which case, that is what is most helpful for you right now. Or it might be that you get some glimpses or even deeper experience of your own divine nature. Your mind may struggle during this process as you begin to move beyond it. This is fine. Just stay calm, stay with your process and know that all is unfolding as it should.

SOUL HEALING PROCESS – EXPRESSING SOUL

Find a peaceful place to sit comfortably with your spine relatively straight and your back supported. Be sure it is a place where you can speak or tone aloud without concern about being overheard or disturbed. Place your palms upturned in your lap or on your knees, whatever feels comfortable and supports your posture. If you have some Aquamarine, wear it or have it lightly touching your body. If you don't have the stone, you may like to open the book to page 33 in the full colour section that features the Aquamarine mandala.

Start the healing by saying, "Of my own free will, I now call upon the Angel of Aquamarine and Daughter of Divine Voice, Bath Kol. I call upon the divine grace of healing and enlightenment, of the sound of my own divine essence. I call upon unconditional love, mercy, healing and protection now. I call upon divine play, truth and expression. Be with me now, bring me healing and support, as I awaken to the expression of my own divine nature. So be it."

Close your eyes, and become aware of the breath as you give yourself permission to journey within. Follow the breath as you travel along a soft blue-green ray of light, deep into the vast, open space that emerges within you now. Imagine a laser-like display of soft blue-green light creating patterns, geometric shapes and formations of light in the vastness before you, like a cosmic light display in a dark night sky.

As you witness this display you notice that it forms a gateway, an opening flooded with light, through which you can enter more deeply into your own divine essence.

Within that gateway you see an angel of sky-blue light with tinges of green in her robes and wings. She glows with ethereal beauty and her eyes are like the ocean, shifting colours of blue and green. This is the Angel of Aquamarine. She fills you with peace and a sense of confidence and clearing. Allow yourself to open your heart to her and receive her energy through her gaze. Drink it in and breathe out and relax as her healing flows through you. You don't have to think or understand, you can just choose to let it happen as it will, according to the higher divine intelligence guiding this process.

As your relax, you become aware of a sound arising all around you, without seeing from where it has come. You can sense it with your inner hearing or you may actually hear. The sound is beautiful, it brings peace and comfort to you, touching your heart. You may hear or sense it as a melody or particular sound, such as "AUM" or "I AM" and you may wish to speak, sing or chant this aloud in your own way, or simply relax further and surrender into the sound, letting it pulse through your being.

You become aware that from this sound, something is birthed. It might be a light, a colour, an image, feeling, symbol or message. It is an expression of your own soul. Be open to receiving what unfolds now, staying with the process, without having to think or understand it for at least forty-four breaths.

When you are ready, become aware of your body in the room. Allow the energy you have received consciously or subconsciously to filter through your entire body. Stay with your breath for at least another nine breaths and when you are ready, just open your eyes.

You have completed your soul healing process.

PSYCHOLOGICAL-EMOTIONAL HEALING WITH THE ANGEL OF AQUAMARINE AND THE ANGEL BATH KOL: CLAIMING YOUR VOICE

Your voice is your key to creation in every sense. If you don't have a clear sense of your own voice, you won't know your opinions, your likes and dislikes. You might be so used to trying to please others or avoid 'making a fuss' that you don't even stop to consider what it is that you like or want. A less obvious, though just as challenging, version of this is those that know only what they don't want, what they don't like, what they judge or criticise in themselves, in others, in a partner, a job, a life style, their finances and so on. This may seem like a strong voice, but it is really just a critic that has hijacked the inner voice, and needs to be silenced with enough love to create space for the genuine voice to emerge.

When you are in possession of your own voice something quite extraordinary happens. You become capable of knowing yourself internally and expressing that self externally. You become a creative force in your own life and relationships. You become capable of exercising the innate power of choice that humanity has in a way that helps you get closer to what you genuinely want, which is, in essence the same thing for all of us, to be who we truly are and realise the magnificence of self.

This is not just the voice in the sense of speaking or singing, or having an opinion (and reserving the right to change one's mind!), although it includes all of those things. To reclaim the voice as creative power means reclaiming your divine self, the creative self, which are one and the same. There is no coincidence that one name for the ultimate divine being is The Creator. When we are playing with our own creative faculty, we are playing with our own divine nature. The voice is the highest creative expression. Sound creates reality, our thoughts and our words, our actions and choices too. Everything is energy and all energy has sound within it, whether we hear it consciously or not.

So you could say everything is sound – and that all creation emerges from sound. It is just that we can only hear it beyond a limited spectrum with our inner hearing or clairaudience. If you have ever been so close to nature, just in the ocean perhaps, resting in the soft swell of the waves, or lying flat out on the Earth, that you could swear you could sense her heart beat, then you are tapping into inner hearing. If you have heard a person speak and you think, "That just doesn't sound right," your inner hearing is detecting the vibration of untruth.

Inner hearing is like inner sight, but instead of seeing, it perceives through the faculty of hearing. It can open up quite naturally as we learn to trust that we can 'hear without hearing' in the typical way.

When I was a very young girl, my mother took me to get my ears tested. I have no idea why! Perhaps I wasn't listening to her very much! I do tend to go into my own world sometimes and not hear the physical world around me. Some of my most powerful meditations have been whilst there is great noise and chaos unfolding around me, though I have to say, I do so enjoy some peaceful quiet.

Anyway, for my hearing test I was placed in a small sound-proof booth with a button to press and a set of headphones. I was given clear instructions. Listen to the headphones and when I hear a sound, press the little red button. I placed on my headphones and heard the small beeps through the headphones, loud at first and then progressively becoming more faint. So I did what I was told. Whenever I "heard" a beep, I pressed that red button. Sometimes I had to listen quite carefully to be sure that there was a beep, and if there was, I pressed the button. After the test, the man doing the testing looked somewhat befuddled. He couldn't understand how I could possibly hear at the range that I was registering. I had been pressing that button in response to sounds that couldn't be registered with the physical ear.

I was very young, and didn't very much enjoy the idea of a test, but I didn't think about what I was doing or what significance it could have. I just followed my instructions – hear sound, press button! I hadn't any conscious recognition of psychic ability, I just received the world around me, in form and as energy, as I did. My mother looked at me curiously and home we went. I never had another hearing test again!

There is energy of sound in our words. The word itself is just a noise, but the sound is the meaning, intent, truth, energy of what is being brought to life through the sound. This is why sometimes I can be speaking extremely calmly and my partner will (quite accurately) pick up on the emotion in what I am saying – because he hears the truth in what is said. I don't have to yell to express anger or to weep to express sadness. The truth can be heard in the vibration of the sound if one is open to hearing it. If you have the ability to hear what is really being said, even whilst the words may sound differently (the classic case being "I'm fine!" when the person obviously is not) then you are tapping into the inner truths of sound. You are listening with your inner hearing.

To claim the truth of your voice, of your own vibration on the inner planes and allow it to shine forth unobstructed to create a truthful, soul-aligned life in the material or physical plane, we often need to learn to let go of emulating the voices of others. They may be role models or inspirations to us. They might be a style icon or a teacher, a mentor or parent. Yet there will be a time in the course of human spiritual development when one must learn to surrender into the divine within, not the guide leading one to it.

When that time is upon us, we must find our courage and faith and head into the inner cave in search of our own divine light and sound, our own true vibration. You see, you weren't created in some cosmic freak accident where you were actually meant to be different and not yourself after all. Just in case you ever wondered about that, I thought I might clarify the situation. You were created with divine purpose and intent. You were created as you, as God-Goddess in the version of you. The more you clear your energy to be ready to accept and radiate this, the more you are living into your soul mission, purpose and destiny for being alive, in a body, here on Earth at this particular moment in time and space.

I had a dream which helped me when such a time was upon me. I dreamed that I was a young woman leaving my mother, who was somewhat frantic at the prospect, and a man who was a bit rough around the edges and quite possibly a gangster of some sort, gave me a beautiful engagement ring. I wasn't so certain of him, but the ring was symbolic to me, and it proved that he knew my soul and that he was trustworthy. It was an antique Aquamarine ring, which glowed blue-green in the light, fit perfectly on my finger and felt like it was just made for me.

Despite the discomfiting emotion of the mother figure in the dream, which represented my own fear about stepping away from what I had learned from my family values and societal conditioning, I felt optimistic about this dream engagement. The young feminine spirit, who held my own values (some of which were quite different to those I had grown up with), could recognise that this rough male suitor was to be trusted. He was my masculine spirit. He wasn't afraid to go against the rules and be tough when something needed to be accomplished. He might not seem gentle and kind, he might seem a bit intimidating actually, but the gift of the ring suggested that he had soul and was interested in loving and honouring my feminine spirit. For me, the antique Aquamarine ring was a symbol of the ancient voice would allow this young feminine spirit to bring through, if she accepted his proposal of marriage. In a nutshell the dream said if you want to sing your soul song, you are going to have to let yourself step away from what you were taught and live your own life. Even if it seems a bit scary at times, and you have enough strength and protection within you to do it.

For us to reclaim our voice, to learn to hear our vibration and let it resonate through our being and into the world, we are going to have to let go of that which would block us from doing so. Then we can create a physical representation of our inner world, where we feel that our inner values and external life are in harmony with each other.

Often it is family programming, shame and doubt, fear and judgement from this lifetime and often many others were we were persecuted, tortured or exiled for speaking our truths.

We are also going to have to trust that there is a part of us that knows how to take care of us. She or he might feel a bit gangster-ish, as though we are taking on society by challenging the norms and living by our own rules, even if society doesn't understand them. Sometimes that is just what we need.

HOW DO I KNOW IF I NEED HEALING
IN THIS WAY AND AT THIS LEVEL OF MY BEING?

There are two phases to reclaiming our voice at an emotional and psychological level. The first is learning to recognise our inner voice and the second is allowing it to manifest unobstructed, untainted, without distortion, in the physical world. First comes first, then the second phase becomes relevant.

If you are not sure who you are, what you are, or even what you are supposed to be learning or doing on this planet, in this body, then you'll need to focus on part one of the healing process, which is learning to recognise your inner self, as it expresses through your inner voice.

This is a really important element of your spiritual journey. We can go back to this phase time and time again as our evolution progresses and we mature spiritually. Who we thought we were expands and old identities can outgrow their usefulness.

Take for example the situation of a man (or woman) at retirement experiencing the loss of a job-related identity that has been his primary sense of self for several decades. Suddenly the loss and concern for how one will now be useful or of value can arise. Not knowing what to do with all the energy and focus that was once poured into work may cause frustration and even depression as the poor ego feels useless, powerless, cast aside.

In truth the person has just outgrown an identity and the soul will want to express itself in another way. Yet if there is no sense of self beyond the old identity, no sense of an inner soul bigger than any role ever was, there can be much despair and suffering in the loss of the identity. It can feel like one is dying, with all the terror and resistance that this can bring up for the ego. Even if there IS a sense of the inner soul, losing an identity to which we have become attached can be an exceptionally painful ego death. Learning to go within and reconnect with the soul vibration, to allow the sound of it to bring us into connection with the part of us that is eternal and peaceful helps us heal and let go, allowing new life, even new identities, to flow.

That is the first part of this healing and an essential spiritual practice to which we will return over and over again as we journey through our human incarnations.

The second phase of the healing applies when we actually do have a sense of who we are internally, and why we are here. We may know we are meant to write, or create or heal or draw communities together. We may know we are meant be a scientist, or a dancer, or a singer. We may know we are meant to be in a relationship and have children, raising a family, or something else altogether different. We are in touch with our inner sound. We KNOW.

The challenge then arises when there is blockage to the expression of our true identity in the external world. So we are a healer without clients. We are a writer without the help of a publisher or distributor. We are a mother without children (biological or otherwise). We are a husband without a wife. We are a dancer without our music or connection with our bodies to be able to dance. We are on the inside what is not yet evident on the outside.

This can be deeply challenging to our sense of faith and trust. We might have to rely a lot on metaphor, of caterpillars breaking down in the cocoon and turning into butterflies eventually in order to keep the faith. Sometimes the challenge when one knows the inner voice, the inner truths, but is yet to see them in the physical world, is to hold on! Have faith, be patient and trust that growth is a process. If you feel it and love it within, and are patient, your birth will be. Your transformation may be of a dramatic nature, and therefore take a little longer in Earth timing to manifest.

I remember coming out of a deeply challenging period where I felt like I essentially dwelled in a sort of underworld. I had been forced out of the realms of light where I would naturally prefer to inhabit, into a dark, womb-like space of the Divine Mother. Although it wasn't of my own personal choice, in terms of 'ego Alana' I did know and accept that my soul was asking something of me by evoking this situation. That didn't mean that I enjoyed it, just that I could value it. Truth was, it was exceptionally difficult for me.

I felt like what I had been was stripped away and I had no clue about what I would become. It just felt beyond me. The manifestation of my passion to succeed in my work had never seemed farther away than it did then. I didn't even expect that my dreams would manifest anymore. I just felt as though I was living in an in-between world and I didn't much like it.

From the soul perspective, I was cast into a world of dark feminine wisdom. I learned a huge amount through that challenging time. I learned about dreams and the unconscious mind and about how to stop looking outside of myself for the light, instead learning how to heal my connection to my own body, learning to find the light from within the body.

I learned a lot from this work, though it was strange and I didn't enjoy it at first. I was taught one of the most important lessons of human experience, which tested my faith and trust over and over again. That is the lesson of patience. Socially it was a very restrictive time, which for me was very difficult, for as much as I love my solitude, I enjoy it most when it is balanced with playful encounters with others.

It felt like, to put it lightly, my whole life was me being trapped inside studying when I could look outside and see the other children playing after school! I was somehow nourished by the inner work, but there were months at a time, and eventually years at a time when I craved the lightness of what I had once known, like an almost unbearable craving for heat and sunlight in the middle of a long cold winter. It was one of my dark nights of the soul, and it lasted for the better part of a decade.

Towards the end of that period, I stumbled across a piece of art in the middle of a shopping mall, in a small gallery shop. Instantly I decided to purchase it though it was somewhat expensive and warranted a call from my bank shortly after purchase asking if the purchase was legitimate or if someone had nabbed my card and run off on a shopping spree!

Somehow, like the dove painting spoke to my mother at the time of my conception, this painting spoke to me just before my spiritual rebirth into the world, though I didn't know that was what was happening at the time. All I knew was that I was captivated by it. It was bright, radiant red, with a huge yellow and white butterfly dominating the centre of the painting, practically bursting off the canvas. The paint was thick and roughly applied and the artwork felt like it was buzzing with pure life force itself. It felt like birth. None of this was conscious at the time. It took me months of gazing at the painting hanging on my wall of my home (which it still does) before I consciously realised that this was what was emerging for me. That it wouldn't be long, and soon that would be my soul bursting forth with new energy, colour, life and power. Which is exactly what happened a year or so following that purchase.

I had to wait, as we often do when inner worlds are gaining enough strength to burst through into physical reality with enough accumulated power that they can trample any obstacle that would otherwise block their manifestation. My patience was rewarded in ways that I feel so humbled and grateful for now. Yet I also know that apart from the patience and the trust, what helped me emerge was the word, the sound, the bridge from my inner world into the physical world that is created by the vibration being strengthened from within, until it spills forth into outer manifestation. This is the second part of the healing – the affirmation, the declaration, that we affirm with as much soul presence as we can muster and we give it sound, we give it words, we give it attention. This is what allows the birth, when the timing is right, to be bold, radiant and a pure alignment of the outer reality with the inner spirit.

If you are still 'cooking' in the cosmic womb, like I was then, gaining the strength and power that you need to bring the inner truths that you know are you into the fullness of manifestation and flow in the physical world, then the second part of this healing process is for you. It's about walking your talk, living in harmony between vision and physical reality. It is where you really feel like you are living your soul in the world. It is worth the work.

PSYCHOLOGICAL-EMOTIONAL HEALING PROCESS – TWO STAGES FOR SOUL RESONANCE

If you have some Aquamarine, please place it on or near your body. You may even wish to lie down and rest it at the base of your throat. If you don't have the stone with you, another option is to simply open this book to page 33 in the full colour section, which features a Crystal Angel Mandala for Aquamarine, and leave it next to you during this process.

Start by sitting or lying comfortably with both palms upwards.

Say, "I call upon the healing Angel of Aquamarine, and divine Angel Bath Kol. I call upon the truthful resonance and sacred sound of my own divine soul. I call upon the healing power of sound and the truth of my own light. Be with me now beloved ones, that my best life may be lived and my truths within may shine as truths in the world of form. Through divine grace, unconditional love and mercy, so be it."

Close your eyes and focus on the breath. Be aware of a soft blue-green light that pulses in your chest, between your heart and throat. Watch it grow to include your heart and your throat. Then it grows again to include your solar plexus, abdominal area and eventually your entire body, until this light is glowing all around you, wider than your body, above your head and beneath your feet.

Stay with this light for at least seven long, slow breaths in and out, or for however long feels appropriate for you.

Then say aloud, "This light is the light of my soul truth. I surrender into it now completely and without fear. I hand over that which no longer serves my most joyful growth with peaceful detachment and trust. I receive that which is truthfully me, beyond what I have been previously able to see, I let go of outgrown identity and I ask to be consciously filled with what is more truthfully me. Through divine grace and my own free will, so be it."

Perceive, visualise or allow the blue green light to radiate more brightly and just let it concentrate itself in the part of your body that you feel needs it the most. You don't have to understand why it centres where it does, just let it go there.

When you are ready say, "I know that I am in truth a soul divine, and that everything in my life is turning out just fine, but if there is a grace that helps me align more swiftly and fully with my soul, may it come to me in time that is perfect and time that is right. Help me translate my inner light into the world of forms that beckons me to it, to shine forth with truth, to let my soul live through it. Help me now build a bridge of sound and light, that the truth within may now take flight, reaching out into the physical world, so in need of its power. I ask for this now, this very hour. Please help me those of unconditional love, Angel of Aquamarine below, and Angel Bath Kol from above. So be it!"

When you are ready, perceive that the radiant blue-green light becomes more powerful again, this time descending from above your head, through you in a vast column of light, wider than your body, descending into the Earth. It is Bath Kol emanating through your body and soul. Say aloud as the light grows and plunges in the Earth, pouring down from heaven through your body, "I AM THAT I AM". Repeat it over and over again for at least several breaths, or however long feels good.

Stay with the flow of light for at least forty-four breaths. Then in your own time, become aware of your body in the room, and open your eyes.

You have finished your psychological and emotional healing process. You may notice your intuitions and interests becoming clearer and stronger over the coming days and weeks. Remember to act on them. This is the soul healing taking place. Don't hold back, don't be scared. We are presented with that which we are ready for – have faith and respond with loving acceptance. It will all work out according to the loving wise playful plan of your own divine guiding light.

PHYSICAL HEALING WITH AQUAMARINE AND ANGEL BATH KOL: THE MEMORY OF THE THROAT

I once had a client who couldn't wear jewellery around her throat. For many years she just felt like she was being strangled. I believe that this was a body memory of a past life where she was either literally strangled (perhaps with a piece of her own jewellery by a disenchanted suitor!) or that she felt strangled from speaking her truth because of wealth (symbolised by jewels around her throat) in a past life.

I have also had experiences of past life recollection where my throat or voice has been the centre of quite a bit of action, where feathers of those in power were ruffled by what I had to say, and times when I had been an oracle and my words carried a lot of power. Political decisions were made based on my interpretation of the signs that I perceived. There was a lot of responsibility on my shoulders! Then there were other times when I had spoken and my words were not heeded and I felt deep sadness and powerlessness at the tragedy that ensued, which I had not been able to prevent. There have been times when I have been releasing old emotions from my body and my throat felt so tight and constricted, and burning, that I could barely speak.

It is not just me who has had such experiences. Many who encounter difficulty in speaking up will have had past life challenges around the throat chakra. Many of those interested in the healing arts in this lifetime will have had the sense of being silenced through beheading or hanging, or threats of such, in other lifetimes. They may have even been silenced through fear of what their speaking out may result in during this lifetime.

All of these memories get lodged in our throats and can produce a powerful but often unconscious block to our soul light radiating freely in our physical life, not to mention eventually causing thyroid problems, tonsillitis, throat infections and so forth as the body attempts to dislodge and release the accumulated toxins.

On a less dramatic level, a clogged throat chakra results in too many thoughts, not enough organisation, too much judgement and an endless to-do list that never seems to get any shorter. I have a dear friend who has entire books of lists. A daunting prospect! Fortunately she has a powerful throat chakra and seems to get through each book before constructing her next book of lists. She is a dynamic, creative force to be reckoned with!

Clearing the throat chakra is a way to wipe the slate clean. What genuinely needs to stay and be done, will be preserved on the soul's list, and all the inessentials that would otherwise lead us down a useless and distracting path will be cleared. It can be a real exercise in trust as we let go of much self-imposed and inessential-to-the-soul busyness and allow ourselves to feel more open and free again. We might feel a bit guilty that we haven't got enough happening if we are used to being overloaded and overwhelmed, yet with a clearer throat chakra we will feel more productive, more creative, clear about what we would like to create. The whole process can then happen more quickly and easily.

HOW DO I KNOW IF I NEED THIS HEALING PRACTICE?

On a physical level if you suffer from throat problems, such as recurring sore throats or neck tension, clearing the throat chakra is an excellent addition to your wellbeing program.

On an energetic level if you need to be more focused, clear and organised, a throat chakra cleanse will help you get there. Be prepared to let go of things that don't feel right after the throat gets cleared and you'll find you have more time for that which is meaningful to your soul purpose, and therefore brings you more fulfilment.

If you struggle to express yourself and not be bullied by others or overwhelmed by your own empathy to other's feelings, losing a connection to your own truths in the process, a regular throat chakra cleanse will help you find your way back to your own truths. To which you are absolutely entitled, I might add.

PHYSICAL HEALING PRACTICE – THROAT CHAKRA CLEARING

Lie comfortably on your back with a piece of Aquamarine (if you have it) lying on or near your throat or heart, resting in the base of the throat or at the palms of your hands (if balancing the stone on your chest/heart area doesn't feel stable). Be warm and comfortable. If you don't have the stone, we'll call on the spirit anyway of course, so the practice will still have an effect. As with the other healing processes in this book, in the absence of the crystal itself you may choose to simply leave the book open to page 40, which features a photo of the stone and have it next to you as you complete the process.

When you are ready, say the following:

"I call upon the healing power of the Angel of Aquamarine and the Angel Bath Kol. I call upon the healing of the blue-green ray of cleansing, truth, discernment and expression. I call upon the natural healing ability of my own body-soul. Please help now beloved ones. Cleanse my throat physical and etheric, through all time and space, through all lifetimes and all ancestral lines. Bring my throat chakra and all of its functions into perfect balance and wellbeing now. Through divine grace, kindness and mercy, so be it!"

Close your eyes and focus on your breath. Let the breath flow in and out of the entire body, as if the entire body could breathe. Then focus your awareness at your throat and allow swirling washes of blue green light to swirl into your throat, washing it inside and flowing out of the front, back and sides of our throat with each inhalation and exhalation.

Inhale the light in. Exhale the light out. Stay with this process for at least forty-four breaths in and out.

When you are ready, say, "I honour the truths of my soul. They support me from within as I live in alignment in the physical world, expressing my truth. I am now free from past trauma and pain, with a willingness to live as myself, bold, bright and true, again. I release old vows, old words spoken and unspoken, thought but not said, and said without thought. I forgive and release old dreams that are not to be, and dreams that yet will be, in alignment with my inner divinity. I choose to let go of withholding and fear, and am no longer afraid to speak my truth aloud and clear. With compassionate intention and divine intervention, I am safe to be me, inside and in the world around me. So be it!"

Allow your body to be wrapped in a beautiful blue-green bubble of light. Take your time and open your eyes.

You have finished your healing process.

You may feel emotions and memories arising during and following this process, or a lot of emotion or intensity in your dreams. These are symptoms of the throat chakra releasing. Be gentle with your body. It can be a great time to journal, to record your dreams and thoughts. These intuitions can be powerful and helpful guides for your life over the coming months and years. So remember to visit your journal and go back and read what you have recorded when you feel an inner nudge (or a clear inner voice saying, "Go and read your journal!") to do so.

PRAYER − AFFIRMATION

To invoke the healing power of Aquamarine and Angel Bath Kol at any time, you can repeat the following affirmation quietly in your mind, or aloud.

"Blue-Green Ray of Divine Truth in Expression,
Manifest my Soul through My Expressed Intention."

18.

SMOKY QUARTZ (Grounding) and ANGEL UZZIEL (Mercy)

THE GIFT OF EMBODIMENT

SPIRITUAL GUIDANCE FROM THE ANGEL OF SMOKY QUARTZ AND THE ANGEL UZZIEL

To come to life in a body is a great spiritual gift, though within the soul it at first causes a rift. You forget that you belong beyond this space and time, you forget you are one with the Creator Divine. Heaven can seem so far away, not connected to your Earth life day after day. Yet hidden within the Earth and this body you hold is the endless light of Christ Consciousness gold. We understand how hard it can be to unearth this treasure, that sometimes your suffering is greater than your pleasure. Yet the spiritual reward in bringing body and soul together as one, brings you to a state where all suffering is undone. Suddenly you are dwelling in eternal light manifest, spiritually you have grown, you have passed the test! And this world becomes Heaven and Heaven becomes Earth, your enlightened body-soul has spiritually rebirthed. Your suffering passes and your bliss does grow, as now you are a divine being, you remember, you know. We help you on this path that you may help others too, to learn to let go of suffering and become what is true. What has suffered can rest, and what is radiant can shine, it all happens perfectly, in accordance with time. For the soul to manifest in this earthly place, it must enter your body through divine grace. Clearing the blocks of depression and pain, accepting the light and letting it reign. We help you to ground, to come to Earth, so that your soul light can manifest and reveal its true worth. Bringing healing truth to this earthly place, helping enlighten the whole human race. Then the Earth will be shown to be, what She is in truth, the Mother, divine and free.

PICTURING SMOKY QUARTZ

Smoky Quartz is translucent quartz with a tinge of palest taupe right through to darkest brown. Even when the colour is very dark, if you hold it up to the light you can see through it. Artificially heated Quartz is usually black and opaque. Natural Quartz is either clear (in shades of smoky brown tones) or with inclusions such as rainbows which create a beautiful healing stone for the entire body. Smoky Quartz can also be found with golden threads of angel hair rutile within it which amplifies its energy.

Smoky Quartz can be found in jewellery or tumbled stones, and most commonly in single points which have been polished. It is relatively inexpensive, though as with most crystals, very high quality pieces cost more.

HEALING PROPERTIES

Smoky Quartz is a 'feel good' stone. It lifts depression and negativity, helps clear fear and any dense vibrational energy from the body, surrounding the user with a feeling of gentle comfort, peace and reassurance. It is both powerful and extremely gentle, not unlike it's associated Angel Uzziel.

Smoky Quartz helps to ground the spiritual energy of the soul into the body, which is where our transformation takes place. The body, when ignited with presence of spiritual light, becomes an alchemical laboratory for spiritual enlightenment. It is capable of such beauty, healing, wisdom and divine bliss! But just like a science experiment, there can be a lot of bubbling and hissing as chemical changes occur when two substances are introduced to each other.

Unlike oil and water, the body and the soul are able to unite in consciousness, becoming an expression of each other, blending and mixing their energies until the body itself is more light than matter, approaching states of golden light and peace. The experiences of this happening can actually be quite disconcerting at first and not particularly pleasant. Further into the process, as the body-soul becomes more refined, this gives way to much more pleasant and sometimes blissful experiences of energy and movement. Initial aches, pains, shaking and hot flashes can eventually be softened into waves of bliss and currents of buzzing energy filling our body and transporting us into beautiful states of feeling.

Rather than turning away from or denying the body to find the Divine, Smoky Quartz encourages those souls on the path to bring the body and soul together in love and light, here in our earthly reality. The earthly world and the body then become instruments through which the divine energy of the soul can express itself for the greater good.

There has to be a great love for the Earth for a soul to take this path, and much spiritual strength to get through the challenges that can present in personal growth and spiritual awakening as the soul incarnates in a body. There are all sorts of emotions which can be difficult to release as the soul enters the body and clears out denser vibrations, transforming the energetic substance of the body into more refined spiritual matter, more suitable for the soul's vibration (which is pure love).

Smoky Quartz helps dissolve and protect the energy field as these energies arise to be released. From fear and even darkest terror, to despair, depression, suicidal thoughts and negative fantasies of violence and destruction (of self or others), to nightmares and general toxicity in mind, emotions and body, Smoky Quartz supports us through it all. These energies will arise as the body releases dense vibration to create space for the soul light to manifest. It is quite a ride when this is happening – and it can be easy to forget the bigger picture and get caught up in believing something is truly wrong. Yet it is through the support of the crystal angels that we can be reminded that we are given only what supports our divine growth and awakening. There are many sources of spiritual support available, we need but ask for them.

Smoky Quartz is the main crystal to use (perhaps along with black tourmaline) for any cases of radiation and its negative impact on our wellbeing. From managing the effects of chemotherapy treatments at one extreme to dealing with the day-to-day reality of living in the stream of radiation from televisions, computer screens, electricity stations and broadcast towers, mobile telephones, wireless internet, microwave ovens and so on. Placing large Smoky Quartz crystals around the home and requesting that they absorb and release excess radiation into the Earth is helpful. These crystals are powerful, having been subjected to extremely high levels of natural Earth radiation in their formation over millions of years. By capturing and returning man-made radiation that could be harmful to us, this crystal serves the greater wellbeing on this planet and her inhabitants.

ABOUT THE ANGEL UZZIEL

Connecting with Uzziel left me speechless for some moments – which you may now be beginning to sense is not so unusual when encountering an angel! The feeling was mentally confounding. I had no clear thought or assessment of what was happening, whilst at the same time my heart was in deep peace and blissful expansion. When connecting with a living being that is not human and not of this human world in a more day-to-day sense, the human mind can get a bit frazzled as it tries to understand what is going on. If there is enough energy the mind will give up and go quiet as the heart takes over. That is the best way to experience an angel. No mind, all heart!

Uzziel translates as "God's Power". He is said to serve under Metatron (who we met in the Clear Quartz chapter). Uzziel unites with Smoky Quartz to bring us the blessings that we need as we go through the often confronting and painful process of spiritual awakening. He brings us hope and restores faith, especially when we have reached those moments where we are in a dark night of the soul and we are wondering if we will ever feel joyful connection or bliss again.

Perhaps most uniquely and importantly, Uzziel is the Angel of Mercy. The concept of mercy was something that I never really understood or thought necessary on the spiritual path for many years. I experienced the divine as loving and benevolent. What did we need mercy for? However, as I grew in my understanding, through my own dreams and spiritual experiences, I realised that mercy is indeed a divine gift and we are absolutely in need of it.

It is not until we connect consciously with power – with our own soul power, with the power of the universal forces and the power all around us and running through us without our ego and its valiant attempts at self-defence – that we begin to understand the need for mercy. It is only in the conscious recognition of our vulnerability and even our fragility that the genuine spiritual value and gift of divine mercy becomes clear.

We have great power to create – sometimes we are like unknowing children wielding sharpest swords. We ask for this, or intend to create that, and if there is attachment involved, we may be making a bed for ourselves that had we had the gift of hindsight, we would have known we would not wish to lie in.

Mercy is that part of divinity that sometimes appears to say "no" when we want it to say "yes", that teaches us through softening the blow of our own error – not so much that we don't learn, but enough that we are not dissuaded from continuing on our path. Mercy is important as we grow in our own power to create and manifest.

In 2011, I was running a class in the Shakti Temple in Sydney. It was a typical gathering and one of the more regular participants had brought some friends with him. One of them was a young man who had no prior experience of either meditation or energy work. As I went about the class, chanting, channelling energy transmissions through my voice and hands and feet, guiding the meditation verbally whilst music played, the divine energy grew and the various participants went off into their own individual experiences of seated meditation or moving dance meditation.

At the end of the process we had a chance to share our experiences and debrief. This young man barely said a word. I could sense that he was holding back and I was disappointed because I would have liked to have helped him through an explanation or two, if possible, but in the moment he chose not to share.

He never returned to the gathering and I heard later that he was deeply disturbed by the energy he felt moving in his body. He had never experienced anything like that before and didn't know what to make of how powerful it felt. Despite my guidance, urging me to accept that if there wasn't some point in it, his body wouldn't have ended up in that chair for the evening, I did feel concerned that I had unwittingly contributed more to his fear than to his awakening.

Sometimes great energy is not a gift but a way to evoke more defensiveness. If you come rushing at someone rather than gently approaching, even if you are rushing to give them a hug, the instinct can unconsciously be to pull back. Sometimes more is attained through gentleness. It all depends on where the soul-ego connection is at and what will best serve. What feeds one may destroy another.

This is why it is so important to allow those that are drawn to a class to come and not push for attendance. It is an attraction, a pull rather than a push, especially with higher intensity energy work. There is always a need for divine mercy. With power there is effect. Even if the power is based in love, there is effect.

So I have learned to call upon divine mercy as a regular practice. You will read it in the healings in this book over and over again. It may well be that what that young man experienced was perfect for him this lifetime. I would have liked to have been an instrument in this path in a gentler fashion, but I simply have to trust and from that experience take the learning that Uzziel is an ally worth calling upon.

SOUL HEALING WITH SMOKY QUARTZ AND ANGEL UZZIEL

Years ago I had a short, violent and disturbing dream that was a confounding but also a great teaching for me. In the dream I was in a class room run by angels and I was having my hand shoved into a blender and macerated into bits! The pain was unbearably excruciating and I suffered visibly and greatly. However the angel instructor simply said, "Wonderful – look at what a mess that is now! We shall have to summon the greatest skill to heal this wound and bring it into wellness again". He was enjoying the challenge of the repair, paying little attention to the suffering of experiencing the wounding.

I awoke from this dream with a start. I had the memory of that unbearable pain and the strange sense of dissociated lack of compassion from the angel instructor of my dream.

Eventually I realised that the dream was trying to teach me about mercy. I needed to learn to honour and acknowledge the deep pain that I was experiencing in my earthly reality (my hand in the blender). I needed to realise that although spiritually this would provide much growth in my abilities as a healer (the angel instructor's excitement at the rewards of successfully completing the healing task) what was missing in me was the compassion and mercy that would allow the body to be held, to soften the horror of the suffering.

From this perhaps something new could emerge – a way of living on the Earth that did not require great terror and suffering in order to grow spiritually, perhaps a more merciful approach to growth that was more calming, compassionate, less violent and more gentle.

Could this not lead to great strides in spiritual growth and even to enlightenment? Of course! But to be aware of the lack of mercy that I had unknowingly been creating (believing that all figures in that dream represented a different part of my own divine self – so that included the rather enthusiastic but clinical angel teacher) was required first. I had to become conscious of my lack of mercy and the need for it before any such growth or development in my own spiritual understanding and approach could occur.

So this dream grabbed my attention in a way that I couldn't ignore, forcing me to confront my own spiritual ruthlessness towards myself and the path. At a time when I was learning to recognise how much power I held, I was also learning to recognise how much mercy I needed for my power to be compassionate, to be based in loving kindness, to be effective without being harsh, to balance my power and temper it with mercy.

SOUL HEALING – DIVINE MERCY AND DIVINE POWER

I have heard a number of spiritual teachers talk about the great honour of receiving a body this lifetime and how they had to fight for it. I chuckle at the idea of souls wrestling each other for the right to incarnate, a bit like parents employing all manner of bribes, manipulations and games in order to get their child into the most elite school. Whilst I don't know about the fight for a body, I do know that no matter what troubles we may experience at a human level about being in a body, the soul has great reverence for the gift of one.

Imagine how you would feel if a generous and powerful benefactor came up to you and said, "Here's a home you can live in for your entire life, it is all yours to do with as you choose, and for the course of your natural life you are allowed to live in as you will. There is no rent, I just want you to have this and live your life." You would probably leap for joy, say, "Yes please! Thank you!" and get on with enjoying your wonderful gift with much gratitude in your heart. Well the soul feels similarly about the body.

What we discover when the spirit moves into this house, however, is that although it is ours, and we are grateful, there may be some work to be done. Perhaps there are parts of the house that need some work to become more inhabitable. We can choose to do this work or not, to the extent that we wish, but if we embrace it, the home becomes a much more enjoyable place to live – it might even become our temple or palace.

Physical houses hold memories and energy, 'if these walls could talk' is the saying, and energetically so too with our body. It holds memories from ancestral lines, and of the Earth herself, from which it has emerged. It holds the light latent in the Earth, her vast consciousness and wisdom, and it is a living house – it will interact with our soul presence.

As the cleansing light of the soul brings its purifying vibration, the living home of the body releases lower density vibrations. Out comes pain, suffering, memories and physical sensations, even as the body-soul is integrating, opening, enlightening and flowing. It can be a great surprise exactly how much pain is released when we are doing deep inner healing work. The soul wants more consciousness, so does the body, but as the saying goes, you can have too much of a good thing!

Mercy helps us keep our enthusiasm or drive for spiritual growth at a level that is manageable. Like a detox diet, too much toxicity in the system may turn that otherwise helpful diet into a death-trap. Cleaning a little at a time first, preparing the body to be in a relatively clear state so that a major detoxification program is something that the system can cope with is more merciful.

Spiritual light is benign but its effects can be destructive and harmful to us if not tempered with kindness. Too much light too soon can trigger fear, cause detox symptoms that are not so enjoyable and the outcome that was desired – more soul and body connection – may be attained through a gentler path, with less struggle and resistance and more actual progress.

When you are growing in your ability to call in the light of your own spirit, to live as a soul, you are gaining spiritual power. To learn how to manage that power is where the lesson of mercy arises. This is what the crystal angels help us master – the art of embodiment. We don't want to ravage the body with light, we want to gently ignite it, to illuminate from within. This can be a far softer, more organic, naturally sustainable and enjoyable way, than by forcing light in through spiritual technologies (such as these healing exercises if done in an immoderate way rather than as suggested – like spiritually over-exercising with light!). I have felt the effects of this in my own body – exhaustion and depletion. I have seen it in teachers and healers that suffered with disease and imbalance. It is not fun, nor is it necessary.

Smoky Quartz supports our body in learning to handle divine energy and process it, to manage the detoxifying effects on the body, mind and emotions with some compassion and gentle yet effective holding. Uzziel carries within his field the energy of divine mercy, which helps us find the balance through which the greatest strides can be made, not through extremes, not through drive, but through a balanced approach where we explore and grow, give ourselves time to integrate and then explore and grow again.

HOW DO YOU KNOW IF YOU ARE HEALING AT A SOUL LEVEL IN THIS WAY?

If you have a strong power drive in your soul, you'll quite likely have big dreams and even bigger determination to simply keep pushing yourself until they manifest. There is undoubtedly an element of strength, commitment and determination that is essential to unlearn old ways and grow spiritually, pulling back the layers as you approach a more pure experience of your own divine self. Yet the force within this can become unbalanced.

Balance allows us to use the innate divine power that we have to play in the world to be with more positive contribution and less harm. We can choose to give our soul truths a voice and to make concrete contributions – in what we create, in how we interact, how we live and so on – that enhance life on this planet. We can use our power drive in service to the soul rather than in service to fear of having to prove something, or in not being good enough, or in fear of not having value unless we create something, for example. We can also use our inner power to be stronger than drive and give ourselves permission to just be. This is vastly helpful to manifestation which often happens despite, rather than because, of our efforts to make it occur faster!

Mercy allows us to learn how to handle our power with consciousness and responsibility. To connect with Mercy as a divine quality helps us trust that we can be safe with power and it won't corrupt us, that we will be able to counter the temptation to go too far with it, and learn instead that power in the true sense isn't about harm, but about love in action.

Many spiritually inclined individuals hold themselves back from their power out of fear that it is the ego and should be avoided. They will have likely had past lives where they had power and the consequences of it were not to their liking. They may be disillusioned by those in positions of political power or authority in this lifetime even, and be unwilling to become like them in anyway, believing that to own their power would result in this happening.

Yet there is a time on the spiritual path to embrace the ego, to infuse it with as much soul as possible and let it play. It is like raising a child and then allowing it to go out into the world, trusting that you have done your absolute best to instil values and awareness that will serve it best. At this point in the journey it is helpful to envision that the ego is meant to connect with and be absorbed into the soul. It is not meant to be pushed away and denied. It is best to learn to balance power and let it serve the higher self than push it away or deny it, where it festers in the shadow and eventually erupts in passive-aggressive behaviour, unconscious harm towards ourselves through addiction or against the world in toxic acting out.

You'll know if this is for you because you will sense that you need to change your relationship to your own power through cultivating more mercy. Or you will feel that power is unclean and to be avoided. Or you will be feeling that you would like a new role model for responsible spiritual power. You may have been very drawn to the first chapter on Quartz and Archangel Metatron as well as this chapter. Perhaps you'll have the sense that there is something of value within you that you have yet to gain the capacity to bring into the world. Or you feel there may lie deep within you something of value that you are yet to consciously discover. All of these places on the path can benefit from an increase in willingness to access and consciously direct our spiritual power, and the mercy that balances this, causing it to be wielded with wisdom, compassion and love.

SOUL HEALING PROCESS – SOUL POWER AND DIVINE MERCY

Find a peaceful place to sit comfortably with your spine relatively straight and your back supported, where you can speak without concern about being overheard or interrupted. If you have any Smoky Quartz, have it anywhere on your body that feels right. If you don't have a piece of the stone, you may like to open this book to page 34 in the full colour section that features a mandala for Smoky Quartz and leave it open next you as you complete the healing process.

Start the healing by saying, "Of my own free will, I now call upon the Angel of Smoky Quartz and the Angel Uzziel. I call upon divine power and divine mercy. I now request special healing and support as I surrender false notions and trauma of power from the past. As I step into my divine power with gentleness and trust, may I find the strength I need to journey within, beyond illusion to the truth of my light. May I access the power that I need to illuminate the Earth's spiritual night. Help me grow with mercy and grace, that my demonstration of power always emerge from my heart space. Help me release harshness and drive that comes from my ego need to survive. May I find instead, power drenched in mercy and grace. May it serve my soul from within and humanity as a whole. May it lift me out of hiding and into luminous life on this Earth. For the greatest good, so be it."

Close your eyes as you give yourself permission to journey within, following the flow of your own breath. Each inhalation draws you deeper into your own centre. Each exhalation allows you to rest and relax there. Let the cycle of the breath continue as your awareness expands and deepens.

Notice two streams of energy flowing before you now. There is a silver light of mercy and a dark smoky light of power. They weave and interact with each other, creating a beautiful dance of light and shadow. As you gaze at these divine forces you notice that they are emanating from a vast cosmic void. This void is open, black and peaceful. These two streams of consciousness flow out of the void like rivers of light. Let yourself move into them now if you choose, bathing first in the energy of mercy, silvery and light, and then be nourished by the dark smoky energy of power, feeling its warmth, nourishment and love.

Allow these lights to balance themselves within you. This does not have to be consciously directed or understood. It can just happen with your permission now. As the lights move through you, and around you, you may notice that there is more of one colour or another in certain parts of your being. Or you may surrender your conscious awareness of the process completely in order to relax with trust, and simply choose to focus on your breath flowing in and out, for forty-four breaths.

When you have completed this part of the healing, simply say, "I now choose to own my power with mercy, in service to my soul truth. I choose to live empowered on this Earth, and to be truly merciful and compassionate. Through my own free will, and with the loving help of the Angel of Smoky Quartz and the Angel Uzziel, so be it."

Move your hands and feet, bringing your awareness completely back into your body and the present moment.

You have completed your soul healing exercise. You can repeat this exercise at any time you feel you need to strengthen or balance your power or your ability to have mercy on yourself or others. This is especially the case if you have been pushing yourself hard or being hard on another for whatever reason.

PSYCHOLOGICAL-EMOTIONAL HEALING WITH THE ANGEL OF SMOKY QUARTZ AND THE ANGEL UZZIEL: ACCEPTING THE BODY

The body may hold within it the dearest spiritual treasures we can imagine, yet if we cannot accept the body or the fact that we are actually bound to live in one this lifetime, then those treasures will not reveal themselves to us.

The body tries to reach to us with its wisdom through dreams and our experiences in meditation, yoga, energy healing sessions, conscious dance and conscious play. Conscious play is that which is undertaken whilst allowing ourselves to be present to what is taking place in that moment, rather than dissociated through alcohol or recreational drug use for example.

If you are having experiences of energy flow, of emotion releasing and a sense of light or opening in the body, seeing light when your eyes are closed, feeling light within your cells, then your body wisdom is speaking to you. Your body wisdom can bring you into a state of bliss and peace, of contentment.

If you have ever felt jealous of the ability of an animal to simply rest and be at peace, then you will have already tapped into a sense of what pure moment, embodied awareness can bring.

I used to envy my cat, when I was a student at university studying endless (and to me, mostly rather boring) legal cases. I had been adopted by a Siamese cat called Tabatha (who just decided to move in and treat me as her owner) at that time, and whilst I would have my nose in a book, she would be curled up in the top desk drawer which I learned to leave open for her. She would snuggle in, fitting just perfectly into that space and promptly fall asleep. Sometimes purring, sometimes dreaming, I would envy her ability to just be, whilst I was pushing myself to do something that didn't seem to bring much benefit to my physical wellbeing at all.

I learned from that to let my body be more often. I was once on spiritual retreat, early on in my twenties, when the mother of one of the women running the retreat came up to me and observed that me just sitting there, not reading, not doing something, not meditating but just being, was so unusual. When my partner finds me in such a situation he virtually always asks me what I am doing, with a bemused expression on his face. My answer of 'nothing' is probably as confounding to him as it is to those women who ask men what they are thinking, only to receive the same response. Once I had a client, an extremely wealthy and successful businessman in his fifties, say to me quite honestly (and with beautiful vulnerability I thought) that he just wanted to know how to sit and watch a sunset. And enjoy the experience. The only way we ever have a hope of getting to that enviable feline place of purring contentment, or the ability to enjoy 'nothing' or to drink in a sunset is to be in the body in that moment.

I still remember when I was coming into my body more consciously this lifetime, after years of it being so clogged up with past lifetime pain, current lifetime trauma, and ancestral karmic imprints that there wasn't much space for my soul to manifest within it. I would step outside and feel the absolute beauty of the day – the crispness of winter, the spiritual electricity of sunlight, sizzling during midsummer, the sharp freshness of autumn as the midday became afternoon, and the beautiful welcoming softness of spring. Suddenly the thought of only experiencing a finite number of these seasons seemed so unbearably and sadly brief. And I had already missed so many by simply not being able to be present, to being back in the past or ahead of myself in the future, living in my mind. It was a sobering moment and it made me appreciate just how much beauty was available through living present in the body. After the earlier part of my incarnation being filled with so much suffering, a karmic agreement my soul had made to 'eat my spiritual vegetables first' this lifetime, so to speak, to finally be able to be in the body and experience the joy of it, rather than only the struggle, was a tremendous and surprising gift.

HOW DO I KNOW IF I NEED HEALING IN THIS WAY AND AT THIS LEVEL OF MY BEING?

It is my experience and belief that our spiritual growth unfolds in spirals. That as we arise in levels of consciousness, sometimes we appear to move back to old issues, yet we are able to approach them more effectively, from a higher place of growth because we have moved that far along our journey. It is a chance to keep coming back to that issue, whilst actually moving forward spiritually, until we outgrow it altogether. At this point it no longer serves our growth and it doesn't arise anymore for us, or if it does, it falls away quickly without distracting us or causing a reaction.

Our journey of soul into the body is of a similar spiralling momentum, spiralling inwards, instead of out. What we find in that inward motion however, as we clear out the old emotional patterning, is vast spaciousness, light and power. We also find an ability to be present. This can be demonstrated when we can just sit and listen to someone speak, really hearing them, without having to interrupt or even throw in our opinion. It can be demonstrated when we are really aware of what is happening in the body at any particular time, including the ability to really take in pleasure and to savour something wonderful, which we may do less often than we realise.

An example of this is the dinner party where some of the guests eat their meal whilst talking about how wonderful the meal was that they ate somewhere else last week or how great they hope the meal will be when they next attend a particular restaurant. Instead of being present and enjoying the feast before them, and being able to honour the energy of their host in creating it, they are off in the past or the future. It denies them the pleasure of the moment, and their host the pleasure of his gift being received.

If we take it a little further and imagine that life is the biggest dinner party ever, and the Divine is the host, well you can imagine how much joy you would provide to the Creator if you really savoured your experiences! I have a client that lives in this way. She is full of robust zest for whatever happens to be going on at the time. I know first-hand how entertaining this is to witness, and I have heard from her guidance how much delight is taken from her way of living. She is a carnival in a body, without being superficial or frivolous in any way. This is one of the gifts that being present, being in the body through acceptance, really committing to life and being here on the Earth brings to us. Life becomes more vivid, it is not boring, it is colourful, it is up and down, sometimes it will feel upside down, and it is a wild ride.

If you need a little more of this – the colour and vibrancy of life – then this healing is for you. If you are at yet another turn of the spiral where you are present but you know you could move more deeply into experience itself, to really drink more of it in, in order to remedy your tiredness, fatigue, emptiness when you feel you are burned out from giving more than you receive or lack of passionate purpose, then this healing is for you.

Finally if you are learning to really accept your body, to learn patience and to make an absolute commitment to being here on the Earth and just giving your life everything you have within you, then this healing will help.

Sometimes we subconsciously hold back from life, from being here on this planet and really just going with it, because we aren't so sure that we really want to be here at all. It is a bit like your soul has moved to another culture and has to get over the culture shock and come on in to the body on Earth, accepting that it is here now, and get on with the task at hand.

Resistance to accepting the body and being alive here on Earth may manifest in thoughts of self-harm including suicidal thoughts. Underlying such thoughts are a hidden message. The message is that something needs to end. In pain and confusion, we might interpret that to mean that our life must end, but actually the message hiding in such thoughts is that the cause of suffering has to be released. This is not life itself. It is the wound within us that needs to heal, the wound that otherwise prevents us from being able to be present to life.

For me, that wound was a sense that I didn't really belong here, that I was so different and too sensitive to bear the pain of this world. Although I didn't have suicidal thoughts, I did have a resistance towards life that manifested as an exceptionally painful withdrawal from the world around me as a coping mechanism. To overcome that withdrawal, to learn to love life even when it was extremely difficult, I had to learn how to move through the wound rather than distance myself from the pain of it. I did this through learning to be present to the pain and allowing it to pass. It took a long time to become capable of that practice. The healing processes here are designed to help you do a similar practice much more quickly.

Resistance to life can show up in more subtle ways too. It might manifest as a reluctance to take heart-centred risks, to act on our dreams or visions, to make connections with others and let others connect with us, or there may be a tendency to hide behind the illusory safety of addictions.

However it manifests, the resolution is essentially the same – it is the courage to say "YES!" to our body, to our life, to our dream or our passion. It means really jumping in, both feet first (or sometimes head first!) and committing to the experience. We know that it is life, we cannot control it, but we can choose to engage with it, to live it and to trust that we will find our way.

This is how we truly come alive and this requires that we first accept that we are indeed in the body, in life. This is the purpose for our psychological and emotional healing process below.

PSYCHOLOGICAL-EMOTIONAL HEALING PROCESS – ACCEPTING EMBODIMENT

If you have some Smoky Quartz, please place it on or near your feet, at the base of your spine or even your lower belly. You may even wish to lie down and place it up to a metre away, directly beneath your feet. As an alternative, leave the book just next to you, open to page 34 where the Crystal Angel Mandala for Smoky Quartz appears in full colour.

Start by sitting or lying comfortably with both palms upwards.

Say, "I call upon the healing Angel of Smoky Quartz, and divine Angel Uzziel. I call upon Mother Earth and my own body-soul. I call upon divine power, peace, mercy and grace. I call on unconditional love. I now choose, of my own free will, to release through all time and space the fear I have held within of being upon this Earth. I release all belief that I am not supposed to be here, that it is a mistake, that I belong elsewhere. I release the fear of being in my body, that I will not be able to bear it, that it will feel suffocating, restraining, painful or distracting from my spiritual path. I release all fear and judgement that my body is not beautiful, that it is sinful, unclean, stupid, a burden, a sack of bones, worthless, illusory and therefore useless, distracting and frustrating. I release all hate I have stored within my body, from me or others, I release any fear of death that my body has experienced, including my own fear and the fears of others. I release the fear, conscious or subconscious, that if I truly engage with life I am turning away from the light, I am not taking my spiritual life seriously and I will get caught up in distraction or pain. I surrender my lack of commitment to my own life out of fear or failure. I surrender fear of suffering and loss, of the emotional experiences that flow through the body. I release this now through divine power and mercy, into the unconditional love of the Earth Mother, so be it."

Close your eyes and focus on the breath. Imagine that you can feel the Earth energy gathering underneath you, whether you are lying on a floor, sitting on a chair, on the first floor, the ground, the beach or in a high rise building. The Earth energy gathers under you, holding and supporting you. Allow yourself to sense that the boundary between you and the Earth energy is softening and become less defined, until you are feeling that you and the energy of the Earth are becoming more harmonised, more at one with each other through your body.

Stay with this experience of blending and being held in the Earth energy. Relax. Let it support you. Let it strengthen you and give you power. Let this energy nourish and restore you. Feel a sense of magnetism, a pulling quality that the Earth has, as she and the Angel of Smoky Quartz begin to draw negativity and pain out of your body and mind and emotions. Just let the energy be sucked out of you and replaced with gentle nourishing love. The presence of Angel Uzziel makes this process gentler and more peaceful. As you release this doubt you start to wonder why you have held back from life. There isn't anything nearly so scary as you once believed. It all seems a bit hard to imagine why you felt that way now. Uzziel blesses you with hope, light and gentle peace.

Together with the Angel of Smoky Quartz you feel a gentle yet pervading sense of love and trust. There is optimism. There is gratitude for the body. You feel uplifted and grounded, energised and relaxed.

Then say aloud, "This life and this body are my sacred gift which I accept completely, surrendering all holding back that I may dive in, live my life and shine bright. May I be assisted with mercy, power and grace, may my embodied life bring more love to the Earth and may I live boldly, kindly and with passionate grace. Through my own free will, so be it."

Perceive, visualise or allow the crystal angels to empower your statement now, encoding it in the cells of your body and every corner of your mind space. Feel the loving response of your body as it is accepted by you, as you love it and serve it, just as it loves and serves you.

Imagine the crystal angels providing a bridge of Quartz along which your mind and body can easily come together in harmony. Let there be a moment of connection that is peaceful, accepting, grateful.

When you are ready, say, "May I always honour and serve the truth held within this body divine. So be it!"

In your own time, become aware of your body in the room, and open your eyes.

You have finished your psychological and emotional healing process.

You may notice that you have emotions continuing to leave after your process, along with a desire to eat or exercise differently, meditate more or dance on the beach! It is good to act on these impulses. They are your body helping your soul find the way to easiest expression of power and manifestation of your soul light, dreams and visions. Your body and soul can work together now, not against each other. Remember this and you'll find a willingness to act on such intuitions. This will serve you well, body and mind and soul.

PHYSICAL HEALING WITH SMOKY QUARTZ AND THE ANGEL UZZIEL: THE BASE CHAKRA

My most conscious physical experience of my base chakra was in the first chakra dance class that I ever did. I was sitting on a cushion in the opening meditation and suddenly I felt a physical sensation of a large coil pulling me into the Earth through the base of my spine. It stretched, and I felt the tension as it 'sprung' for a moment until my mind caught on to was happening, got really excited, pulled me out of the altered state of awareness that I needed to be in to feel the subtle energy so strongly, and I lost it!

I have never again experienced it in quite the same way, which is a disappointment. But that moment was enough to prove that the chakras are not just conceptual energy centres, they are literal and real, and I had just felt one. Not the energy of it – which we will discuss in a moment – but the actual structure of the base chakra itself.

I often say to clients to imagine their base chakra as one of those old Victorian hoop skirts starting at the base of their spine instead of their waist, or a really large upside down bowl that they can sit on, and digs deep into the Earth. So even if you don't have an actual experience of the chakra directly, you can imagine it energetically which will help you connect.

The base chakra is where the action of embodiment takes place, where our soul really engages with and takes root on the Earth, living a physical life as a body-soul, which is quite incredible when you really think about it. The chakras below the heart are essential for us to live as physical beings on this Earth. I have met highly evolved spiritual beings in meditation which have no such chakras, not needing them to live in the spiritual dimensions where they resided, which were not of the Earth. However, for us spiritual boot campers on Earth, the base chakra is essential. It is what gives our soul the legs and feet it needs to literally walk upon the Earth.

When the base chakra is open and connected, we enjoy our body. Physical life nourishes us and brings us energy, gives us opportunities to grow through challenge and express our light in material ways. Our sexual energy brings us joy and helps keep us energised. Our legs and feet are strong and powerful and we can move – symbolically and actually. When the base chakra is clogged with ancestral fear, with old emotional patterns from this or other lifetimes, our existence is so much less fun! We may have to overeat and become heavy as we subconsciously attempt to ground ourselves on the Earth. We may become spaced out or vague, lacking in commitment, presence, purpose and passion in life. We might feel as though we don't have a firm foundation or a strong anchor holding us in place from within, so we get blown about by circumstances outside of our control. We lose our firm foothold in life and perhaps slip off our path, walking the paths that others feel we should, rather than those that hold genuine meaning for us.

With a strong and open base chakra, we are able to generate and hold on to energy without hoarding through fear. That energy could be money, life force, power or emotional energy. The base chakra is our foundation and you could consider this exercise for the body and soul connection to be like an energetic pedicure and reflexology treatment! Good for the feet and the base chakra, which when strong, effectively supports the entire being. Just like a ballet dancer supporting her entire body weight on her toes.

HOW DO I KNOW IF I NEED THIS HEALING PRACTICE?

Unless you are already an incredibly grounded, earthy person, this healing will benefit you. Even then, it can assist you in cleansing the base chakra which will allow you to call in more of your spirit. If you find it difficult to access spirit, rather than to ground, then you may like to include a piece of Selenite or Clear Quartz above your head as well as Smoky Quartz below your feet for this healing, calling on the Angel of Selenite and the Angel of Clear Quartz as well.

For me, grounding has always been more challenging than spiritual connection. Learning to connect and stay present in my body is far less natural for me than conscious connection with spiritual beings. Once in a deep meditation my soul explained that I was like a big toe dipped into the earthly realms. The soul was this vast being beyond me, and my embodiment as Alana, which already felt quite vast in many ways, was just one big toe. It also explained why I could struggle to keep my awareness in my body. Have you ever tried putting all your awareness in one big toe? Not so easy! But of course to learn how to do this would bring great power and grace. So of course, it is worth the effort to master it. This is my gift and my challenge.

This may be similar for many of you who are naturally more attuned to the non-physical worlds. Learning to come into the body and be present to this physical reality as much as the non-physical realities might be your particular learning edge. In which case this entire chapter will serve you greatly.

Or perhaps you are at the other side of the growth process, learning how to expand beyond your very embodied awareness, into the non-physical parts of you. This healing will help you too because it will help you begin to recognise the non-physical reality of the physical body – that it is so much more than it appears to be.

That is the gift of working with the chakras. It helps to ground those of us who tend towards disembodiment and expand those that tend to embodiment at the expense of expanded spiritual awareness. They are the place in the energy body where these two extremes meet and are healed.

PHYSICAL HEALING PRACTICE – BASE CHAKRA CLEARING

Choose a place where you can lie comfortably and also stand.

Lie on your back with a piece of Smoky Quartz (if you have it) lying on or near your feet or at the base of the spine. If you don't have the stone, we'll call on the spirit anyway of course, so the practice will still have an effect. Another option is to leave the book open to page 40 in the full colour section that features a photo of the stone.

When you are ready, say the following:

"I call upon the healing power of the Angel of Smoky Quartz and the Angel Uzziel. I call upon the healing of the Earth herself. I call upon the natural healing ability of my own body-soul. Please help now beloved ones, to cleanse my base chakra through all time and space, through all lifetimes and all ancestral lines. Bring my base chakra into perfect balance and wellbeing now, that I may walk my soul light this lifetime, living my highest spiritual destiny. Through divine grace, kindness and mercy, so be it!"

Close your eyes and focus on your breath. Let the breath flow in and out of the entire body, as if the entire body could breathe. Then focus your awareness at the base of your spine and allow your awareness to expand if you wish to include your legs and feet.

The crystal angel appears before you as a beautiful rich red-brown clay like energy. Inhale the energy in through the soles of the feet and the base of the spine. It gathers negative energy and programming, and then very slowly exhale the energy out through the soles of the feet and base of the spine. Stay with this process for at least four repetitions.

When you are ready, say, "I call upon the light within Smoky Quartz and ask for healing now."

Stay with the breath and let the light of Smoky Quartz do its work. Imagine it rising up from the Earth, flowing in an upwards motion until it is out through the crown of your head, where it spills over each side and deep into the Earth, rising up and flowing out, falling down and descending over and over again. It is a cleansing flowing river of smoky light and love. Stay with this process for at least four repetitions.

Allow your body to be wrapped in a rich bubble of Smoky Quartz light now, turned softly golden and when you are ready, stand up slowly, taking your time. Really feel your feet on the earth, and bounce on the four corners of your feet – heels, toes, each side of the foot. If you cannot do this, simply intend to feel where your energy connects with the earth in four places – front, back, and each side.

Take four breaths in and out as you do this final grounding and when you are ready, simply open your eyes.

You have finished your healing process.

I recommend that you make sure you drink enough water and get adequate minerals in your diet. You may like to consult with a health care practitioner or your own intuition about this. To support the body at such a time will allow your healing to be that much more effective and have a long lasting positive impact in your life.

PRAYER – AFFIRMATION

To invoke the healing power of the Angel of Smoky Quartz and Angel Uzziel at any time, you can repeat the following affirmation quietly in your mind, or aloud.

"My Soul Embodied, Is Free within This Divine Temple Alight."

THE END IS JUST ANOTHER BEGINNING

SPIRITUAL GUIDANCE FROM THE CRYSTAL ANGELS

We your angels love you without condition
We help you discover and fulfil your divine life mission
We remind you to let go of your fear and feel free
We help you remember your innate divinity

We reach to you from the heavenly spheres
We are always with you, drawing you near
We guide you from deep within this loving Earth
Helping your soul light in this world to birth

All that is unique, beautiful and wise
The divine soul that dwells behind your eyes
If you ever need reminding that we are always together
Just keep your eyes open for a single white feather

It is one way we tell you
That our presence is true
That we have always loved you, we love you still
We love you unconditionally, and always will

PRAYER – AFFIRMATION

To invoke the healing power of all the crystal angels, at any time, you can repeat the following affirmation quietly in your mind, or aloud.

"Crystal Angels Help me through unconditional love
With the power of Earth below and Heaven above!"

AND FROM HERE?

Every ending is another beginning, beloved. If you wish to continue our journey together you may enjoy the other books in the Crystal series.

Alana shares the ancient wisdom teachings of the Ascended Masters for spiritual growth in *Crystal Masters 333: Initiation with the Divine Power of Heaven and Earth*.

In *Crystal Goddesses 888: Manifesting with the Divine Power of Heaven and Earth*, Alana guides you into a world of abundance, prosperity and manifesting your soul destiny through the Divine Feminine wisdom.

The stunning *Crystal Mandala Oracle* deck features all the artwork from the three first books in this series, *Crystal Angels 444*, *Crystal Masters 333*, and *Crystal Goddesses 888* with fresh new messages channelled by Alana in a powerful 'download' from higher guidance! Enjoy this powerful card set as a way to take your healing journey through *Crystal Angels 444* into an accessible form of regular divine guidance with beautiful crystal mandalas and inspirational messages of love.

With more books in the series coming soon, stay up-to-date with the new release titles by joining Alana's monthly e-newsletter by visiting **www.alanafairchild.com**.

ABOUT ALANA

When something is natural for you, especially if it has been that way since childhood, you can assume that it is natural for everyone. It took me some years to realise that my sensitivity, healing ability and natural conscious connection to the higher planes of spiritual guidance was unusual.

It wasn't long after that realisation that I stepped away from a career as a lawyer (spiritual law was always more interesting to me) and I began my vocation as a spiritual healer and teacher.

From the earliest memories I had, I was always in conscious connection with Spirit. It has always been as natural as breathing to me and is probably the gift that I am most grateful for this lifetime – though I have gratitude for plenty.

I felt the call to spiritual guidance at age nine, and began offering advice to my fellow classmates in a school-yard healing centre (under the tree, by the back gate in the playground). I remember at the time thinking, "I need more life experience to be able to do this properly!" This was quite a thought for a nine-year-old. Yet I knew that sitting under that tree in the playground like a wise old sage (instead of a primary-school girl) offering some sort of wisdom was exactly what I was meant to be doing.

Not so many years later, as a young woman in my teens, I realised that my soul was a shaman and a priestess on this Earth. The shaman is one who ventures into alternative realities to bring back wisdom, truth and insight for healing in this Earthy reality. The priestess is one who honours the bridge between the inner and outer worlds, between heaven and Earth, keeping the bridge open and helping others to learn how to walk that bridge, drawing the Earth and heaven closer together.

The role of the modern shaman priestess is to keep the sacred intact and awaken it in the world. It is about living with head in the heavens and feet on the Earth and pulling the two together into oneness through all parts of her Being, in service of love.

My own sense of my ancient spiritual connection has manifested as a full-time vocational dedication to living, walking and talking the path of the soul, with special attention to healing for those seeking to carve out a life of individuality, courageously breaking with mass opinion in favour of independent thought and personal spiritual integrity (a bit of rebellion can go a long way to finding your own truth, then you don't need to be the rebel quite so much, you can just be).

My work as a shaman and priestess is expressed in soul whispering, being a divine voice channel and a healer, teaching, dancing and singing (and playing!) with an international client base and a broad product range including DVDs, CDs and the beautiful "Kuan Yin Oracle" and "Isis Oracle" decks.

To learn more about Alana and her work, visit her online at: **www.alanafairchild.com**

ABOUT THE ARTIST

Jane Marin is an accomplished artist, intuitive healer/coach, past life regressionist, author and Reiki/Seichim Master/Teacher.

She holds diplomas in Child Psychology, Hatha Yoga Teaching, Bach Flower Essences and Certificates in Past Life Regression, Journal Therapy, Angel Therapy™, Crystal Light Healing Practitioner Level III, and Motivational Kinesiology IV.

Her background in dance prompted her to explore the healing powers of music and dance leading her to the ancient art of bellydance. She has been teaching this form of dance since 2004.

Jane's spiritual art and photography can now be purchased in our online shop as can her beautiful coffee table books.

Jane is the author of "The Me Book - A Journey of Self-discovery", published in 2011 by Balboa Press to compliment her popular "Me Book" workshops.

The crystal mandalas from this book, as well as those in *Crystal Goddesses 888* and *Crystal Masters 333* have now been released as an oracle card deck, with messages by Alana Fairchild: *Crystal Mandala Oracle* released by Blue Angel Publishing.

THEMATIC INDEX BY CHAPTER

1. CLEAR QUARTZ (The Master Healer) and ARCHANGEL METATRON (King of Angels)

THE GIFT OF POWER

addiction
Atlantis
computers
confusion
Crown Chakra
depression
digestion
empowerment
fatigue
fear of power
headaches
helplessness
immune system
power
purpose
responsibility
Solar Plexus Chakra
Soul Star Chakra
spiritual growth
strength
technology
tiredness

2. ARAGONITE (Sacred Rest) and ARCHANGEL REMIEL (Carer of the Soul)

THE GIFT OF REST

chronic fatigue syndrome
depression
fatigue
fear of death
fear of letting go
feminine wisdom
financial stress
mind
procrastination
pushing
relaxation
rest
rushing
safety
stress
struggle
stuck
transition

3. PINK CALCITE (Unconditional Acceptance) and ARCHANGEL ANAEL (Angel of the Heart)

THE GIFT OF UNCONDITIONAL ACCEPTANCE

abuse
acceptance
bad body image
body
conditioning
denial
despair
eating disorders
forgiveness
grace
grief
Heart Chakra
hope
judgement
love

loving your body
martyr
new patterns
opening the heart
pain
programming
regret
sadness
self-abuse
self-acceptance
self-hate
self-love
sexual abuse
victim
weight
weight obsession

4. SELENITE (Peace) and ARCHANGEL MELCHIZEDEK (Angel of Peace)

THE GIFT OF HIGHER CONSCIOUSNESS

angelic contact
calm
cellular memory
christ consciousness
Crown Chakra
detachment
divine plan
healers
higher consciousness
letting go
nervous system
peace
perfection
sensitive
sensitivity
solutions
spiritual connection

spiritual growth
spiritual protection
surrender
why?
wisdom

5. LABRADORITE (Uniqueness) and ARCHANGEL IAHEL (Angel of Solitude)

THE GIFT OF INDIVIDUALITY

conformity
courage
cutting cords
fitness
individuality
negativity
outcast
past life healing
protection
rebel
seeker
self-belief
socialising
solitude
soul talents
time for you
weight loss
wellbeing

6. BLUE OBSIDIAN (Clarity) and ANGEL AMITIEL (Angel of Truth)

THE GIFT OF CLARITY

anger
avoidance
awakening
blessing

blockages
childhood
clarity
confusion
dance
deception
detoxification
emotions
fake
freedom
I AM
injustice
intuition
lies
mudras
protection
psychic attack
resistance
self-knowledge
trust
truth
victim

7. POLYCHROME JASPER (Playfulness) and ANGEL CALIEL (Angel of Laughter)

THE GIFT OF DIVINE PLAY

adventure
balance
cats
chakra balance
change
commitment
darkness
efficiency
exertion
fun
higher guidance
in a rut

inner child
inspiration
irresponsibility
joy
karma
laughter
learning to play
pets
presence
rainbow
seriousness
spice of life
spirit guides
spontaneous
stress
struggle
time
unplug
worry

8. LAPIS LAZULI (Insight) and ARCHANGEL MICHAEL (Protection)

THE GIFT OF VISION

ancient wisdom
clairvoyance
courage
curses
danger
demon
Divine Masculine
Egypt
eye health
gossip
grace
hormones
mysteries
protection
psychic ability

psychic attack
self-destruction
soul purpose
spiritual teachers
spiritual tests
strength
Third Eye Chakra
unconscious mind
vision

9. PICTURE JASPER (Earth Wisdom) and ARCHON BARBELO (Prosperity)

THE GIFT OF SUPPORT

abundance
addiction
alchemy
ascension
body
connecting to Earth Mother
Divine Mother
enlightenment
envy
flow
freedom
goddess
golden body
inner child
jealousy
letting go
light body
love
masculine and feminine balance
mother issues
peace
prosperity
purification
receiving
reprogramming beliefs

resources
safety
struggle
support
thrills
trust

10. CARNELIAN (Life Force) and ANGEL ISDA (Food)

THE GIFT OF NOURISHMENT

abundance
acceptance
accidents
anger
anorexia
birth
body issues
bulimia
closeness
cold hands and feet
cold house
collectors
commitment
daydreaming
depression
inflammation
disembodied
dissociation
eating disorders
emptiness
fantasy bond
fatigue
fear
fertility
food
getting into your body
ghost lover
golden body
grounding

guilt
hips
hoarding
hunger
ideal partner
impure
in your head
inner child
innocence
intimacy
loneliness
low energy
nourishment
nutrients
other worlds
ovaries
overeating
plastic surgery
rage
relationship issues
replenishment
sacred chakra
self-love
sensuality
sexual abuse
sexual organs
sexuality
shame
spacey
star children
starvation
suicidal thoughts
trauma
trust
unclean
vague
vitality
warmth
weight issues
weight loss
womb

11. TURQUOISE (Amulet) and ARCHANGEL GABRIEL (Strength)

THE GIFT OF SPIRITUAL AUTHORITY

authority
baptism
clearing
cults
deception
discernment
divine purpose
divine will
ears
ego
emotional cleansing
energy
fear
freedom
good fortune
habits
healing the ears
holding back
immune system
inner hearing
inner knowing
leadership
lies
luck
meditation
mental programming
messages
mind control
moon
patience
protection
psychic clearing
responsibility
self-doubt
self-expression
self-reliance

strength
thinking for one's self
throat chakra
trust
truth
vision
vows
will
wisdom

12. PIETERSITE (Knowledge) and ANGEL RAZIEL (Mysteries)

THE GIFT OF HIGHER UNDERSTANDING

altered states
authenticity
body
channelling
chaos
chi gung
creativity
discernment
divine support
driving
endurance
energy
exhaustion
flexibility
focus
Heart Chakra
high level spiritual guidance
higher guidance
insight
judgement
learning
life force
meditation
mind power
obstacles

peace
physical challenges
power
pushing
rainbow bridge
rest
shadow healing
shaman
soul connection
spiritual connection
spiritual tests
stability
stillness
storm energy
strength
the master
transformation
transitions
trust
truth
wisdom
yoga

13. TIGERS EYE (Courage) and ANGEL ADNACHIEL (Adventure)

THE GIFT OF INDEPENDENCE

addiction
adventure
aliveness
anxiety
boldness
boredom
children
community
confidence
confusion
courage
creativity
curiosity

dependence
despair
digestion
direction
Divine Masculinity
divine timing
doubt
dreams
efficiency
empowerment
energising
energy
failure
faith
fear
fighter
force
forgiveness
freedom
independence
instincts
intuition
moderation
nightmares
paralysis
passion
play
power
presence
procrastination
productivity
purpose
risk
safety
self-belief
self-care
self-worth
sensitivity
Solar Plexus
spiritual warrior
spontaneous
stomach

talents
teenagers
trust
validation
warmth
weakness
wildness

14. BLACK TOURMALINE (Cleansing) and ANGEL LAHABIEL (Protection)

THE GIFT OF PURIFICATION

aggression
attachment
attack
blockages
boundaries
cleansing
compassion
confidence
constipation
cults
curses
darkness
death
detoxification
dreams
elimination
emotional cleansing
entities
evil
evil eye
fear
gentleness
grace
healing
higher consciousness
humiliation
judgement - non-judgement

karma
letting go
love
lymphatic system
magic
manifestation
negativity
obstacles
opportunities
past
peace
pets
power
protection
psychic attack
psychic protection
radiation
rebirth
self-sabotage
sensitivity
shame
spirit beings
spiritual rescue
tall poppy syndrome
victims
walls

15. MALACHITE (Evolution) and ARCHANGEL RAPHAEL (Healing)

THE GIFT OF ONENESS

adaptability
adventure
adventure
aliveness
beauty
brain
Chi
comfort zone
courage

dance
detoxification
drumming
enlightenment
exercise
faith
fear - fearlessness
fitness
flexibility
grace
healing
healing ability
healing fear
healing talent
heart
hormones
hot hands
inner child
life force
love
negativity
power
projection
reassurance
Reiki
reprogramming
risk
safety
security
sexual attraction
shadow
Shakti
spiritual defence
spiritual intelligence
strength
trust
truth
unlearning
vitality

16. ROSE QUARTZ (Unconditional Love) and ANGEL BALTHIEL (Healing Jealousy)

THE GIFT OF HEART HEALING

aggression
anger
compassion
Crown Chakra
disciple - devotee
emotional healing
empath
envy
fear
fighting
forgiveness
grief
guru
hate
heart attack
Heart Chakra
heart disease
inner child
insecurity
jealousy
journalling
judgement
letting go
love
moving on
opening
past pain
peace
possessiveness
psychic
relationships
sadness
self-harm
self-worth
sensitivity
sexuality

spiritual gift
spiritual light
spiritual release
spiritual rescue
suffering
trauma
unconditional love
violence

17. AQUAMARINE (Expression) and ANGEL BATH KOL (Voice)

THE GIFT OF HIGHER CREATIVITY

art
assertiveness
Buddha
Christ
clairaudience
clairvoyance
clarity
coming out of the closet
communication
community
confusion
courage
creativity
dark night of the soul
depression
direction
Divine Feminine
Divine Masculine
divine purpose
divine timing
enlightenment
expression
fantasy
fear of death
God
grace

heart
holding back
holy spirit
Holy Trinity
I AM
identities
individuality
inner hearing
light
losing your job
manifestation
mantra
moving forward
OM
patience
power
public image
public opinion
public profile
revelation
Saraswati
self-worth
shame
singing
Solar Plexus
sound
speaking in public
speaking up
stuck
talking from the heart
the cosmic womb
the void
Throat Chakra
throat problems
thyroid
truth
uniqueness
walking your path
white dove

18. SMOKY QUARTZ (Grounding) and ANGEL UZZIEL (Mercy)

THE GIFT OF EMBODIMENT

acceptance
Base Chakra
bigger picture
body
body issues
compassion
contentment
detoxification
dissociation
divine timing
earth
earth connection
eating disorders
ego
exhaustion
fatigue
fear
gentleness
incarnation
instincts
living your dreams
manifestation
mental over-work
mercy
over-eating
power
presence
radiation
rebirth
rest
self-harm
service
shame
smell the roses, watch the sunset
spirals
spiritual connection
starvation

suicidal tendencies or thoughts
the void
too much too soon
violence on the spiritual path
weight issues

INDEX

Note to reader: The page numbers listed below refer to the page number on which the chapter dealing with each theme begins.

abundance, 163, 179

abuse, 71

acceptance, 71, 179, 323

accidents, 179

adaptability, 267

addiction, 43, 163, 229

Adnachiel, 229

adventure, 133, 229, 267

aggression, 249, 285

alchemy, 163

aliveness, 229, 267

altered states, 211

Amitiel, 115

ancient wisdom, 147

Angel Adnachiel, 229

Angel Amitiel, 115

Angel Balthiel, 285

Angel Bath Kol, 303

Angel Lahabiel, 249

Angel Raziel, 211

Angel Uzziel, 323

angelic contact, 85

anger, 115, 179, 285

anorexia, 179

anxiety, 229

Aquamarine, 303

Aragonite, 57

Archangel Anael, 71

Archangel Caliel, 133

Archangel Gabriel, 195

Archangel Iahel, 99

Archangel Isda, 179

Archangel Melchizedek, 85

Archangel Metatron, 43

Archangel Michael, 147

Archangel Raphael, 267

Archangel Remiel, 57

Archon Barbelo, 163

art, 303

ascension, 163

assertiveness, 303

Atlantis, 43

attachment, 249

attack, 249

authenticity, 211

authority, 195

avoidance, 115

awakening, 115

bad body image, 71

balance, 133

Balthiel, 285

baptism, 195

Barbelo, 163

Base Chakra, 323

Bath Kol, 303

beauty, 267

bigger picture, 323

birth, 179

Black Tourmaline, 249

blessing, 115

blockages, 115, 249

Blue Obsidian, 115

body issues, 179, 323

body, 71, 163, 211, 323

boldness, 229

boredom, 229

boundaries, 249

brain, 267

Buddha, 303

bulimia, 179

Caliel, 133

calm, 85

Carnelian, 179

cats, 133

cellular memory, 85

chakra balance, 133

change, 133
channelling, 211
chaos, 211
Chi Gung, 211
Chi, 267
childhood, 115
children, 229
Christ consciousness, 85
Christ, 303
chronic fatigue syndrome, 57
clairaudience, 303
clairvoyance, 147, 303
clarity, 115, 303
cleansing, 249
Clear Quartz, 43
clearing, 195
closeness, 179
cold hands and feet, 179
cold house, 179
collectors, 179
comfort zone, 267
coming out of the closet, 303
commitment, 133, 179
communication, 303
community, 229, 303
compassion, 249, 285, 323
computers, 43
conditioning, 71
confidence, 229, 249
conformity, 99
confusion, 43, 115, 229, 303
connecting to Earth Mother, 163
constipation, 249
contentment, 323
courage, 99, 147, 229, 267, 303
creativity, 211, 229, 303
Crown Chakra, 43, 85, 285
cults, 195, 249
curiosity, 229
curses, 147, 249
cutting cords, 99
dance, 115, 267

danger, 147
dark night of the soul, 303
darkness, 133, 249
daydreaming, 179
death, 249
deception, 115, 195
demon, 147
denial, 71
dependence, 229
depression, 43, 57, 179, 303
despair, 71, 229
detachment, 85
detoxification, 115, 249, 267, 323
digestion, 43, 229
direction, 229, 303
discernment, 195, 211
disciple - devotee, 285
disembodied, 179
dissociation, 179, 323
Divine Feminine, 303
Divine Masculine, 147, 229, 303
Divine Mother, 163
divine plan, 85
divine purpose, 195, 303
divine support, 211
divine timing, 229, 303, 323
divine will, 195
doubt, 229
dreams, 229, 249
driving, 211
drumming, 267
ears, 195
earth connection, 323
earth, 323
eating disorders, 71, 179, 323
efficiency, 133, 229
ego, 195, 323
Egypt, 147
elimination, 249
emotional cleansing, 195, 249
emotional healing, 285
emotions, 115

empath, 285
empowerment, 43, 229
emptiness, 179
endurance, 211
energising, 229
energy low, 179
energy, 195, 211, 229
enlightenment, 163, 267, 303
entities, 249
envy, 163, 285
evil eye, 249
evil, 249
exercise, 267
exertion, 133
exhaustion, 211, 323
expression, 303
eye health, 147
failure, 229
faith, 229, 267
fake, 115
fantasy bond, 179
fantasy, 303
fatigue, 43, 57, 179, 323
fear - fearlessness, 267
fear of death, 57, 303
fear of letting go, 57
fear of power, 43
fear, 179, 195, 229, 249, 285, 323
feminine and masculine balance, 163
feminine wisdom, 57
fertility, 179
fighter, 229
fighting, 285
financial stress, 57
fitness, 99, 267
flexibility, 211, 267
flow, 163
focus, 211
food, 179
force, 229
forgiveness, 71, 229, 285
freedom, 115, 163, 195, 229

fun, 133
Gabriel, 195
gentleness, 249, 323
getting into your body, 179
ghost lover, 179
God, 303
Goddess, 163
golden body, 163, 179
good fortune, 195
gossip, 147
grace, 71, 147, 249, 267, 303
grief, 71, 285
grounding, 179
guilt, 179
guru, 285
habits, 195
hate, 285
headaches, 43
healers, 85
healing ability, 267
healing fear, 267
healing talent, 267
healing the ears, 195
healing, 249, 267
heart attack, 285
Heart Chakra, 71, 211, 285
heart disease, 285
heart, 267, 303
helplessness, 43
high level spiritual guidance, 211
higher consciousness, 85, 249
higher guidance, 133, 211
hips, 179
hoarding, 179
holding back, 195, 303
holy spirit, 303
Holy Trinity, 303
hope, 71
hormones, 147, 267
hot hands, 267
humiliation, 249
hunger, 179

I AM, 115, 303
Iahel, 99
ideal partner, 179
identities, 303
immune system, 43, 195
impure, 179
in a rut, 133
in your head, 179
incarnation, 323
independence, 229
individuality, 99, 303
inflammation, 179
injustice, 115
inner child, 133, 163, 179, 267, 285
inner hearing, 195, 303
inner knowing, 195
innocence, 179
insecurity, 285
insight, 211
inspiration, 133
instincts, 229, 323
intimacy, 179
intuition, 115, 229
irresponsibility, 133
Isda, 179
Jasper (Picture), 163
Jasper (Polychrome), 133
jealousy, 163, 285
journaling, 285
joy, 133
judgement - non-judgement, 249
judgement, 71, 211, 285
karma, 133, 249
Labradorite, 99
Lahabiel, 249
Lapis Lazuli, 147
laughter, 133
leadership, 195
learning to play, 133
learning, 211
letting go, 85, 163, 249, 285
lies, 115, 195

life force, 211, 267
light body, 163
light, 303
living your dreams, 323
loneliness, 179
losing your job, 303
love, 71, 163, 249, 267, 285
loving your body, 71
low energy, 179
luck, 195
lymphatic system, 249
magic, 249
Malachite, 267
manifestation, 249, 303, 323
mantra, 303
martyr, 71
masculine and feminine balance, 163
meditation, 195, 211
Melchizedek, 85
mental over-work, 323
mental programming, 195
mercy, 323
messages, 195
Metatron, 43
Michael, 147
mind control, 195
mind power, 211
mind, 57
moderation, 229
moon, 195
mother issues, 163
moving forward, 303
moving on, 285
mudras, 115
mysteries, 147
negativity, 99, 249, 267
nervous system, 85
new patterns, 71
nightmares, 229
nourishment, 179
nutrients, 179
Obsidian, 115

obstacles, 211, 249
OM, 303
opening the heart, 71
opening, 285
opportunities, 249
other worlds, 179
outcast, 99
ovaries, 179
overeating, 179, 323
pain, 71
paralysis, 229
passion, 229
past life healing, 99
past pain, 285
past, 249
patience, 195, 303
patterns (new), 71
peace, 85, 163, 211, 249, 285
pets, 133, 249
physical challenges, 211
Picture Jasper, 163
Pietersite, 211
Pink Calcite, 71
plastic surgery, 179
play, 229
Polychrome Jasper, 133
possessiveness, 285
power, 43, 211, 229, 249, 267, 303, 323
presence, 133, 229, 323
procrastination, 57, 229
productivity, 229
programming, 71
projection, 267
prosperity, 163
protection, 99, 115, 147, 195, 249
psychic ability, 147
psychic attack, 115, 147, 249
psychic clearing, 195
psychic protection, 249
psychic, 285
public image, 303
public opinion, 303

public profile, 303
purification, 163
purpose, 43, 229
pushing, 57, 211
Quartz, 43
radiation, 249, 323
rage, 179
rainbow bridge, 211
rainbow, 133
Raphael, 267
Raziel, 211
reassurance, 267
rebel, 99
rebirth, 249, 323
receiving, 163
regret, 71
Reiki, 267
relationship issues, 179
relationships, 285
relaxation, 57
Remiel, 57
replenishment, 179
reprogramming beliefs, 163, 267
resistance, 115
resources, 163
responsibility, 43, 195
rest, 57, 211, 323
revelation, 303
risk, 229, 267
Rose Quartz, 285
rushing, 57
sacred chakra, 179
sadness, 71, 285
safety, 57, 163, 229, 267
Saraswati, 303
security, 267
seeker, 99
Selenite, 85
self-abuse, 71
self-acceptance, 71
self-belief, 99, 229
self-care, 229

self-destruction, 147
self-doubt, 195
self-expression, 195
self-harm, 285, 323
self-hate, 71
self-knowledge, 115
self-love, 71, 179
self-reliance, 195
self-sabotage, 249
self-worth, 229, 285, 303
sensitive, 85
sensitivity, 85, 229, 249, 285
sensuality, 179
seriousness, 133
service, 323
sexual abuse, 71, 179
sexual attraction, 267
sexual organs, 179
sexuality, 179, 285
shadow healing, 211
shadow, 267
Shakti, 267
shaman, 211
shame, 179, 249, 303, 323
singing, 303
smell the roses, 323
Smoky Quartz, 323
socialising, 99
Solar Plexus Chakra, 43, 229, 303
solitude, 99
solutions, 85
soul connection, 211
soul purpose, 147
Soul Star Chakra, 43
soul talents, 99
sound, 303
spacey, 179
speaking in public, 303
speaking up, 303
spice of life, 133
spirals, 323
spirit beings, 249

spirit guides, 133
spiritual connection, 85, 211, 267, 323
spiritual defence, 267
spiritual gift, 285
spiritual growth, 43, 85
spiritual intelligence, 267
spiritual light, 285
spiritual protection, 85
spiritual release, 285
spiritual rescue, 249, 285
spiritual teachers, 147
spiritual tests, 147, 211
spiritual warrior, 229
spontaneous, 133, 229
stability, 211
star children, 179
starvation, 179, 323
stillness, 211
stomach, 229
storm energy, 211
strength, 43, 147, 195, 211, 267
stress, 57, 133
struggle, 57, 133, 163
stuck, 57, 303
suffering, 285
suicidal tendencies or thoughts, 179, 323
support, 163
surrender, 85
talents, 229
talking from the heart, 303
tall poppy syndrome, 249
technology, 43
teenagers, 229
the cosmic womb, 303
the master, 211
the void, 303, 323
thinking for oneself, 195
Third Eye Chakra, 147
thrills, 163
Throat Chakra, 195, 303
throat problems, 303
thyroid, 303

Tigers Eye, 229
time for you, 99
time, 133
tiredness, 43
too much too soon, 323
transformation, 211
transition, 57, 211
trauma, 179, 285
trust, 115, 163, 179, 195, 211, 229, 267
truth, 115, 195, 211, 267, 303
Turquoise, 195
unclean, 179
unconditional love, 285
unconscious mind, 147
uniqueness, 303
unlearning, 267
unplug, 133
Uzziel, 323
vague, 179
validation, 229
victim, 71, 115, 249
violence on the spiritual path, 323
violence, 285
vision, 147, 195
vitality, 179, 267
vows, 195
walking your path, 303
walls, 249
warmth, 179, 229
weakness, 229
weight issues, 179, 323
weight loss, 99, 179
weight obsession, 71
weight, 71
wellbeing, 99
white dove, 303
wildness, 229
will, 195
wisdom, 85, 195, 211
womb, 179
worry, 133
yoga, 211

Kuan Yin Oracle
Blessings, Guidance and Enlightenment
from the Divine Feminine

Kuan Yin. Radiant with Divine Compassion.

The 44 cards in this deck guide you to a place of inner peace and beauty. Kuan Yin's energy reaches out to you from each card. The messages, inspired by her presence and guiding voice, contain her wisdom to help us live a loving and enlightened life that is practical, spiritual and positive. The guidance in the messages and the practical exercises for each card nourish you on your spiritual path, help you realise that you are a divine Soul and learn to love, trust and live your highest destiny this lifetime.

Artwork by Zeng Hao
Features 44 cards and detailed 144-page guidebook, packaged in a hardcover box set.

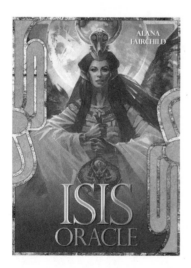

Isis Oracle

Awaken the High Priestess Within...

The High Priest or Priestess within you walks the path of divine love, power and wisdom. This is the path of spiritual self-mastery where we are initiated through the darkness of struggle into the light of love. Learn to apply the Ancient Mystery teachings of Isis in practical ways to help you navigate through the experiences and challenges in your daily life. Allow the Goddess, this sacred priestess, initiate, magician and healer to help you reactivate your own soul talents of healing, magic and more as you journey with her from darkness and uncertainty into light, love and power.

Artwork by Jimmy Manton
Features 44 cards and detailed 220-page guidebook, packaged in a hardcover box set.

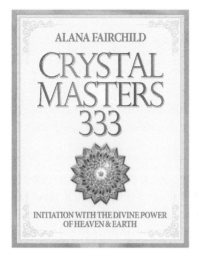

Crystal Masters 333
Initiation with the Divine Power of Heaven and Earth

You have wise spiritual guides from the spiritual worlds of Crystals and Ascended Masters. They are ready to help you on your path of spiritual growth now.

In *Crystal Masters 333*, Alana Fairchild continues the highly successful Crystal Spirituality Series, which began with *Crystal Angels 444*. She shares her unique approach to crystal healing, combining the natural healing properties of each crystal and its 'crystal angel' or 'spirit' with wisdom teachings from the loving Ascended Masters, such as Mother Mary, Kuan Yin, Jesus, the Buddha, Mary Magdalene and Merlin. Together they help you take the next steps on your path of spiritual growth, by preparing you with the teachings and tools you need to successfully navigate the demands of spiritual initiation.

Initiation is a path of advanced spiritual growth. When you are highly committed to your spiritual path and personal growth this lifetime, you will be on the path of initiation. This path can be very challenging but offers incredible rewards including the awakening of spiritual talents, assistance in bringing your divine light to the world and support in your own role as a healer and spiritual leader on the earth. Each chapter deals with a powerful precious stone and its heavenly angel and features spiritual teachings and stories from Alana's own life and work, as well as a healing process to help you fully harness the therapeutic potential of that stone and connect directly with the Ascended Masters, to receive their wisdom and blessings.

You will delve deeply into a variety of topics including aligning with divine will, healing the child within, planetary healing, spiritual communication, enlightenment and spiritual growth, the light body, the golden body, and much more.

You have important healing work to do on yourself and for the planet. 'Crystal Masters 333' is written for you, to help you successfully complete your task, with greater happiness and fulfilment.

Featuring 18 full-colour Crystal Master Mandalas by artist Jane Marin.
Paperback book, 384 pages.

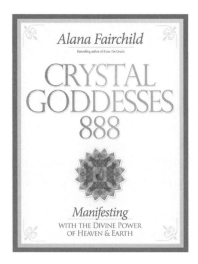

Crystal Goddesses 888
Manifesting with the Divine Power of Heaven and Earth

You have wise spiritual guides from the mystical worlds of Crystals and Goddesses. They are ready to help you now.

Manifesting from your soul feels good. It isn't about forcing the world to bend to your will, it is about co- creating with the power of life itself. When you manifest from your soul, you not only bring your visions to life, but you become more alive too. You are healing yourself through the process of creation whilst your world transforms along with you. This book is your guide to the many ways you can manifest from your soul. From exploring the power of sound and light, to embracing darkness and healing through joy, celebrating being different, honouring being a rebel and expressing your passion as well as your compassion, you will be offered many ways to heal and manifest your divine destiny.

Crystal Goddesses 888, the next volume in the highly successful Crystal Spirituality Series, will connect you to the power of heaven in the form of the wild and loving divine feminine (and her many faces as goddesses from different spiritual traditions), and the power of the earth in the form of crystals that support each goddess in bringing her gifts of healing to you. With real life stories from the author to make the material practical and accessible, this book guides you with humour and love to take the next step on your path, creating your own version of heaven on earth. Whether you are new to all this, or have been on your conscious path for years, you'll find a wealth of treasures in here. May you blossom wildly on your beautiful life journey, held in the grace of the wild feminine spirit that loves you unconditionally.

Featuring 18 full-colour Crystal Master Mandalas by artist Jane Marin.
Paperback book, 384 pages.

Crystal Mandala Oracle
Channel the Power of Heaven & Earth

This unique oracle deck is encoded with crystal frequencies, and the high vibrational energy of angels, ascended masters and goddesses, to empower you to channel the divine healing power of Heaven and Earth.

In this stunning, stand-alone deck, you will work with the vibrant crystal mandalas by Jane Marin, as featured in Alana Fairchild's popular books *Crystal Angels 444, Crystal Masters 333* and *Crystal Goddesses 888.* Alana shares loving spiritual guidance from the angels, masters and goddesses to help you integrate the frequencies of the crystals and higher beings that are featured in each of the cards. The Crystal Angels will help you heal your body, mind and soul. The Crystal Masters will support your spiritual growth and help you successfully pass through spiritual tests and initiations. The Crystal Goddesses will empower you to embody your spirit and express your soul purpose in the world.

This powerful deck will enhance your connection to the sacred worlds of higher beings and crystal energy, opening your heart to divine beauty and empowering your soul with loving consciousness.

Artwork by Jane Marin.
54 cards and 244-page guidebook set, packaged in a hardcover box.

For more information on this or other
Blue Angel Publishing titles,
visit our website at:
www.blueangelonline.com